WOMEN PRIESTS

WOMEN PRIESTS

A Catholic Commentary
on the
Vatican Declaration

edited by
Leonard Swidler
and
Arlene Swidler

PAULIST PRESS
New York / Ramsey / Toronto

Library of Congress
Catalog Card Number: 77-83572

ISBN: 0-8091-2062-3

Published by Paulist Press
Editorial Office: 1865 Broadway, New York, N.Y. 10023
Business Office: 545 Island Road, Ramsey, N.J. 07446

Printed and bound in the
United States of America

Contents

Contents

PART I

PROLEGOMENA

Introduction
Roma Locuta, Causa Finita?

Roma locuta, causa finita? It might in the matter of the Roman Declaration on the ordination of women priests more accurately be stated: *Roma locuta, causa stimulata!* A gradual increase in the number of Catholics in favor of women priests has been recorded in France from 1968 to 1976: 25% in 1968, 28% in 1970, 30% in 1974, 37% in 1976, with 42% of secular priests polled in 1976 in favor also.[1] The jump from 1974 to 1976 probably reflects the snowballing discussion the subject has been experiencing in recent years. Unfortunately no post-Declaration poll is available for France. In the United States a poll was taken in 1974, showing 29% of Catholics in favor of women priests, almost the same figure as in France at that time. Then in February and March, 1977, after the Declaration, a Gallup poll of U.S. Catholics was conducted on the same question in three stages, with the following results in favor of women priests: February 18—31%; March 4—36%; March 18—41%. As Father Andrew Greeley pointed out, there was a 10% favorable increase within a month in the wake of the Vatican Declaration.[2]

Of course truth is not something that normally is determined by votes of the people. However, there is a special pertinence to the above impertinences. One of the major arguments of the Declaration against women priests is that because the priest is to be an image of Christ (a male), a woman could not be such an image, for the "faithful could not recognize it with ease" (par. 27). But now it would seem a rapidly approaching majority of the faithful would recognize a woman priest as an image of Christ. Further, since, as the Pontifical Biblical Commission pointed out (IV,2) and the Vatican Declaration itself intimated (par. 13), the Bible does not settle the question of women priests one way or the other, the Declaration places a strong emphasis on Tradition as the norm determining the acceptability of women priests. But even in very traditional pre-Vatican II theology manuals a "certain criterion" listed for determining what is Catholic Tradition is the "consensus of the faithful": *"Consensus fidelium est certum Traditionis et fidei Ecclesiae criterium."*[3] It would seem that a major shift in the *"consensus fidelium"* favorable to women priests is rapidly approaching.

It would be inappropriate to pose some sort of crisis-creating contradiction between this Vatican Declaration and the burgeoning shift in the *"consensus fidelium"* on women priests. As Karl Rahner recently pointed out, "the Declaration, despite its approval by the Pope, is not a definitive decision; it is fundamentally reformable; it can (which does not *a priori* mean 'must') be erroneous."[4] Rahner goes on to offer a careful analysis of what the present book is all about. He asks what the Catholic theologian's attitude ought to be toward the present Declaration, and replies: She or "he must bring to such a decree the appropriate respect; he likewise has however not only the right but also the duty to probe it critically and in certain circumstances to contradict it. The theologian respects this decree in that he attempts to evaluate as objectively as possible the arguments it puts forth . . . even to the possibility that he would judge its basic position in fact to be in error. There is (not counting earlier times) a whole series of declarations in the 19th and 20th centuries by the Roman Congregation of the Faith which among others have been shown to be in error or at least long since left behind. Such progress in knowledge is absolutely necessary for the Church's effective proclamation, and factually is absolutely unthinkable without such a critical collaboration of theologians."[5]

However, Rahner also cautions that too much is at stake to let this critical process drift on too slowly: "Indeed one may well say that such a revision process in the last 150 years has not infrequently proceeded too slowly—to the injury of the Church—because theologians have exercised their inalienable office too fearfully and even under the threat of ecclesiastical disciplinary measures. With today's increasingly rapid evolution and change of consciousness in civil society such a revision process in these circumstances is all the more urgent and demands even more than before the honest and courageous work of the theologian, even when it is tedious and above all when little thanks and recognition from the side of the Roman Magisterium can be reckoned with."[6]

This book, then, is a scholarly attempt by forty-four North American Roman Catholic theologians to enter into serious dialogue with the Congregation For the Teaching of the Faith concerning its Declaration on women priests. In so doing they are, as Rahner put it, exercising not only their right, but, more importantly, their duty. Indeed, Vatican II called upon not only professional theologians, but "all Catholics wherever necessary to undertake with vigor the task of renewal and reform. . . . Their primary duty is to make a careful and honest appraisal of whatever needs to be renewed and done in the Catholic household itself" (Ecumenism Decree, 4).

Setting In Time and Space

The Vatican Declaration on women priests did not fall out of some abstract logical Roman world, nor did it result from discussions and actions of ordaining women by non-Roman Catholic Churches, nor even from the Women's Liberation Movement (though the latter two were contributory influences). Rather, it came as a response to the movement for full Christian personhood for all Catholics, women included, flowing from the creative thought and actions of Vatican II. The Council's notions of participation of the laity in all aspects of the life of the Church, of collegiality, of the Church as the People of God, naturally led women to seek full exercise of their gifts as first-class members of that Church, of that People. That logically meant some women would be expected to experience a call to the priesthood—and in a non-discriminatory Church they ought to be able to have that call tested and respond to it if found authentic. Thus it was long before the birth of the Women's Liberation Movement (c. 1969) or before Catholics were talking seriously to non-Catholics who ordained women that pioneer Catholic women and men began to raise the issue of women priests.

This question-raising began at least with the petition to the Preparatory Commission of the Second Vatican Council (which began in 1962) submitted by the Catholic laywoman, Gertrude Heinzelman, a Swiss lawyer and member of St. Joan's International Alliance, which in its 1963 and 1964 Conventions also petitioned the Council concerning women priests.[7] About the same time a most thorough-going Catholic study of the question of women priests was completed by the Dutch Father Haye van der Meer, S.J., as his doctoral dissertation written under the direction of Karl Rahner, S.J., in Austria.[8] In 1963, this time in Peru, another Catholic study was published, by Father José Idigoras, S.J.[9] By the end of Vatican II more and more journal articles began to appear;[10] in 1967 Sister V.E. Hannon in England completed another book-length study of women priests,[11] and in 1970 Ida Raming earned her doctorate of Catholic theology in Germany with her dissertation, an analysis of the canon law mandating only male priests.[12] All of these studies concluded in favor of women priests. By this time studies and articles began to appear with ever growing rapidity, as is outlined in the bibliographical essay in the present book.

As far off as India the Catholic Church's concern for women in official Church ministries, including deaconate and priesthood, could be found up to the eve of the Vatican Declaration: "The present situation, therefore, in which all women are excluded from her ministries, only because they are women, should be rectified. This step should be taken without hesitation because: a) theological research recognizes that no valid reasons can be given against the installation of women in lay ministries, nor against their ordination as deacons (whereas the admission of women to the presbyterate remains a matter of discussion)."[13] Even stronger: "In the new order which Christ has created, women share fully in all the aspects of his redemptive priesthood. This implies of necessity that women should also participate in the sacramental priestly ministry."[14] And this in a periodical published by the Catholic Bishops Conference India which goes to all bishops, priests, religious and many Catholic laity of India. This issue was a special one on "Ministries In the Church," and was so enthusiastically received that it had to be reprinted. It was the result of many months of serious study on the part of various scholars and consultants of church groups, some of which were directed by a number of Catholic bishops of India in person or through representatives. Then the issue was distributed to all the Catholic bishops of the Far East.

It should now be clear that the impetus of the Catholic movement for women priests did not initially, nor does it now exclusively, come from America, as was suggested by a spokesman at the Vatican press conference upon the release of the Vatican Declaration.[15]

At the present time a large and strong support for women priests has developed in America, as is only partially indicated by the above-mentioned

polls; a flood of articles, statements and open letters in response to the
Declaration which are favorable to women priests has poured forth from
Catholic organizations, theologians and laity.

Foreign Critiques of the Declaration

But as before the Declaration, so also after, Catholic support for women
priests comes from many places in the Catholic world. Hence, to put the
present book in a spacial context as well as a temporal one, a number of representative brief quotations from geographically scattered Catholics outside
of America in response to the Vatican Declaration are presented here. Because of distance and the relative shortness of time after the Declaration almost only European reactions were available at the time of printing. There is
one response from Brazil, one from India, and the rest are spread over Germany, Switzerland, Netherlands, Belgium, France, Spain, and England.

Mission

One response came in terms of the Church ministries women are performing, particularly in developing countries—much as was stated in the Fall
of 1976: "The Church in India in her missionary situation cannot afford to
neglect the rich resources of women, and their great capacity for many ministries must be fully utilized."[16] The Catholic Radio of the Netherlands took
up this theme when it broadcast that, "This Declaration must be resented as
a slap in the face by certain women in pastoral positions, and nuns who, for
the most part, in particular in developing countries and in the immense extent
of Brazil and elsewhere, are nothing other than the image of Christ and his
representative in carrying the Good News there where a priest rarely pene-
trates."[17]

A nun from the very country mentioned, Brazil, raised a challenge to the
Declaration from a very poignant, personal, and pastoral point of view: "if I
consider the reality of a country like Brazil where the population is dispersed
in an immense territory, and where there exists the need of apostolic work to
respond to the needs of that portion of the People of God who display a great
desire to know Jesus Christ, I clearly perceive a call in that situation. And
that call is to a person who is not a priest, a nun for example, able to carry
out a sacramental ministry in the overcrowded towns or in the strung out
regions where at times the priest would not be able to appear but every two
or three years.

"Why should that nun who is engaged in the pastoral task not be able to
proceed to celebrate the eucharistic mysteries with the lay people she has cat-
echized and with whom she lives in a community of faith?

"That impossibility is far from being evident when I read the Gospel,
and I believe it is necessary to attempt to criticize it more and more in light
of the situation and the concrete needs of 1977. It is above all necessary to
discern Jesus' will of salvation for ALL humanity. *What does it say to us
today?*"[18]

Ecumenism

The Declaration was charged with ecumenical insensitivity on a broad geographical basis, ranging at least from Spain, France, and England to Belgium. At one end of the spectrum was a moderate chiding by Henri Fesquet of the Catholic daily *Le Monde* for the omission of ecumenical concern: "Finally, it is difficult *not* to take seriously the arguments of those non-Catholic Churches which do ordain women. Is it not opportune, after all, to begin to probe the historical, exegetical and philosophical motifs used to justify that which in the highest degree is the result of a mentality and a subjective affectivity? Rome, whether it knows it or not, has a celibate theology. Not only does it not wish to ordain women priests, it also refuses the exercise of the priesthood to Western married priests."[19]

The London *Tablet* even more strongly criticized the dearth of ecumenical awareness throughout the Declaration: "Where the Holy Office's old style is likely to be most clearly discerned, especially in the English-speaking world, is in the almost complete ignoring of the ecumenical aspect of the question. It is of course widely and reasonably argued that the recent Anglican departure from age-old practice in the matter has also been heedless of ecumenical considerations, but recent correspondence between the Pope and Archbishop Coggan, together with informal high-level talks, have, while recognising Anglican change as a 'new and grave obstacle,' shown anxiety not to take it as a pretext for closing doors so heroically prised open in the past decade. There is no trace of this anxiety in the declaration, which uses the words 'ecumenical problem' only once, on page 4, very much *en passant*. This is in line with the fact—an open secret—that the Secretariat for Promoting Christian Unity was not consulted about the text."[20]

A Spanish Professor of Ecumenism found not only violation of the ecumenical spirit by omission, but also by commission: "From the ecumenical point of view it seems to me that after Vatican II at least one can no longer say: 'there is a continuous tradition in time *universal* in the East and West . . . in not conferring priestly ordination except on males.' The Anglican, Lutheran, Calvinist Churches . . . they also are Churches (Ecumenism Decree 3, 19) and they recognize the ordained ministry of women."[21]

But a Belgian criticism of the Declaration's ecumenical violations was strongest of all, accusing Rome of a haughty attitude: "How will the sister-churches react to the haughty attitude of Rome affirming alone a doctrine contrary to others and invoking on this point 'its fidelity to the Lord,' as though this fidelity is not also their concern? Was it really necessary to write a statement, and in such a peremptory manner, on this subject? Would it not have been better to seize, in all humility and thanksgiving, this occasion of walking along together towards Unity by searching with other Christian Churches, and with their help, another dimension, possibility and ministerial perspective that may exist for today's world, so much transformed by profound social changes?"[22]

Bible

Many commentators on the Declaration criticized its use of the Bible, both in general and in specifics. On the moderate side was the critique raised by Father Yves Congar, who in an interview responded: "If someone asks me, Is it [male priests only] of divine law? I know nothing about it! But if I am pressed, I would rather say it is not. For what is of divine law? That which is in the Bible, what is attested to there. But in the Bible there is nothing formal or explicit, nothing for or against."[23] One Spanish Scripture Professor succinctly concluded, "Does the living and existential reading of the Bible oblige us definitively to exclude women priests? We believe not."[24] Another Spanish theologian stressed the socio-cultural context of biblical statements and its pertinence in this matter: "I believe that the historical data of the lack of women in the ministerial priesthood is profoundly conditioned by the socio-culture. . . . Theoretically I see no major difficulty preventing the ministerial priesthood of women."[25] Karl Rahner made much the same point about the importance of the culture and social environment in the question of women priests: "In a brief essay it is not possible to spell out in detail the historical material that makes it understandable that Jesus and the Apostles in their concrete cultural and social milieu could not think of (without undertaking the then impossible) appointing women as community leaders and presiders at the eucharistic celebrations—indeed that such a development in that situation could not even turn up as a possibility."[26]

Another Spanish biblical scholar hammered at the uncritical method interpretation employed by the Declaration: " 'Women should keep silent in the church.' This expression of 1 Cor 14:34-35 which, when read in its context, cannot be other than a rubric for the well-ordering of the liturgical assembly, or at most a condescension to the social conventions of the moment, has been raised up by theology to a categorical principle which is powerful, even absolute. In virtue of it women remain excluded from the sacrament of Orders and even the use of speech in church. . . .

"Here we have a typically uncritical use of the Bible which ignores a series of relativizing principles that a healthy hermeneutics has been introducing into the reading of the Sacred Scripture."[27]

A Swiss theologian and a German theologian, Hans Küng and Gerhard Lohfink, pungently applied a *reductio ad absurdam* to the Declaration's biblical interpretation method: "Are we to think that only married and gainfully employed Jews (whenever possible fishermen from Lake Gennesaret) will now be considered for the office of priest or bishop in the Catholic Church? It is hard not to be ironic when faced with the hermeneutic employed in the recent Roman Declaration on the Ordination of Women. Its determining principle: norms are derived directly from historical facts. 'Jesus Christ did not call any women to become part of the Twelve'—and so the Church can admit no women to priestly ordination. Such a hermeneutic is dangerous. Used consistently, it leads not only to oddities like the above but to a rocking of the entire constitution of the Church. For in the judgment of serious exegetes the calling of the Twelve is not a calling to ecclesiastical office; the historical Paul 'ordained' no priests at all, not even men; Peter and all the apostles, according to the unambiguous witness of Paul, took their wives on their mission journeys. . . ."[28]

Tradition

If the use of the Bible by the Declaration was roundly criticized by many Catholic scholars, perhaps even more so was its use of the notion of tradition. The anger of the commentators was often evident here. Perhaps the mildest reproof came from a Spanish theologian who wrote that, "The tradition which is presented here is no more than custom and not the tradition which was presented at Vatican II."[29] A Swiss Professor of Theology in effect accused the Congregation of the Faith here of right-wing reactionarism: "The concept of tradition which is used here also appears doubtful. It recalls ultimately, in its rigidity and its misdirectedness, the conception of Archbishop Lefevre, which was rejected without equivocation by Rome."[30]

A Dutch Catholic called the Vatican to return to Vatican II's notion of tradition: "The Biblical Commission already previously declared that Scripture does not exclude the ordination of women. But the Congregation for the Teaching of the Faith has cooked up a new recipe: tradition, understood as separated from Scripture. That conception of tradition was abandoned by nearly all theologians of the period following the Vatican Council II."[31] A group of Belgian Catholics also charged the Declaration with abandoning Vatican II and falling into the primitive logical error of *petitio principii*: "The document had to rely on Tradition taken as an independent factor, and apart from the Scriptures. This way of arguing—which we presume would have been definitively abandoned since Vatican II—reveals itself in this case as begging the question: the same authority that by its own action created and perpetuated a tradition now tries to justify it by arguing with this sole historical fact, the fact of a custom of which she bears alone the responsibility."[32]

The German theologian Karl Rahner calmly dismissed the claim that the tradition of only male priests was necessarily divine when he stated, "that the actual attitude of Jesus and the apostles in the strict sense of the word implies a norm of divine revelation does not appear to be proved. This praxis (even if it has stood unchallenged for a long time) can clearly be understood as a 'human' tradition, as other traditions in the Church which once were unchallenged, stood for a long time, and then nevertheless through a social and cultural evolution became obsolete."[33]

An Indian Jesuit argued that ordaining priests was an early change in tradition warranted by pastoral need; true to primary concern of missionary countries to preach the gospel, the priest advocated ordaining women on similar grounds—with a homey footnote: "I hope the Vatican 'No' to women's ordination will not be the last word that comes from Rome. . . . Tradition has been constant. But what happened in the early centuries of the Church? When the faithful grew in numbers and the Bishops—successors of the Apostles—could not cope with the work, could not attend to the Sacramental needs of the believers, helpers—priests—were ordained. Tradition was changed.

"Need should be the strongest argument today. When priests are not enough in many parts of the world, ordained ladies, especially Sisters, could come to our rescue. The sacramental life of the Christians is a forceful reason to alter tradition. . . . Some priests have to say two, three and at times even four Masses on Sundays, in far away places. If some of our Bishops should have to do a similar task, their tired feet and bodies would give their learned minds additional wisdom and courage to cast their votes in favour of women's ordination."[34]

Sexism

In the wake of the Declaration a professor at the Catholic University of Louvain, Belgium, raised in a very personal way the question of discrimination against women, sexism, in the Catholic Church. She reflected: "I ask myself, if I had to have a daughter again, would I bring her to be baptized in a Church which practices discrimination against women."[35] In the French Catholic paper *Le Monde* the specific charge of sexism was levelled at the Declaration: "If the document recalls—and very rightly so—that the admission of women to the ministry does not reside in a personal right, nor even in the dignity of the person called, even less in her superiority, it then bases this condition (and this is a test of prime importance) *on sex*. This is precisely the definition of sexism, a sexism that has become largely condemned and abandoned."[36]

Authority of the Declaration

Just what authority the Declaration was to be given was often the subject of reflection ranging from analytic to even sarcastic comments by Catholic theologians. One of the milder analyses—which still found the Declaration far from definitive in authority—came from Spain. The editorial spoke about the need to interpret the data of Revelation, taking into account the sociocultural circumstances, what is of permanent value and what is not, and then added: "The document undertakes this task of interpretation, but its reasoning does not produce very convincing results. . . . The arguments have a relative validity. They express in every case a preference and a greater congruence in favor of a male priesthood, but not an absolute incompatibility of women with the sacred ministry."[37]

Another Spanish Professor of Theology insisted on the ambiguity of the question of women priests, that it therefore should be declared 'open' and further studied: "It is well known that in these questions it is not possible to describe the position as definitive. There is a collective process which has to follow its course. There are arguments for and arguments against. Today neither one nor the other appears to be doctrinally clearly proven. In such cases it seems to me prudent to leave the 'question open,' in the hope that 'additional reflection'—and the same cultural and social evolution—will offer more mature data which will allow a more elaborated decision."[38]

Still another Spanish theologian—one who had previously published substantively on women in the Church—dismissed the persuasiveness of the Declaration: "The Sacred Congregation of the Faith, withal, does not have the competence to fix doctrinally such a question. A matter of such seriousness belongs to the Pope in person or in an Ecumenical Council. This document then is reduced to a Declaration, clothed with the authority lent by the commission and favorable perusal of Paul VI, but whose fundamenal force lies in the theological arguments it adduces. These are not convincing."[39]

The English Catholic *Month* likewise found the Declaration unconvincing in its arguments that attempted to project the past into the future: "But it [the Declaration] aims to go further, believing that these same arguments are so theologically well-founded that no change in the traditional practice is possible. At this point, it becomes open to criticism; it is only as good as its theology. In all the areas into which the Declaration delves, there are counter-arguments and amplifications to be put to the positions it expresses."[40]

The Spanish Catholic weekly periodical *Vida Nueva* in putting out a special issue on "El Sacerdocio de la Mujer" insisted on entering into dialogue with Rome on the subject of the Declaration: "In the case at hand, the Roman document on the priesthood of women, we feel obliged to offer to the proper authority a humble reflection as an act of service, of better service: that of an intelligence which does not refuse to obey, but which also refuses to suffocate itself at the same time. Nothing more and nothing less."[41]

Herbert McCabe, O.P., editor of England's *New Blackfriars* could hardly contain his scorn for the Declaration. He wrote: "We refer, of course, to the ludicrous Declaration on Women and the Priesthood which takes about 6000 words to say that nothing must ever happen for the first time. It is full of superb non-sequiturs of which my favourite is the argument that the equality of the sexes is irrelevant since the priesthood is not a human right. The argument, of course, is not whether anybody has a 'right' to the priesthood but whether anybody has the right to refuse it to someone *simply* on the grounds of her sex."[42]

Writing in a French Catholic journal from Lyon, editor Donna Singles took an equally firm stand but developed it with less acidity. She closed her long editorial with the following: "We are persuaded that the last word has not yet been said, that the Church is embarked, whether it wants to or not, upon a process which places it more and more in the position of having to accept and welcome the presence of women at all levels of public life of the Church and in all actions of the New Covenant. The institution cannot return to the past. It is already too late, for the idea is well launched now that there is no solid theological reason prohibiting Christian women from participation in all areas of the life of the Church. One day it will happen. The walls of resistance are already beginning to collapse. Is it, the more the Magisterium resists, the more it seems to give the impression that it is not in accord with the profound will of Christ? Too harsh an image? Perhaps, but the categorical refusal of the Magisterium to ordain women makes one think that it is perhaps motivated by some sentiments connected more to a nostalgia for the past and to personal reluctance than to the will of the disciple to follow his master."[43]

But the statement on the authority of the Declaration that combined most of all a firm stance, nuanced respect with biting humor, and an optimistic outlook was made by Sister María Jesús Romero, President of the Spanish Conference of Women Religious. In somewhat terse language she wrote: "Although it is not a dogmatic definition, it is a document which merits our complete attention. It demands our obedience (though this should not be thought to be enthusiastic), but does not prohibit our reflection (though this should not be understood as less respectful).

"To begin to speak about equality between man and woman in order immediately to determine on an inequality reminds one of the classical system of 'yes, but. . . ,' which some readers would find positively distasteful. In fact, between equality and inequality there is introduced an element of asymmetry: the man and the woman are equal but different, but they are different in different ways. . . .

"For the future one can not only think about the *possibility*, but also the *need* to ordain women."[44]

Consultation

Though Vatican spokesmen said various persons were consulted during the writing of the Declaration, in standard Vatican fashion no names or other specific information was forthcoming; all was veiled in secrecy. The apparent lack of consultation was vigorously condemned by Catholic theologians and groups. The Swiss theologian Küng and the German Lohfink wrote: "Obviously only ordained men collaborated on this document. The Vatican Committee on Women in Church and Society was forbidden to discuss the ordination of women. The papal Biblical Commission, however, supported another viewpoint. The Secretariat for Christian Unity, although competent in ecumenism, was not even consulted. To say nothing of a consultation of the bishops! Was it thought that the 'Faith of the Church' could be expressed by such means? It is as if there had never been a Vatican II with its calls for collegiality and serious curial reform."[45]

Spreading the charge of non-consultation even further, the French Catholic Bernard Lauret wrote: "A brief additional word. Outside of the priesthood the Declaration wishes for the sake of the Church that Christian women would become fully aware of the greatness of their mission: Today their role is of capital importance, both for the renewal and humanization of society and for the rediscovery by believers of the true face of the Church. Very well, but the Vatican also preaches by example! If among others one looks at the 1975 *Annuario Pontificio*, not a single woman will be found among the members of the Secretariat of State, nor many in the ten Congregations which make decisions for the life of the Church. Those women who are found there are listed only among the 'consultors' but not among the members."[46]

But perhaps the most significant charge of lack of consultation came from Denmark where the Council of the World Union of Catholic Women's Organizations (WUCWO), representing all national Catholic women's organizations around the world, met in the Spring of 1977: "The Council regrets that in spite of the statement it had made, according to which a large number of women should have been consulted during the preparatory stage of the editing and publication of the Declaration, WUCWO was not consulted. And further, the Council emphasizes that WUCWO represents 127 organizations, existing in 60 countries of six continents (about 30 million women)."[47] Their complaint made waves all the way to the Congregation of the Faith, which granted their leaders a two-hour interview.

Organization Statements

Besides the many statements by individual Catholic theologians and editorial stances mentioned already, a number of Catholic organizations issued strong statements in response to the Declaration—all these of course are in addition to the many statements by American Catholic organizations.[48]

In Germany the executive committee of the *Katholische Frauengemeinschaft Deutschlands* expressed "concern" about the Declaration in a letter to Cardinal Joseph Höffner, the President of the German Bishops' Conference. They urged the Cardinal to forestall a definitively negative decision concerning women priests by taking up the matter in the German Bishops' Conference and in Rome.[49]

St. Joan's International Alliance, Belgian section quickly (February 7, 1977) issued a statement "deploring the Declaration issued by the Congregation. . . . It expresses its regrets that it is not able to accept the arguments—already refuted by numerous theologians—invoked as a support of that decision."[50]

In the Netherlands "among the groups studying questions concerning women in the Church and society are those made up of several faculties of theology, both Catholic and Protestant. They met on the national level several times during 1976. During one of the last meetings, on February 5, 1977, the Inter-University Commission 'Feminism and Theology' sent the following telegram to the Congregation For the Teaching of the Faith: 'We received a sudden and profound shock by the Declaration of the Congregation For the Teaching of the Faith concerning the admission of women to the priesthood. What arrogance not to take account either of the conclusions of the Pontifical Biblical Commission, or of the experience of the women pastors of the entire world, or of the conclusions of theologians of great faith and solid competence.' "[51]

Another international Catholic organization, Women and Men In the Church, issued a long critical statement on the Vatican Declaration. They closed thus: "The international group 'Femmes et Hommes dans l'Eglise' regrets to declare that this document is not the fruit of an authentic research. It appears rather as a justification—by all means—of a pre-conceived thesis that is no longer defensible with the usual arguments. The Group appeals to the Christian community as a whole and sees as a sure sign of justice, solidarity and hope in Christ that some persons manifest openly to proper authorities their regret and disavowal of this document."[52]

But the most important organization statement issued was that of the 30 million-strong WUCWO's Council referred to above. They reported that in response to the requests of many of their members they formulated a letter to the Congregation of the Faith. Besides regretting their not being consulted, the note vigorously criticized the Declaration on many levels. It stated in part: "The Council likewise emphasizes that its approach is not concerned simply with the discussion of the accession of women to the priesthood: the content of the Declaration presents in effect in subliminal fashion an image of woman and a theology which contradicts the statements of Pius XII, John XXIII and Paul VI, the open perspectives of Vatican II and at the same time are not congruent with the gospel. The content of the Declaration likewise implicitly runs counter to the 'signs of the times' which vigorously support the rising consciousness of women today concerning their personal dignity and their participation in society and the Church.

"The Council foresees the negative impact the Declaration of the Congregation For the Teaching of the Faith will have on the women's organizations and movements, Christian and otherwise, and on the Christian Churches before the world.

"The Council deplores the contradiction which is apparent between the Declaration and numerous stands the Church has taken (notably on the occasion of the Women's International Year) for the promotion and support of equality between men and women in society on the one hand and on the other the refusal of that equality in the bosom of the Church. The Council declares that these contradictions hurt and demoralize women.

"In conclusion the Council of WUCWO wishes to bring its full and entire collaboration to the studies and actions which will be undertaken in the Church to clarify the situation and resolve these problems. Magleas, Denmark, April 3, 1977."[53]

Not only was this strong note sent to the Congregation of the Faith, but an elected delegation of the Council of WUCWO, led by their General President, Elizabeth Lovatt-Dolan, had a two-hour interview with the Secretary, Under-secretary, and two experts of the Congregation For the Teaching of the Faith on June 28, 1977. The representatives of the Congregation reportedly showed themselves very interested in the Council's work and reflections, and indicated they wished to consult with WUCWO in the future, and that they would report the discussion to the proper authorities.

# # # # # #

The present book contains the Declaration on the Question of the Admission of Women to the Ministerial Priesthood by the Sacred Congregation For the Teaching of the Faith, the Commentary on it also released through the same Congregation, and the 1976 Report of the Pontifical Biblical Commission on women priests. The latter two documents are found in an appendix. The Declaration is printed here with boldface numerals added throughout, locating the correspondingly numbered essays commenting on that portion of the Declaration. Including the four introductory essays there are fifty essays of commentary on the Declaration by forty-four Catholic scholars of North America. It is worth noting that of the forty-four scholars twenty-eight are women and sixteen men; seventeen are laywomen, eleven are sisters, twelve are priests, and four are laymen.

Each essay is signed, and responsibility for it is assumed only by the author, for naturally there are differences of view among the scholars writing here; a book like the present one is part of what theological dialogue is all about. And in this particular case, as Karl Rahner so aptly put it: "Even after this Declaration the discussion over the present problem may and must go on; this discussion is not at an end and it cannot consist only of an apology for the basic thesis and arguments of the Declaration. The Declaration is an authentic but fundamentally revisable and reformable Declaration of the Roman Magisterium which the theologian must respond to with respect but also with the right and duty of a critical evaluation."[54]

L.S.

July 14, 1977
Bastille Day

Philadelphia, Pennsylvania
City of Sisterly and Brotherly Love

Notes

1. *Femmes et Hommes dans l'Eglise*, No. 22 (March, 1977), p. 16. Address: Rue de la Prévoyance 58, Brussels, Belgium.

2. Cf. *Origins*, Vol. 8, No. 47 (May 12, 1977), p. 742. The poll found more support for women priests among men than among women, and that the majority of those under thirty years of age were in favor of women priests. Cf. also Andrew Greeley's Universal Press Syndicated column published in *The Church World* (May 26, 1977), p. 21.

3. Ad. Tanquerey, *Synopsis Theologiae Dogmaticae Fundamentalis* (New York: Benziger Brothers, 1937), p. 752.

4. Karl Rahner, "Priestertum der Frau?" *Stimmen der Zeit*, Vol. 105, No. 5 (May, 1977), p. 293.

5. *Ibid.*, p. 294.

6. *Ibid.*

7. Cf. *Wir schweigen nicht länger! We Won't Keep Silence Any Longer* (Zurich, 1964). This is a collection of essays in either German or English by a number of Catholic women—Swiss, German, and American—who deal with the status of women in the Catholic Church. It includes the petition by Dr. Heinzelman, and resolutions on the same subject passed by St. Joan's International Alliance at its 1963 and 1964 conventions. ("St. Joan's Alliance grew from the Catholic Woman's Suffrage Society founded in London in 1911, the only association of Catholics to work for woman's suffrage . . . and enjoys consultative status with the United Nations.") Cf. "Now Hear

This" (Dr. Gertrude Heinzelmann's Request to the Vatican Council), *Commonweal* (October 5, 1962), p. 31.

8. Haye van der Meer, *Priestertum der Frau?* (Freiburg: Herder Verlag, 1969). Translated by Arlene and Leonard Swidler, *Women Priests in the Catholic Church?* (Philadelphia: Temple University Press, 1973). The dissertation, however, had been finished in 1962.

9. The work of Father Idigoras, *La Mujer dentro del Orden Sagrado*, appeared in mimeographed form in Lima, Peru in 1963. It is summarized under the title ,of *La femme dans l'ordre sacré* in *Informations Catholiques Internationales*, November 15, 1963.

10. Cf. e.g., Rosemary Lauer, "Women and the Church," *Commonweal* (December 20, 1963), pp. 365-68; P. Jordan, "Women-priests Stirs Controversy," *Catholic Messenger* (April 16, 1977), p. 8; E. Gibson, "Women as Clergy?" *Ave Maria* (July 24, 1965), pp. 5-8; Gertrude Heinzelman, "The Priesthood and Women," *Commonweal* (January 15, 1965), pp. 504-8; Mary Daly, "A Built In Bias," *Commonweal* (January 15, 1965), pp. 508-11; D. Lowery, "Should Women Be Priests? *Ligorian* (May, 1965), pp. 20-25; B. Damian, "The Priesthood for Women?" *Friar* (February, 1966), pp. 14-17; Rosemary Lauer, "Women Clergy for Rome?" *Christian Century* (September 14, 1966), pp. 1107-10; Arlene Swidler, "The Male Church," *Commonweal* (June 24, 1966), pp. 387-89; Cecelia Wallace, "How Women Were Excluded," *National Catholic Reporter* (January 5, 1966), p. 6. These are only a few of just the American articles in these years dealing with women priests. Kathryn E. Kirby has annotated over a hundred such in a research paper submitted to the Department of Library Science of the Catholic University of America in January, 1970, entitled: "The Status of Women in the Church Vatican II—1968 Annotated Bibliography."

11. V. E. Hannon, *The Question of Women and Priesthood* (London: G. Chapman, 1967).

12. Ida Raming, *Der Ausschluss der Frau vom priesterlichen Amt* (Cologne: Böhlau, 1973). Translated into English by Norman R. Adams, *The Exclusion of Women From the Priesthood* (Metuchen, N.J.: Scarecrow Press, 1976).

13. "Statement of Recommendations by the Pastoral Consultation on Ministries in the Church," *Word and Worship* (Bangalore, India), Vol. 9, No. 5 (July, 1976), p. 331.

14. "Conclusions of Interdisciplinary Research Seminar on Ministries in the Church," *ibid.*, p. 297.

15. "L'Église réaffirme son opposition à l'ordination sacerdotale des femmes," *Le Monde* (February 2, 1977).

16. *Word and Worship*, p. 331.

17. Interview With Yves Congar, "Non, cela ne s'est jamais fait," *Réforme* (February 19, 1977), p. 10.

18. *Femmes et Hommes*, p. 22.

19. Henri Fesquet, "Points de vue sur la femme dans l'Église," *Le Monde* (March 1, 1977), p. 15.

20. *The Tablet* (London) (February 5, 1977), p. 136.

21. Ana Maria Schlüter Rodes, Professor of Ecumenism, Member of the Community of Bethany, "El Sacerdocio de la Mujer, A Debate," *Vida Nueva* (March 5, 1977), p. 26.

22. "Déclaration du groupe international Femmes et Hommes dans l'Eglise," *Femmes et Hommes*, p. 5.

23. Congar, *Réforme*, p. 10.

24. Felipe Fernández Ramos, Professor of Bible at the University of Salamanca, *Vida Nueva*, p. 31.

25. Josep Perarnau, Professor of Theology at Barcelona and Valencia, *Vida Nueva*, p. 24.

26. Rahner, *Stimmen der Zeit*, p. 298.

27. Antonio Gonzalez Lamadrid, Biblical Scholar, *Vida Nueva*, p. 30.

28. Hans Küng and Gerhard Lohfink, "Keine Ordination der Frau?" *Theologische Quartalschrift* (Tübingen), Spring, 1977.

29. Felipe Fernandez Ramos, *Vida Nueva*, p. 31.

30. Jospf Bommer, *Luzerner Neuste Nachrichten* (January 31, 1977).

31. Andre Lascaris, "La peur des femmes," *De Bazuin* (February 4, 1977).

32. *Femmes et Hommes*, p. 4.

33. Rahner, *Stimmen der Zeit*, p. 299.

34. J.D. Calvo, S.J., "Women's Ordination," *The Herald* (Calcutta), February 18, 1977, p. 7.

35. Interview with Professor Emma Vorlat in *Knack Magazine* (February 9, 1977).

36. Marie-Thérèse van Lunen-Chenu, "Vieux rêves et anciens refus," *Le Monde* (March 1, 1977), p. 15.

37. "Documento sobre del sacerdocio de la mujer Observaciones," *Colligite* (October-December, 1976), pp. 338-39. This editorial was obviously written and published after January, 1977.

38. Jordi Piquer, Professor on the Theology Faculty of Barcelona, *Vida Nueva*, p. 29.

39. Manuel Acalá, S.J., Professor of Ethics, Grenada Theology Faculty, *Vida Nueva*, p. 33. Cf. Manuel Acalá, "El Problemo de la Ordenacion Ministerial de la Mujer a Partir del Vaticano II, in *Teologia y mundo. Homenaje a K. Rahner* (Madrid: Ed. Cristiandad, 1975), pp. 577-612; and Manuel Acalá, "Por Que Discriminacion Sexual en la Iglesia?" *Razon y Fe* (October, 1975), pp. 195-207.

40. *The Month* (March, 1977), p. 75.

41. This issue of *Vida Nueva* (March 5, 1977), devotes sixteen pages to this question. The periodical is illustrated with photos, having a format not unlike Time Magazine. The cover of this issue is a photo of a woman dressed in Mass vestments standing by an altar. Six years earlier *Vida Nueva* (February 6, 1971) also ran a cover with a photo of a woman priest and devoted a section of the issue to the topic. The 1977 special issue printed the Vatican Declaration and the comments of ten Spanish theologians; two agreed with the Declaration and eight disagreed. The issue was edited by Maria Lopez Vigil, an Associate Editor.

42. Herbert McCabe, "Comment," *New Blackfriars* (February, 1977), p. 54.

43. Donna Singles, "Le 'Non' à l'ordination des femmes, expression de la volonté du Christ?" *Effort diaconal* (Lyon), May-June, 1977, p. 5.

44. María Jesús Jurado Romero, President of the Spanish Conference of Women Religious, *Vida Nueva*, p. 35.

18   *Prolegomena*

45. Küng and Lohfink, *Theologische Quartalschrift,* Spring, 1977.

46. Bernard Lauret, *Témoignage Chrétien* (February 3, 1977), p. 20.

47. "Note des Reactions du Conseil sur la Declaration de la Congregation pour la Doctrine de la Foi," Cir. Speciale-77/ORG, Annexe 1, issued July, 1977, by WUCWO headquarters in Paris.

48. Among many, the following organizations in America made public statements favorable to the ordination of women: St. Joan's International Alliance, Women's Ordination Conference, Leadership Conference of Women Religious, National Coalition of American Nuns, National Association of Women Religious, Priests For Equality, and the Liturgical Conference.

49. Catholic Press Service (Kathpress), Bonn, February 15, 1977.

50. *Femmes et Hommes*, p. 22.

51. *Ibid.*, p. 18.

52. *Ibid.*, p. 5.

53. "Note des Reactions du Conseil," *op. cit.*

54. Rahner, *Stimmen der Zeit*, p. 301.

The Juridical Significance of the Declaration

Francis G. Morrisey

The statement issued by the Sacred Congregation for the Doctrine of the Faith is identified as a "declaration." In order to understand better the significance of this term, it is important to remember that the word "declaration" is used in many senses.

In general, we can state that a declaration is an interpretation of existing law or facts, or a reply to a contested point of law. There are at least four basic types of declarations.[1]

The first type is known simply as a *declaration*. Generally speaking, it is not a new law, and must be interpreted in the light of existing legislation. One such declaration that was misunderstood in recent years was the joint declaration of the Sacred Congregation for the Clergy and the Sacred Congregation for the Discipline of the Sacraments on the question of first confession and first communion (May 24, 1973).[2] Since this particular text was simply presented as a declaration, it did not constitute new law. If the legislator had intended it to be otherwise, he would have used a different form of pronouncement, such as a "decree."

The second type of declaration is the *authentic interpretation* or declaration. A very important example of this type of document was the declaration of the Sacred Congregation for the Doctrine of the Faith, June 26, 1972.[3] This was proposed as an authentic declaration, and, consequently, did not require further promulgation (can. 17, par. 2) and was retroactive. This particular declaration was concerned with norms relative to the return of priests to the lay state.

The third type of declaration is the *extensive declaration*, which, to a certain extent, modifies the law. This type must be promulgated according to the norms of law and is not retroactive. There have not been too many examples of this type of declaration in recent years.[4]

The Roman Congregations have also lately been issuing *declarations on moral issues*, such as the one on sexual ethics, December 29, 1975.[5] These declarations are not of the legislative order, but pertain more directly to matters of faith and morals.

In addition to these types of declarations, the word is also used in other juridical circumstances. In cases of procedure, a declaration may be used to state that a penalty has already been imposed by the law; in cases of nullity, a declaration of nullity states that a given act is null and void and has been so from the beginning.

19

With the exception of the extensive declaration, all of these documents have one thing in common: they do not create new law, but simply restate existing legislation and apply it to new circumstances. The same can be said about the present Declaration regarding the ordination of women to the ministerial priesthood. The law has not been changed; however, new or different reasons are presented in an attempt to justify maintaining the legislation as it exists. This particular statement would be placed, it seems, in the first category of declarations.

In one sense, the document changes nothing in the legislation regarding the ordination of women to the ministerial priesthood. On the other hand, the legal or juridical position is reinforced by making the legislator's intention known and by trying to clarify any doubts about his position. However, this very clarification can raise some other problems that must be considered. One of these is: what does the document signify or represent? It is a re-statement of a juridical norm, but a re-statement based on arguments which are not primarily of the juridical order.

From a legislative point of view, it would be oversimplistic to state that because the Declaration was not preceded by some form of public universal consultation, it does not have legal value. Indeed, it is not presented primarily as a juridical text. In fact, with very few exceptions, the present legislative system of the Church does not *require* previous consultation with specifically-designated persons.[6] Or course, any good legislation will not be the result of arbitrary decisions, but will be based upon a consensus expressing what is felt best for the public good. It goes without saying, though, that the mere fact of consensus does not always make a thing right or opportune on a long-range basis.

Looking at the subject matter of this Declaration, and replacing it in its broad *juridical* context, it would have been inopportune even to consider this particular aspect of the status of women in the Church until the more fundamental points of basic equality between men and women have been settled in other areas of ecclesiastical legislation.

To ask whether the document is binding is another question. A declaration generally has no more juridical effect than the law which it wishes to clarify. In this instance, the law itself is quite clear and positive (can. 968, par. 1), and concerns validity. Therefore, just as the law is binding, the Declaration is binding as a source of interpretation. The question to be asked is whether the ordination of women is only a matter of ecclesiastical law, or whether it is also a matter related to the Divine will. The presumption had been in the past that the prescription allowing only males to receive ordination was not simply of ecclesiastical law.[7] Like any other presumption, however, it stands until it is reversed. The presumtion could only be reasonably reversed, if at all, after serious, objective study and investigation. This is not a matter of a few months, or even of a few years. Conclusions of research have to be tested and verified. Likewise, in a question of such particular importance, these conclusions would have to be accepted by the teaching Magisterium of the Church as part of the Christian heritage.

By its very nature as a declaration, the statement does not close the door definitively on the question. It simply states that at the present time, "the Church, in fidelity to the example of the Lord, does not consider herself authorized to admit women to priestly ordination."[8] The text states that "the various arguments capable of clarifying this important problem have been submitted to a critical examination,"[9] but it does not refer to the manner in which these arguments were examined or evaluated. The conclusion, in the light of many pronouncements of the Holy Father himself,[10] was to be expected. It might possibly be questioned whether the matter was completely and exhaustively studied; but study alone is not the only way of understanding truth.

Looking to the future, it could be stated that since the Declaration calls for a "deepening understanding of the respective roles of men and of women," that much can be done to help clarify the juridical status of all the members of the Church. The Declaration will certainly be a stimulus to this type of work, and this will probably be its greatest contribution to the development of the question.

Notes

1. Cf. Francis G. Morrisey, *The Canonical Significance of Papal and Curial Pronouncements* (Hartford, Ct.: Canon Law Society of America, 1974), p. 10.

2. Cf. *Acta Apostolicae Sedis*, 65 (1973), p. 410.

3. Cf. *ibid.*, 64(1972), pp. 641-643. For a commentary on declarations see Raoul Naz, "Déclaration," in *Dictionnaire de Droit canonique* (Paris, Letouzey et Ané), IV, cc. 1059-1061.

4. One example of such an extensive declaration is found in the response of the Sacred Congregation of the Holy Office, November 16, 1934, on the application of certain prescriptions of canon 2367 on the absolution of the accomplice to other cases not immediately envisaged in the penal legislation of this particular canon; cf. *A.A.S.*, 26(1934), p. 634. Another example of such a declaration, although it is not specifically presented as such, is to be found in a response of the Pontifical Commission for the Interpretation of the Decrees of the Second Vatican Council, February 14, 1974, in *A.A.S.*, 66(1974), p. 463, on the necessity of motivating decrees of ratification in second instance in cases of nullity of marriage.

5. The English translation of this declaration may be found in *Origins*, 5(1975-1976), pp. 485, 487-494. The response of the Sacred Congregation for the Doctrine of the Faith regarding Sterilization, March 13, 1975, and made public in May, 1976 (cf. *Origins*, 6(1976-1977), pp. 33, 35) is a response, and not a declaration since it was not intended for the general public.

6. In some instances, a legislator is required to have the deliberative vote of his council before proceeding to perform certain acts (e.g., certain specified financial transactions; cf. cans. 1530-1532, etc.); in other instances, a consultative vote is required (e.g., in relation to certain appointments, to

admission to religious Institutes, etc.; cf. cans. 543, 403, etc.); finally, in some cases, no form of consultation is prescribed, although it is rarely prohibited; the norms regarding the selection of Bishops prohibit consultation of groups, although the individuals concerned may be consulted—cf. Norms of March 25, 1972, Art. XII, 1, in *A.A.S.*, 64(1972), p. 390.

7. For an example of such arguments, cf. F.M. Cappello, S.J., *Tractatus Canonico-Moralis de Sacramentis*, IV, *De Ordine* (Rome: Marietti, 1947), p. 249. Cappello, in this instance, states that we must be rather cautious about invoking such reasons.

8. Cf. Declaration, par. 5.

9. Cf. *ibid.*, par. 4.

10. Cf. letter of Pope Paul VI, November 30, 1975, in *A.A.S.*, 68(1976), pp. 599-600, to the Archbishop of Canterbury.

Internal Indecisiveness

Carroll Stuhlmueller

In this Declaration the Sacred Congregation for the Doctrine of the Faith manifests a low profile of authority. Not only was the form of a "Declaration" chosen instead of a papal "Motu Proprio" or "Encyclical," but significant qualifying words or phrases lessen the internal certitude within the document. The Declaration claims to have made "a critical examination" of "various arguments capable of clarifying this important problem." As a result, its own negative conclusions have had to be modified and its supporting reasons presented as less than probative. Because earlier publications have contributed to a more nuanced Declaration, new books and articles will continue the dialog and move the issue towards still greater certitude in the Magisterium and the Church at large.

We cite examples of indecisiveness within the document. Already in the "Introduction" it is *not* directly and definitively stated that women cannot be ordained. Rather, we read that "the Church . . . does not *consider herself authorized* to admit women to priestly ordination" (italics added). The door is left open. With new and further clarification the Church could *consider herself authorized.* This indirect style recalls a statement in Pope Pius XII's encyclical, *Humani Generis* about polygenism (namely, the hypothesis that human beings existed after Adam not descended from him, or that "Adam" signifies several first parents collectively). Pius XII declared that "it is not apparent ("nequaquam appareat") how this position can be adjusted to those other statements which the sources of revelation and the acts of the Church's Magisterium propose about original sin . . . " *(Enchiridion biblicum:* Rome, 1956, n. 617). The statement implicitly admits that further investigation might make it apparent and even certain. In any case "appareat" is a weak word in ecclesiastical documentation.

Within the "Introduction" the Declaration admits: "we are dealing with a debate which classical theology scarcely touched upon." Chapter One states moreover that the ordination of men only was "a principle . . . not attacked . . . a law . . . not challenged." The subject then of women's ordination bears comparison with the doctrine of the inspiration of the Bible. This religious truth received practically no attention in papal or conciliar documents till Pope Leo XIII's encyclical *Providentissimus Deus* (18 Nov., 1893). Since then it has undergone important development into what is now termed "the social character of inspiration" (cf., James T. Burchaell, *Catholic Theories of Biblical Inspiration Since 1810.* Cambridge University Press, 1969; J.L. McKenzie, "The Social Character of Inspiration," *Catholic Biblical Quarterly*, Vol. 24 [1962], pp. 115-124; C. Stuhlmueller, "The Search for

23

God's Word," *Cross Currents*, Vol. 20 [Summer, 1970], pp. 301-314). Just as our study into the doctrine of inspiration has led to a much broader base and a wider sharing of this charism within the society of Israel, investigations into priesthood are deepening the roots and extending the base of this sacred office. In both cases the initial document from the Magisterium does not settle the question but focuses research.

In Chapter Two the Declaration concedes that a scrutiny into the Gospels and the attitude of Christ leads to "facts [which] do not make the matter immediately obvious. . . . We have here a number of convergent indications." The word *indications* is very weak, especially in serious controversial dialog. Furthermore, the Declaration adds that "a purely historical exegesis of the texts cannot suffice."

Because the results of Chapter Two on "the attitude of Christ" are so inconclusive, one is surprised that the all-important "Introduction" appeals to "the example of the Lord" as the reason why the "Church . . . does not consider herself authorized. . . ." The same indecisive reasoning appears again in Chapter Three concerning "The Practice of the Apostles." Here we read: "They could therefore have envisaged conferring ordination on women, if they had not been convinced of the duty of *fidelity to the Lord on this point*" (italics added). Yet in Chapter Two this significant point is "not immediately obvious" and amounts to "a number of convergent indications." Chapter Four, moreover, recalls "this attitude of Jesus and the Apostles which has been *considered* as normative by the whole of tradition up to our own day" (italics added). The word "considered" weakens a statement which could have read more simply and more forcefully "which has been normative." This hesitation about tradition is more apparent when we recall the earlier admission in the Declaration that "we are dealing with a debate rarely mentioned by the Fathers and Scholastics (whom the Declaration in Chapter One admits were often prejudiced in their attitude towards women), "which classical theology scarcely touched upon," a "question [which] has not been raised again." In other words, the two shortest and weakest chapters in the Declaration become the principal basis for the negative conclusion.

The authors of the Declaration must have been conscious of this internal indecisiveness. Roman documents must be exegeted carefully; qualifying phrases which blunt the directness of the conclusions are deliberately introduced. When the document comes to "the final analysis" in Chapter Four, the authors state that it is the "Magisterium . . . [which] decides what can change and what must remain immutable." Evidently reasons from Scripture and Tradition were not sufficiently cogent to close the case. If the biblical, patristic and scholastic basis is not presented as probative and if the theological debate has only begun, then these admissions of the Magisterium deny ordination for women only for now and invite further research. Through this new study and through the extension of women's pastoral role in the Church, which the Declaration declares very desirable, the indecisiveness will turn towards certitude.

A Tale of Two Documents

John R. Donahue

For those Catholics concerned about ordination of women for the ministerial priesthood the period from July, 1976, through January, 1977, was the
"best of times" and the "worst of times." Advocates of such ordination were
encouraged by published reports in late June of some results of the April,
1976, meeting of the Pontifical Biblical Commission.[1] Most startling to some
observers were the three votes attributed to the Commission: (1) a unanimous
(17-0) vote that the New Testament does not settle in a clear way and once
and for all whether women can be ordained priests, (2) a 12-5 vote in favor of
the view that scriptural grounds alone are not enough to exclude the possibility of ordaining women and (3) a 12-5 vote that Christ's plan would not be
transgressed by permitting the ordination of women.[2] For those opposed to
the ordination of women the "best of times" came on January 27, 1977, with
the publication by the Sacred Congregation for the Doctrine of the Faith of
the Declaration (*Inter Insigniores*) on the Question of the Admission of
Women to the Ministerial Priesthood which declared Catholic teaching to be
that "the Church, in fidelity to the example of the Lord, does not consider
herself authorized to admit women to priestly ordination."[3]

Catholics and non-Catholics, lay people and scholars alike, are therefore
confronted by an apparent conflict between an official Roman statement
(hereafter, referred to as the Declaration) and the report of an official
Roman Commission. Where the Biblical Commission says that the New Testament leaves the question open, the Congregation states that it is precisely
the will of Christ as attested in the New Testament which determined early
Church practice and subsequent tradition. Independent of one's judgment
about which view is more faithful to the New Testament and also independent of one's sympathies, in order to understand the difference between the
two documents some comments must be made about the Vatican offices
which issued the documents.

The Biblical Commission and Its "Report"

The Pontifical Biblical Commission, the oldest of the formal commissions of the modern papacy, was established by Leo XIII on October 30,
1902, in order to oversee proper biblical interpretation and to foster biblical
studies.[4] In the early decades of its history it was associated with a series of
responsa or decrees which were in opposition to modern trends of biblical interpretation. It has also issued instructions, of which the most famous is the
1964 *Instruction on the Historical Truth of the Gospels*.[5] Prior to 1971 the

only *formal members* of the Commission were the 10 or more Cardinals, even though from its inception the Commission employed for its deliberations consultors or experts in biblical studies. On June 27, 1971, in his *Motu Proprio* (Apostolic Brief), *Sedula Cura*, Paul VI promulgated a new set of regulations for the Commission.[6] In place of the Cardinal members, the Commission was to be composed of a Cardinal-President, a Secretary proposed by the President, and twenty formal members who were to be "scholars of the biblical sciences from various schools and nations."[7]

In its recognition of the need for trained scholars in the discussion of biblical questions and in its "internationalizing" of a Vatican office, the reorganization was seen as a progressive move. At the same time the re-organization weakened whatever independent status the Biblical Commission possessed. The Cardinal President was to be the Cardinal Prefect of the Congregation for the Doctrine of the Faith (Franjo Šeper). The Biblical Commission itself was to be in effect a sub-commission of this same Congregation and whatever conclusions it reached were to be transmitted "for the use of the Congregation on Doctrine."[8] The Biblical Commission could no longer issue any independent reports; its only formal vehicle of communication was through the Congregation on Doctrine. In this light the apparent ignoring of the Biblical Commission's report by the Congregation of the Doctrine makes some sense, even if it does not evoke much assent. In the mind of the Congregation the work of the Biblical Commission is merely advisory. It is not seen as a consultative body of experts which may arrive at unexpected or unhoped for conclusions which would be normative in any discussion.[9]

The report of the Biblical Commission which was made public July, 1976 is not really an official or finished document but the unofficially leaked portions of sections of the Commission's deliberations. The question of the ordination of women occupied the Biblical Commission prior to and during its plenary sessions of April, 1975 and 1976. Given the time spent and the high quality of scholarship represented by members of the Commission, one could have hoped for a more thorough and adequate biblical statement on women. The Report cannot be read with this expectation. Its introduction and four sections comprise answers to specific questions, rather than organic parts of a finished piece. Because of the secrecy which surrounds the work of all Vatican Offices, the actual questions posed are unknown. Like the problems behind Paul's letters, the questions must be deduced from the often cryptic answers to them.[10]

At the same time the Report does summarize major aspects of the best New Testament scholarship on women. Also the significance of the Report is not in the cogency or polish of the public statement but in the votes which accompanied it. In spite of its official status as a subcommission of the Congregation on Doctrine, and in face of public and clearly articulated statements about what was and was to be the official teaching on women's ordination, the Commission arrived at a conclusion different from that of the Congregation.[11] Whatever the ecclesiastical status of the report, the conclusions and the votes of the Commission are signs of an emerging pluralism in Catholic thought as well as of a changing relationship between the official Magisterium and theologians.[12]

The Congregation and Its Declaration

The Congregation for the Doctrine of the Faith under whose direct authority the Declaration was issued has a long and important history. It was founded by Paul III in 1542 as "The Sacred Congregation of the Roman and Universal Inquisition," was later called the Holy Office, and, on December 7, 1965, was re-organized by Paul VI and given its present name.[13] Though at this time some of the more harsh juridical procedures of the Congregation were mitigated, it still functions as a overseer of orthodoxy.

Given the history and juridcal status of this Congregation and given the public statements of Paul VI over the past three years, the conclusion of the Congregation should have come as a surprise to no one. From all indications it was sometime in early 1975 that Paul VI mandated the Congregation to prepare a statement on women's ordination.[14] From this same period onward the position of Paul VI became increasingly clear. On April 18, 1975, he stated that "women did not receive the call to the apostolate of the twelve and therefore to the ordained ministry."[15]

In the exchange of letters with the Archbishop of Canterbury, especially in the letter of November 30, 1975, Paul VI expressed, in brief form, what was to be the substance of the argument in the Declaration: the example of Jesus in choosing only men is determinative of Church doctrine and practice.[16] The only new elements in the final Declaration are certain expansions of this statement and the addition of the theological argument on the natural resemblance between Christ and the minister of the Eucharist. All of this suggests that during that very period when the Biblical Commission was studying the matter, the conclusions, the general shape of the argument and perhaps the actual formulation of the final Declaration of the Congregation were nearing completion.

In this light a discrepancy between the Commission's Report and the Congregation's Declaration is not surprising. What is, however, a bit surprising is the apparent absence of any formal participation in the deliberations by the Secretariat for Christian Unity. The initial contacts on the issue between Anglicans and Catholics took place through this Secretariat. However, when the Declaration was released there was no one present representing this Secretariat, and the Swiss Journal *Orientierung* reports that the Declaration hit the Secretariat members "like a bolt from the blue."[17] Such an apparent lack of communication between Roman offices dealing with a critical issue is surprising in view of the regulation of Paul VI in his 1967 reform of the Curia that when business falls under the province of a number of departments, it is to be discussed "on the basis of consultation of the departments concerned."[18]

This glance at the offices involved and at some of the events of the past few years suggests that the Declaration of January 27 cannot be seen as the end product of serious and sustained reflection and study on the part of a wide representation of the Magisterium[19] Just as the Biblical Commission's Report cannot be read as the best discussion of the scriptural evidence bearing on the question, the Declaration of the Congregation can not be read as if it were the best presentation of the available considerations either against or for the ordination of women.

Two Documents Compared

While it is impossible to know whether and how the Report of the Biblical Commission was used by the Congregation, there are a number of places where common material is treated. We will attempt to describe some of the areas of common concern and indicate points of agreement as well as significant difference.

I. The Attitude of Jesus

The basic argument of the Declaration is that in his call of the twelve men Jesus was not influenced by any cultural prejudice against women and deliberately did not entrust "the apostolic charge" to women, not even to his mother. The Declaration also rejects the view that Mt 19:28 ("You will sit on the twelve thrones, judging the twelve tribes of Israel") with its eschatological symbolism is basic to an understanding the ministry of the Twelve.[20]

The Report also stresses the newness of Jesus' attitude toward women which is "in striking contrast to the contemporary usages of the Jewish world." While the Report admits *the fact* that Jesus chose a group of twelve men, it stresses that these are chosen "who, after the fashion of the twelve patriarchs of the Old Testament, would be leaders of the renewed people of God." Though the Report recognizes the masculine character of leadership in the early Church, it does not root this in the intention of Jesus, and asks, "Must we conclude that this rule must be valid forever in the Church?" The Report never alludes to the question of the ordination of Mary since there is not enough evidence in the New Testament even to address this question. Finally, the Report stresses the eschatological framework of Jesus' total ministry, as well as of his choice of the Twelve, when it says, "Jesus inaugurates in the framework of the present world the order of things that constitutes the final horizon of the kingdom of God."

The Report therefore exercises exegetical reserve in regard to the intention of Jesus. The argument of the Declaration that Jesus was free of certain cultural prejudices in regard to women and therefore consciously excluded them freely from leadership suffers from both poor logic and poor exegesis. The accounts of the call and the mission of the Twelve simply do not provide the kind of information required to arrive at the intention of Jesus.[21] Likewise the overlooking of the eschatological significance of the Twelve is a serious defect of the Declaration. If the choice of "the Twelve" is dictated by the eschatological consciousness of Jesus that the end is near, then his choice can scarcely be seen as prescriptive for a long period of Church history.[22]

II. Practice of the Early Church

The Declaration holds that the apostolic community remained faithful to the attitude of Jesus in excluding women. Though women worked with St. Paul, he never envisaged "conferring ordination" on these women, and he clearly distinguished between "my fellow workers" and "fellow workers of God" who participated in the "official and public proclamation of the message." Paul's prohibitions in 1 Cor 14:34-35 and 1 Tim 2:12 are not the expression of cultural fact but of a different nature and concern "the official function of teaching in the Christian assembly."

The Report differs on almost all of these points and also adds a fuller picture of ministry in the New Testament. The Report does not use the anachronistic language of "conferring ordination" in describing ministry in the early Church, nor does it gives the impression that the different forms of ministry arose in continuity with the explicit intention of Jesus. It mentions the choice of the Twelve and states that, upon leaving the earth, "he also delegated to a group of men whom he had chosen the responsibility to develop the kingdom of God and the authority to govern the Church." This group is the basis of a community which has continued the work of Christ, but there is no statement that this group explicitly determined the shape of ministry in the early Church.

The report gives a much fuller picture of the role of women in the early Church. They participate in the work (*kopian*) of evangelization. Phoebe is not described in the weak language of the Declaration, "in the service of the Church," but as a deacon. The Report mentions the possibility that the Junias of Rom 16:7 who is ranked with the apostles may be a woman, and it alludes to the significant role of women in the Gospel of John.[23] The Report does not make the dubious distinction between "my fellow worker" and "fellow worker of God."[24] Finally Paul's prohibitions of 1 Cor 14:34-35 are evaluated in the following way. "It is possible that they refer only to certain concrete situations and abuses. It is possible that certain other situations call on the Church to assign to women the role of teaching which these two passages deny them, and which constitute a function belonging to the leadership." In comparing what the two documents say about the early Church it is clear that the Declaration is selective in its description of the roles of women in the early Church and that when it does mention them, it minimizes them.

III. The Use of Nuptial Imagery

Both documents call attention to those texts in which Christ is related to the Church as bridegroom to bride. The Declaration then goes on to make a theological extension of this image not found in the New Testament: the priest represents Christ the groom and therefore must be male. In the New Testament the image is used only of Christ and the Church and never extended into the area of ministry.

IV. Principles of Exegesis

The Report begins with a number of cautions on addressing the question of the ordination of women: (1) woman does not constitute the principal subject of biblical texts, (2) the very posing of the question in terms of "priesthood" and celebration of the Eucharist is "somewhat foreign to the Bible" and derives from a perspective of a later conception of the priesthood, and (3) the Church is now in the process of broadening its concept of the priesthood beyond that of the eucharistic ministry. With these exegetical cautions the Report is rather tentative in its conclusions, suggesting in different ways that the New Testament provides a background for theological reflection and questioning whether all New Testament practices can be directly normative for present Church life.

The Declaration also admits the limitation of the data provided by the New Testament; however, it responds to this limitation not with the exegetical reserve of the Report, but with the statement that a purely historical exegesis of Scripture cannot suffice to reach the ultimate meaning of the mission of Jesus and the ultimate meaning of Scripture, and that "it is the Church through the voice of her Magisterium that, in these various domains, decides what can change and what can remain immutable." While Catholic exegetes would agree that the *ultimate* meaning of Scripture is beyond the province of exegesis and would recognize the authority of the Magisterium in articulating authentic tradition, Catholic exegetes would also recall the hermeneutical guidelines of par. 12 of the Vatican II Degree on Revelation which stress the need for scientific and historical exegesis in order to find what the sacred writers really intended.[25]

Conclusion

The documents discussed reveal not only different conclusions on the admission of women to the priesthood; they reveal different ways of looking at the biblical material. In the Declaration the exegesis is selective and is marshalled to support the current teaching of the Magisterium.[26] Such exegesis will convince no one who is not disposed to agree with the Declaration on grounds other than the strength of its exegesis. The Report of the Biblical Commission is necessarily tentative and limited by the questions posed to it. Both documents leave an unfinished agenda. The mainly negative conclusion of the Biblical Commission (there is nothing in the New Testament which prohibits the ordination of women) can be supplemented by positive considerations not simply by biblical scholars but also by theologians, especially in the area of ecclesiology.[27] One relatively untapped area of biblical and theological reflection will be to ask how the different forms which ministry assumed in the early Church were in response to different social and religious demands of the emerging communities. From its very beginning the Church embodies a principle of sacramental adaptation. The question can then be raised as to what forms ministry must take today in response to different social and religious demands.[28] The Declaration of the Congregation also leaves an unfinished agenda. In its call for attention to the symbolic dimension of scriptural language "which affects man and woman in their profound identity and through which the mystery of God is revealed" the Declaration implicitly calls for the use in theology and exegesis of not only the tools of historical method and critical reflection but also for engagement in anthropology and the phenomenology of symbol and of psychology as a way to sound the depths of what Scripture says about the mystery of man and woman and how they are to minister to the body of Christ in the world. The Report of the Biblical Commission and the Declaration of the Congregation are not the end but the beginning of a task of study and reflection which will continue to engage the whole Church.[29]

Notes

1. "Biblical Commission Report. Can Women Be Priests?" *Origins*, Vol. VI, No. 6 (July 1, 1976), pp. 92-96. For press reports see *National Catholic Reporter*, Vol. XII, No. 34 (July 2, 1976), p. 15; John T. Muthig, *Our Sunday Visitor*, Vol. LXV, No. 3336 (June 27, 1976), p. 3.

2. The questions voted on comprise the final three paragraphs of the report.

3. *The National Catholic Register* (Los Angeles), February 13, 1977, contained the headline, "Women Priests Ban Acclaimed." Cardinal William Baum of Washington, D.C., stated: "I thank our Lord for the firm and clear guidance which the Holy Father has given to us in approving and confirming the teaching of this declaration." *Origins* Vol. VI, No. 34 (Feb. 10, 1977), p. 548, published also in *L'Osservatore Romano*, English edition (Feb. 24, 1977), p. 7.

4. B.N. Wambacq, "Pontifical Biblical Commission," *New Catholic Encyclopedia*, Vol. XI, pp. 551-554; *Enchridion Biblicum* (Rome: A. Arnodo, 1961), pp. 64-68; *Rome and the Study of Scripture* (St. Meinrad, Indiana: Grail Publications, 1962), pp. 33-34.

5. *Catholic Biblical Quarterly*, Vol. XXVI (1964), pp. 299-304 (Latin Text); pp. 305-312 (English Text).

6. *Acta Apostolicae Sedis*, Vol. LXIII (1971), pp. 665-669; *Origins*, Vol. I, No. 8 (July 29, 1971), pp. 149-151; D. Stanley, "Pontifical Biblical Commission," *New Catholic Encyclopedia: Supplement*, 1967-1974, Vol. XVI, pp. 357-358.

7. *Sedula Cura*, No. 3. A list of the members can be found in the *Annuario Pontificio* (1973), p. 1036.

8. *Ibid.*, No. 10. Stanley, *op. cit.*, p. 358. Vatican watchers can observe the reduction of the Commission's official standing by noting that prior to 1972 the Biblical Commission was listed first among the "Commissioni e Comitati Permanente" (*Annuario Pontificio* [1970], p. 1069). After the reorganization it (along with the International Theological Commission) was listed as a sub-committee of the Sacred Congregation on the Doctrine of the Faith and no longer appears first in the list of commissions, but inconspicuously in the middle.

9. In a press conference on June 28, 1976, a Vatican spokesman made the following statement: "The proper agencies of the Holy See follow and study all those major questions which are significant, among which must be included the question of the ordination of women. It should be noted that the fact a question is studied in no way signifies that a change is foreseen. In the

case of the priesthood for women, the study bears solely on the manner of presenting the traditional teaching and practice of the Church as it has been clearly recalled by the Holy Father on many occasions." *Documentation Catholique*, Vol. LXXIII, No. 1704 (Sept., 1976), p. 770.

10. A major problem facing anyone writing about Vatican statements is the practice of secrecy which surrounds the workings of all Vatican offices. This secrecy extends often not only to matters of necessary confidentiality but to the most mundane matters of when a cetain study was begun, who was consulted, who participated in the drafting, etc. The Biblical Commission's Report is a "leaked" document made public "after a source unrelated to the commission made it available to the press" (*Origins*, Vol. VI, No. 6, p. 92). It is directed not to the general public but to those who mandated the study, presumably the Pope or the Congregation on Doctrine.

11. The ordination of women has become a topic of intense research and discussion in Catholicism only in the past decade. See Ann E. Patrick, "Women and Religion: A Survey of Significant Literature, 1965-1974," *Theological Studies*, Vol. XXXVI (Dec., 1975), pp. 737-765 (also published in *Women: New Dimensions*, ed. Walter Burghardt, S.J. [New York: Paulist Press, 1976] pp. 161-189). With the emergence of reflection on the possibility of women's ordinations official Church statements which earlier had not addressed the question became increasingly negative on the possibility; see E.J. Kilmartin, S.J., "Full Participation of Women in the Life of the Catholic Church," in *Sexism and Canon Law*, ed. James Coriden (New York: Paulist Press, 1977) pp. 109-135, and Nadine Foley, O.P., "Woman in Vatican Documents 1960 to the Present," *ibid.*, pp. 82-108; H.M. Legrand, O.P., "Views on the Ordination of Women," *Origins*, Vol. VI, No. 29. (Jan. 6, 1977), pp. 459-468. *Infra*, Notes 14-16.

12. R. A. McCormick, S.J., "Notes on Moral Theology," *Theological Studies*, Vol. XXXVIII (March, 1977), pp. 84-100 has a superb summary of the recent literature on this topic.

13. U. Beste, "Doctrine of the Faith, Congregation for the," *New Catholic Encyclopedia*, Vol. IV, pp. 944-946. The decree of reorganization (*Integrae Servandae*) is found in the *Acta Apostolicae Sedis*, Vol. LVII (1965), pp. 952-955 = *The Pope Speaks*, Vol. XI (1966), pp. 13-16.

14. See the report by Desmond O'Grady, *National Catholic Reporter*, Feb. 4, 1977, p. 17, who states, "In mid-1975 Pope Paul asked the Doctrinal Congregation to prepare a statement."

15. Address to the committee studying the Church's response to the International Woman's Year. *Origins*, Vol. IV, No. 45 (May 1, 1975), pp. 718-719.

16. *Origins*, Vol. VI, No. 9 (Aug. 12, 1976), pp. 129-132.

17. A. Ebneter, "Keine Frauen im Priesteramt," *Orientierung*, Vol. XLI, No. 3 (Feb. 15, 1977), p. 26.

18. "Reorganizing the Roman Curia," Apostolic Constitution, *Regimini Ecclesiae Universalis*, Aug. 15, 1967. *Acta Apostolicae Sedis*, Vol. LIX (1967), pp. 885-928 = *The Pope Speaks*, Vol. XII (1967), pp. 393-420, No. 13.

19. As noted, serious study of the question of the ordination of women is relatively recent in Catholicism. Legrand and Patrick (*supra*, n. 11) mention some of the recent studies; see also, A.M. Gardner, S.S.N.D. (ed.) *Women and Catholic Priesthood* (New York: Paulist Press, 1976), esp. the

bibliography on pp. 199-208; compiled by Donna Westly and R. T. Barn-house, M. Fahey, S.J., B. Oram and B. Walker, O.P., "The Ordination of Women to the Priesthood: An Annotated Bibliography," *Anglican Theological Review*, Supplementary Series, No. 6 (June, 1976), pp. 81-106. Though the press reported that members of the Theological Commission, bishops, other theologians and women were consulted, no specifics were ever made available about who was actually consulted and how they were consulted. See, Report of Interview with Fr. Richard Malone of the NCCB staff, The *Baltimore Catholic Review*, (Feb. 4, 1977), p. B-2. The International Theological Commission never formally considered the question, nor did the Papal Commission on Women. See, M-T van Lunen-Chenu, "La Commission pontificale de la femme," *Études*, Vol. CCCXLIV (June, 1976), 879-891.

20. Mt 19:28 (Lk 22:30) is mentioned only in note 10 which says that in these texts it is "only a question of their participation in the eschatological judgment." The importance of this text cannot be so minimized. It is the only place in the New Testament where "the Twelve" is on the lips of Jesus in giving a mandate to the disciples (Mk 14:20, the sole other place where Jesus speaks of "the Twelve," is a prediction of Judas' betrayal). See R. Brown, *Priest and Bishop* (New York: Paulist Press, 1970), p. 55; and R. H. Fuller, "Pro and Con: The Ordination of Women," in *Toward a New Theology of Ordination*, ed. M. H. Micks and C. P. Price (Alexandria: Virginia Theological Seminary, 1976), p. 2; and the essay by Elisabeth Fiorenza, pp. 114-122.

21. It is generally admitted that Mk 3:13 where it says Jesus called those "whom he wanted" is a redactional comment of the Evangelist. These words are not found in the Matthean (5:1) nor the Lukan (Lk 6:13) parallels. The literal historicity of the call narratives is also disputed. The following authors agree that Mk 3:13-14 are mostly redactional, i.e., due to the Evangelist, and can not be used as a historical description of Jesus' intentions. R. Pesch, Das *Markusevangelium, Part I*, Herders theologischer Kommentar zum Neuen Testament (Freiburg: Herder, 1976), pp. 202-209; Vincent Taylor, *The Gospel According to Mark*, 2nd ed. (London: Macmillan, 1966), p. 229, says, "The narrative appears to have been constructed *ad hoc* on the basis of existing tradition"; D. E. Ninehan, *Saint Mark* (Baltimore: Penguin Books, 1963), p. 116. In its exegesis the Vatican Declaration does not always seem aware of the different levels of the traditions about Jesus as they are described in the 1964 *Instruction* (*supra*, n. 5).

22. Fuller, *op. cit.*, p. 2.

23. R. E. Brown, "Roles of Women in the Fourth Gospel," *Theological Studies*, Vol. XXXVI (Dec., 1975), pp. 688-700 (also in *Women: New Dimensions*, pp. 112-124). Brown is a member of the Biblical Commission.

24. For a more extended critique of this distinction see, J. R. Donahue, "Women, Priesthood and the Vatican," *America*, Vol. CXXXVI (April 2, 1977), pp. 286-287.

25. "Dogmatic Constitution on Divine Revelation," in *The Documents of Vatican II*, ed. Walter Abbott (New York: Herder and Herder, 1966), par. 12. In his commentary on this section Alois Grillmeir notes that "the *determinata adiuncta*, the particular circumstances, the situation from which the sacred writer speaks or in which the text has grown," must be the starting point of exegesis, "and he further notes: "This must all be established by his-

torical critical methods. *Divino afflante* firmly urged this." *Commentary On The Documents Of Vatican II*, ed. H. Vorgrimler (New York: Herder and Herder, 1969), Vol. III, p. 221.

26. The understanding of the relation of theology to the Magisterium which seems to be at work in the Declaration is that expressed in the 1950 encyclical of Pius XII, *Humani Generis:* "It is also true that theologians must always go back to the sources of divine revelation; for it pertains to their office to show how *(qua ratione)* the teachings of the living Magisterium are contained, either explicitly or implicitly, in the Sacred Scriptures and divine Tradition." No. 21, in *The Encyclical "Humani Generis"* trans. A. C. Cotter (Weston, Mass: Weston College Press, 1952), also in Denzinger-Schön-metzer, *Enchridion Symbolorum* (Freiburg: Herder, 1962), No. 3886.

27. For recent New Testament studies see the surveys by, A. Lemaire, "The Ministries in the New Testament," *Biblical Theology Bulletin*, Vol. III (1973), pp. 133-166; and R. Schnackenburg, "Apostolicity: the Present Position of Studies," *One Christ*, Vol. VI (1970), pp. 243-273.

28. See Anne Carr, "The Church in Process: Engendering the Future," in *Women and Catholic Priesthood*, pp. 66-88.

29. McCormick, *op. cit.*, p. 99, writes: "Finally—and this is delicate—something must be done to liberate Roman congregations from a single theological language and perspective. . . . More radically, one can wonder whether congregations as such should be involved in doing theology." The Declaration on Women, published after McCormick wrote these words, confirms his view.

PART II

SACRED CONGREGATION
FOR THE DOCTRINE OF THE FAITH

Declaration
On the Question of the Admission of Women
to the Ministerial Priesthood

DECLARATION
ON THE QUESTION OF THE ADMISSION OF
WOMEN TO THE MINISTERIAL PRIESTHOOD

INTRODUCTION
THE ROLE OF WOMEN IN MODERN SOCIETY
AND THE CHURCH

1. Among the characteristics that mark our present age, Pope John XXIII indicated, in his Encyclical *Pacem in Terris* of 11 April 1963, "the part that women are now taking in public life . . . This is a development that is perhaps of swifter growth among Christian nations, but it is also happening extensively, if more slowly, among nations that are heirs to different traditions and imbued with a different culture".[1] Along the same lines, the Second Vatican Council, enumerating in its Pastoral Constitution *Gaudium et Spes* the forms of discrimination touching upon the basic rights of the person which must be overcome and eliminated as being contrary to God's plan, gives first place to discrimination based upon sex.[2] The resulting equality will secure the building up of a world that is not levelled out and uniform but harmonious and unified, if men and women contribute to it their own resources and dynamism, as Pope Paul VI recently stated.[3](1)

2. In the life of the Church herself, as history shows us, women have played a decisive role and accomplished tasks of outstanding value. One has only to think of the foundresses of the great religious families, such as Saint Clare and Saint Teresa of Avila. The latter, moreover, and Saint Catherine of Siena, have left writings so rich in spiritual doctrine that Pope Paul VI has included them among the Doctors of the Church. Nor could one forget the great number of women who have consecrated themselves to the Lord for the exercise of charity or for the missions,(2) and the Christian wives who have had a profound influence on their families, particularly for the passing on of the faith to their children.

3. But our age gives rise to increased demands: "Since in our time women have an ever more active share in the whole life of society, it is very important that they participate more widely also in the various sectors of the Church's apostolate".[4] This charge of the Second Vatican Council has already set in motion the whole process of change now taking place: these various experiences of course need to come to maturity. But as Pope Paul VI also remarked,[5] a very large number of Christian communities are already benefitting from the apostolic commitment of women. Some of these women are called to take part in councils set up for pastoral reflection, at the diocesan or parish level; and the Apostolic See has brought women into some of its working bodies.

4. For some years now various Christian communities stemming from the sixteenth-century Reformation or of later origin have been admitting

women to the pastoral office on a par with men. This initiative has led to pe-
titions and writings by members of these communities and similar groups,(3)
directed towards making this admission a general thing; it has also led to
contrary reactions. This therefore constitutes an ecumenical problem, and the
Catholic Church must make her thinking known on it, all the more because
in various sectors of opinion the question has been asked whether she too
could not modify her discipline and admit women to priestly ordination. A
number of Catholic theologians have even posed this question publicly, evok-
ing studies not only in the sphere of exegesis, patrology and Church history
but also in the field of the history of institutions and customs, of sociology
and of psychology.(4) The various arguments capable of clarifying this important problem have been submitted to a critical examination. As we are
dealing with a debate which classical theology scarcely touched upon, the current argumentation runs the risk of neglecting essential elements.

   5. For these reasons, in execution of a mandate received from the Holy
Father and echoing the declaration which he himself made in his letter of 30
November 1975,[6] the Sacred Congregation for the Doctrine of the Faith
judges it necessary to recall that the Church, in fidelity to the example of the
Lord, does not consider herself authorized to admit women to priestly ordination. The Sacred Congregation deems it opportune at the present juncture to explain this position of the Church. It is a position which will perhaps
cause pain but whose positive value will become apparent in the long run,
since it can be of help in deepening understanding of the respective roles of
men and of women.

1

THE CHURCH'S CONSTANT TRADITION

   6. The Catholic Church has never felt that priestly or episcopal ordination can be validly conferred on women. A few heretical sects in the first centuries, especially Gnostic ones, entrusted the exercise of the priestly ministry
to women: this innovation was immediately noted and condemned by the Fathers, who considered it as unacceptable in the Church.[7](5) It is true that in
the writings of the Fathers one will find the undeniable influence of prejudices
unfavourable to women, but nevertheless, it should be noted that these prejudices had hardly any influence on their pastoral activity, and still less on their
spiritual direction.(6) But over and above considerations inspired by the spirit
of the times, one finds expressed—especially in the canonical documents of
the Antiochian and Egyptian traditions—this essential reason, namely, that
by calling only men to the priestly Order and ministry in its true sense, the
Church intends to remain faithful to the type of ordained ministry willed by
the Lord Jesus Christ and carefully maintained by the Apostles.[8](7)

   7. The same conviction animates mediaeval theology,[9] even if the Scholastic doctors, in their desire to clarify by reason the data of faith, often present arguments on this point that modern thought would have difficulty in admitting or would even rightly reject.(8) Since that period and up to our own

time, it can be said that the question has not been raised again, for the practice has enjoyed peaceful and universal acceptance.(9)

8. The Church's tradition in the matter has thus been so firm in the course of the centuries that the Magisterium has not felt the need to intervene in order to formulate a principle which was not attacked, or to defend a law which was not challenged. But each time that this tradition had the occasion to manifest itself, it witnessed to the Church's desire to conform to the model left to her by the Lord.

9. The same tradition has been faithfully safeguarded by the Churches of the East. (10) Their unanimity on this point is all the more remarkable since in many other questions their discipline admits of a great diversity. At the present time these same Churches refuse to asociate themselves with requests directed towards securing the accession of women to priestly ordination.

2

THE ATTITUDE OF CHRIST

10. Jesus did not call any woman to become part of the Twelve.(11) If he acted in this way, it was not in order to conform to the customs of his time, for his attitude towards women was quite different from that of his milieu, and he deliberately and courageously broke with it.

11. For example, to the great astonishment of his own disciples Jesus converses publicly with the Samaritan woman (cf. Jn 4:27); he takes no notice of the state of legal impurity of the woman who had suffered from haemorrhages (cf. Mt 9:20-22), he allows a sinful woman to approach him in the house of Simon the Pharisee (cf. Lk 7:37 ff.); and by pardoning the woman taken in adultery, he means to show that one must not be more severe towards the fault of a woman than towards that of man (cf. Jn 8:11). He does not hesitate to depart from the Mosaic Law in order to affirm the equality of the rights and duties of men and women with regard to the marriage bond (cf. Mk 10:2-11; Mt 19:3-9).

12. In his itinerant ministry Jesus was accompanied not only by the Twelve(13) but also by a group of women: "Mary, surnamed the Magdalene, from whom seven demons had gone out, Joanna the wife of Herod's steward Chuza, Susanna, and several others who provided for them out of their own resources" (Lk 8:2-3). (13) Contrary to the Jewish mentality, which did not accord great value to the testimony of women, as Jewish law attests, it was nevertheless women who were the first to have the privilege of seeing the risen Lord, and it was they who were charged by Jesus to take the first paschal message to the Apostles themselves (cf. Mt 28:7-10; Lk 24:9-10; Jn 20:11-18), in order to prepare the latter to become the official witnesses to the Resurrection.

13. It is true that these facts do not make the matter immediately obvious. This is no surprise, for the questions that the Word of God brings before us go beyond the obvious. In order to reach the ultimate meaning of the mission of Jesus and the ultimate meaning of Scripture, a purely histori-

cal exegesis of the texts cannot suffice. But it must be recognized that we have here a number of convergent indications that make all the more remarkable the fact that Jesus did not entrust the apostolic (14) charge[10] to women.(15) Even his Mother, who was so closely associated with the mystery of her Son, and whose incomparable role is emphasized by the Gospels of Luke and John, was not invested with the apostolic ministry. This fact was to lead the Fathers to present her as the example of Christ's will in this domain; as Pope Innocent III repeated later, at the beginning of the thirteenth century, "Although the Blessed Virgin Mary surpassed in dignity and in excellence all the Apostles, nevertheless it was not to her but to them that the Lord entrusted the keys of the Kingdom of Heaven".[11](16)

3

THE PRACTICE OF THE APOSTLES

14. The apostolic community remained faithful to the attitude of Jesus towards women.(17) Although Mary occupied a privileged place in the little circle of those gathered in the Upper Room after the Lord's Ascension (cf. Acts 1:14), it was not she who was called to enter the College of the Twelve at the time of the election that resulted in the choice of Matthias: those who were put forward were two disciples whom the Gospels do not even mention.

15. On the day of Pentecost, the Holy Spirit filled them all, men and women (cf. Acts 2:1; 1:14), yet the proclamation of the fulfilment of the prophecies in Jesus was made only by "Peter and the Eleven" (Acts 2:14).(18)

16. When they and Paul went beyond the confines of the Jewish world, the preaching of the Gospel and the Christian life in the Greco-Roman civilization impelled them to break with Mosaic practices, sometimes regretfully.(19) They could therefore have envisaged conferring ordination on women, if they had not been convinced of their duty of fidelity to the Lord on this point. In the Hellenistic world, the cult of a number of pagan divinities was entrusted to priestesses.(20) In fact the Greeks did not share the ideas of the Jews: although their philosophers taught the inferiority of women, historians nevertheless emphasize the existence of a certain movement for the advancement of women during the Imperial period. In fact we know from the book of the Acts and from the Letters of Saint Paul that certain women worked with the Apostle for the Gospel (cf. Rom 16:3-12; Phil 4:3). Saint Paul lists their names with gratitude in the final salutations of the Letters. Some of them often exercised an important influence on conversions: Priscilla, Lydia and others; especially Priscilla, who took it on herself to complete the instruction of Apollos (cf. Acts 18:26); Phoebe, in the service of the Church of Cenchreae (cf. Rom. 16:1). All these facts manifest within the Apostolic Church a considerable evolution vis-à-vis the customs of Judaism. Nevertheless at no time was there a question of conferring ordination on these women.

17. In the Pauline Letters, exegetes of authority have noted a difference

between two formulas used by the Apostle: he writes indiscriminately "my fellow workers" (Rom 16:3; Phil 4:2-3) when referring to men and women helping him in his apostolate in one way or another; but he reserves the title "God's fellow workers" (1 Cor 3:9; cf. 1 Thess 3:2) to Apollos, Timothy and himself, thus designated because they are directly set apart for the apostolic ministry and the preaching of the Word of God.(21) In spite of the so important role played by women on the day of the Resurrection, their collaboration was not extended by Saint Paul to the official and public proclamation of the message, since this proclamation belongs exclusively to the apostolic mission.

4

PERMANENT VALUE OF THE ATTITUDE OF JESUS AND THE APOSTLES

18. Could the Church today depart from this attitude of Jesus and the Apostles, which has been considered as normative by the whole of tradition up to our own day?(22) Various arguments have been put forward in favour of a positive reply to this question, and these must now be examined.

19. It has been claimed in particular that the attitude of Jesus and the Apostles is explained by the influence of their milieu and their times. It is said that, if Jesus did not entrust to women and not even to his Mother a ministry assimilating them to the Twelve, this was because historical circumstances did not permit him to do so. No. one however has ever proved—and it is clearly impossible to prove—that this attitude is inspired only by social and cultural reasons. As we have seen, an examination of the Gospels shows on the contrary that Jesus broke with the prejudices of his time, by widely contravening the discriminations practised with regard to women. One therefore cannot maintain that, by not calling women to enter the group of the Apostles, Jesus was simply letting himself be guided by reasons of expediency. For all the more reason, social and cultural conditioning did not hold back the Apostles working in the Greek milieu, where the same forms of discrimination did not exist.(23)

20. Another objection is based upon the transitory character that one claims to see today in some of the prescriptions of Saint Paul concerning women, and upon the difficulties that some aspects of his teaching raise in this regard. But it must be noted that these ordinances, probably inspired by the customs of the period, concern scarcely more than disciplinary practices of minor importance, such as the obligation imposed upon women to wear a veil on the head (24) (1 Cor 11:2-16); such requirements no longer have a normative value. However, the Apostle's forbidding of women "to speak" in the assemblies (cf. 1 Cor 14:34-35; 1 Tim 2:12) is of a different nature, and exegetes define its meaning in this way: Paul in no way opposes the right, which he elsewhere recognizes as possessed by women, to prophesy in the assembly (cf. 1 Cor 11:5); the prohibition solely concerns the official function of teaching in the Christian assembly.(25) For Saint Paul this prescription is bound up with the divine plan of creation (cf. 1 Cor 11:7; Gen 2:18-24).(26) It would

be difficult to see in it the expression of a cultural fact. Nor should it be forgotten that we owe to Saint Paul one of the most vigorous texts in the New Testament on the fundamental equality of men and women, as children of God in Christ (cf. Gal 3:28). Therefore there is no reason for accusing him of prejudices against women, when we note the trust that he shows towards them and the collaboration that he asks of them in his apostolate.(27)

21. But over and above these objections taken from the history of apostolic times, those who support the legitimacy of change in the matter turn to the Church's practice in her sacramental discipline. It has been noted, in our day especially, to what extent the Church is conscious of possessing a certain power over the sacraments, even though they were instituted by Christ. She has used this power down the centuries in order to determine their signs and the conditions of their administration: recent decisions of Popes Pius XII and Paul VI are proof of this.[12] However, it must be emphasized that this power, which is a real one, has definite limits. As Pope Pius XII recalled: "The Church has no power over the substance of the sacraments, that is to say, over what Christ the Lord, as the sources of Revelation bear witness, determined should be maintained in the sacramental sign".[13] This was already the teaching of the Council of Trent, which declared: "In the Church there has always existed this power, that in the administration of the sacraments, provided that their substance remains unaltered, she can lay down or modify what she considers more fitting either for the benefit of those who receive them or for respect towards those same sacraments, according to varying circumstances, times or places".[14](28)

22. Moreover, it must not be forgotten that the sacramental signs are not conventional ones. Not only is it true that, in many respects, they are natural signs because they respond to the deep symbolism of actions and things, but they are more than this: they are principally meant to link the person of every period to the supreme Event of the history of salvation, in order to enable that person to understand, through all the Bible's wealth of pedagogy and symbolism, what grace they signify and produce. For example, the sacrament of the Eucharist is not only a fraternal meal, but at the same time the memorial which makes present and actual Christ's sacrifice and his offering by the Church. Again, the priestly ministry is not just a pastoral service; it ensures the continuity of the functions entrusted by Christ to the Apostles and the continuity of the powers related to those functions. Adaptation to civilizations and times therefore cannot abolish, on essential points, the sacramental reference to constitutive events of Christianity and to Christ himself.

23. In the final analysis it is the Church, through the voice of her Magisterium, that, in these various domains, decides what can change and what must remain immutable.(29) When she judges that she cannot accept certain changes, it is because she knows that she is bound by Christ's manner of acting.(30) Her attitude, despite appearances, is therefore not one of archaism but of fidelity: it can be truly understood only in this light. The Church

makes pronouncements in virtue of the Lord's promise and the presence of the Holy Spirit, in order to proclaim better the mystery of Christ and to safeguard and manifest the whole of its rich content.

24. This practice of the Church therefore has a normative character: in the fact of conferring priestly ordination only on men, it is a question of an unbroken tradition throughout the history of the Church, universal in the East and the West, and alert to repress abuses immediately. (31) This norm, based on Christ's example, has been and is still observed because it is considered to conform to God's plan for his Church.

5

THE MINISTERIAL PRIESTHOOD
IN THE LIGHT OF THE MYSTERY OF CHRIST

25. Having recalled the Church's norm and the basis thereof, it seems useful and opportune to illustrate this norm by showing the profound fittingness that theological reflection discovers between the proper nature of the sacrament of Order, with its specific reference to the mystery of Christ, and the fact that only men have been called to receive priestly ordination. It is not a question here of bringing forward a demonstrative argument, but of clarifying this teaching by the analogy of faith.(32)

26. The Church's constant teaching, repeated and clarified by the Second Vatican Council and again recalled by the 1971 Synod of Bishops and by the Sacred Congregation for the Doctrine of the Faith in its Declaration of 24 June 1973, declares that the bishop or the priest, in the exercise of his ministry, does not act in his own name, *in persona propria:* he represents Christ, who acts through him: "the priest truly acts in the place of Christ", as Saint Cyprian already wrote in the third century.[15] It is this ability to represent Christ that Saint Paul considered as characteristic of his apostolic function (cf. 2 Cor 5:20; Gal 4:14). The supreme expression of this representation is found in the altogether special form it assumes in the celebration of the Eucharist, which is the source and centre of the Church's unity, the sacrificial meal in which the People of God are associated in the sacrifice of Christ: the priest, who alone has the power to perform it, then acts not only through the effective power conferred on him by Christ, but *in persona Christi*,[16] taking the role of Christ, to the point of being his very image, when he pronounces the words of consecration.[17](33)

27. The Christian priesthood is therefore of a sacramental nature: the priest is a sign,(34) the supernatural effectiveness of which comes from the ordination received, but a sign that must be perceptible[18] and which the faithful must be able to recognize with ease.(35) The whole sacramental economy is in fact based upon natural signs, on symbols imprinted upon the human psychology: "Sacramental signs", says Saint Thomas, "represent what they signify by natural resemblance".[19] The same natural resemblance is required for persons as for things:(36) when Christ's role in the Eucharist is to be

expressed sacramentally, there would not be this "natural resemblance" which must exist between Christ and his minister if the role of Christ were not taken by a man.(37) In such a case it would be difficult to see in the minister the image of Christ.(38) For Christ himself was and remains a man.

28. Christ is of course the firstborn of all humanity, of women as well as men: the unity which he re-established after sin is such that there are no more distinctions between Jew and Greek, slave and free, male and female, but all are one in Christ Jesus (cf. Gal 3:28). Nevertheless, the Incarnation of the Word took place according to the male sex: this is indeed a question of fact, and this fact, while not implying an alleged natural superiority of man over woman, cannot be disassociated from the economy of salvation: it is, indeed, in harmony with the entirety of God's plan as God himself has revealed it, and of which the mystery of the Covenant is the nucleus.

29. For the salvation offered by God to men and women, the union with him to which they are called—in short, the Covenant—took on, from the Old Testament Prophets onwards, the privileged form of a nuptial mystery: for God the Chosen People is seen as his ardently loved spouse. Both Jewish and Christian tradition has discovered the depth of this intimacy of love by reading and rereading the Song of Songs;(39) the divine Bridegroom will remain faithful even when the Bride betrays his love, when Israel is unfaithful to God (cf. Hos 1-3; Jer 2).(40) When the "fullness of time" (Gal 4:4) comes, the Word, the Son of God, takes on flesh in order to establish and seal the new and eternal Covenant in his blood, which will be shed for many so that sins may be forgiven. His death will gather together again the scattered children of God; from his pierced side will be born the Church, as Eve was born from Adam's side. At that time there is fully and eternally accomplished the nuptial mystery proclaimed and hymned in the Old Testament: Christ is the Bridegroom; the Church is his bride, whom he loves because he has gained her by his blood and made her glorious, holy and without blemish, and henceforth he is inseparable from her. This nuptial theme, which is developed from the Letters of Saint Paul onwards (cf. 2 Cor 11:2; Eph 5:22-23) to the writings of Saint John (cf. especially Jn 3:29; Rev 19:7, 9), is present also in the Synoptic Gospels: the Bridegroom's friends must not fast as long as he is with them (cf. Mk 2:19); the Kingdom of Heaven is like a king who gave a feast for his son's wedding (cf. Mt 22:1-14). It is through this Scriptural language, all interwoven with symbols, and which expresses and affects man and woman in their profound identity, that there is revealed to us the mystery of God and Christ, a mystery which of itself is unfathomable.(41)

30. That is why we can never ignore the fact that Christ is a man. And therefore, unless one is to disregard the importance of this symbolism for the economy of Revelation, it must be admitted that, in actions which demand the character of ordination and in which Christ himself, the author of the Covenant, the Bridegroom and Head of the Church, is represented, exercising his ministry of salvation—which is in the highest degree the case of the Eucharist—his role (this is the original sense of the word *persona*) must be

taken by a man. This does not stem from any personal superiority of the latter in the order of values, but only from a difference of fact on the level of functions and service.

31. Could one say that, since Christ is now in the heavenly condition, from now on it is a matter of indifference whether he be represented by a man or by a woman, since "at the resurrection men and women do not marry" (Mt 22:30)? But this text does not mean that the distinction between man and woman, insofar as it determines the identity proper to the person, is suppressed in the glorified state; what holds for us holds also for Christ. It is indeed evident that in human beings the difference of sex exercises an important influence, much deeper than, for example, ethnic differences: the latter do not affect the human person as intimately as the difference of sex, which is directly ordained both for the communion of persons and for the generation of human beings. (42) In Biblical Revelation this difference is the effect of God's will from the beginning: "male and female he created them" (Gen 1:27).

32. However, it will perhaps be further objected that the priest, especially when he presides at the liturgical and sacramental functions, equally represents the Church: he acts in her name with "the intention of doing what she does". In this sense, the theologians of the Middle Ages said that the minister also acts *in persona Ecclesiae*, that is to say, in the name of the whole Church and in order to represent her. And in fact, leaving aside the question of the participation of the faithful in a liturgical action, it is indeed in the name of the whole Church that the action is celebrated by the priest: he prays in the name of all, and in the Mass he offers the sacrifice of the whole Church. In the new Passover, the Church, under visible signs, immolates Christ through the ministry of the priest.[20] And so, it is asserted, since the priest also represents the Church, would it not be possible to think that this representation could be carried out by a woman, according to the symbolism already explained? It is true that the priest represents the Church, which is the Body of Christ. But if he does so, it is precisely because he first represents Christ himself, who is the Head and Shepherd of the Church. The Second Vatican Council[21] used this phrase to make more precise and to complete the expression *in persona Christi*. It is in this quality that the priest presides over the Christian assembly and celebrates the Eucharistic sacrifice "in which the whole Church offers and is herself wholly offered"[22](43)

33. If one does justice to these reflections, one will better understand how well-founded is the basis of the Church's practice; and one will conclude that the controversies raised in our days over the ordination of women are for all Christians a pressing invitation to meditate on the mystery of the Church, to study in greater detail the meaning of the episcopate and the priesthood, and to rediscover the real and pre-eminent place of the priest in the community of the baptized, of which he indeed forms part but from which he is distinguished because, in the actions that call for the character of ordination, for the community he is—with all the effectiveness proper to the sacraments—

the image and symbol of Christ himself who calls, forgives, and accomplishes the sacrifice of the Covenant.

6

THE MINISTERIAL PRIESTHOOD ILLUSTRATED BY THE MYSTERY OF THE CHURCH

34. It is opportune to recall that problems of sacramental theology, especially when they concern the ministerial priesthood, as is the case here, cannot be solved except in the light of Revelation. The human sciences, however valuable their contribution in their own domain, cannot suffice here, for they cannot grasp the realities of faith: the properly supernatural content of these realities is beyond their competence.

35. Thus one must note the extent to which the Church is a society different from other societies, original in her nature and in her structures. The pastoral charge in the Church is normally linked to the sacrament of Order: it is not a simple government, comparable to the modes of authority found in States. It is not granted by people's spontaneous choice: even when it involves designation through election, it is the laying on of hands and the prayer of the successors of the Apostles which guarantee God's choice; and it is the Holy Spirit, given by ordination, who grants participation in the ruling power of the Supreme Pastor, Christ(44) (cf. Acts 20:28). It is a charge of service and love: "If you love me, feed my sheep" (cf. Jn 21:15-17).

36. For this reason one cannot see how it is possible to propose the admission of women to the priesthood in(45) virtue of the equality of rights of the human person, an equality which holds good also for Christians. To this end use is sometimes made of the text quoted above, from the Letter to the Galatians (3:28), which says that in Christ there is no longer any distinction between men and women. But this passage does not concern ministries: it only affirms the universal calling to divine filiation, which is the same for all. Moreover, and above all, to consider the ministerial priesthood as a human right would be to misjudge its nature completely: baptism does not confer any personal title to public ministry in the Church. The priesthood is not conferred for the honour or advantage of the recipient, but for the service of God and the Church; it is the object of a specific and totally gratuitous vocation: "You did not choose me, no, I chose you; and I commissioned you . . ." (Jn 15:16; cf. Heb 5:4).(46)

37. It is sometimes said and written in books and periodicals that some women feel that they have a vocation to the priesthood. Such an attraction, however noble and understandable, still does not suffice for a genuine vocation. In fact a vocation cannot be reduced to a mere personal attraction, which can remain purely subjective. Since the priesthood is a particular ministry of which the Church has received the charge and the control, authentication by the Church is indispensable here and is a constitutive part of the vocation: Christ chose "those he wanted" (Mk 3:13). On the other hand,

there is a universal vocation of all the baptized to the exercise of the royal priesthood by offering their lives to God and by giving witness for his praise.

38. Women who express a desire for the ministerial priesthood are doubtless motivated by the desire to serve Christ and the Church. And it is not surprising that, at a time when they are becoming more aware of the discriminations to which they have been subject, they should desire the ministerial priesthood itself. But it must not be forgotten that the priesthood does not form part of the rights of the individual, but stems from the economy of the mystery of Christ and the Church. The priestly office cannot become the goal of social advancement; no merely human progress of society or of the individual can of itself give access to it: it is of another order.

39. It therefore remains for us to meditate more deeply on the nature of the real equality of the baptized which is one of the great affirmations of Christianity: equality is in no way identity, for the Church is a differentiated body, in which each individual has his or her role. The roles are distinct, and must not be confused; they do not favour the superiority of some vis-à-vis the others, nor do they provide an excuse for jealousy; the only better gift, which can and must be desired, is love (cf. 1 Cor 12-13). The greatest in the Kingdom of Heaven are not the ministers but the saints.

40. The Church desires that Christian women should become fully aware of the greatness of their mission: today their role is of capital importance, both for the renewal and humanization of society and for the rediscovery by believers of the true face of the Church.

41. *His Holiness Pope Paul VI, during the audience granted to the undersigned Prefect of the Sacred Congregation on 15 October 1976, approved this Declaration, confirmed it and ordered its publication.*

42. Given in Rome, at the Sacred Congregation for the Doctrine of the Faith, on 15 October 1976, the feast of Saint Teresa of Avila.

FRANJO CARDINAL ŠEPER
Prefect

✠ Fr. Jérôme Hamer, O.P.
Titular Archbishop of Lorium
Secretary

Notes

1. *Acta Apostolicae Sedis* 55 (1963), pp. 267-268.

2. Cf. Second Vatican Council, Pastoral Constitution *Gaudium et Spes*, 29 (7 December 1965): *AAS* 58 (1966), pp. 1048-1049.

3. Cf. Pope Paul VI, Address to the members of the Study Commission on the Role of Women in Society and in the Church and to the members of the Committee for International Women's Year, 18 April 1975: *AAS* 67 (1975), p. 265.

4. Second Vatican Council, Decree *Apostolicam Actuositatem*, 9 (18 November 1965): *AAS* 58 (1966), p. 846.

5. Cf. Pope Paul VI, Address to the members of the Study Commission on the Role of Women in Society and in the Church and to the members of the Committee for International Women's Year, 18 April 1975: *AAS* 67 (1975), p. 266.

6. Cf. *AAS* 68 (1976), pp. 599-600; cf. *ibid.*, pp. 600-601.

7. Saint Irenaeus, *Adversus Haereses*, I, 13, 2: *PG* 7, 580-581; ed. Harvey, I, 114-122; Tertullian, *De Praescrip. Haeretic.* 41, 5: *CCL* 1, p. 221; Firmilian of Caesarea, in Saint Cyprian, *Epist.*, *75: CSEL* 3, pp. 817-818; Origen, *Fragmentum in I Cor.* 74, in *Journal of Theological Studies* 10 (1909), pp. 41-42; Saint Epiphanius, *Panarion* 49, 2-3; 78, 23; 79, 2-4: vol. 2, *GCS* 31, pp. 243-244; vol. e, *GCS* 37, pp. 473, 477-479.

8. *Didascalia Apostolorum*, ch. 15, ed. R. H. Connolly, pp. 133 and 142; *Constitutiones Apostolicae*, bk. 3, ch. 6, nos. 1-2; ch. 9, nos. 3-4: ed. F. H. Funk, pp. 191, 201; Saint John Chrysostom, *De Sacerdotio* 2, 2: *PG* 48, 633.

9. Saint Bonaventure, *In IV Sent.*, Dist. 25, art. 2, q. 1, ed. Quaracchi, vol. 4, p. 649; Richard of Middleton, *In IV Sent.*, Dist. 25, art. 4, n. 1, ed. Venice, 1499, f° 177r; John Duns Scotus, *In IV Sent.*, Dist. 25: *Opus Oxoniense*, ed. Vives, vol. 19, p. 140; *Reportata Parisiensia*, vol. 24, pp. 369-371; Durandus of Saint-Pourçain, *In IV Sent.*, Dist. 25, q. 2, ed. Venice, 1571, f° 364v.

10. Some have also wished to explain this fact by a symbolic intention of Jesus: the Twelve were to represent the ancestors of the twelve tribes of Israel (cf. *Mt* 19:28; *Lk* 22:30). But in these texts it is only a question of their participation in the eschatological judgment. The essential meaning of the choice of the Twelve should rather be sought in the totality of their mission (cf. *Mk* 3:14): they are to represent Jesus to the people and carry on his work.

11. Pope Innocent III, *Epist.* (11 December 1210) to the Bishops of Palencia and Burgos, included in *Corpus Iuris, Decret. Lib.* 5, tit. 38, *De Paenit.*, ch. 10 *Nova:* ed. A. Friedberg, vol. 2, col. 886-887; cf. *Glossa in Decretal. Lib.* 1, tit. 33, ch. 12 *Dilecta*, v° *Iurisdictioni*. Cf. Saint Thomas, *Summa Theologiae*, III, q. 27, a. 5 ad 3; Pseudo-Albert the Great, *Mariale*, quaest. 42, ed. Borgnet 37, 81.

12. Pope Pius XII, Apostolic Constitution *Sacramentum Ordinis*, 30 November 1947: *AAS* 40 (1948), pp. 5-7; Pope Paul VI, Apostolic Constitution *Divinae Consortium Naturae*, 15 August 1971: *AAS* 63 (1971), pp. 657-664; Apostolic Constitution *Sacram Unctionem*, 30 November 1972: *AAS* 65 (1973), pp. 5-9.

13. Pope Pius XII, Apostolic Constitution *Sacramentum Ordinis: loc. cit.*, p. 5.

14. Session 21, chap. 2: Denzinger-Schönmetzer, *Enchiridion Symbolorum* 1728.

15. Saint Cyprian, *Epist.* 63, 14: *PL* 4, 397 B; ed. Hartel, vol. 3, p. 713.

16. Second Vatican Council, Constitution *Sacrosanctum Concilium*, 33 (4 December 1963): ". . . by the priest who presides over the assembly in the person of Christ . . ."; Dogmatic Constitution *Lumen Gentium*, 10 (21 November 1964): "The ministerial priest, by the sacred power he enjoys, moulds

and rules the priestly people. Acting in the person of Christ, he brings about the Eucharistic Sacrifice, and offers it to God in the name of all the people . . ."; 28: "By the powers of the sacrament of Order, and in the image of Christ the eternal High Priest . . . they exercise this sacred function of Christ above all in the Eucharistic liturgy or synaxis. There, acting in the person of Christ . . ."; Decree *Presbyterorum Ordinis*, 2 (7 December 1965): ". . . priests, by the anointing of the Holy Spirit, are marked with a special character and are so configured to Christ the Priest that they can act in the person of Christ the Head"; 13: "As ministers of sacred realities, especially in the Sacrifice of the Mass, priests represent the person of Christ in a special way"; cf. 1971 Synod of Bishops, *De Sacerdotio Ministeriali* I, 4; Sacred Congregation for the Doctrine of the Faith, *Declaratio circa catholicam doctrinam de Ecclesia*, 6 (24 June 1973).

17. Saint Thomas, *Summa Theologiae*, III, q. 83, art. 1, ad 3: "It is to be said that [just as the celebration of this sacrament is the representative image of Christ's Cross: *ibid.* ad 2], for the same reason the priest also enacts the image of Christ, in whose person and by whose power he pronounces the words of consecration."

18. "For since a sacrament is a sign, there is required in the things that are done in the sacraments not only the 'res' but the signification of the 'res' ", recalls Saint Thomas, precisely in order to reject the ordination of women: *In IV Sent.*, dist. 25, q. 2, art. 1, quaestiuncula 1^a, corp.

19. Saint Thomas, *In IV Sent.*, dist. 25, q. 2, quaestiuncula 1^a ad 4um.

20. Cf. Council of Trent, Session 22, chap. 1: *DS* 1741.

21. Second Vatican Council, Dogmatic Constitution *Lumen Gentium*, 28: "Exercising within the limits of their authority the function of Christ as Shepherd and Head"; Decree *Presbyterorum Ordinis*, 2: "that they can act in the person of Christ the Head"; 6: "the office of Christ the Head and the Shepherd". Cf. Pope Pius XII, Encyclical Letter *Mediator Dei:* "the minister of the altar represents the person of Christ as the Head, offering in the name of all his members": *AAS* 39 (1947), p. 556; 1971 Synod of Bishops, *De Sacerdotio Ministeriali*, I, 4: "[The priestly ministry] . . . makes Christ, the Head of the community, present . . .".

22. Pope Paul VI, Encyclical Letter *Mysterium Fidei*, 3 September 1965: *AAS* 57 (1965), p. 761.

PART III

COMMENTARIES

1
Woman, Human and Ecclesial?

M. Nadine Foley

The Sacred Congregation for the Doctrine of the Faith opens its Declaration by citing the authority of Pope John XXIII's encyclical "Peace on Earth"[1] and the pastoral constitution "The Church in the Modern World"[2] from Vatican Council II. These are followed by an allusion to Pope Paul VI's statement to the members of the Vatican Study Commission on the Role of Women in Society and in the Church present in an audience with members of the Committee for the International Women's Year on April 18, 1975.[3] In this way the Declaration brings to the fore a sampling of current Church observations on women to set the tone for the exposition which follows. The selected texts respectively make three points which are typical of the allusions to women found in contemporary Vatican texts: (1) the development and expansion of the social roles of women is a phenomenon of our times, stemming from women's growing consciousness of their human dignity; (2) discrimination according to sex, whether social or cultural, is contrary to God's intent and must be overcome; and (3) equality of rights must aim at that effective complementarity between men and women which will build an harmonious and unified world according to the design of the Creator.

(1) The development and expansion of the social roles of women is a phenomenon of our times.

In "Peace on Earth" Pope John XXIII identified three characteristics of the contemporary world: the working classes have gradually gained ground in economic and public affairs; women are now taking a part in public life; in the modern world human society has taken on an entirely new appearance in the field of social and political life.[4] All three trends are embraced in one principle set forth by Pope John: "Thus in very many human beings the inferiority complex which endured for hundreds of thousands of years is disappearing, while in others there is an attenuation and gradual fading of the corresponding superiority complex which had its roots in social-economic privilege, sex or political standing."[5] The importance of this principle lies in its acknowledgment that phenomena evident in social, economic and political life of people today are part of an evolution in human consciousness coextensive with the history of humankind. This insight is compatible with the emphasis that "The Church in the Modern World" places upon the task of the Church to scrutinize the signs of the times and to interpret them in the light of the Gospel. For, it continues, ". . . we can already speak of a true social

53

and cultural transformation, one which has repercussion on man's religious life as well."[6] If the position of women is subject to true social and cultural transformation, then it follows that that development has implications for the religious life of the Church, the people of God. This fact of cultural change, something which occurs in varying patterns and degrees in different societies, is set forth in the statement from "Peace on Earth" quoted in the Declaration. The part which women are now taking in public life ". . . is a development that is perhaps swifter among Christian nations, but it is happening extensively, if more slowly, among nations that are heirs to different traditions and imbued with a different culture."[7] As quoted in the Declaration, this statement stands as an observation on the cultural phenomena of the times as social institutions outside the Church are being affected. In context, however, the statement expands upon one aspect of a growing development in human consciousness toward liberation from the superiority/inferiority complexes which have dominated human relationships throughout a long history.

The distinction is important. The tendency to observe changes in the social roles of women in isolation from other cultural phenomena is one of many ways in which women, and issues affecting women, continue to be marginated in the widely-based concern for human development which is a challenge and a responsibility for society and Church today. Human development, which is largely concerned with eliminating the superiority/inferiority relationships which have governed and controlled persons, races, societies and nations is the crying need of the present day. Its imperative makes serious claims upon the Church's ministry.

Papal and synodal documents such as "On the Development of Peoples,"[8] "Peace on Earth,"[9] "A Call to Action,"[10] "Justice in the World,"[11] and "The Evangelization of the Modern World"[12] present to the people of God challenges in ministry unprecedented in the Church's history. Merely to reflect upon the obstacles outside and within the Church which are listed as possible hindrances to evangelization in "The Evangelization of the Modern World"[13] is to realize the crises affecting the Church's mission today.

It is also to call into question the adequacy of the prevailing structures of ministry in the Church to meet the demands of the present and the future. To have issued this Declaration at the present time and in separation from the wider concerns about ministry which the contemporary world poses to all the people of God, women and men, illustrates the continuing problem. Women are consistently treated in separation from the mainstream of ecclesial issues.[14] They are also categorized as a group and treated without respect for their individual gifts of nature and of grace.

Despite this Declaration the Church has still to address the implications of the development and expansion of the social roles of women for its own ministry in the world today. It must do so by situating women within the people of God as fully participating members of the ecclesial community by virtue of their Baptism. The development and expansion of the social roles of women is symbolic of their deeper realization of their personhood which calls the teaching Church to a reexamination of its theological anthropology. The reconsideration will not be adequate without women theologians participating in the endeavor. For women are the bearers of the experience which has implications for the Church today.

(2) Discrimination according to sex, whether social or cultural, is contrary to God's intent and must be overcome.

The Declaration refers to the Second Vatican Council which, "enumerating in its Pastoral Constitution *The Church in the Modern World* the forms of discrimination touching upon the basic rights of the person which must be overcome and eliminated as being contrary to God's plan, gives first place to discrimination based upon sex."[15] The text cited states, ". . . with respect to the fundamental rights of the person, every type of discrimination, whether social or cultural, whether based on sex, race, color, social condition, language or religion is to be overcome and eradicated as contrary to God's intent."[16] The notion that "The Church in the Modern World" intended that "first place" belongs to sex among the possible bases for discrimination in society today is a curious claim. Later in the same document "first place" is given to race.[17] The emphasis of the Pastoral Constitution seems better placed upon the fact that the several forms of discrimination cited are *contrary to God's intent.*

What is contrary to the divine plan must seemingly be eradicated not only from the economic and political fields, nationally and internationally, but also from the Church. In paragraph three the Declaration quotes the "Decree on the Apostolate of the Laity" to the effect that women must assume more active roles in the Church. "Since in our time women have an ever more active share in the whole life of society, it is important that they participate more widely also in the various sectors of the Church's apostolate."[18] More recently the Synod of Bishops in their document "Justice in the World" have spoken similarly. "We also urge that women should have their own share of responsibility and participation in the community life of society and likewise of the Church."[19]

The argument for promoting the participation of women in the life and work of the Church appears to be one of achieving a correspondence between developments in society at large and those within the Church. It is at the same time an apparent acknowledgment that social organization within the Church should follow upon and reflect what is happening outside its ranks in this respect.

The sources are weak in indicating why this should be so. The insurance of basic human rights is the reason offered for the Church's concern that discrimination in all its forms should be eliminated in society. A firm commitment to such a project for itself might inspire the Church to become a paradigm of social organization in which the rights and responsibilities of women are reflected in their sharing fully and equally with men in the Church's life and mission. Yet the Church agenda is tentative. *Because* women are becoming more active in society today, they should also begin to share more widely in the Church's apostolate.

The argument has its positive value insofar as it respects the fact that the Church is enculturated as a human institution, that true social and cultural transformation has a repercussion within the Church. It is deficient, however, since as an operative principle it renders the Church a follower rather than a leader in proclaiming and manifesting the full equality of human persons achieved through the redemptive mission of Jesus Christ which the Church serves.

(3) Equality of rights must aim at that effective complementarity between men and women which will build an harmonious and unified world according to the design of the Creator.

The Declaration cites the statement of Pope Paul VI to the Committee for the International Women's Year and other women gathered with them on April 18, 1975. He spoke of equality among men and women.

> . . . to speak of equalization of rights does not resolve the problem, which is much more profound: it is necessary to aim at an effective complementarity, so that men and women bring their proper riches and dynamism to the building of a world, not levelled and uniform, but harmonious and unified, according to the design of the Creator, or, to use the terms of the Holy Year, renewed and reconciled.[20]

This quotation neatly summarizes the prevailing official Church teaching on the fundamental relationships between women and men to be achieved and maintained. The key phrases are "effective complementarity," *"proper* riches and dynamism," and "according to the design of the Creator." There is an abundance of contemporary material from Vatican sources to expand upon the meaning of these phrases, and the presuppositions upon which they are founded.

At the root lies the position that in the order of creation, especially as Genesis 2 recounts the origin of man and woman, the sexes have been established in a relationship of fundamental complementarity. Philosophically this means that males and females have their respective proper or specific natures. From the natural, divinely-established complementarity of male and female, or from their respective proper natures, flow certain necessary characteristics appropriate to each. Correspondingly certain social roles, especially in the family, must be guarded and defended by the Church.

Generally Vatican statements do not devote tracts to elucidating the special qualities and roles of men. But there are many devoted to the specific nature, characteristics and proper roles of women. In his "A Call to Action" Pope Paul VI says,

> We do not have in mind that false equality which would be in contradiction with woman's proper role, which is of such capital importance, at the heart of the family, as well as within society. Develop-

ments in legislation should on the contrary be directed to protecting
her proper vocation and at the same time recognizing her independence as a person, and her equal rights to participate in cultural,
economic, social and political life.[21]

Again in 1972 the Holy Father said, ". . . women's authentic liberation does
not consist in a formalistic or materialistic equality with the other sex, but in
recognizing what the female personality has that is essentially specific to it:
woman's vocation to be a mother"[22] In his address on "Reconciliation/the
Way to Peace," delivered at Christmas time in 1974 the Holy Father spoke
of the qualities of women.

> We rejoice especially on the eve of International Women's Year,
> proclaimed by the United Nations, at the ever wider participation
> of women in the life of society, to which they bring a specific con-
> tribution of great value, thanks to the qualities God has given them.
> These qualities of intuition, creativity, sensibility, a sense of piety
> and compassion, a profound capacity for understanding and love,
> enable women to be in a very particular way the creators of recon-
> ciliation in families and in society.[23]

The several kinds of statements about women typical of Church pronouncements today are derived from two kinds of evidence: that which ultimately has its source in the consciousness and experience of women and is
reflected and observed in changing social roles; and that deduced from long
standing principles of divine order and nature that have remained unchallenged throughout a considerable history. Recognizing the former, the
Church attempts to accept it in terms of limitations imposed by the latter.
The result is a consistent qualifying of women's equality and rights according
to what is perceived as "proper" to her nature. The data from experience is
accordingly judged valid to the extent that it is compatible with the accepted
principles. The principles themselves remain largely unexamined in terms of
insights available from the human sciences and biblical studies as these dis-
ciplines have developed in the last century.

Many women and men today proceed differently with the same data.
Given their experience, their aspirations away from the superiori-
ty/inferiority structures which have typified human interactions for centuries,
they question the absolutism of principles which are incompatible with their
experience. Experience shows that not every woman has gifts and traits complementary to those of a particular man. There is a growing awareness that
individual persons are complementary to one another or not irrespective of
sex differentiation, that to insist otherwise is to subject individuals to the
oppression of sex role stereotyping. There is reason therefore to question a
doctrine which would assign behavioral traits, especially nurturing qualities,
to women as necessarily typical of all without differentiation. There is further
reason to question that women can fill only those roles in society and Church

which conform to their presumed natural competencies.

⟨ The problem seems to be that women are commonly treated in terms of their roles, especially that of motherhood, rather than in the light of their essential human personhood and variety of personal gifts. Paragraph three of the Declaration which speaks of the decisive roles played in the Church by women through their religious consecration or through their rearing of families is particularly telling in this respect.[24] The fact that there is no place for the single laywoman in this enumeration raises the key question. What value does the woman have in herself, apart from her association with a male Church or with a male partner in marriage? Until this question is answered in the only way it can be answered there seems little point in writing treatises on women in ministerial priesthood or in any other *role*. The needed ontology is missing.

And finally if the doctrine is presumably rooted in a divine order established in revelation there is reason to reexamine the biblical interpretation which seems to support an anthropology at variance with contemporary human experience.[25]

The texts cited in the first paragraph of the Declaration under the heading "The Role of Women in Modern Society and the Church" undoubtedly are intended by the authors to document the Church's awareness and affirmation of the developments furthering the status of women today, as well as its commitment to the elimination of discrimination based upon sex. The negative position on the ordination of women to ministerial priesthood is then not to be construed as stemming from opposition to women's advance toward social equality or from discrimination on the basis of sex within the Church. It derives from a view of what is proper to women in terms of maintaining an effective complementarity with men in the offices of the Church⟨ Equality of rights based upon the effective complementarity flowing from the design of the Creator is then the principle providing the critical difference for the positions developed later in the Declaration. It is not, however, the completely adequate reason since the base of the discussion changes, and the special influx of the "light of revelation" is invoked. "The human sciences, however valuable their contribution in their own domain cannot suffice here, for they cannot grasp the realities of faith: the properly supernatural content of these realities is beyond their competence."[26]

Women's experience in moving from the superiority/inferiority dominances to which they have been subjected throughout history is a "new thing" emerging in the consciousness of peoples today. Pope John XXIII recognized it and saw its importance. He did not elaborate on it in "Peace on Earth" as he did on the implications of persons striving for economic and political liberation. That is unfortunate. But the reality persists and is the unique possession of women who strive to bring it to the life of the Church as a contribution to its own agenda of continuing reformation. The "new thing," like new wine, cannot be put in old wineskins. Because it cannot, the context in which the Sacred Congregation attempts to establish a position on women in ministerial priesthood is inadequate.

Notes

1. "Pacem in Terris," *Acta Apostolicae Sedis* 55(1963), pp. 267-268; "Pacem in Terris" (Washington, D.C.: United States Catholic Conference, 1963), p. 11.
2. "Gaudium et Spes, 29" (December 7, 1965); *AAS* 58 (1966), pp. 1048-49; *The Documents of Vatican II*, ed. by Walter M. Abbott and Joseph Gallagher (New York: The Guild Press, 1966), pp. 227-228.
3. *AAS* 67 (1975), p. 265; "Women/Disciples and Co-Workers," *Origins* 4 (May 1, 1975), p. 718.
4. *AAS* 55 (1963), pp. 267-268; NCWC text, pp. 11-12.
5. *Ibid.*
6. *AAS* 58 (1966), pp. 1027-1028; *The Documents of Vatican II*, pp. 201-202.
7. *AAS* 55 (1963), pp. 267-268; NCWC text, p. 11.
8. "Populorum Progressio," *AAS* 59 (1967), 256-299; "On the Development of Peoples" (Washington, D.C.: United States Catholic Conference, 1967).
9. See note 2.
10. "Octogesima Adveniens," *AAS* 63 (1971), pp. 400-444; "A Call to Action" (Washington, D.C.: United States Catholic Conference, 1971).
11. "De Justitia in Mundo," (November 30, 1971); *AAS* 63 (1971), pp. 923-941; Synod of Bishops, "The Ministerial Priesthood" and "Justice in the World" (Washington, D.C.: National Conference of Catholic Bishops, 1971), pp. 33-52.
12. Synod of Bishops, "The Evangelization of the Modern World," (Washington, D.C.: United States Catholic Conference, 1973).
13. *Ibid.*, pp. 3-4.
14. This is illustrated by the special document "The Role of Women in Evangelization" from the Pastoral Commission of the Vatican Congregation for the Evangelization of Peoples. See *Origins* 5 (April 22, 1976), pp. 702-707. The Synod of Bishops study document "The Evangelization of the Modern World" has six pages of guidelines and practical applications for promoting evangelization today (pp. 14-18). A wide range of issues is set forth, but there is no reference to women either as requiring special attention in evangelization or as having a particular role to play. The issuing of a separate treatise on women's role in evangelization suggests that what is said in general of the Church's responsibility cannot be addressed to women without distinctions. Yet the issues of evangelization are well known to women in ministry and they perceive their ability to respond in ways not now open to them. This is the development in women's consciousness which must be addressed *within* the Church.
15. Declaration, par. 1.
16. *AAS* (1966), pp. 1048-1049; *The Documents of Vatican II*, pp. 227-228.
17. *Ibid.*, pp. 1080-1081; and p. 266. The latter reads ". . . discrimination on the grounds of race, sex, nationality, religious or social conditions."
18. "Apostolicam Actuositatem, 9" (November 18, 1965); *AAS* 58 (1966), p. 846; *The Documents of Vatican II*, p. 500.

19. "Justice in the World," p. 933; and p. 44.

20. *AAS* 67 (1975), p. 265; "Women/Disciples and Co-Workers," p. 718.

21. "A Call to Action," pp. 410-411; and p. 8.

22. "The Right to Be Born," An Address to the Italian Catholic Jurists, *The Pope Speaks*, Vol. XVII, No. 4 (1973), p. 335.

23. *Origins* 4 (December 26, 1974), 431. See also Pope Paul VI, "Women/Disciples and Co-Workers," *Origins* 4 (May, 1975), p. 719; "The Role of Women in Contemporary Society," *The Pope Speaks*, Vol. XIX (December 8, 1974), 314; and especially "The Role of Women in Evangelization" from the Pastoral Commission of the Vatican Congregation for the Evangelization of Peoples, *Origins*, 5 (April 22, 1976), pp. 703-704.

24. *Origins* 6 (February 3, 1977), pp. 519-520.

25. See Report of the Pontifical Biblical Commission, "Can Women Be Priests?" *Origins* 6 (July 1, 1976), pp. 92-96. "In Genesis 1 man and woman are called together to be the image of God (Gen. 1, 26f.) on equal terms and in a community of life. It is in common that they receive rule over the world. Their vocation gives a new meaning to the sexuality that man possesses as animals do" (p. 92). This kind of insight needs to be brought to bear upon the developing knowledge of human sexuality unknown before the present time.

26. Declaration, par. 34. This is a truth that involves much complexity. Pertinent to it are the kinds of issues raised by Avery Dulles, S.J. in his address to the Catholic Theological Society of America June 12, 1976. Cf. "What Is Magisterium?" *Origins* 6 (July 1, 1976), pp. 82-88.

2
Women in the Life of the Church

Elizabeth Carroll

The life of the Church continues the earthly life of Jesus. It depends upon the force of the Spirit revealing, animating, empowering, just as Jesus did.[1] Jesus laid the basis of the Church by attracting and forming disciples, women as well as men.[2] Jesus counted upon women to understand and integrate his message, to act upon it and to proclaim it.[3]

By admitting women to Baptism the early Church acknowledged the full potentiality of the female to live the new life of the risen Christ, to receive and be driven by the charisms of the Holy Spirit, and to fulfill the promise of their Creator as imaging God.[4]

Throughout the history of the Church cultural conditions and human failures have prevented women from fulfilling their potential and from having their services honestly named.[5] The Declaration singles out two "foundresses" and two Doctors of the Church for mention.[6] It is noteworthy that the Law of the Church has not upheld the prerogatives of leadership based on such "foundresses"[7] nor has the teaching authority of the Church built upon the truth inherent in the fact that if women are among the Doctors of the Church they are thereby acknowledged as part of the magisterium.[8]

The truth is that today women are performing most of the functions which Jesus mandated to his disciples as ways of being like him. At home and in innumerable Church functions women serve in that provision of food which was so often for Jesus a setting for friendship, acceptance of the outcast, and teaching.[9] Women continue in works from personal nurture to community organizing to help people accept and form bonds of mutual supportive services.

Jesus commissioned his apostles to preach the Gospel.[10] Today, according to the Sacred Congregation for the Evangelization of Peoples, one-third of those "engaged directly in evangelization" are men, two-thirds are women. The Congregation declares that: ". . . the history of the missions has for a long time borne witness to the very large role played by women in the evangelization of the world." This congregation details some of the areas in which women participate in the pastoral work of the Church:

> In how many parishes already does not a Sister, in the absence of a priest, preside over the liturgical assembly of the faithful on Sundays and weekdays, and exhort and instruct them in their Christian duties.[11]

Even in parishes within which priests reside women are performing important pastoral activities as team members or as staff. In some parishes they regularly deliver homilies, thus bringing feminine experience into reflection on the Scriptures.[12] An example of the leadership being afforded women in this field is the appointment of a woman as chairperson of the Homiletics department of a major seminary.[13] From teachers of prayer and moral decision-making in the home and nursery school to professors of theology in university and seminary, women are at present shaping much of the perception of the message of Jesus. Women, moreover, are increasingly active in the preaching and directing of retreats, in spiritual direction, even of priests, in leading shared prayer and group study of spirituality and of Scripture. Women are engaged in many parishes as "ministers of liturgy," helping to prepare liturgies, to train persons for their participation in them, to make their meaning explicit.

In fields relating closely to jurisdiction women have been authorized to serve as Chancellor of the diocese, as Vicars for Religious, as directors of diocesan departments.[14]

In the Catholic tradition the life of Jesus is transmitted not only through hearing his word but through the sacraments. A considerable amount of the work of preparing persons for the sacraments is in the hands of women. The instruction of catechumens and of catechists of catechumens, the delicate task of preparing children for first communion and first confession, the youth ministry that precedes Confirmation all enlist the talents of women on a very large scale. As the document of the Council for Evangelization, *The Role of Women in Evangelization*, indicates:

> It is often a Sister too whose presence makes it possible to have the Blessed Sacrament reserved; and she distributes it to the faithful both during Mass and outside of Mass when necessary.

> There are cases where Sisters are permanently in charge of parishes, with the authorization of the Bishop, and administer baptism as well as preside at marriages as the Church's official witness.[15]

One of the distinguishing marks of Jesus' ministry and a locus of his presence was its welcome to sinners and the abandoned, its outreach to the needy.[16] In the experience of St. Paul Christ declared himself as the person of the persecuted.[17] In Matthew's scene of the Last Judgment the Son of Man identifies himself with the hungry, the homeless, the sick, the prisoner.[18] Today in the administration and service of institutional works, hospitals, refuges for the unwanted, training centers for the afflicted and delinquent, women continue to extend that welcome, thus "being" Christ for those in need. In one-to-one visits with the psychologically depressed, the guilt-ridden, the aging, women help persons to that conversion of heart which is integral as means and end to every sacramental grace.[19]

Women's services in the Church today present an anomoly. As regards offices of leadership their work can be rendered "official" by an exceptional authorization, an indult. In the sacramental order their emerging roles constitute a challenge to the understanding of sacrament. Does God forgive sins confessed to a person whose ministry has helped the sinner to conversion of heart? Or does God forgive only sins absolved by an ordained priest with appropriate faculties? Is it respectful of the mercy of Jesus or the humanness of women to allow women to anguish over the incompleteness of their reconciling mission (in forgiveness of sin or sacrament of anointing) because no priest is available? Is the ministry of a woman who in day-by-day loving service gathers a parish for prayer, scriptural remembering, and distribution of the Eucharist the locus for the full presence of Christ? Or do the words of consecration alone provide the sacramental union of Christ with and among his people?

People see a natural resemblance to Jesus in the love conveyed, the service rendered, the self shared, much more than they look to a physical characteristic like sex.[20] The fact that people in physical, psychological, and spiritual need accept the ministry of women belies the contention that women cannot be recognized as images of Christ.[21]

Matthew represents Jesus as declaring, "It is enough that the disciple should grow to be like the teacher. . . ."[22] Women as well as men will be accepted as bearing a natural resemblance to Christ as they grow like their teacher, Jesus, as they "put on the Lord Jesus Christ."[23]

Notes

1. "Constitution on the Church," nos. 4-8, in *The Documents of Vatican II*, ed. W.M. Abbott (New York: Association Press, 1966), pp. 20-22; Mt 4:1; Mark 1:10, 12; 4:14.

2. E.g., Lk 11:27-28; 8:21: Mary, the mother of Jesus, "heard the word of God and kept it"; Lk 10:39: Mary of Bethany; especially Lk 8:1-3; 24:10; Mk 15:40-41; 16:9; Mt 27:55-56; Jn 19:25: On the way, women as well as the Twelve accompanied Jesus.

3. E.g., Lk 2:52: Mary "kept all these things in her heart"; Jn 11:17-31: Martha's dialogue with Jesus on the resurrection; Jn 4:5-42: Jesus' interaction with the Samaritan woman.

4. Gal 3:27-28 represents a baptismal text, emphasizing the equality of all baptized. See also Gen 1:26-27; "Constitution on the Church," *loc. cit.*

5. The Church rose out of the patriarchal culture of the Jews. Despite the initiatives of Jesus in cutting through the legal impediments on women, cultural habits prevailed, to be reinforced in the dualism of patristic thought and the turmoil of Germanic migrations. Both men and women lacked insight into the non-Christlike structure; men fell into *machismo* or chauvinism, women into timidity and manipulation.

6. St. Clare and St. Teresa; St. Catherine of Siena and St. Teresa.

7. The Code of Canon Law (c. 506) requires that elections of many religious superiors of women to be valid must be presided over by a man, in

all cases may be required to have a man presiding, and in some instances need men as tellers.

8. In B. Forshaw, "Doctors of the Church," *New Catholic Encyclopedia* (1967), Vol. 4, it is stated that there are no women who are Doctors of the Church, nor was it likely that any would be because of the "link between the title and the teaching office of the Church." Yet Pope Paul in 1970 in his homily on St. Teresa went to great length to explain that in her case "Doctor of the Church" was not a matter of "a title entailing hierarchical teaching functions." See *Pope Speaks* Vol. 15 (1970), p. 221; see also *Spiritual Life*, Vol. 16 (1970) pp. 210-263; see also *Acta Apostolica Sedis*, Vol. 62 (1970), pp. 594f.

9. On Jesus' application to himself and to women of the verb *diakonein*, to serve, see Elizabeth Carroll, "Women and Ministry," *Theolgical Studies,* Vol. 36, No. 4 (Dec., 1975), p. 662.

10. Mk 16:16.

11. Pastoral Commission of the Sacred Congregation for the Evangelization of Peoples, *The Role of Women in Evangelization* (Rome, March, 1976), No. 5.

12. Elizabeth Carroll, Report to Committee on Women of the Canon Law Society of America, Bethesda, Md., April 15-17, 1977.

13. Aquinas Institute (Order of Preachers), Dubuque, Iowa.

14. Carroll, *op. cit.* A woman is Chancellor in the diocese of Nelson, British Columbia. Vicars for Religious are women in Denver, Providence, Youngstown, New Ulm, and Detroit. Canada lists women as constituting 27% of directors of diocesan departments.

15. Pastoral Commission, *op. cit.*

16. Mt. 9:10; Lk 5:12-14; 7:36-50; 8:43-48, etc.

17. Acts 9:4-5; 22:8; 26:15.

18. Mt 25:31-46.

19. Mt 18:3; Lk 17:4.

20. One woman pastoral associate affirms this influence on attitudes as she writes, "This town would not favor the ordination of women, but (because of my long service here) they would like *me* to be ordained."

21. Declaration, par. 26.

22. Mt 10:25.

23. Rom 13:14.

3
Ecumenism and the Lack Thereof
Arlene Anderson Swidler

The Commentary on this Declaration is somewhat less oblique than the Declaration itself in its reference to the ecumenical problems involved in the ordination of women. It opens, "The question of the admission of women to the ministerial priesthood seems to have arisen in a general way about 1958, after the decision by the Swedish Lutheran Church in September of that year to admit women to the pastoral office."[1]

The distinction between that 1958 decision and the earlier admission of women to ministry in various other church groups is standard. Haye van der Meer, for example, summarizes what he considers the primary reason for reconsidering the question in the Catholic Church by saying, "There are now, at least in the Scandinavian churches, women on whom the bishops have imposed hands and upon whom the Mass vestments have been conferred. That means that now, even among Christians who make the same efforts as we do to deal with the full tradition of their churches . . . the opinion prevails that the female priestly office does not contradict the essence of Christianity."[2]

The assertion that the question of women in the ministerial priesthood arose in (or about) 1958, however, is quite misleading. It assumes, as does the Declaration itself,[3] that such a "question" can be directed to the Catholic Church solely by ecclesiastical decisions, never by either the findings of individual scholars or the reflections of officially constituted church commissions.

In reality, the question arose in the Anglican Church decades earlier. Canon C.C. Raven favored the ordination of women in his book *Women and Holy Orders* published in 1928. Ordination of women—first as deaconesses, later as priests—has been on the agendas of Lambeth Conferences since 1920.[4] Naturally Episcopalians are displeased when their decision to ordain women is treated in Roman circles as facile and unconsidered. The ecumenical officer of the Episcopal Church in this country, Peter Day, responded with some asperity to an anonymous Vatican description of the decision to ordain women as simply the result of a head count: "The question of diaconate for women is now under discussion in the Roman Catholic Church among theologians of the highest repute. This was where the Episcopal Church began its deliberations in 1871."[5]

Ignoring these early discussions within the Anglican communion (though that church itself took the findings of its official commissions quite seriously) seems to suggest once again that the question of the ordination of women is unrelated to research and theological reflection. This impression is confirmed by the Declaration's statement that because the problem is ecumenical, the Catholic Church must make its thinking on the matter known.[6] There is no hint that the Declaration is simply a laying out of a present position as a basis for dialogue either within or without the Catholic Church.

A second unfortunate attitude—one characterized by the Lutheran publication *Forum Letter* as "of particular offense to Lutherans"[7]—assumes that the Swedish Lutheran ordination of women in 1958 raises no "strictly theological problem" inasmuch as Lutherans have rejected the sacrament of Orders.[8] The assumption that it is only when confronting sacramental issues that Christians concern themselves deeply with tradition and the teachings of the Gospel must sound strange indeed to all our Christian sisters and brothers who have observed the inordinate amount of theologizing and sermonizing Catholics have devoted to Mary the Mother of Jesus over the centuries.

In the following sentence the Commentary is simply inaccurate: the Anglican ordinations in 1971 are not the first within communities that claim apostolic succession, for the Church of Sweden has retained episcopacy and the apostolic succession since pre-Reformation times.[9]

The next paragraph of the Commentary states that the ordination of what have come to be known as the Philadelphia Eleven was "afterwards declared invalid by the House of Bishops." The women ordinands in that case had neither the permission of the Bishop of Pennsylvania, in whose diocese the ordinations occurred, nor the approval of their own diocesan authorities; the ordinations seem clearly to have been canonically irregular. However, they cannot be said to have been declared invalid—or even canonically irregular—by the House of Bishops simply because the bishops had no such power. This meeting was neither an ecclesiastical court nor a legislative session. In fact, if the House of Bishops had authority to legislate without the concurrence of the House of Deputies its own 1972 vote favoring the ordination of women to the priesthood could have settled the matter then and there.

The August 1974 issue was clearly the matter of the breaking of collegiality on the part of the ordaining bishops rather than any theological question of the capability of women for Holy Orders. In addition, the bishops were merely expressing their opinion, as the opening of the relevant paragraph makes clear: "Further, we express our conviction that the necessary conditions for valid ordination to the priesthood in the Episcopal Church were not fulfilled. . . ."[10]

Prior to the voting, the Bishop of West Missouri, speaking from notes, is reported to have told the assembly, in the words of others present, that "contemporary ecumenical discussion tends simply to define as valid that which is duly recognized by a communion of the Church," as well as argued that the ordinations were invalid on traditional grounds because of a defect in the intention of the officiating bishops.[11] Admittedly the situation was both confusing and confused. Nevertheless, it is inaccurate to say that the House of Bishops declared the Philadelphia ordinations invalid.

In summary, the unwary might assume from the Commentary that a) the Church of Sweden's decision to ordain women is irrelevant to our proceedings because Lutherans don't take all this very seriously; b) the Episcopalians rather rushed into the whole thing; c) ordinations which don't fulfill the requirements of church canons are not ordinations at all. Each of these impressions woud strengthen the over-all effect of the Vatican Declaration on the average reader. At the same time these inaccuracies have alienated members of the Lutheran and Episcopalian Churches, who, along with the Orthodox, must be the partners in future dialogue on the question.

The point must also be made that, although the ecumenical dimensions of the changing role of women have been pointed out often enough,[12] the Catholic Church has shown little interest in dialogue on the subject.

In this country the Catholic Church has participated in eight bilateral consultations, all founded in the 1960s and all but one, the Southern Baptist-Catholic consultation, still active. The participation of women in these dialogue teams has been only token despite a good deal of urging and correspondence from American Catholic women.[13] Of the three consultations which involve other "liturgical" churches, two—the Orthodox-Roman Catholic Consultation and the Lutheran-Catholic Consultation—have never had any women members from either side.

The Roman Catholic-Presbyterian Consultation Group produced several statements concerning women in 1970 and 1971.[14] A committee of the Catholic Theological Society of America, chaired by Avery Dulles, SJ, in reviewing the work of all the bilaterals up to 1972, called these statements on the status of women "a sincere and promising fruit of courageous ecumenical dialogue" and recommended that other bilateral consultations take advantage of the statements, which "provide an excellent example of how this important and delicate matter can be forthrightly and prudently handled."[15]

However, only the Anglican-Roman Catholic Consultation, lately augmented with its first female participants, has since taken up the question of ordination of women. In a special meeting in June of 1975 it formulated a statement which stressed, among other things, the gravity of the question: ". . . problems relating to the doctrine of God, of the Incarnation, and Redemption are at least indirectly involved in its solution, so that any decision, whether for or against the ordination of women, will in fact require the Church to explain or develop its essential tradition in an unprecedented way."[16] In October of the same year it described the ecumenical task as an inquiry into whether one church can recognize another amid differences, whether such controverted issues may perhaps represent different manifestations of God's grace.[17]

Unfortunately, the timing of these studies probably restricted the intellectual freedom which leisurely discussion fosters. As the June statement itself pointed out, the ordination question was expected to be proposed at the Episcopal General Convention the following year; the time for initiating a shared searching and reflection was long past. Once the Episcopal Church has integrated women priests into its structures and experiences, dialogue can begin again, but it will be of a different order. The opportunity to move forward together has been lost.

Notes

1. Commentary, par. 1.
2. Haye van der Meer, SJ, *Women Priests in the Catholic Church?* trans. A. and L. Swidler (Philadelphia: Temple University Press, 1973), pp. 6-7.
3. Declaration, par. 4. The Declaration states here that the "initiative" of "admitting women to the pastoral office on a par with men" "constitutes an ecumenical problem."
4. A helpful chronology of relevant documents and actions in the Anglican Communion can be found in Emily C. Hewitt and Suzanne R. Hiatt, *Women Priests: Yes or No?* (New York: Seabury, 1973), pp. 102-104.
5. Peter Day, Letter to the Editor, *Ecumenical Trends*, Vol. 6, No. 2 (February, 1977), p. 28.
6. Declaration, par. 4.
7. "That Vatican Declaration," *Forum Letter*, Vol. 6, No. 4 (April 18, 1977), p. 5.
8. Commentary, par. 2.
9. This is mentioned briefly in John Reumann's "Editor's Introduction" to Krister Stendahl, *The Bible and the Role of Women*, trans. Emilie T. Sander (Philadelphia: Fortress Press, 1966), p. vii. Stendahl, now Dean of Harvard Divinity School, is a member of the Church of Sweden; this study was prepared for the Swedish Church Assembly of 1958. Both the Stendahl essay and the Reumann introduction in this small book are helpful.
10. Harvey H. Guthrie, Jr., Edward G. Harris, and Hays H. Rockwell, "A Personal Report on the Meeting of the House of Bishops of the Episcopal Church in Chicago on August 14 and 15, 1974, and Some Reflections on Process and Theology," (mimeographed, Sept. 3, 1974), p. 4.
11. *Ibid.*, p. 2.
12. Cf., e.g., Arlene Swidler, "An Ecumenical Question: The Status of Women," *Journal of Ecumenical Studies*, Vol. 4, No. 1 (Winter, 1967), pp. 113-115.
13. An Ad Hoc Committee of the U.S. Section of St. Joan's International Alliance, for example, has corresponded over the years with the president and various staff members of the National Conference of Catholic Bishops as well as a number of bishops chairing bilateral consultations. Responses have varied from sympathetic acknowledgment of clerical clubbiness to an occasional show of hostility, but the proportion of women has not increased.
14. These are most easily accessible in the *Journal of Ecumenical Studies:* "The Ordination of Women," part of a longer paper in Vol. 7, No. 3 (Summer, 1970), pp. 686-690; "Women in Church and Society," in the same issue, pp. 690-91; and "Women in the Church," in Vol. 9, No. 1 (Winter, 1972), pp. 235-41.

15. *Proceedings of the Twenty-Seventh Annual Convention of the CTSA* (Bronx: Manhattan College, 1973), pp. 205-6.

16. "ARC Consultation on Ordination of Women," *BCEIA Newsletter,* Vol. 4, No. 4 (October, 1975), p. 4.

17. "ARC Statement on the Ordination of Women," *BCEIA Newsletter,* Vol. 5, No. 2 (April, 1976), p. 4.

4
Studies on Women Priests
Anne E. Patrick

Public discussion of the women's ordination issue by Roman Catholic scholars has increased dramatically in the last several years. The works cited below are especially important. Scrutiny of them will afford a sense of the range and significance of the arguments in favor of altering the current discipline, many of which seem to have been ignored or glossed over by the Declaration.

For an overview of Catholic literature in English on the ordination question published during the decade after Vatican Council II, cf. my "Women and Religion: A Survey of Significant Literature, 1965-1974," *Theological Studies*, Vol. 36 (December, 1975), pp. 737-765 (cf. especially pp. 752-757). In general, this survey concludes, early works served to establish the importance of the question, while subsequent writings analyzed materials from Scripture and tradition and focused on the pastoral dimensions of the issue. Symbolic considerations have frequently been brought into the discussion by both advocates and opponents of women's ordination, and recent arguments emphasizing the need to symbolize the fact that the image of God is both male and female are seen to "entail an important shift in the discussion. Rather than asking whether it is right to *include* women in official ministry, a number of writers are inquiring, at least implicity, whether it is wrong to continue *excluding* them" (p. 757).

Since this earlier survey covers the literature through 1974, attention will here be given primarily to more recent works available in English. For almost annually issued (since 1969) comprehensive bibliographies of book and periodical literature (many hundreds of items) from all major European languages on women in the Church, including ordination, see: Werkgroep "Samenwerking van Man en Vrouw in de Kerk," *Literatuurlijst Man en Vrouw in Kerk en Maatschappij* (St. Janssingel 21, 's-Hertogenbosch, Netherlands, 1969ff.).

The December 1975 issue of *Theological Studies*, edited by Walter Burghardt, S.J., has recently been reprinted as *Woman: New Dimensions* (New York: Paulist, 1977). Besides the bibliographic survey mentioned above, this volume contains several essays pertinent to the ordination question, especially "Women and Ministry" by Elizabeth Carroll, R.S.M. (pp. 660-687) and "Roles of Women in the Fourth Gospel" by Raymond E. Brown, S.S. (pp. 688-699). Carroll's article is cited in the Vatican Commentary on the Declaration, note 52. In addition to the Burghardt volume, then, the following resources are particularly significant:

(1) Haye van der Meer, S.J., *Women Priests in the Catholic Church?* tr. by Arlene and Leonard Swidler (Philadelphia: Temple University Press, 1973). A student of Karl Rahner, S.J., van der Meer completed this doctoral thesis in 1962 and published it as *Priestertum der Frau?* in 1969. He concludes from his investigations of arguments from Scripture, tradition, the magisterium, and speculative theology that "Catholic dogmatic theologians may not hold that according to the present position of theology it is already (or still) established on a scholarly basis that 'office' should, by divine law, remain closed to women" (p. 9). Van der Meer does not find difficulty with the idea of women representing Christ, and he also observes that there is something "significantly feminine not only in the Church as bride receiving, but in the Church as imparting, as dispensing life" (p. 149). He further argues that to claim that women cannot *administer* sacraments on account of their sex logically entails that one must find it problematic for men to *receive* sacraments. The English edition of van der Meer's book is enhanced by a bibliographic survey in the "Translators' Foreword," as well as by the translators' overview of developments since the thesis was written. For the recent thought of Rahner on this question, cf. his *The Shape of the Church to Come* (New York: Seabury, 1974), where he observes that since Christian community leadership should be linked with sacramental and liturgical life, this will require women's serving in priestly roles in communities where they are leaders (p. 114).

(2) Anne Marie Gardiner, S.S.N.D., ed., *Women and Catholic Priesthood: An Expanded Vision. Proceedings of the Detroit Ordination Conference* (New York: Paulist, 1976). This volume features major papers by Elizabeth Carroll, R.S.M., ("The Proper Place for Women in the Church"), Margaret Farley, R.S.M. ("Moral Imperatives for the Ordination of Women"), and Anne Carr, B.V.M. ("The Church in Process: Engendering the Future"), as well as responses by C. Stuhlmueller, R. Ruether, G. Tavard, E. Hewitt, R. McBrien, and E. Fiorenza. In "Synthesis of the Ordination Conference," Mary Daniel Turner, S.N.D. calls attention to themes recurrent in the discussion: "(1) the need for a reinterpretation of the priesthood within today's pastoral needs, (2) a concern for bonding among women, and (3) an emphasis on fidelity to the tradition of the Church" (p. 136). This volume commends itself not only because of the historical significance of the 1975 Detroit Conference, which was attended by over 1200 persons, but also because of the quality of theological and pastoral thinking displayed in the proceedings. In particular, the discussion of "justice" by Farley and that of "tradition" by Carr bear examination because they bring out dimensions of these concepts often ignored in superficial treatments of the ordination question. (For a brief discussion of the "tradition" aspect of the ordination question, cf. my "Conservative Case for the Ordination of Women," *New Catholic World*, Vol. 218, No. 1305, May-June 1975, pp. 108-111). The Gardiner volume also contains several appendices, including a selected bibliography of works published from 1965 to 1975, as well as the text of Archbishop Bernardin's statement of 1975 reiterating the teaching

that "women are not to be ordained to the priesthood" (p. 195).

(3) Ida Raming, *The Exclusion of Women from the Priesthood: Divine Law or Sex Discrimination?*, tr. by Norman R. Adams, preface by Arlene and Leonard Swidler (Metuchen, NJ: Scarecrow Press, 1976). First published in Germany in 1973 (*Der Ausschluss der Frau vom priesterlichen Amt: Gottgewollte Tradition oder Diskriminierung?*), Raming's historical study investigates the juridical and doctrinal foundations of canon 968, section 1, of the Code of Canon Law and concludes that the traditional arguments supporting the law are invalid.

(4) Roger Gryson, *The Ministry of Women in the Early Church*, tr. by Jean Laporte and Mary Louise Hall (Collegeville, MN: The Liturgical Press, 1976). The often-heard notion that women's ordination is a pecularly "American" concern seems contradicted by the fact that several of the key resources for the discussion were originally published in Europe. Gryson's book first appeared as *Le ministère des femmes dans l'Église ancienne* (Gembloux: Éditions H. Duculot, 1972). It endeavors to be an exact, objective account of the ministerial situation during the first six centuries and points to the need for further research on the question of why "Jesus did not mandate women to preach the gospel with apostolic authority" (p. 133), the question presumed by the Declaration to be settled (cf. par. 10 and following, "The Attitude of Christ"). Gryson notes that "it is not out of place to ask whether the Jewish mentality at that period was ready to listen to the preaching of a woman" (p. 133). He concludes that to decide the question of the attitude of Jesus and the question of the reasons for the discipline of the early Church will require "a serious study of the image and the juridical status of woman in the different milieus of ancient society where the Church was born and developed . . . [and] a parallel study . . . devoted to the understanding of woman herself in the primitive Church" (p. 114). For a brief discussion of the status of women in the ancient Semitic, Egyptian, Hellenistic, and Roman worlds, and a thorough analysis of the status of women in early Judaism see: Leonard Swidler, *Women In Judaism: The Status of Women In Formative Judaism* (Metuchen, N.J.: Scarecrow Press, 1976).

(5) An important cluster of resources is the literature generated by the Declaration itself. Early responses were carried widely in the secular and religious press, and there is indication that instead of settling the issue, the Declaration has promoted further research and discussion. An especially useful article is "Women, Priesthood and the Vatican" by John R. Donahue, S.J., *America*, Vol. 136 (April 2, 1977), pp. 285-289. Donahue raises questions about the Declaration's use of Scripture, tradition, and theology, and observes that current pastoral practice in many parts of the world includes women in ministerial roles formerly denied them on the same grounds as ordination to priesthood. He writes: "The tradition of the church is, therefore, already in the process of change at the level of practice, and the contemporary *ecclesia orans* ("church praying") or the *sensus fidelium* ("understanding of the faithful") has as much to teach the church as official declarations" (p. 289).

Also very significant is the "Open Letter to the Apostolic Delegate" from the Pontifical Faculty of the Jesuit School of Theology in Berkeley, which appeared in *Commonweal*, Vol. civ, No. 7 (April 1, 1977), pp. 204-206. This document builds on an American tradition of loyal opposition ("We dissent not because we disassociate ourselves in any way from the Catholic Church or from the Roman Pontiff, but because we feel ourselves very much united with both. Dissent in our culture is the protest of those who belong," p. 204) and states that "it is our judgment that the conclusion of the Declaration is not sustained by the evidence and the arguments alleged in its support, and that it could sanction within the Church a practice of serious injustice" (*ibid.*). These theologians maintain that the injustice of the present discipline does not lie in the fact that any particular woman is denied orders, for no one can claim a "right" to ordination. Instead, they state, "the issue of justice is engaged when an entire class of Catholics is antecedently excluded on principle even from the possibility that Christ might call them to this ministry . . ." (p. 205). They note that the Declaration itself acknowledges the growing awareness of women's rights as a major development in contemporary moral thought, and yet "retards that movement and commits the people of God to abiding and exclusive government by men" (p. 205). Recalling examples of "serious mistakes" made in the past by Roman Congregations, they declare that "in its decision, the Roman Congregation may well be repeating in its own form and through its insufficient sensitivity to the issues involved, such condemnations as those of the Chinese Rites, of the Copernican understanding of the solar system, and of the early emerging biblical movement at the turn of the century" (*ibid.*).

(6) Finally, mention should be made of the forthcoming report of the Taskforce on the Status of Women in Church and Society of the Catholic Theological Society of America. Chaired by Sara Butler, M.S.B.T., this committee will present to the June 1977 meeting of C.T.S.A. its evaluation of the arguments for and against the ordination of women to pastoral office which have appeared in recent Catholic "consensus statements." Such statements include official church documents, resolutions prepared by Catholic organizations, and reports of ecumenical consultations.

Without attempting to draw out all of the implications of this burgeoning literature, some observations are in order here. For one thing, this literature testifies to the fact that women have found their theological voice, and are employing it in channels formerly inaccessible to them. Careful research, clear and cogent argumentation, fidelity to tradition, pastoral sensitivity, and a sense of vocation to preach the gospel in today's world—such are the features of much that Catholic women have written on the ordination question. These qualities are, of course, present also in much that Catholic men have written, and the fact that so many "established" male scholars have devoted energy to the question evinces the growing reality of a partnership between men and women in the church.

Also, in contrast to the more narrowly-based arguments for maintaining the status quo, studies open to the question of changing the discipline tend to take account of a broad range of data: scriptural and historical research, the findings of the "human sciences," and reflection on contemporary experience. Whereas references to contemporary pastoral needs and to justice issues are not developed in most of the literature defending current practice, the more "progressive" literature tends to integrate the conclusions of recent Vatican documents on evangelization and justice into the discussion about ordination. What is especially at issue here seems to be a difference in understanding the nature of the activity of the Holy Spirit in the Church. This difference might be summed up in the question: Is the Spirit given mainly to protect the past of which we are "sure" or to guide us into an uncertain future, confident that God will make up for what is lacking in our best human efforts? Given a Church whose history records both conceptual and structural development, the currently available defenses of present practice do not argue convincingly against the possibility that in our times the Spirit calls women as well as men to pastoral office in the Roman Catholic Church. On the other hand, the arguments in favor of women's ordination are convincing many faithful Catholics that such vocations are, at this point in history, more than "mere possibilities."

5
The Church Fathers and the Ministry of Women

Carolyn Osiek

The Declaration's interpretation of the evidence regarding the Church Fathers' attitude to women in ministerial roles implies a number of underlying assumptions that are highly problematic. Let us consider each statement in turn.

"The Catholic Church has never felt that priestly or episcopal ordination can be validly conferred on women." At later times the definition and boundaries of the "Catholic Church" are clearer. In the first centuries of Christianity they are not so clear. As first used by Ignatius of Antioch in his letter to the Smyrneans (8.2), the expression "Catholic Church" seems to have meant the association of Christian communities with whom he was in communion across the Empire from Antioch to Rome. To say that in the following years there was a clear consensus of doctrine that distinguished this Christian tradition from others is misleading. The Christology of Justin Martyr and other theologians in Rome in the next two generations after him was not that of the later dogmatic pronouncements of Nicea, Ephesus, and Chalcedon; the differences between Tertullian's theology in his earlier "orthodox" period and his later "Montanist" period are not totally definable; the *Acts of Perpetua and Felicitas*, accepted by the Catholic Church, show Montanist tendencies; many aspects of the theology of Clement of Alexandria can be construed as "Gnostic"; the theology of some of the Desert Fathers showed similarities to Gnosticism. This does not exhaust the list of possible examples. When speaking of the first centuries of the Christian faith as does the paragraph quoted above, caution must be applied to be sure that a certain fluidity of concept is maintained.

"A few heretical sects in the first centuries, especially Gnostic ones. . . ." The Commentary on the Vatican Declaration (par. 10) expands the interpretation: in "some heretical sects" we find "attempts" to have women exercise priestly ministry, but these are "very sporadic occurrences." Again, the interpretation of the data is misleading. We know that the Marcionite and Montanist Churches had women in prominent ministerial roles as did many Gnostic communities. Most of the evidence for these groups comes only from the heresiologists precisely because the majority of the books and documents written by such groups perished with them in the eventual triumph of the Catholic Church as it gained political ascendancy as well as doctrinal

75

clarity. The discovery in this century of a wealth of Gnostic literature, particularly from Nag Hammadi in Upper Egypt, has added much information about the theology and spirituality of communities from which it came, but very little knowledge of their ecclesiastical organization.[1] Consequently we must rely almost exclusively on the writings of their opponents for accurate information of this sort about them, and the Church Fathers who wrote polemical treatises against the "heretics" were anything but objective. One of their favorite tactics was to insinuate sexual impropriety and delusion on the part of women who exercised church leadership, exactly as does the Commentary on the Declaration by its passing statement that these "very sporadic occurrences" of women in ministry are associated with "rather questionable practices," a suggestion which, given the tendency to rhetorical exaggeration on the part of the same heresiologists and the strong stress on sexual continence on the part of most of these "heretical" groups, is often not credible. Many Gnostic gospels were written under the authority of a woman, and some of the second-century apocryphal acts of apostles portray women as important evangelizers.[2] While such literature was long recognized as pseudepigraphical, it nevertheless shows women exercising roles which must have been credible in the Christian communities from which they came: teaching, preaching, even performing miracles.[3] We know of many women, some in traditions based on New Testament times, who were prophets and teachers in Gnostic and Montanist communities: Marcellina, Helene, Salome, Mariamne.[4]

The Declaration goes on to say that these heretical sects "entrusted the exercise of the priestly ministry to women." It is unclear in the Declaration itself, just as it is in most texts of the period of church history which we are considering, precisely what "priestly ministry" does and does not include. As the statement of the Pontifical Biblical Commission on the question points out (Introduction, #2), the New Testament knows no specialized office of *hiereus*, or priest in the later sense, and never connects authorization to perform the Eucharist with the office of apostle, bishop, or presbyter. The early Church Order known as the *Didache* expressly allows itinerant prophets to celebrate Eucharist in the form and wording that they wish (10.7). Ignatius of Antioch (*Smyrneans* 8.1) says that there can be no Eucharist without the bishop that is *bebaia*: reliable and, in that sense, valid or authorized. An examination of the role descriptions of ministers in the early Church reveals that attention is focused not on authority to perform the Eucharist but on authority to preach and teach, and therefore to be recognized as a teacher of sound doctrine.[5]

The Declaration notes seven texts in the Church Fathers in which information is found about the exercise of "priestly ministry" by women.[6] Irenaeus (*Adversus Haereses* 1.13.2) describes part of the Gnostic liturgy of the Marcosians in which women offer the cup at the altar; Marcus is depicted as a charlatan and the women in question as deranged. Tertullian (*De Praescriptione Haereticorum* 41.5) satirizes the lightness and lack of seriousness of heretical groups by mocking their lack of structure. Another proof in his estimation of their lack of genuineness is the arrogance of their women who dare to teach, refute, exorcize, promise healing, and perhaps even baptize. No eucharistic celebration is mentioned in this passage. The letter of Firmilian recounts the tale of a woman of the generation before him who exercised prophetic powers and performed Baptism and Eucharist in the accepted way and with the correct formulae, apparently not in a heretical church but in a situation well known to the bishop. (He of course considered such liturgical actions invalid.) This occasion may be considered exceptional, but those described by Irenaeus, Tertullian, and Epiphanius are not; they are rather practices of long standing in some Christian communities. Origen's remarks on 1 Cor. 14:34-35 concern the right to prophesy or teach in the assembly; they are directed against the Montanists' women prophets. Epiphanius' account of the prophecy and leadership of Priscilla and Quintilla speaks of the Montanists' practice of admitting women "into the clergy" (*en klērō*) as presbyters and bishops but does not specify what the offices entailed (*Panarion* 49.2-3). His description of the Collyridians is more specific. In this case groups of women assemble and perform priestly functions (*hierourgein*) in honor of the Virgin Mary (*Panarion* 78.2-3, 79.2-4). Of these seven references cited by the Declaration, three concern the exercise of a eucharistic function, two that of baptizing, and four that of the authority to preach or teach. There is no one model of ministry used in these texts. Moreover, once we see the variety of roles included here in the exercise of priestly ministry, we must also see that it is simply not accurate to state as the Commentary does (par. 10) that we know of these roles being exercised by women only from the above texts. There are other texts by some of the same authors as well as passages in Church Order collections such as the *Apostolic Constitutions* which condemn a woman's right to teach, baptize, or offer Eucharist.[7] The controversy over the question was more widespread than the impression left by the Declaration.

"This innovation," continues the Commentary, was noted and condemned. Considering the information we have about the evangelizing activities of women in apostolic times, it is impossible to label the whole role of women as prophets and teachers an innovation. To say that women's further role in baptizing and celebrating Eucharist during the first centuries of the Church was an innovation is to accept the classical position of the heresiologists that all "heresies" originated later than the true teaching of the apostles and were in opposition to this apostolic teaching which was absolutely clear and unified from the beginning. Such a conception of the origins of church history is highly questionable in the light of recent scholarship.[8] The same monolithic conception of church history is implied later in the Declaration: "this attitude of Jesus and the Apostles . . . has been considered as normative by the whole of tradition up to our own day" (par. 18); and in the Commentary (par. 11) the custom is referred to as "the constant and universal practice of the Church." One wonders how a practice can have been constant and universal if all the statements regarding it are negative and imply that the practice needed to be defended.

"This innovation was immediately noted and condemned by the Fathers, who considered it as unacceptable in the Church." Certainly those Church Fathers cited, inasmuch as they speak on the subject, did consider official ministry for women unacceptable, with the exception of the limited role of deaconess admitted by Epiphanius for the Baptism and visiting of women— the same role assigned to them by the contemporary *Apostolic Constitutions*.[9] It is then necessary to ask *why* the Fathers considered the practice unacceptable. There are two obvious reasons given within the texts themselves. The first is that they considered it predominantly a practice of heretics, and in the mindset and literary style of most of their writings, anything connected with the heretical must be wrong. This brings us to the question: did the heresiologists reject ministry for women on principle or because it was considered a practice tainted with heresy? The latter alternative was suggested long ago in regard to the Montanists[10] and must be kept as a live possibility in regard to other heretical groups who differed more radically than they from orthodox or Catholic tradition.

The second reason contained within the texts themselves for the Church Fathers' rejection of women in ministry is their appeal to a select group of Scripture passages which can be interpreted to support the natural inferiority of women: Gen. 3:16 and 1 Cor. 11:3, 8; and especially 1 Cor. 14:34-35 and 1 Tim. 2:11-15, which base submissive behavior of women in the Christian assembly on the argument from the order of creation and the fall. Origen's commentary on 1 Corinthians, #74 interprets 1 Cor. 14:34-35 to include even prophecy, allowing women to prophesy (as in 1 Cor. 11:5) only outside the assembly; he also invokes 1 Tim. 2:12 and Titus 2:3, as well as Gen. 3:16 in #71. Tertullian in *de Baptismo* 17.4-5 invokes the authority of 1 Cor. 14:34-35, as he also does in *Contra Marcionem* 5.8.11, where he forbids women to speak in the assembly even in order to learn. Again in *de Virginibus Velandis* 9.1, probably written when Tertullian was a Montanist, he still assumes that women cannot perform any priestly function and again appeals to 1 Cor. 14:34-35 and 1 Tim. 2:12. The *Apostolic Constitutions* 3.6 quotes 1 Cor. 14:34 and 1 Cor. 11:3 against women teaching and 3.9 again cites 1 Cor. 11:3 and Gen. 3:16 against women baptizing or having any part in the priesthood. When the Montanists against whom Epiphanius writes justify their inclusion of women as bishops and presbyters on the authority of Gal. 3:28, he quotes against them Gen. 3:16; 1 Cor. 14:34-35; 1 Cor. 11:8; and 1 Tim. 2:14 (*Panarion* 49.2-3). As the Commentary on the Declaration admits (par. 12), St. Thomas Aquinas still uses the same scriptural bases for his exclusion of women from priesthood: because woman is in a state of subjection (*quia mulier est in statu subiectionis*) even though at that point such an argument is called "scarcely defensible today." We are thus left with conclusions based on authorities whose reasons are admitted to be no longer viable. Indeed the appeal to the natural inferiority of women runs counter to the current voice of the teaching Church. Both the Declaration and the Commentary fail to wrestle with this fundamental problem of appeal to scriptural statements which seem to stand in opposition to a contemporary vision of human dignity recognized by the Church. That is the most serious problem arising from this section of the Declaration.

There is however an additional problem of no little seriousness, namely that the reasons advanced by the Church Fathers in these texts all rest on an appeal to a hierarchy of authority between man and woman: woman cannot be a priest because she is subordinate to man; priesthood is therefore seen only in terms of authority and dominance. How well do such arguments hold against a more comprehensive notion of priesthood and ordained ministry for which we are striving today?

Notes

1. For texts, see Werner Foerster, ed., *Gnosis: A Selection of Gnostic Texts*, trans. R. McL. Wilson, 2 vols. (Oxford: Clarendon, 1972 and 74), especially vol. 2.

2. See Edgar Hennecke, *New Testament Apocrypha*, ed. by Wilhelm Schneemelcher, trans. R. McL. Wilson, 2 vols. (Philadelphia: Westminster Press, 1963 and 65); Roger Gryson, *The Ministry of Women in the Early Church*, trans. Jean'Laporte and Mary L. Hall (Collegeville, Minn.: Liturgical Press, 1976), pp. 15-16.

3. *Acts of Paul and Thecla; Acts of John* 82-83.

4. On Marcellina: Irenaeus, *Adv. Haer.* 1.25.6, and Epiphanius, *Panarion* 27.6; Mariamne: *Acts of Philip* 94-95, and Hippolytus, *Refutatio* 5.7.1; 10.9.3; on them and others: Origen, *Contra Celsus* 5.62; Augustine, *de Haer.* 27.

5. See Raymond Brown, *Priest and Bishop: Biblical Reflections* (New York: Paulist Press), 1970, pp. 13-45.

6. Declaration, n. 7: Irenaeus, *Adv. Haer.* 1.13.2 (Foerster, *Gnosis*, I, pp. 200-201); Tertullian, *Praes.* 41.5 (Ante-Nicene Fathers III, p. 263); Firmilian of Caesarea in Cyprian, Ep. 74(75) (Ante-Nicene Fathers V, p. 393); Origen on 1 Cor. 14, frag. 74, reconstructed by Claude Jenkins in *Journal of Theological Studies* 10 (1909), pp. 41-42 (Gryson, *The Ministry of Women*, pp. 28-29); and Epiphanius, *Panarion* 49.2-3 on the Quintillians or Montanists; 78.2-3 and 79.2-4 on the Collyridians.

N.B. Sources in the original languages are given in the notes of the Declaration itself. Where English translations are readily available, they are given above in parentheses and in following notes. Ante-Nicene Fathers henceforth = ANF.

7. Cf. Tertullian, *de Bapt.* 17.4-5 on teaching and baptizing (ANF III, p. 677); *de Virg. Vel.* 9.1 on teaching, baptizing, and offering Eucharist (ANF IV, p. 33); *Con. Marc.* 5.8.11 on teaching; Epiphanius, *Panarion* 42.4 on baptizing; *Didascalia Apostolorum* and parallel texts in *Apostolic Constitutions* 3.9 on baptizing (ANF VII, p. 429) and 3.6.1-2 on teaching (ANF VII, pp. 427-8).

8. See for example, Walter Bauer, *Orthodoxy and Heresy in Earliest Christianity*, ed. George Stecker, trans. Robert Kraft and Gerhard Krodel (Philadelphia: Fortress Press, 1971); James M. Robinson and Helmut Koes-

ter, *Trajectories through Early Christianity* (Philadelphia: Fortress Press, 1971); Robert L. Wilken, *The Myth of Christian Beginnings: History's Impact on Belief* (Garden City: Doubleday, 1971).

    9. *Panarion* 79.3; *Apostolic Constitutions* 3.15 (ANF VII, p. 431); 8.20 (p. 492).

    10. Labriolle, Pierre de, " 'Mulieres in Ecclesia Taceant'; un aspect de la lutte antimontaniste," *Bulletin d'ancienne littérature et d'archéologie chrétiennes* 1 (1911), pp. 3-24; 103, 122; 292-298; especially pp. 120-122.

6
Use the Other Door;
Stand at the End of the Line
Bernard P. Prusak

No one deny that women were baptized in early Christianity or that they participated in the Eucharist. But the assertion that the prejudices unfavorable to women had hardly any influence on pastoral activity seems problematic, especially in light of instructions such as the following found in *The Apostolic Tradition* of Hippolytus of Rome (c. 215):

> Let the women stand in the assembly (*ekklēsia*) by themselves, both the baptized women and the women catechumens. But after the prayer (of the faithful) is finished the catechumens shall not give the kiss of peace for their kiss is not yet pure. But the baptized shall embrace one another, men with men and women with women. But let not men embrace women. Moreover let all the women have their heads veiled with a scarf but not with a veil of linen only, for that is not a (sufficient) covering.[1]

Women were definitely to keep their particular place, which was one step behind laymen. In the *Didascalia Apostolorum* which expanded upon *The Apostolic Tradition* we read that presbyters were to sit in the eastern part of the church with the bishop in their midst, and the laymen were to sit nearby with the women behind.[2] In 1947, long before the matter of ordaining women clearly emerged as an issue, Alphonsus Raes, S.J., of the Pontifical Institute of Oriental Studies already recognized such directives as a manifestation of the inferiority attributed to women in early Christianity.[3] He noted that among the Coptic Christians of Egypt a high wall or screen was used further to separate women from the rest of the community. Much later, in Medieval Europe, the north side of the church was the side for women. According to Remigius of Auxerre (d.c. 908) the North was the region of the devil. Joseph Jungmann pointed out the modifications made in the direction which a deacon faced when proclaiming the gospel so that the symbolism of facing north might be retained without having to tolerate a deacon reading toward the women's side of the church.[4]

A woman could gain stature in the early Christian community by the degree to which she was removed from any sexual exercise. Such was true of deaconesses who were employed for the baptism of women and for home visitations to places where the visit of a deacon might scandalize non-believers.[5] In the Communion procession the bishop received first, then the presbyters, deacons, subdeacons, readers, chanters, ascetics, and, among the women, the deaconesses, the virgins, the widows, then the children, and finally all the people, which would mean men and then women. When entering and leaving the assembly men used a door where a deacon stood guard and women one where a subdeacon was doorkeeper.[6] In such details it is hard to distinguish cultural and theological perspectives. However, we have elsewhere suggested that the patristic church inherited and expanded a tradition that envisioned women as secondary creations and even more crucially as seductive sirens and sources of sin through their sexual and procreative functions.[7]

The influence of such Fall motifs found in the Intertestamental Pseudepigraphal literature is unmistakable in the early Fathers of the Church. Justin Martyr cites the Watcher legend of *1 Enoch* which amplifies Genesis 6.[8] Irenaeus works with the "Adam and Eve story" of Genesis 3 but includes the embellishments found in the *Apocalypse of Moses* and the *Life of Adam and Eve*.[9] Both Clement of Alexandria and Origen likewise connect the first sin with sexuality and have concomitant prejudice toward women.[10] However, Clement seems to have admitted women into his lectures and recognized their capacity for wisdom.[11] (We must remember that his lectures would have meant little to working class persons; they were upper-class oriented.) Tertullian's writings are filled with preoccupations about the dress of women, especially that they be veiled at prayer. Tertullian interprets the Pauline directive of 1 Corinthians (11:4-10): "It is right that a face which was a snare to angels should wear some mark of a humble guise and obscured beauty."[12] He believed that the destruction brought about by the female sex imposed ignominy and the need for expiation on every woman alive.[13] I would suggest that such theological perspectives, which served to buttress the cultural practices of a patriarchal society, cannot be discounted in analyzing the pastoral practice and discipline of the patristic period. Why did women have to sit behind men? Why did they enter and leave by a different door? Why were their heads to be covered? To a certain degree such practices reflected the protective barriers placed around women and still encountered in certain cultures even in our time. That sons were not similarly protected by restrictions reveals a double standard which was theologically expressed in the identification of women as seductive sirens. That leads us to the issue of pastoral direction.

The unofficial Commentary on the Declaration by the Congregation for the Doctrine of the Faith[14] suggests one can find proof that misogynist prejudice did not affect the Fathers' spiritual direction by simply glancing through the correspondence that has come down to us. It is true that the Fathers often wrote to women and offered guidance. The letters of the Cappadocians reveal that fact. Likewise, John Chrysostom wrote seventeen letters to the widow and deaconess Olympias. Among the letters of Augustine we find those addressed to Italica, Proba, Juliana, Felicitas and her community of consecrated virgins, Sapida, and Fabiola.[15] In one letter to Proba he devotes much effort to discussing prayer.[16] But it is the upper class widow or virgin who usually attracts his praise: in his estimation womanly happiness means growing great in mind, not becoming big with child.[17] Proba and Juliana were thus especially praiseworthy for bringing their granddaughter/daughter to virginity.

At the same time, Augustine does not see what help woman would offer man if the purpose of procreation were eliminated.[18] Unlike chapter five of the canonical Epistle to the Ephesians, there is no real notion of love between husband and wife as persons in Augustine's work on *The Good of Marriage*, although chapter three makes some allowance for mutual companionship between older people who marry. Augustine simply does not seem to accept a woman in her full potential, as one who can integrate femininity, even motherhood, and full personhood.

The same is true of Augustine's contemporary, Jerome. For him only those women become holy who cease being married women by imitating virginal chastity within the very intimacy of marriage.[19] Jerome was certainly interested in giving pastoral guidance to women. He often offered it even when it was unsolicited. But again one must take into consideration the content of his spiritual direction. For example, he writes to a woman whom he has never met and vividly suggests how she may be guilty of some rather saucy conduct.[20] The sexual fantasies and flirtations which he describes are really the product of his imagination but reveal his image of a woman.

In her analysis of his epistles Rosemary Ruether suggests that Jerome really invited women to an asceticism which sought to crush their "femaleness" so as to substitute it with a "virile" dedication to a higher pursuit of wisdom.[21] But at least he recognized their ability for such. Marcella, one of Jerome's students, assumed his role as interpreter of the Scriptures after his departure from Rome.[22] His heroine was the widow Paula who left behind her grown children in Rome to live an ascetic life in Bethlehem. She outdid Jerome in her asceticism. In her praise he noted that she never entered a bath except when dangerously ill.[23]

What is one to conclude with regard to the present debate about the ordination of women? First, it is clear that contexts differ. Augustine and Jerome simply were not able to ask the question as it is being asked today. They were still solving other questions which predetermined their more fundamental attitudes on women. Secondly, it seems that the issue of whether sexuality, marriage, family, holiness, and ministry are compatible must be faced squarely. A look at the sources reveals that married laywomen sat directly behind married laymen. Admittedly laymen fared inifintely better in practice and theory but both still came last in the communion procession and in the estimation of many Fathers. If the relational and service potential of fully embodied or incarnate persons is not confronted, the issue is narrowed to arguing for the ordination of women religious, widows, and consecrated virgins. Clergy-laity would remain as a caste distinction but the ranks of the clergy would be diversified. The positions to be overcome by the Roman Catholic lobby for the ordination of women are thus infinitely more complex than those faced by the Episcopal Church.

Notes

1. *The Apostolic Tradition*, xviii, 2-5. Translation from *The Treatise on The Apostolic Tradition of St. Hippolytus of Rome*, ed. Gregory Dix (London: S.P.C.K., 1968), p. 29.

2. *Didascalia et Constitutiones Apostolorum* II, 57, 3-5, ed. by Franciscus Xaverius Funk, Vol. I (Paderborn: Libraria Ferdinandi Schoeningh, 1905—Torino: Bottega I' Erasmo, anastatic edition 1970), pp. 158-161.

3. *Introductio in Liturgiam Orientaliem* (Rome: Pont. Institutum Orientalum Studiorum, 1947), p. 31.

4. *The Mass of the Roman Rite*, tr. by Fancis A. Brunner, rev. by Charles K. Riepe (New York: Benziger, 1959), pp. 270-272.

5. *Didascalia* III, 12, 1-4; *Const. Apost.* III, 16, 1; *Funk* I, pp. 208-211.

6. *Const. Apost.* VIII, 11, 11; *Funk* I, pp. 494-495.

7. B. P. Prusak, "Woman: Seductive Siren and Source of Sin? Pseudepigraphal Myth and Christian Origins," in *Religion and Sexism: Images of Woman in the Jewish and Christian Traditions*, ed. by Rosemary R. Ruether (New York: Simon and Schuster, 1974), pp. 89-116.

8. *II Apology* 5:3ff.

9. See *Adversus Haereses* 4, 40, 3; 5, 24, 4; 5, 21, 1.

10. Clement, *Stromateis* 3, 14-17; *Protrepticus* 11; Origen, *Commentary on Canticles* 3.

11. *Paedogogus* 1, 4; *Stromateis* 4, 18 & 19.

12. *Against Marcion* 5, 8.

13. *De Cultu Feminarum* 1, 1.

14. *Origins*, Vol. VI, No. 6 (Feb. 3, 1977), pp. 524-531; see below, pp. 325ff.

15. See *Ep.* 92, 99, 130, 131, 150, 210, 211, 263, 285.

16. *Ep.* 130.

17. *Ep.* 150.

18. *De Genesi ad literam* 9, 7.

19. *Against Helvidus* 21 (*On the Perpetual Virginity of the B.V.M.*).

20. *Ep.* 117.

21. "Misogynism and Virginal Feminism in the Fathers of the Church," in *Religion and Sexism*, p. 176.

22. *Ep.* 127, 7f.

23. *Ep.* 108.

7
Fidelity in History
Jean M. Higgins

In this portion of the text, the Declaration sums up its most important evidence from the patristic period. Beyond mere condemnations of innovations, beyond any hint of cultural prejudices, the Declaration finds an "essential reason" expressed in certain documents of central significance.

This reason is that "by calling only men to the priestly Order and ministry in its true sense, the Church intends to remain faithful to the type of ordained ministry willed by the Lord Jesus Christ and carefully maintained by the Apostles." The "canonical documents"[1] in which the Declaration finds "this essential reason" are named in footnote 8. A respectful commentary on the sentence in the text must include a close inspection of the references in that footnote.

We start with the fifth and last: "Chrysostom, *De Sacerdotio*, 2, 2: PG 48, 633." Chrysostom there is praising the advantages of being appointed bishop. He writes:

> You will be doing that which the Lord told Peter would make him surpass the rest of the apostles. For He said: "Peter, lovest thou me more than these?" Yet He might have said to him: "If thou lovest me, practice fasting, sleeping on the ground, and prolonged vigils, defend the wronged, be as a father to orphans, and supply the place of a husband to their mother." But as a matter of fact, setting aside all these things, what does He say? "Tend my sheep." For those things which I have mentioned might easily be performed by many even of those who are under authority, women as well as men: but when one is required to preside over the Church, and to be entrusted with the care of so many souls, the whole female sex must retire before the magnitude of the task, and the majority of men also; and we must bring forward those who to a large extent surpass all others.

The argument is that a bishop's care for so many souls is a task of such magnitude that only outstanding persons can accomplish it. That rules out the majority of men, and all women. Women might perform many other ministries; but, as persons "under authority," they could never preside over the Church.

The text clearly shows the status of women in fourth-century Antioch, and something of Chrysostom's own esteem for women. But over and above such "considerations inspired by the spirit of the times," it unfortunately says nothing about Christ's will for an all-male priesthood or about the Church's intent to remain faithful to that will. We must turn to the other four texts of footnote 8.

The first of these is "*Didascalia Apostolorum*,[2] ch. 15, ed. R.H. Connolly, p. 133":

> It is neither right nor necessary therefore that women should be teachers, and especially concerning the name of Christ and the redemption of His passion. For you have not been appointed to this, O women, and especially widows, that you should teach, but that you should pray and entreat the Lord God. For He, the Lord God, Jesus Christ our Teacher, sent us the Twelve to instruct the People and the Gentiles; and there were with us women disciples, Mary Magdalene and Mary the daughter of James and the other Mary; but He did not send them to instruct the people with us. For if it were required that women should teach, our Master Himself would have commanded these to give instruction with us. But let a widow know that she is the altar of God; and let her sit ever at home, and not stray or run about among the houses of the faithful to receive. For the altar of God never strays or runs about anywhere, but is fixed in one place.

This paragraph is a part of "Chapter XV: How Widows ought to deport themselves." The immediately preceding paragraph (pp. 132-33) gives the context:

> Every widow therefore ought to be meek and quiet and gentle . . . not be talkative or clamorous, or forward in tongue. . . . And when she is asked a question by any one, let her not straightway give an answer, except only concerning righteousness and faith in God; but let her send them that desire to be instructed to the rulers. And to those who question them let them [the widows] make answer only in refutation of idols and concerning the unity of God. But concerning punishment and reward, and the kingdom of the name of Christ, and His dispensation, neither a widow nor a layman ought to speak; for when they speak without the knowledge of doctrine, they will bring blasphemy upon the word. . . . For when the Gentiles who are being instructed hear the word of God not fittingly spoken, as it ought to be, unto edification of eternal life—and all the more in that it is spoken to them by a woman—how that our Lord clothed Himself in a body, and concerning the passion of Christ: they will mock and scoff, instead of applauding the word of doctrine; and she shall incur a heavy judgment of sin.

This represents that patristic pastoral advice and spiritual direction in which the Declaration discovers "hardly any influence of prejudices unfavorable to women." But our concern is only to uncover the "essential reason" which the Declaration finds here expressed. Unfortunately, again, there is not a word in the text about "ordained ministry" or "priestly Order and ministry in its true sense," but only about who "should be teachers," "should teach," "instruct the people," "give instruction."

The text clearly says that widows should not teach and instruct pagans, except on certain specific topics: "righteousness," "faith in God," "idolatry," "the unity of God." It says the same about lay men (132,19) for the same reason: namely, that if "they speak without knowledge of the doctrine, they will bring blasphemy upon the word."

We must remember that this reflects third century Syria. Many of the ordinary people would not be able even to read. In Chapter IV, for instance, the rule has to be laid down for choosing a bishop: "*If it be possible*, let him be instructed and apt to teach; *but if he know not letters*, let him be versed in the Word and advanced in years."[3]

Obviously it was taken for granted that women would not be among the instructed; hence the expectation that the Gentiles would laugh if Christian mysteries were expounded to them by a woman. Within the community, however, a woman who was known to be capable could teach and instruct, as we read in Chapter XVI: "When she who is being baptized has come up from the water, *let the deaconess* receive her and *teach and instruct* her how the seal of baptism ought to be kept unbroken in purity and holiness."[4]

In this context, the passage quoted does relate that Jesus sent no women out to teach. But the conclusion it draws is that "it is neither right *nor necessary therefore* that women should be teachers." "For *if it were required* that women should teach," Jesus would have sent them.[5]

The fact that Jesus did not send women is used as proof that widows *can* live in the service of the Church without taking up the ministry of teaching. The text is a warning to widows that their acceptance into this order[6] did not automatically authorize them to be speakers for the Church. They had been qualified for their order by their situation and by their personal virtues. Education was not a prerequisite. If they felt that as "approved widows" they must also be missionaries, they might do more harm than good, speaking of things they had never studied. The same caution is laid down about uninstructed lay men.

The third text cited in footnote 8: "*Constitutiones Apostolicae*, bk. 3, ch. 6, nos. 1-2" is substantially a repetition of the one we have just considered.[7] The first two sentences have been replaced by:

We do not permit our "women to teach in the Church"; but only to pray and hear those that teach.

After referring to Jesus' not sending the women, it adds:

For "if the head of the wife be the man," it is not reasonable that the rest of the body should govern the head." Let the widow therefore own herself to be the altar of God . . . etc.[8]

The added material is from 1 Corinthians 14:34 and 11:3. It reminds us that when St. Paul wrote those lines of 1 Corinthians, he made no claim that they represented the teaching or example of Jesus; he argued from the Old Law, from the natural subordination of women, and from what was being done in the other churches.

So neither the reference to the *Didascalia* nor to the same passage as modified in *Constitutiones Apostolicae* speak of the Church's intention of being faithful to Christ by ordaining only men. On the contrary, the passage offers a brilliant example of how the Church has adapted its structures to cultural changes. The order of "widows" no longer exists, and in missionary churches of many lands well-trained women, religious and lay, preach on any average Sunday.[9] Meanwhile, in every nation, educated women, many with both ecclesiastical and secular academic degrees, teach and instruct at all levels, including graduate faculties of theology in Catholic universities and pontifical seminaries. In recent years, the names of two women have been added to the select list of Doctors of the Church.

The second text appealed to in footnote 8: "*Didascalia Apostolorum*, ch. 15, ed. R.H. Connolly, p. 142" reads:

That a woman should baptize, or that one should be baptized by a woman, we do not counsel, for it is a transgression of the commandment, and a great peril to her who baptizes and to him who is baptized. For if it were lawful to be baptized by a woman, our Lord and Teacher Himself would have been baptized by Mary His Mother, whereas He was baptized by John, like others of the people. Do not therefore imperil yourselves, brethren and sisters, by acting beside the law of the Gospel.

Unfortunately, instead of focusing on "priestly Order and ministry in its true sense," this text speaks exclusively about Baptism. That a woman should baptize is "a transgression of the commandment," is not "lawful," is "beside the law of the Gospel," and is "a great peril." The same passage is copied and adapted considerably in the third text of footnote 8, "*Constitutiones Apostolicae*, bk. 3, ch. 9, nos. 3-4":

Now as to women's baptizing, we let you know that there is no small peril to those who undertake it. Therefore we do not advise you to do it; for it is dangerous, or rather wicked and impious. For if the "man be the head of the woman," and he be originally ordained for the priesthood, it is not just to abrogate the order of the creation, and leave the principal to come to the extreme part of the body. For the woman is the body of the man, taken from his side and subject to him, from whom she was separated for the procreation of children. For, He says, "he shall rule over thee." For the principal part of the woman is the man, as being her head.

But if in the foregoing constitutions we have not permitted them to teach, how will any one allow them, contrary to nature, to perform the office of a priest? For this is one of the ignorant practices of the Gentile atheism, to ordain women priests to the female deities, not one of the constitutions of Christ. For if baptism were to be administered by women, certainly our Lord would have been baptized by His own mother, and not by John; or when he sent us to baptize, He would have sent along with us women also for this purpose. But now He has nowhere, either by constitution or by writing, delivered to us any such thing; as knowing the order of nature, and the decency of the action; as being the Creator of nature, and the Legislator of the constitution.

This fourth-century reworking of the *Didascalia* in its first paragraph adds quotes from 1 Cor 11:3 and from Genesis 3:16 to provide the reasons why women may not baptize: namely, because they are subject to men by nature and by the curse of God. These are not part of the "essential reason" sought by the Declaration.

But in the second paragraph of this text we finally come for the first time to an explicit statement about "priesthood." The argument is a fortiori: we [the fourth-century Arian redactor pretending to be the Twelve Apostles] have not allowed women to teach; how shall we allow them to perform the office of a priest?

Still, strange to say, the one special work of the priesthood, reserved to males by nature and by the will of Christ, turns out to be the work of administering Baptism. So even this one text which might have confirmed the doctrine of the Declaration is another example of how the Church's fidelity to Christ has always involved adapting laws and practices to changing circumstances. For, since the eleventh century, women do baptize.[10]

Some further reflections seem called for. The fourth-century translator and interpolator may not have known that the original was not really written by the Apostles. But he certainly knew that what he himself was adding was not by the Apostles. Thus, ironically, the Declaration offers as a witness to the unchangeable tradition of Christ and the Apostles someone who was deliberately modifying the records to make them better reflect his own views.

Again, we notice that even this bold interpolator does not quote any words of Jesus actually forbidding women to baptize. His appeal to Jesus (like that of the Declaration itself) is an attempt to shift the burden of proof to those who encourage women. He says: "He [Jesus] has nowhere, by constitution or in writing, delivered to us any such thing." Thus Paul's "All things are lawful for me" (1 Cor 6:12; 10:23) becomes "All things, unless specifically allowed, are forbidden."

He argues—in an early inversion of the classic pattern: "Potuit; decuit;

non fecit; ergo." "Jesus *could* have sent women to baptize; he *should* have at least had his own mother baptize him: But he *did* neither: therefore no one may." The Declaration follows him in this.

Such argumentation reminds one of those sectarians who refuse even today to have buttons on their coats, because there is no evidence that Jesus wore buttons. In a Vatican document, it represents a singular but enthusiastic conversion of Rome to the norm of *scriptura sola.*

If the Declaration were serious about presenting the *Didascalia* and the *Constitutiones* as normative for our understanding of Holy Orders, it would have had to impose the wearing of beards on all priests (*Didascalia*, ch. II, p. 10); the proving of all bishops, that they had chaste wives and obedient children (ch. IV, p. 32); the ordination of female deacons ("thou hast need of the ministry of a deaconess for many things . . . . Let a woman be devoted to the ministry of women and a male deacon to the ministry of men," ch. XVI, p. 148)[11]; and the re-ordering of ecclesiastical dignities so as to honor the bishop as God the Father, the male deacon as Christ, whereas the female deacon "shall be honored by you in the place of the Holy Spirit; and the presbyters [today's priests] shall be to you in the likeness of the Apostles" (ch. IX, p. 86).

In fact, of course, there is little hope of discovering Christ's will for ministry today by debating third and fourth century canon law. Nor are we likely to get much positive inspiration from meditating on things Christ did not do (ordain women, free the slaves, wear buttons, build schools and hospitals). Christ in the Gospels makes many positive statements about the kind of persons he wants to represent him: their humility, their poverty, their charity.[12] And he describes explicitly the kind of ecclesiastic he knew and did not approve of: men of ambition, hypocrisy, lovers of money, honor, and power.[13] The more we meditate on these statements and try to live by them, the more likely it is we shall find or create "the type of ordained ministry willed by our Lord Jesus Christ." It is by calling to "priestly Order and ministry in its true sense" those who best meet these criteria that the Church can show itself faithful in the future.

Notes

1. The Declaration uses this phrase not of books within the canon of Sacred Scripture, but of summaries of ecclesiastical practice (canon law). Although it claims to find its material "especially in the canonical documents of the Antiochian *and Egyptian* traditions," all five works cited in footnote 8 are from the region of Antioch (Syria).

2. This work pretends to be written by the twelve Apostles, but is in fact a description of the customs of the Syrian Church of the third century. Cf. R.H. Connolly, *Didascalia Apostolorum* (Oxford: Clarendon Press, 1929), pp. lxxxvii-xci.

3. *Ibid.*, p. 30.

4. *Ibid.*, p. 146.

5. I repeat Connolly's translation of the first sentence: "It is neither right nor necessary therefore that women should be teachers . . ." because the Declaration uses Connolly. But in fact a more accurate rendition is that of Achelis-Flemming (cf. Connolly's praise of this "fullest and most careful study of the *Didascalia*," pp. v and xxii): "Es ist also nicht nötig oder gar dringend erforderlich": "It is therefore not necessary or even urgently called for"; *Die syrische Didaskalia* übersetzt und erklärt von Hans Achelis und Johannes Flemming (*Texte und Undersuchungen* 25, 2 [NF 10, 2]; Leipzig: J.C. Hinrichs, 1904), p. 77; 274-282.

6. Criteria for the enrolling of widows are discussed as early as 1 Timothy 5, 9-16.

7. The first six books of the "Apostolic Constitutions" are a translation and reworking of the *Didascalia* in the late fourth-century. The author removes references to Christ's divinity, and so is presumed to have been an Arian. The Council *in Trullo* (692) rejected the book as "falsified by the heretics." Cf. Connolly, p. xx; B. Altaner, *Patrology* (New York: Herder and Herder, 1961), p. 59.

8. Other minor changes in the text are the omission of "He, the Lord God, Jesus Christ" (offensive to Arian ears); and the insertion of a longer list of women, including "our Lord's mother and His sisters" (which takes six columns of notes to explain in the *Patrologia Graeca*, I, 769-774).

9. "Third Instruction on the Correct Implementation of the Constitution on the Sacred Liturgy" (Liturgiae Instaurationes), Sacred Congregation for Divine Worship, 5 September, 1970, 6e.

10. The same prohibition against women baptizing is found in Tertullian "De Baptismo" 17. "De Virginibus Velandis" 9, and in the Fourth Council of Carthage, canon 100. A decision of Urban II (1088-1099) is the first record of an exception being allowed for emergencies: "Baptismus sit, si instante necessitate femina puerum in nomine Trinitatis baptizaverit" (Epistola 271: PL 151, 529).

11. The complete ordination ritual is given in *Constitutiones Apostolicae* Bk. VIII, Ch. 19-20: "Concerning a deaconess, I Bartholomew make this constitution: O bishop, thou shalt lay thy hands upon her in the presence of the presbytery, and of the deacons and deaconesses and shalt say: 'O Eternal God, the Father of our Lord Jesus Christ, the Creator of man and of woman, who didst replenish with the Spirit Miriam . . . do Thou now also look down upon this Thy servant, who is to be ordained to the office of the deaconess . . .' " (PG I, 1115-1118, translation from *The Ante-Nicene Fathers*, volume 7, edd. Robert and Donaldson (Buffalo: Christian Literature Company, 1886), p. 492.

12. Mt 10:7-39; Mk 10:35-45; Lk 9:57—10:7; 22:24-27; Jn 15:9-17.

13. Mt 23:1-39; Lk 11:37-52.

8

Non-Conclusive Arguments:
Therefore, Non-Conclusion?

Francine Cardman

If modern thought "would have difficulty in admitting or would even rightly reject" the reasons advanced by medieval theologians for the Church's practice of not ordaining women, what present weight can be given the scholastic doctors' opinion that this practice is normative for the Church? By its approval of the disjunction of reasons and conclusions, the Declaration asks that assent to its teaching be given on the basis of an argument from "fittingness" and, implicitly but more fundamentally, an appeal to the authority of the magisterium. Not only does the Declaration misuse its medieval sources by taking this position, it also calls into question the nature of doctrinal development, the foundations of theological reflection and argument, and the locus of discernment and decision-making in the Church.

Development of Doctrine and Discipline:
The Hermeneutics of Tradition[1]

Neither the practice and discipline of Christian life (liturgy and prayer as well as ethics and asceticism) nor the process of doctrinal formulation (whether the result of theological reflection on the life, death, and resurrection of Jesus Christ or as the legitimation of disciplinary developments) arose in a vacuum. Each interacted with the other and both were in turn shaped by their socio-cultural context. For instance: a penitential system with an accompanying sacramental theology took its start from the practice of a one-time repentance and forgiveness for post-baptismal sin; papal primacy became a matter of doctrine only after papal practice had made it a fact; transubstantiation was found to be an apt expression for the kind of eucharistic piety long dominant in the Western Church; and the medieval doctors' discussion of women and orders was predicated on current practice and its systematization in canon law.[2] Christian doctrine, then, is rooted in Christian experience: discipline influences doctrinal development and is itself reinforced by doctrine; in unusual situations doctrine is formalized into dogma.[3]

The development of doctrine and discipline is not a homogeneous process. It is, rather, heterogeneous, even discontinuous.[4] The process is not organic, hence not irreversible. Awareness of the often unreflective or unintentional process by which doctrine and discipline have interacted in the Church's history can be a hermeneutical key to interpreting the continuing significance of a tradition. In assessing past disciplinary or doctrinal developments, it is important to recognize that, as Avery Dulles puts it, "no doctrinal decision of the past directly solves a question that was not asked at the time."[5] Prior to the present day discussion of women and priestly ordination, the question rested somewhere in the area between discipline and doctrine. Practice disallowed the ordination of women, and some doctrinal positions (e.g., some understandings of the Mass as sacrifice, or priesthood interpreted according to an Old Testament model) seemed to validate the practice. Not only do these peripherally related doctrinal statements fail to touch the question as it is being posed today, but there is also no properly dogmatic assertion that would forbid the ordination of women. The rereading of central Christian dogmas in light of the present hermeneutical situation could, on the other hand, even come to *require* that women be allowed the possibility of ordination. What is being called for in the current situation, therefore, is not the reassertion of practice but the reexamination of it. Once past practice or doctrinal interpretation is perceived as being in conflict with a more basic dogmatic principle—as, for instance, the understanding of the human nature of Jesus Christ as it was classically formulated at Chalcedon—it becomes not only possible but also necessary to change it.[6] Rather than looking to the past, Christian tradition "points forward" and "constantly propels the Church to move into the promised future and prepare for eschatological life that is to come."[7]

Arguments and Conclusions: Theological Method[8]

If the opinions of medieval masters are to have any bearing on the current discussion, they must be viewed in their historical context and in light of their authors' intentions and method. The Declaration cites the opinions of Bonaventure and Duns Scotus, along with the lesser figures of Richard of Middleton and Durand of Saint-Pourcain. Thomas Aquinas' views, dependent as they are on the assumption of the natural inferiority of women, are apparently among those which the Declaration would consider "rightly rejected," as they are not mentioned.[9] The conclusions reached by Thomas, Bonaventure and Scotus represent three major types of argument about the ordination of women and several kinds of theological method. The arguments are essentially similar to those being proposed today. For Thomas, the argument is sacramental: women may not be ordained because the sacrament of order signifies preeminence and women are incapable of signifying this, as they are in a state of subjection. For Bonaventure, it is biblical or typical: the priest represents the male Christ and acts in his *persona*, symbolizing particularly Christ's role as spouse (husband) of the Church, and women can no more be husbands than they can typify the male Christ. And for Duns Scotus, the argument is neither sacramental nor from biblical typology: the Church does no injustice to women in not ordaining them because it is following the will of Christ rather than its own opinions on this matter. The will of Christ is also put forward by Richard of Middleton and Durand of Saint-Pourcain as justification for not ordaining women.

Voluntarism is the best designation for the kind of theological method employed by Duns Scotus and others like him on the question of women and orders. The growth of canon law in the medieval period also contributed to the blurring of reasons and facts in theological argumentation about the ordination of women. For it was particularly in the area of the sacraments that canon law had considerable influence on the elaboration of theology.[10] This meant that actual practice often served as the "reason" offered for theological conclusions in medieval discussions of the sacraments. But whenever the argument was in the least reflective, the method employed assumed an integral connection between faith and reason. This is certainly the case in Thomas and even Bonaventure. Thomas' testimony is omitted by the Declaration as apparently unacceptable. Bonaventure's is misrepresented: for, finally unable to construct a tight or persuasive argument for not ordaining women, Bonaventure admits that his view is only the "sounder and more prudent opinion of the doctors," a point not mentioned by the Declaration or its Commentary.[11] In contrast to the method of Thomas and Bonaventure is that of Duns Scotus. For Scotus, only the will of Christ himself prohibits the ordination of women, for apart from Christ's will, reason would find great injustice in denying both women and the Church the good that could come from their ministry. Again the Declaration and Commentary misrepresent their sources, for no reference is made to the second part of Scotus' statement where the question of injustice and pastoral benefits is raised.[12] But more importantly, in relying on the type of argument offered by Duns Scotus, the Declaration seems to approve the voluntarism of his theology. By endorsing conclusions that have been divorced from their arguments, the Declaration promotes a kind of fideism and seeks a response of obedience to its discernment of the will of Christ.

Because the Declaration assumes that its interpretation of the tradition will be authoritative, it can appeal in a later section to the analogy of faith as further support for its position. As employed in Catholic theology, the analogy of faith is an internal argument from the interconnection of doctrines.[13] Its use in the Declaration is in keeping with the disjunction of reasons and conclusions already noted. The argument from fittingness or convenience convinces only those who are already convinced—whether by the preceding four sections of the Declaration or by prior preferences. In prescinding from demonstrative argument, the Declaration considers its efforts with the analogy of faith as illustrative rather than probative: those who already share the vision will be moved by the sketch, those who do not, will not be. In appealing to the analogy of faith, the Declaration begs the question: it presumes that there is a sufficient body of faith about the ordination of women to make a judgment about the question with ease; and it suggests that a pattern can be found in this body of faith apart from the ordinary processes of reasoned argument.

The Declaration's disjunction of faith and reason extends beyond internal theological argument to the relationship of other forms of human knowledge to theology. Although it alludes to psychological and biological evidence when referring to differences of sex vs. ethnic differences, the Declaration is consistent in its isolation of theology from other forms of human thought when it insists that "problems of sacramental theology . . . cannot be solved except in the light of Revelation."[14] However valuable they may be in their own right, "the human sciences . . . cannot suffice here, for they cannot grasp the realities of faith: the properly supernatural content of these realities is beyond their experience." Similarly, the Church is seen as "a society different from other societies, original in her nature and in her structures." Equality of rights, though an acceptable ideal in the human realm, has no place in the supernatural society that is the Church.[15] Because of this, "the priestly office cannot become the goal of social advancement; no *merely human* progress of society or the individual can of itself give access to it: it is *of another order*" (emphasis mine). Not only are arguments unrelated to conclusions, reason to faith, but human reality has little bearing on the Church except as the substratum in which the Church functions.

Followed to its logical end, the Declaration resolves the question of women's ordination on the basis of authority, for it is only through the authoritative magisterium that the will of Christ for the Church is known.

Magisterium and Discernment: Who Reads the Signs of the Times?

By relying, in the final analysis, on an argument from authority, the Declaration raises the question of magisterium: who is "the Church . . . [which] does not consider herself authorized to admit women to priestly ordination"; who is the Church which "through the voice of her magisterium . . . in these various domains decides what can change and what must remain immutable"; and how does this Church "know" that "when she judges that she cannot accept certain changes, it is because she . . . is bound by Christ's manner of acting"? Or, put another way, who or what is magisterium?

At present a considerable debate is shaping up in the Church as to the nature of magisterium.[16] The actual collaboration of bishops and theologians at Vatican II—such that the council would have been impossible without it—led to expectations of collegiality and co-responsibility that were dashed against the rock of *Humanae vitae*. In this encyclical, as well as in the Declaration in Defence of the Catholic Doctrine on the Church against Certain Errors of the Present Day (*Mysterium Ecclesiae*), the Declaration on Certain Questions Concerning Sexual Ethics (*Persona humana*), and the present Declaration on the Question of the Admission of Women to the Ministerial Priesthood (*Inter insigniores*), the problem of the relationship of theologians and bishops in the teaching office of the Church has become acute. There is growing opinion that, in contrast to a 19th century neo-scholastic and Roman theology of magisterium, both bishops and theologians are jointly under responsibility to the Word of God.[17] If bishops and popes make official declarations of what the Church already believes, it is the task of theologians, according to Dulles, not merely to defend these teachings but especially to "discover what hasn't yet been taught."[18] *Gaudium et spes* noted that it is the task of the Church, the People of God, to labor "to decipher authentic signs of God's presence and purpose in the happenings, needs, and

96 *Commentaries*

desires in which this People has a part along with other men of our age."[19] Because the present is as much a *locus theologicus* as the past or the future, there is need for discernment in the Church, for a magisterial function directed toward reading the signs of the times. Magisterium that represented the insights of the faithful as well as the cooperation of theologians and bishops would enable the Church to be responsive to its changing historical context.

Institutional change, in the Church as in other human societies, occurs in three major stages: innovation, articulation, and adoption. Pastoral practice is already undergoing considerable innovation as women share in many forms of ministry; the continued evolution of practice will in time make an argument of fittingness work in the direction of ordination of women to the priesthood. Theological reflection on the ordination of women is only now beginning to mature; a new level of discourse, beyond the old arguments and the appeal to authority, must evolve before the process of articulation can be completed. The time for magisterial decision is not yet, and even the Declaration is not a final pronouncement on the question; adoption will come as the Church learns to live toward the future.

Notes

1. Tradition (capitalized) is the Gospel of Jesus Christ made present in the Church by the Holy Spirit; it is to be distinguished from tradition, which includes both the traditionary process and that which is handed on (often referred to as "apostolic tradition"). I have attempted to define the various meanings of "tradition" and to raise the question of a hermeneutics of tradition in "Tradition, Hermeneutics, and Ordination," in *Sexism and Church Law*, ed. James Coriden (New York: Paulist Press, 1977).
2. For the relation of canon law and scholastic theology on the question of women and orders, see George Tavard's essay, "The Scholastic Doctrine," in this volume. I have traced the development of the topic as a question in medieval theology in "The Medieval Question of Women and Orders," forthcoming in *The Thomist*.
3. In his multi-volume history of the Christian tradition, Jaroslav Pelikan defines doctrines as "what the church of Jesus Christ believes, teaches, and confesses on the basis of the word of God": *The Emergence of the Catholic Tradition (100-600)* (Chicago: University of Chicago Press, 1971), p. 1. What is believed is always more than what is taught, which is also more than what is confessed by dogmatic statement. For perceptive explorations of the process of doctrinal development, see Pelikan, *Development of Doctrine: Some Historical Prolegomena* (New Haven: Yale University Press, 1969), and Maurice Wiles, *The Making of Christian Doctrine* (Cambridge: Cambridge University Press, 1967).
4. Avery Dulles, "The 'Irreformability' of Dogma," in *The Survival of Dogma* (Garden City, NY: Doubleday, 1973), p. 208. See also John T. Ford's comments on homogeneity and development in "Newman on 'Sensus Fidelium' and Mariology," *Marian Studies*, Vol. 28 (1977), pp. 144-45.

5. Dulles, "The Hermeneutics of Dogmatic Statements," *Survival*, p. 185.

6. For the process by which a maxim conditioned by a socio-cultural situation comes into conflict with a more universal and fundamental moral principle, and the application of this to the Declaration's argument, see Karl Rahner, "Priestertum der Frau?" *Stimmen der Zeit*, Vol. 195, No. 5 (March, 1977), pp. 191-201.

7. Dulles, "The Magisterium in a Time of Change," *Survival*, p. 126. See also his presidential address to the Catholic Theological Society of America, "What is Magisterium," *Origins*, Vol. 6, No. 6 (July 1, 1976), pp. 81, 83-88.

8. The debate unleashed by David Tracy's study of pluralism in theology and theological method in *Blessed Rage for Order* (New York: Seabury Press, 1975) indicates the profundity of the question of theological method and underscores the Declaration's disregard of the same. For one response to Tracy, see Avery Dulles, "Method in Fundamental Theology," *Theological Studies*, Vol. 37, No. 2 (June, 1976), pp. 304-16.

9. Thomas' explanation is set out in *Commentum in 4 Librum Sententiarum*, Dist. 25, q. 2, a.1. The Supplement to the *Summa* (Q. 39, a.1) merely repeats this treatment.

10. See Joseph de Ghellinck, *Le Mouvement theologique du XIIe siecle* (2nd ed., Brussells, 1969), pp. 52-65, 203-13, 416-510, 537-47.

11. That woman's incapacity for ordination is *de facto* as well as *de jure* is only a "probable" opinion according to Bonaventure (*saniorem opinionem et prudentiorem doctorum*). The Declaration only quotes that part of Bonaventure's statement which attributes the non-ordination of women to the incapacity of their nature rather than the Church's decision.

12. Read in its entiety, Scotus' explanation takes on a different tone: "The Church would not have presumed to deprive the entire sex of women, without any fault of their own, of an act which could licitly have been theirs, and which might have been ordained for the salvation of woman and others in the Church through her, for it would seem a very great injustice, not only to the entire sex but also to a few (specific) persons; but now, if by divine law ecclesiastical order could licitly belong to woman, this would be for their salvation and the salvation of others through them."

13. See Leo Scheffczyk, "Analogia Fidei," *Sacramentum Mundi*, Vol. 1, pp. 25-27. The idea of the analogy of faith can be recognized in Catholic theology from the time of Vatican I, but the expression only gains currency with Leo XIII. For Protestant theology the term refers to a hermeneutical principle in scriptural interpretation. The two views come into conflict when Karl Barth challenges the Catholic usage of *analogia entis* and by extension *analogia fidei*—see Hans Urs von Balthasar, *The Theology of Karl Barth* (New York: Holt, Rinehart, & Winston, 1971), pp. 93-100, 147-50.

14. It is worth noting that the same kind of argument appears in the Declaration On Certain Questions Concerning Sexual Ethics. According to that document, sociological surveys of sexual practices are useful for discovering facts, "but facts do not constitute a criterion for judging the moral value of human acts." Similarly, the moral norms affirmed in the document "must be faithfully held and taught" because the Church "knows with certainty that they are in complete harmony with the divine order of creation

and with the spirit of Christ, and therefore also with human dignity."

15. See the essay by Margaret Farley in this volume, "Discrimination or Equality? The Old Order or the New?" pp. 310-315.

16. Richard A. McCormick, S.J., surveys the major positions to date in "Notes on Moral Theology," *Theological Studies*, Vol. 38, No. 1 (March, 1977), pp. 84-100.

17. *Ibid.*, pp. 90-97.

18. Dulles, "Doctrinal Authority in the Church," *Survival*, p. 98.

19. *Gaudium et spes* 11, in *Documents of Vatican II*, ed. Walter M. Abbott, S.J. (New York: Association Press, 1966), p. 209.

9

The Scholastic Doctrine

George H. Tavard

As treated by the three major scholastic doctors, Thomas Aquinas, Bonaventure and John Duns Scotus, the question of the ordination of woman is more canonical than theological. All three reflect about the fact of non-ordination, which they try to justify with suitable theological arguments. We will therefore examine the *Decree* of Gratianus, which embodies the canonical legislation of the Middle Ages, and to which all three refer, before looking at the argumentation of the three great theologians.

1. Gratianus's *Decretum*[1]

Part I, dist. 23 of the *Decree* treats several points of liturgical discipline. *Chapter 25*, to which the three theologians refer, states that religious women are not allowed to handle sacred vessels and vestments or to act as thurifers around the altar. This "plague" must be abolished everywhere. Chapter 29 takes up another relevant point: "No woman, however learned and holy, may presume to teach men in an assembly (*in conventu*). No layman may dare to teach in the presence of clerics, except at their request." Let us also take notice of two chapters, 22 and 32, which, irrelevant as they may seem to us, weighed in the theological argumentations: both forbid clerics to let their hair grow.

These canons should be related to another section of the *Decretum:* Part *II, causa 23, question 5*, apropos married women who wish to take a vow of continence, discusses the proper hierarchy of authority. No married woman may take such a vow without her husband's consent, for "it is the natural order among men (*hominibus*) that females should obey males and children parents, for there is no justice in the higher obeying the lower" (chapter 12). Further, "the image of God is in man (*homine*) in such a way that there be only one lord, the origin of all others, having the power of God as God's vicar, for every king is in God's image; and thus woman is not made in God's image" (ch. 13). The reference is of course to Eve being formed from Adam, who alone qualifies as the source of humankind and as the image of God. Chapter 15 should be quoted in its entirety:

> Since the male is the head of his wife as Christ is the head of the male, a woman who does not obey her husband, that is, her head, is guilty of the same crime as a male who does not obey Christ, his head. It is blasphemous against the word of God to despise the first

point and make nothing of it, and to insult the gospel of Christ, as when a Christian woman, who is, by divine law, subject, wants to dominate her husband in spite of the law and fidelity of nature, while even pagan women, in keeping with the universal law of nature, obey their husbands.

Chapter 18 adds: "Adam was deceived by Eve, not Eve by Adam. It is fair that the one whom she called to sin should now assume her governance, lest she fall again through female weakness." And chapter 19: "Woman must veil her head, for she is not God's image. But, to show that she is subject and because sin began through her, she must carry this sign: not to hold her head free in the church, but covered by a veil in respect for the bishop, and not to have the authority to speak, for the bishop stands for the person of Christ. On account of original sin, she must be seen as an inferior before the bishop, who is the vicar of the Lord, as before a judge." Chapter 19 repeats the point that woman is made from man.

Thus medieval canon law embodied an anthropology in which woman was by nature inferior to the male of the race: her secondary status in the Church was seen as naturally flowing from her inferior status in nature. It was with this basic material that the scholastic theologians had to work.

2. *Thomas Aquinas*[2]

The *Sentences* of Peter Lombard do not include a discussion of woman in their section on who can or cannot receive the sacrament of Orders. Nor do the first *Commentaries on the Sentences*. Thus the *Glossa* of Alexander of Hales does not even mention the problem. But the question is raised, a little later, in the influential *Commentaries* written by St. Thomas Aquinas and by St. Bonaventure.

St. Thomas's treatment of the question comes from his first major work, the *Commentary on the Sentences, book IV, dist. 25, quest. 2, art. 1*. The text of the *Summa theologica, III, suppl., quest. 39, art. 1*, which was added to the unfinished summa after Aquinas's death, quotes the commentary word for word. Therefore we do not really know how Thomas would have treated the question had he lived long enough to finish the summa. The solution he has left us is from his youth; and Thomas modified many of his positions between the commentary and the summa.

Aquinas begins by mentioning three arguments in favor of the ordination of woman: (1) Women have been prophets in the Old Testament; and prophecy is a higher function than priesthood. (2) Women have been in positions of spiritual authority, like abbesses, or Debora, or the women martyrs; therefore they can have authority in the Church. (3) The power of Orders, being spiritual, lies in the soul, not in the body; and the soul is the same for both sexes.

The *Sed contra*, which provides the basis for Thomas Aquinas's position, argues from 1 Tim. 2:12 ("I do not permit a woman to teach in the assembly or to dominate a man") and from the liturgical practice of the clerical tonsure: such a shaving of the head is not appropriate to women, in keeping with 1 Cor. 11:6.

Having found the problem solved by this combination of Scripture and custom, Thomas Aquinas explains theologically that woman is naturally unable to receive the sacrament of Orders because the sign-quality of the sacrament cannot be found in her. For this sign indicates eminence and authority, and woman is in a natural position of subjection and inferiority (*in statu subjectionis*).

Aquinas adds that wherever such terms as *diaconissa* (deaconess) and *presbytera* (priestess) are used, they must have a non-sacramental meaning. And he refutes the previous arguments: (1) prophecy is not a sacramental sign, and so there is no difficulty about woman prophesying; (2) the authority of abbesses is not "ordinary" but delegated, and it is justified by the danger of cohabitation between men and women; and Debora had temporal, not priestly, power. Curiously enough, argument (3), about the non-sexuality of the soul, is left unanswered.

3. *Bonaventure*[3]

St. Bonaventure's examination of the question is more complete. In his *Commentary on the Sentences, IV, dist. 25, art 2, quest. 1*, he lists, as usual, arguments pro and con before stating his own position. Four arguments favor the ordination of males only: (1) Since woman must wear a veil on her head when she prays (1 Cor., 11:5), the clerical tonsure is not appropriate to her. (2) Only the male is the image of God by virtue of sex (*ratione sexus*); and the sacrament of Orders can be given only to the image of God, because it makes man (*homo*) somehow divine. (3) Woman cannot have spiritual authority, because she is not allowed to speak in church (1 Tim. 2:12). (4) All the Orders prepare ultimately for the episcopate; but woman cannot be a bishop, since a bishop is the husband of his Church, and a woman cannot be a husband.

Four arguments for the ordination of woman are also presented: (1) The example of Debora shows that a woman can have jurisdiction, and therefore the priestly power. (2) Abbesses have the authority to bind and to loose; they could therefore also receive the sacerdotal Order. (3) Orders are received in the soul; and, in her soul, woman is as much the image of God as the male. (4) There is no higher perfection than that of the religious vocation and no greater strength than that of martyrdom; women have been admitted to both; therefore they can also be admitted to a sacred Order.

In his own solution, Bonaventure begins with the remark that the common opinion rejects the admission of women to sacred Orders on the strength of Gratianus's *Decree*, dist. 23, ch. 25, which forbids women to handle sacred vessels (see above). He also notes the opinion of some, called Cataphrygians, for whom woman has the capacity for ordination, even if she is never ordained in fact; but he also argues, like Thomas, that the words *diaconissa* and *presbytera* have no sacramental meaning. His own judgment is that it is "the saner and the more prudent opinion" to think that women not only must not but also cannot be ordained either *de jure* or *de facto*. The reason for this is "not so much the Church's decision (*institutio*)" as the non-congruity of the sacrament of Orders with the female sex. "For the person ordained must signify Christ as mediator, and the mediator can be signified only in the male sex and through the male sex." Why this should be so, however, Bonaventure does not make clear. He concludes only that males alone can "naturally represent and actually carry the sign (of the mediator) by virtue of the reception of the character (of the sacrament)." "This position is more probable, and can be confirmed by many texts of the Fathers."

The four arguments in favor of the ordination of women are then refuted. (1) Debora had temporal, not spiritual, authority. (2) Abbesses, unlike priests, have no "ordinary" authority; power (*regimen*) may be appropriate for women, but the spiritual significance of Orders is not. (3) The sacrament of Orders is received indeed in the soul, but only inasmuch as the soul is joined to a body; and the sign dimension belongs to the visible realm, and therefore to the body. (4) The religious vocation and martyrdom belong to the level of sanctifying grace (*gratia gratum faciens*) where there is no difference between men and women; but the sacrament of Orders pertains to another level (that of *gratia gratis data*): it may well be reserved to one sex because it is not a purely interior grace but has exterior significance.

It seems clear that Bonaventure is more aware than Thomas Aquinas of the difficulties of the problem. His conclusion is less absolute, since he considers it only "more probable" than its opposite. He does not stress the inferiority of woman. Yet he dare not ascribe the impediment of sex for ordination to a decision of the Church. At the same time, Bonaventure does not argue from Scripture. He rather sees the impediment as a theological conclusion based on congruity, and, more specifically, on the natural symbolism of womanhood, which he considers to be incompatible with the sacramental symbolism of Orders.

4. *John Duns Scotus*[4]

His treatment of the question is found in both the *Opus oxoniense* and the *Reportata parisensia*, at the classical locus of the *Sentences, IV, dist. 25, quest. 2*. There are some differences between the two, which I will indicate. Above all, Duns Scotus brings new material to bear on the question in relation to his predecessors.

Only two arguments favorable to the ordination of women are presented at the beginning of the question, in both places. But the first is new: (1) It is based on Gal. 3:28 ("In Christ Jesus there is neither slave nor freeman, neither male nor female"); "therefore there is no difference between female and male in the law of Christ, as between serf and free; therefore this sacrament of the evangelical law, which a male can receive, can also be received by a female, as with serf and free." (2) The second argument is the one about *presbytera* and *diaconissa* being used in old canons. Against ordination, Duns Scotus refers, like his predecessors, to (1) the canon about woman not handling sacred vessels, and (2) 1 Cor. 11:6 about the shame of a woman shaving her hair, and the relevant canon about the clerical tonsure.

Duns Scotus's own position begins with a clearer distinction than either Thomas or Bonaventure had made between congruency (is ordination proper or not?), liceity (is it allowed by the Church's discipline?), and validity (is there in woman a basic incapacity to receive ordination?). Applying this to the problem, Duns Scotus considers that the point at stake is the third one: it is a matter of validity. But his reason for this understanding of the case is new:

> One should not hold it to be decided by the Church, but it comes from Christ. The Church would not presume to deprive the entire female sex, without any guilt on its part, of an act which might licit- ly pertain to it, being directed toward the salvation of woman and of others in the Church through her. For this would seem to be an extreme injustice both toward the entire sex and toward a few spe- cific persons. If by divine law the ecclesiastical Order could licitly be fitting to woman, it could be for the salvation of women and of others through them. But what the Apostle says in 1 Tim. 2:12, "I do not permit a woman to teach," speaking of the public doctrine in the Church, he does not say on his own authority; but, "I do not permit," because Christ does not permit (*Opus oxoniense, ad locum*).

To support this, Duns Scotus argues from the non-ordination of the Mother of Jesus, and from natural reason: "Nature does not permit women, at least after the fall, to hold a position of superiority in the human race." Duns Scotus then formulates a philosophical objection: the ordaining bishop being of the same species as a hypothetical woman-ordinand, nothing can stop the effect of ordination from taking place in the woman. But, he responds, the ef- fect is not automatic, for it is a contingent action (which depends on certain conditions).

The opposite arguments are then easily refuted: (1) There is no distinc- tion of male and female as far as grace and glory are concerned; but the order of the Church is not that of grace and glory, for it follows the law of nature. (2) A *presbytera* is not a priest, but may be the wife of a Greek priest, or else an elderly lady; a *diaconissa* is not a deacon, but a nun who is desig- nated by an abbess to read the gospel.

There is no essential difference between the *Opus oxoniense* and the *Reportata parisiensia* on the question. In these also the decision not to ordain women is attributed "not to the Church's institution or the Apostles' pre- cept," but to Christ himself, for neither the Apostles nor the Church could withdraw from women the possibility of ordination if it was given to them by Christ. But Duns Scotus is now more explicit on the appropriateness of this decision of Christ. Ordination is not allowed to women "on account of the weakness of their intellect and the mutability of their will . . . . For a doctor must have a quick intellect for the knowledge of truth, and a stable will for the affirmation of the truth." The non-congruity of woman's ordination follows also from the analogy of nature, in which woman is naturally subject to the male. This natural subjection has been reinforced by the fall, so that, by Christ's will, woman "is not capable (non est *materia capax*) of receiving ordination."

To his refutation of the philosophical argument about the effect of an act when the agent is of the same kind as the receiver, Duns Scotus now adds the theological argument that the ordaining bishop is only a secondary agent of ordination; the primary agent is God, who himself decides to whom this sacrament may be given, and who has reserved it to males.

Given the forcefulness of John Duns Scotus's argumentation, which comes out much more strongly in the *Reportata parisiensia*, another addition to the treatment of the matter is indeed surprising: the possibility is admitted that "Mary Magdalen was an apostle (*apostola*), and like a preacher (*tamquam praedicatrix*), and a supervisor of all penitent women." But this would have been a personal privilege granted to Mary by Christ: Duns Scotus does not see it as a precedent for ordinations of women in the future.

The references to other scholastics contained in footnote 9 of the Declaration would add nothing of substance. Both Richard of Middleton (Franciscan, between Bonaventure and Duns Scotus) and Durandus of St-Pourcain (Dominican, d. 1334) ascribe to Christ himself the restricion of the sacrament of Orders to males. Durandus, who gives the usual arguments, affirms that "it pertained to Christ to institute the sacraments both as to their ministers and as to their recipients" (IV, dist. 25, q. 2). He also picks up the point made by Duns Scotus about injustice. The restriction must come from Christ, because the Church could not be guilty of "causing prejudice" to women. And the reason behind Christ's decision must be one of congruity: "A position of predominance over males is not fitting for women, but rather a state of subjection, on account of the weakness of their body and the imperfection of their mind."[5] The idea has not been strengthened by this reformulation. For the congruity now depends on a point of fact: is woman physically weaker and intellectually less perfect than the male?

Conclusion

It appears clearly from a careful reading of the three major scholastic theologians that what weighed the most in their approach to the matter was the canonical tradition. The theologians do little more than try to find legitimate reasons for the legislation. They seek for such reasons in the order of nature and the analogy between the sacraments and nature, in some scriptural texts, especially taken from the Pastoral Epistles, and in what seemed to them the appropriate symbolism of the priestly functions compared to the symbolism of womanhood.

At the same time, their positions are not identical. The theology of St. Thomas is tied more than the others to a belief in woman's basic inferiority. But the positions of St Bonaventure and of John Duns Scotus are considerably more flexible. Both hold that the legislation goes back to Christ himself. But Bonaventure does not see this as a certainty: it is only "more probable." And Duns Scotus introduces two points that may well be ultimately incompatible with his own conclusion: first, the admission that there could be a basic injustice in the legislation; second, the admission that Mary Magdalen may have been truly an Apostle.

Furthermore, on the related problem of the ordination of children, Duns Scotus formulates a notion which could be applied to the question of the ordination of women, although he himself does not make this application. This is the idea that laws can change "especially when a new reason brings about contrary practices" (*Opus oxoniense, IV, dist. 25, quest. 3*). This principle is itself borrowed from Gratianus's *Decree, part I, dist. 4, ch. 3*, where it instances a broader axiom: "In laws affected by time, whatever the thought of those who instituted them, once they have been instituted and applied, one must not pass judgment about them, but one must judge according to what they are." As surviving in the present code of canon law, this principle is now formulated: "Custom is the best interpreter of laws" (canon 29). Changing customs therefore call for changing the laws. The changing customs of our society as regards the status of woman and the changing sensitivity of Catholic women toward the problem of ordination force us to take a new look at the legislation and the theology of ordination. Practices that were formerly believed to pertain to nature are now recognized to derive from culture. In addition, the contemporary reading of Scripture has rendered untenable the assumption that Jesus handed down a finished sacramental system. The argument from symbolism, which seems the most solid of the medieval discussion, is itself not persuasive; for symbols vary with varying cultures, and people can be educated into new readings of symbols. The vanishing of the former symbolism of womanhood obliges us to take seriously John Duns Scotus's insight that there would be an injustice in "depriving the entire female sex, without any guilt on its part, of an act which might licitly pertain to it. . . ."

As this study shows, it would be fallacious to base upon scholastic theology the continuation of the negative legislation on ordination of woman, as scholastic theology was based chiefly upon the negative legislation. And scholastic theology itself contains the seeds of a positive judgment about the question.

Notes

1. For Gratianus's *Decretum* I have used *Corpus juris canonici emendatum et notis illustratum, Gregorii XIII Pont. Max. jussu editum* (Paris, 1587). In *Part II, causa 15, q. 3,* Gratianus sums up the canonical tradition: "Women cannot be promoted, not only to the priesthood, but even to the diaconate." But this text is not quoted by any of the theologians I have been able to look up. The canonical tradition has been investigated by Ida Raming: *The Exclusion of Women from the Priesthood: Divine Law or Sex Dis-*

crimination? (Metuchen, N.J.: Scarecrow, 1976). There is no systematic study of the theological tradition in the Middle Ages; but elements of the problem, especially as treated by Thomas Aquinas, have been examined in Haye van der Meer: *Women Priests in the Catholic Church?* (Philadelphia: Temple Univ., 1973).

2. I have used the text of St Thomas's *Commentary on the Sentences* in *Doctoris Angelici Divi Thomae Aquinatis Opera Omnia*, Vol. 11 (Paris: Vives, 1874).

3. *Doctoris Seraphici S. Bonaventurae Opera Theologica Selecta*, tome 4 (Quaracchi: Coll. S. Bonaventurae, 1949).

4. *J. Duns Scotus: Opera Omnia*, Vol. 9 (Hildesheim: Olms, 1968); this reproduces the *Questiones in lib. IV Sententiarum* (Lyon: Durand, 1939). For the *Reportata parisiensia*, I use vol. 11 of the same edition.

5. Durandus: *Commentarium in Sententias Lombardi* (Paris: Petit, 1527).

10
Eastern Orthodoxy and the Ordination of Women

Michael A. Fahey

Not surprisingly the Declaration by the Vatican Doctrinal Congregation on the ordination of women appeals to the tradition and practice of the "Churches of the East." For Catholics to prescind from the views of the Eastern Churches in this regard would be to undo the careful work of dialogue between these "sister Churches" begun at Vatican II and dramatically continued by the several encounters of Pope Paul VI and the late Ecumenical Patriarch Athenagoras I.[1]

The Vatican statment notes with respect to the East: "The same tradition [namely the tradition which has never admitted that priestly or episcopal ordination can be validly conferred on women] has been faithfully safeguarded by the *Churches of the East.*" The expression "Churches of the East" is however somewhat ambiguous. One could at first assume that the reference is to those Oriental Christians in full communion with Rome but with different liturgical and disciplinary traditions, such as the Melkites and the Maronites; sometimes called "Uniates," these are the subject of an entire decree of Vatican II, *Orientalium Ecclesiarum*. But from the context and from the examples cited in the semi-official Commentary on the Declaration, it is clear that the reference is specifically to the Orthodox Churches and indirectly to the ancient Eastern Churches, the non-Chalcedonian Churches such as the Nestorians, Jacobites, Armenians and Copts. The special status of these Churches is discussed in Vatican II's decree on ecumenism, *Unitatis Redintegratio*, especially paragraphs 13 and 14. These Churches include those divided from the great Church since the councils of Ephesus (A.D. 431) or Chalcedon (451), but espceially those Churches not in full communion because of the "breakdown of ecclesiastical communion between the Eastern Patriarchates and the Roman See." In conformity with modern research, Vatican II assigned no date to this breakdown inasmuch as the estrangement was slow but constant after Constantinople became the New Rome.[2]

The remark in the Declaration focuses on what the Churches of the East in our present juncture of church life think about the ordination of women. One should not forget either that millions of these so-called "Eastern" Orthodox actually live in the Americas, Western Europe and other parts of the world. The theological influence of these diaspora Orthodox is often more pronounced than those living in the East.

The Vatican Declaration provides an unassailable description of fact, namely that women in the East (apart from some fringe group heretics) have never been ordained bishops or presbyters. The text notes that the Eastern tradition "has been faithfully safeguarded." In one sense, this expression is rather curious because it implies a conscious reflective guarding in safe-keeping when in fact, except for very rare cases, and up to modern times we are dealing with an unreflective practice. For that reason the text is also misleading when it appeals to "canonical documents of the Antiochian and Egyptian traditions" (three references are given) which refer to the "essential reason" for not ordaining women: because Christ had called only men to the priestly Order and ministry in its true sense and the Church intends to remain faithful to the type of ordained ministry willed by the Lord Jesus Christ and carefully maintained by the Apostles. This is not the sort of nuanced historical statement one would hope for in a document of this moment.[3]

The Vatican text continues with regard to the Churches of the East: "their unanimity on this point is all the more remarkable since in many other questions their discipline admits of great diversity." Actually, the exact opposite could be stated just as correctly. One could have written: Their unanimity on this point (i.e., of never admitting women to priesthood or episcopate) is *not at all* remarkable since today the Eastern Orthodox Churches consider themselves strictly bound to abide by previous synodal, canonical decisions, so that its theologians and hierarchs experience great difficulties in formulating new solutions to questions without direct precedents. In light of this particular difficulty it will be important to follow closely the deliberations at the forthcoming Pan-Orthodox Great and Holy Council, an event which will be for the Orthodox similar to the experience of Vatican II for Catholics, to see how they proceed to find creative solutions to new issues.[4]

The Vatican Declaration is quite accurate, however, in noting that these Churches of the East "refuse to associate themselves with requests directed toward securing accession of women to priestly ordination." This is a crucial and critical issue for the Vatican: the problem of grappling with this delicate ecumenical problem of sharp and severe Orthodox opposition to women's ordinations. It is important to cite several of these vigorously negative condemnations of the issue of women's ordination as expressed by representative Orthodox hierarchs and theologians.

The semi-official Commentary on the Vatican text refers to one of these warnings made by Athenagoras of Thyateira, Archbishop for the Orthodox in Great Britain. "It is the same people," writes Athenagoras, "who preach the ordination of women and who cast doubt on, deny, or ignore the mystery of the holy Eucharist, the apostolic succession, and the infallibility of the Church."[5]

Closer to home, Archbishop Iakovos, Orthodox Primate of North and South America, in his enthusiastic support of the Vatican Declaration, seems to see those Anglicans and Catholics who favor this development as influenced by a Protestantizing diminution of ordained priesthood into a sort of simple pastoral directorship. He writes: Christ "did not choose or call women to celebrate the Eucharist, the principal raison d'etre of the priesthood. If the priesthood is nothing more than pastoral directorship of the Church, then we serve neither Christ nor His people, but our own glorified and narrowed views that empty the Church of its divine mission and the priesthood of its essential character."[6] Notable here is the close association of the meaning of the priesthood with the celebration of the Eucharist, underlining the strong liturgical roots of Orthodox theology.

Even more strongly opposed are the Orthodox theologians. We will restrict ourselves to citing two distinguished Orthodox theologians currently teaching in the United States. Father Maximos Aghiorgoussis of the Holy Cross Greek Orthodox School of Theology in Brookline, Mass., in his booklet *Women Priests?* published after the decision of the Episcopal Church to ordain women, remarks: "I cannot but condemn this uncharitable act perpetrated not only against the people within the Anglican communion who do not accept this decision, but also against the Churches of apostolic tradition, and especially the Eastern Orthodox Church."[7] He judges the Episcopal Convention of betraying the gospel and the great apostolic tradition of the Church and continues: "As far as the Orthodox are concerned, the ordination of women to the Holy Priesthood is untenable since it would disregard the symbolic and iconic value of male priesthood, both as representing Christ's malehood and the fatherly role of the Father in the Trinity, by allowing female persons to interchange with male persons a role which cannot be interchanged."[8]

No less severe are the judgments of the Orthodox Church of America in the person of Thomas Hopko, associate professor of dogmatics at St. Vladimir's Seminary, New York, who refers to the "distortions and abnormalities" of having women as priests since women have a "unique mode of human being and action" which is incompatible with exercising sacerdotal positions in the community.[9]

These Orthodox theologians, despite their appeals to earlier Church traditions, do not perceive the paradox noted by Professor Norris that their arguments about the representational role of male priests is virtually unprecedented in tradition. Rather than being a "traditional" reason for denying ordination to women it is, in Norris' words, "genuinely novel, untraditional," demanding the most sceptical scrutiny.[10]

We have cited some of these typical modern Orthodox objections by hierarchs and theologians because they provide a useful context in which to understand the preoccupation of the Vatican Declaration. But rather than allowing ourselves to be frightened by these strong objections, out of a sense of charitable commitment to one another, we must ask whether Orthodox and Catholics are indeed being faithful to the deepest traditions of their Churches and whether we perhaps may not have allowed our personal interpretations of historical phenomena to narrow our perceptions.

There is another sense, however, in which the Vatican Declaration is addressing not simply what the Orthodox Churches are *now* saying about the ordination of women but also what the whole liturgical tradition of the East both before and after its alienation from the See of Rome tells us about the

nature of ordination. In this regard it is methodologically infelicitous of the
Vatican Declaration to have prescinded completely from the question of the
ordination of women as deaconesses in the past and its possible restoration.
Putting in parentheses for the time being the history and theology of the ordination of women as deaconesses has somewhat distorted the total liturgical
tradition of the East in order to make it serve the present preoccupation of
the Vatican Declaration. This is untypical of much of the excellent studies of
the Byzantine and other Oriental liturgies undertaken by such scholars as the
Roman Catholics Matheos, Taft, Vagaggini, Macomber and Gryson which
approach the liturgies from the perspective of truly Eastern preoccupations.

For what has been determined by scholars, although sometimes not
widely known even among the Orthodox, is that from the third and fourth
century on women were ordained as deaconesses by imposition of hands
(*cheirotonia*) and that this ordination clearly had a sacramental character.
This liturgical practice lasted in Byzantium up to the twelfth century and in
Syria up to the fifteenth century. We are indeed fortunate today to have excellent documentation of this material, though much of it has not yet been
properly disseminated and assimilated even by theologians.

Why, it may be asked, is the question of the sacramental ordination of
women as deaconesses in the Byzantine churches important in discussing a
document about the access of women to the presbyteral or episcopal offices
of the Church? Precisely because it illustrates that for many centuries the
Church did indeed administer, to use the language of the Vatican Declaration, an ordained ministry which was *not* (directly at least) willed by the Lord
Jesus Christ. This fact relativizes many of the Declaration's arguments about
the need to imitate the choices of Jesus Christ in regard to ordained ministers. Furthermore, the decline of ordinations of deaconesses in the Orthodox
Churches presents us with an example of a living tradition which has by and
large died out. We have the possibility then of a tradition not preserved
rather than of a dangerous innovation being added to the Church today. The
development of the ordination of women as deaconesses in the Eastern
Churches illustrates tellingly the ability of the Church to respond creatively
to a new situation which may not have had direct New Testament precedents. The ordination of women as deaconesses shows the freedom which the
Byzantine Church perceived for structuring its sacramental ministry to meet
the needs of the present.

For many centuries our perception of the ministries of women in the early
Church remained undifferentiated. It was not always clear how widows, virgins and deaconesses differed one from the other. The Louvain historian,
Roger Gryson, has outlined the history of our gradual understanding of the
ministry of women from earliest times.[11] In the course of this research it
became clearer and clearer that deaconesses had certain ordained functions,
liturgical functions we would say today, which they did not share with virgins
or widows as such. The English theologian C.H. Turner has clearly separated
out for us what were the roles of widows, virgins and deaconesses in the early
Church.[12]

Particular attention has turned to the so-called "church orders" of the early Church, collections of liturgical and disciplinary decisions. In two of these "orders" we have clear descriptions of women being ordained with laying on of hands by a bishop. The *Didascalia Apostolorum* (II, 26, 6) from the first half of the third century indicates that deaconesses were ordained as deacons were with a proper liturgical imposition of hands (*cheirotonia*) and that these women had liturgical and pastoral ministries toward other women (though not toward men). Their liturgical "competence" was directed toward assisting in the Baptism of women through anointings. There is no indication that these women were given a commission to preside at the Eucharist. They did receive a sort of extra liturgical commission to care for sick women. But in liturgical rank they enjoyed positions of honor, *axiomata*, which ranked them only after the bishops, presbyters and deacons.

From the fourth century on references to deaconesses multiplied in the East (except in Egypt). In another church order, the *Apostolic Constitutions* (VIII, 19-22), dated toward the end of the fourth century, we have a rite of ordination for deaconesses which mentions *cheirotonia*. Again, the liturgical functions of these women are restricted to the anointing of women in baptism and the welcoming of women at the door of the church and catechetical instruction. By the end of this century deaconesses were definitely considered part of the clergy; in fact, they were bound by the same strict marriage regulations as other major clerics.

It is sometimes argued by individual Orthodox theologians today that the ceremony of ordination for deaconesses was not truly a sacramental ordination (*cheirotonia*) but a *cheirothesia*, in other words not an imposition of hands but a simple blessing. This opinion has been refuted by studies which indicate that prior to the eighth century the two words *cheirotonia* and *cheirothesia* were not distinguished but were used interchangeably.[13]

The most important liturgical study on this question of the ordination of deaconesses in the Byzantine tradition was recently published in Italian by the liturgical scholar Cipriano Vagaggini, O.S.B., of S. Anselmo in Rome (an article which hopefully will be soon translated into English).[14] By a minute study of the references in the church orders and especially by the Byzantine liturgical rite of ordination contained in the *Codex Barberiano greco* 336, in use in Byzantine circles from the eighth to the fourteenth centuries, Vagaggini has established the important following conclusions: (1) After the distinction *cheirotonia* and *cheirothesia* (a simple blessing or *eulogia*) was introduced, deaconesses were receiving true imposition of hands. (2) The ordination of deaconesses took place at the foot of the altar inside the sanctuary. This rubric was as obligatory as it was for bishops, presbyters and deacons, but forbidden to subdeacons and lectors. (3) The moment of ordination for deaconesses came at the end of the first anaphora, as part of the prayer for distribution of communion. (4) The prayer of petition used in the ordination rite includes the traditional reference to "divine grace" as in the other ordinations. (5) Women were given the deacon's *horarion* or stole by the bishop at the end of the *cheirotonia*. (6) Deaconesses communicated from the chalice right after the deacons, and this communion took place in the sanctuary itself. Vagaggini also notes that some Byzantine traditions allowed the deaconesses to distribute communion in certain circumstances which could be regarded as a form of *potestas in eucharistiam*.[15]

We clearly have much to learn about the traditions of the past. At the same time both East and West need to grow in a more profound understanding of tradition, that it is not simply an inflexible transmission of past principles regardless of the cultures out of which they arose. The Church's stewardship (*oikonomia*) requires adaptation to changing pastoral situations. The particular contribution of the Orthodox in this search will be to remind us that no single Declaration from a single source can settle what needs to be explored in a synodal fashion.

Notes

1. For a history and documentation of the recent Catholic and Orthodox efforts at reunion see the volume, in Greek and French, *Tomos Agapis. Vatican—Phanar (1958-1970)* (Rome: Vatican City Press, 1971).

2. One of the clearest and most accurate descriptions of this estrangement can be seen in W. de Vries, *Les structures ecclésiales vues dans l'histoire des sept premiers conciles oecuméniques* (Paris: Cerf, 1974).

3. The weakness of this argument is found in the text of the Jesuit School of Theology at Berkeley, "Letter to the Apostolic Delegate on the Vatican Statement about the Ordination of Women," *Origins*, 6, No. 42 (April 7, 1977), pp. 661-665, here p. 663.

4. See, *Towards the Great Council. Introductory Reports . . .* (London: SPCK, 1972). A list of the topics to be explored at the coming council as worked out at the preparatory meeting at Chambésy, Geneva, 21-28 November 1976, is found in *Documentation Catholique*, 74 (16 Jan., 1977), pp. 91-92.

5. This text from the *Orthodox Herald* is reproduced in the *Osservatore Romano*, June 17, 1975. See also, "Catholics and Russian Orthodox at Trent, 23-28 June 1975," cited in *Osservatore Romano* and in *Documentation Catholique*, 71 (1975), p. 707.

6. *Orthodox Observer* (New York City), 43 (16 Feb., 1977), p. 1.

7. *Women Priests?* (Brookline, Mass.: Holy Cross Press, 1976), p. 1.

8. *Ibid.*, p. 5.

9. "On the Male Character of Christian Priesthood," *St. Vladimir's Theological Quarterly*, Vol. 19, No. 3 (1975), pp. 147-173. See also the strong reactions of the senior Orthodox colleague at the same school, A. Schmemann, "Concerning Woman's Ordination: A Letter to an Episcopal Friend," *St. Vladimir's Theological Quarterly*, Vol. 17 (1973) 239-243.

10. R. A. Norris, Jr., "The Ordination of Women and the 'Maleness' of Christ," *Anglican Theological Review*, Supplementary Series, Number 6 (June 1976), pp. 69-80, especially p. 70.

11. Roger Gryson, *The Ministry of Women in the Early Church*, trans. J. Laporte and M. L. Hall (Collegeville: Liturgical Press, 1976). The French

original appeared in 1972. The English translation also contains Gryson's response to objections of M. Martimort concerning Gryson's interpretation of the section cited from the *Apostolic Constitutions.* Martimort is opposed to interpreting these texts as proof of an ordination.

12. C. H. Turner, "Ministries of Women in the Primitive Church: Widow, Deaconess and Virgin in the First Four Christian Centuries," H. N. Bate, ed., *Catholic and Apostolic* (London: Nowbray, 1931), pp. 316-351. A recent reliable work on deaconesses is the article by A. Kalsbach, "Diakonisse," *Reallexikon für Antike und Christentum,* 4 (1959), cols. 917-928.

13. Cyrille Vogel, "Chirotonie et chirothésie. Importance et relativité du geste de l'imposition des mains dans la collation des ordres," *Irénikon,* Vol. 45 (1972), pp. 7-21; 207-238. For an Orthodox perspective see the article (in Greek) of E. D. Theodoron, "Hē 'cheirotonia' ē 'cheirothesia' tōn diakonissōn," *Theologia,* Vo. XXV (1954), pp. 430-469; 576-601; Vol. XXVI (1955), pp. 57-76.

14. "L'ordinazione delle diaconesse nella tradizione greca e bizantina," *Orientalia Christiana Periodica,* Vol. 40 (1974), pp. 145-189. The text of the rite is found on pp. 177-178.

15. *Ibid.,* p. 185; an important summary on pp. 188-189. An interesting study is to compare the text of this Byzantine ritual of ordination for deaconesses with a Romano-German Pontifical text dating from the 10th century, available in English translation in J. Massyngberde Ford, "Order for the Ordination of a Deaconess," *Review for Religious,* Vol. 33 (1974), pp. 308-314, with documentation of original sources.

11
The Twelve

Elisabeth Schüssler Fiorenza

The Vatican Declaration and Commentary not only argue that Jesus did not call any woman to become a member of the Twelve, but they also seek to refute the apologetic arguments explaining why Jesus could not have done so. In order to understand the thesis of the Declaration, therefore, one must also analyze the counterarguments proposed.

It is often maintained that Jesus could not call a woman to be one of the twelve apostles because the customs of the time would not permit this. The Declaration correctly argues that Jesus did not follow the societal and religious customs of the time and therefore could have chosen a woman, but did not do so. The authors are however aware that exegetically it could be maintained that Jesus called women to apostleship and to discipleship but not to the circle of the Twelve. In defense of their position the authors especially address the counter-argument that the Twelve are the foundational group of the renewed Israel and the symbolic representation of the twelve tribes. Since the twelve tribes were a patriarchal institution women were not able to fulfill this symbolic representational function.

Against this contention the Declaration and Commentary argue the following: First, only little importance is given in the NT to the symbolic understanding of the Twelve, since Mark and John do not refer to it. Second, the eschatological symbolism of the Twelve is not decisive for Jesus' understanding, since it is pronounced only at a relatively late stage of his public ministry. Third, the number twelve in Mt 19:28//Lk 22:30 could simply mean the whole of Israel. Fourth, these two synoptic texts deal only with a particular aspect of the mission of the Twelve, namely, the eschatological judgment of Israel, while it is their main task to preach the gospel (Mk 3:14; 6:12). These exegetical arguments of the Declaration and Commentary assume that the concept of the Twelve is uniform in the different writings of the NT and that it is formulated by Jesus himself as a blueprint plan for the future Church.

The Vatican Commentary concludes its arguments with a counterthesis: The Twelve represent within the messianic community Jesus and his work and not the twelve tribes of Israel. "That is the *real* (italics mine) reason why it is fitting that the Apostles should be men." In other words, women are excluded from the male circle of the apostles not because they unable to represent the patriarchally constituted Israel but because they are not fit to represent Christ and his work. This counter-thesis is an attempt to establish the biblical foundation for the "natural resemblance" thesis developed later in the Declaration. This counter-thesis indicates that not the *historical* datum that no woman was a member of the Twelve but the assumed *theological* reasoning behind this fact is decisive for the argument of the Vatican Declaration. The counter-thesis further assumes that the Twelve and the apostles are exactly the same circle of people and that priests and bishops stand in direct succession to them.

However, the authors are well aware that their interpretation of the NT texts and the conclusions deduced from it for the ordination of women to the priesthood are not cogent in themselves. Therefore they caution that the NT evidence has to be understood from the perspective of the Church's constant praxis to exclude women from the sacramental priesthood. The authors fail to see that they thus not only relinquish the biblical foundation of the argument but they also declare the constant tradition and practice of the Church to be intrinsically discriminatory against women.

In the following I should like to analyze the NT texts and their understanding of the Twelve in order to show that neither the thesis nor its presuppositions or its supporting arguments do justice to the NT texts.

I. The earliest traditions

The Vatican Declaration and Commentary appear to assume that the terms "apostles" and the Twelve are coextensive categories as if they connote the very same circle and function of the disciples. Yet this assumption goes against the NT evidence and the scholarly consensus that the apostles and the twelve were different circles and only in the course of time did they come to be identified.[1] Originally the word "apostle" described a function and was not restricted to any group like the Twelve. Only at a later stage of the tradition are the Twelve called apostles (cf. Mk 6:30; Mt 10:2; Apoc 21:14). Not every apostle is a member of the Twelve, and it is unclear at what point of the tradition the Twelve were also understood as apostles. Paul and Barnabas, for instance, are known as apostles in early Christianity (cf. Acts 14:4, 14), but they definitely did not belong to the circle of the Twelve.

The NT literature indicates that the Twelve are firmly rooted in the tradition and are already traditional figures of the past towards the end of the first century (cf. Apoc 21:14). The terms used are "the Twelve," "the twelve disciples," the "twelve apostles" and "the Eleven." It is astonishing that direct references to the Twelve are rare in the Pauline writings (one in a traditional formula) and the Johannine literature (four) and completely absent in the Catholic and Pastoral Epistles. In the Pastorals Paul has become the apostle par excellence.

The Declaration assumes that the male character of the Twelve is essential for their function and mission. We must therefore ask whether the Twelve's mission and function necessitates that they are males. Do the early traditions about the Twelve emphasize the male character of the Twelve and do they reflect on it? Moreover, is the function and mission of the Twelve according to the NT traditions continued in the structure and leadership of the

Twelve? Did the Twelve have successors, and if so did they have to be male? In other words, do we find any evidence in the NT that the male character is intrinsic to the function and mission of the Twelve and therefore intrinsic to the apostolic office of the Church?

1 Cor 15:5 and the Q saying Mt 19:28 (cf. Lk 22:30) are the two oldest texts of the NT that refer to the Twelve. In 1 Cor 15:3-5 Paul quotes a tradition which he has already received.[2] This pre-Pauline tradition maintains that the resurrected Lord appeared first to Cephas and then to the Twelve. The text refers to the Twelve as a fixed and well known group, since it does not speak of Peter and the Eleven. The text also does not reflect the defection of Judas as the resurrection narratives of the Gospels do when they consistently refer to the Eleven. Furthermore, the traditional formula of 1 Cor 15:3-5 does not indicate whether this group of the Twelve existed already before Easter as a definite circle of disciples in the ministry of Jesus or whether it was constituted by the resurrection appearances and commission of the Lord.

The Pauline account parallels 1 Cor 15:5 with 15:7, which refers to the appearance of the risen Lord to James and then to "all the apostles." It is not clear whether or not Paul parallels 1 Cor 15:5 with 15:7 or whether he had already found this parallel in his tradition.[3] In any case, the present text appears to combine two different traditions and to speak of two different groups, namely, the Twelve and the apostles. As Peter stands out from the Twelve, so does James among the apostles. However neither the pre-Pauline tradition nor the Pauline text reflect upon the gender of the Twelve.

The very old saying Mt 19:28 (par. Lk 22:30) has a quite different form and setting in Matthew and Luke. Even though the Matthean and Lukan form of the saying are redactional,[4] the contrast between present sufferings and future glory is common to both. In its original form the saying is an eschatological promise to the disciples who followed Jesus. This Q-logion[5] explicitly interprets the number twelve. When in the new world the Son of Humanity will be revealed in all his splendor and glory, the followers of Jesus also will sit "on twelve thrones and judge (or rule) the twelve tribes of Israel" (Mt 19:28). The text clearly does not underline the historical existence of a group of twelve men but the function of the disciples of Jesus in the eschatological future vis-a-vis Israel. The faithful disciples will share with Jesus in the exercise of authority and power when the kingdom is established. Since at the time of Jesus only two and a half tribes still existed, the number twelve is clearly symbolic in character.

The number twelve refers backwards to the ancient constitution of Israel of twelve tribes as well as forward to the eschatological restitution of the people of God. The "maleness" of the disciples is not explicitly mentioned in this Q-logion. It could be inferred that the leaders of the renewed Israel must be male if the text mainly referred to and symbolized the ancient constitution of Israel, which in its religious and political form was patriarchal. Yet the logion's main thrust is not historical but rather points to the eschatological future. The promise is given to the disciples not because they are male but because of their faithful discipleship. Moreover the Q-saying does not postulate a continuum between Jesus—the Twelve—and the Church, but between Jesus—the Twelve—and the eschatological kingdom of God. The NT, however, gives us no indication that Jesus conceived of the kingdom as a male patriarchal institution.

The essential character of the Twelve is eschatological-symbolical and not historical-masculine, as Apoc 21:14 indicates. According to this text the eschatological city, the New Jerusalem, is patterned after the twelve tribes of Israel. "And the wall of the city had twelve foundations and on them the twelve names of the twelve apostles of the Lamb." Here the twelve apostles are not the foundation of the Church but of the New Jerusalem as an eschatological reality. Finally, it cannot be argued as the Commentary does that the Q-saying was formulated only late in the ministry of Jesus and therefore did not have a great impact on the mission and the function of the Twelve. Since the present position of the saying in Matthew and Luke is editorial, we no longer know when it was formulated. From a tradition-historical point of view, it could have been spoken by Jesus, since it reflects the heart of his eschatological preaching.

II. The Markan and Lukan understanding of the Twelve

The Commentary maintains that not the eschatological symbolic function but the historical mission of the Twelve is decisive. The Twelve represent Jesus to the messianic people of God and carry on his ministry and work. The Commentary bases this interpretation of the Twelve's function primarily on the Gospel of Mark. "As Jesus before them, the twelve were above all to preach the Good News (Mk 3:14; 6:12). Their mission in Galilee (Mk 6:7-13) was to become the model of the universal mission (Mk 12:10; cf. Mt 28:16-20). Within the messianic people the twelve represent Jesus."

The two main "prooftexts," Mk 3:13-19 and 6:6b-13, are according to most scholars formulated by the Markan redaction.[6] They do not necessarily reflect the intention of Jesus but definitely spell out the Markan theological understanding of the Twelve. While the Commentary stresses that the Twelve were above all sent out to preach the Good News, the Markan texts stress that the specific power and authority given to the Twelve is that of exorcism.[7] Mk 3:14 mentions their mission to preach but underlines that power is given to them to cast out the demons. According to the commissioning scene (Mk 6:6b-13) they are neither explicitly authorized (v. 7b) nor commissioned (vv. 8-10) to preach. Their preaching is only mentioned in the concluding statement in v. 12. But in the concluding verse 13 Mark stresses again their power to heal and to cast out demons. A careful reading of the text indicates that in Mark's view the Twelve are primarily sent and have received the power of exorcism and healing, while Jesus is the one who proclaims the gospel of the kingdom (1:14f.).

It should be noted that this theological emphasis of Mark on the empowerment of the Twelve to cast out demons is completely neglected by the Commentary. Moreover, in Mark not only the Twelve preach (*keryssein*), but also John the Baptist (1:4, 7), those who are healed (1:45; 5:20) or witnesses of a healing (7:36) and the post-Easter community as a whole (13:10; 14:9). Further, the preaching activity of the Twelve addresses Israel. Since Mark does not know of a post-Easter commissioning of the Twelve (Mt 28:16-20) to universal mission, it could be inferred that Mark intends to limit the preaching of the Twelve to the Galilean misson. Finally, Mk 3:13-19 and 6:6b-13 do not stress that the Twelve have *to be* like Jesus but demand that as the disciples of Jesus the Twelve have *to do* what Jesus did. In Mark's view Jesus is the teacher with great authority and power. His power is demonstrated by exorcisms and healing-miracles. If the disciples are in Mark the functional successors of Jesus, then it is not their maleness that makes the Twelve representatives of Jesus. Their preaching, exorcising and healing activity is the continuation of Jesus' mission.

Important too is the fact that Mark does not differentiate between but rather identifies the Twelve and the disciples.[8] A comparison of Mk 11:11 with 11:14, and Mk 14:12.14 with 14:17 speaks for the overlapping of both groups. Mk 4:10 does not provide a sufficient textual basis for a clear cut distinction between the Twelve and the disciples, since such a separation cannot be maintained for the subsequent passages (Mk 6:35-44; 7:17; 9:28; 10:10). Since Mark does not stress the apostolic character of the Twelve, even though he is aware of it (cf. 3:14 and 6:30) he clearly is not concerned with the theological foundation of apostolic ministry. He primarily understands the Twelve as disciples and attributes to them no distinctive function and mission other than discipleship. The mission of the Twelve to do what Jesus did is therefore according to Mark not restricted to the Twelve but is a task of all disciples.

The second part of the Gospel therefore stresses again and again that the disciples have to suffer the same consequences as Jesus had to suffer for his preaching and mission. Just as the way of Jesus led to suffering and eath, so does the way of the true disciple. Connected with each passion prediction are statements stressing that no possibility of discipleship exists apart from taking upon oneself its consequence of suffering. Yet again and again the Twelve with their leading spokesman Peter betray that they do not understand and even reject Jesus' insistence on suffering discipleship.

The twelve disciples who were called "to be with him" (Mk 3:14) desert Jesus in the hour of his suffering (14:50), and Peter denies him three times (14:66-72). They are not found under the cross of Jesus, nor at his burial, and it remains unclear whether they receive the message of the resurrection (Mk 16:7-8). In marked contrast to the twelve disciples, the women disciples who followed Jesus from Galilee to Jerusalem (cf. 15:40f.) remained faithful until the end.

Not the Twelve but the women followers prove to be the true disciples of Jesus. The women not only accompany Jesus on his way to suffering and death but they also *do* what he had come to do, namely, to serve (*diakonein* cf. 10:42-45 and 15:41). Finally: While the twelve disciples are unable to understand and to accept Jesus' teaching that he must suffer, it is a woman who according to Mark shows such perception and acts accordingly (14:3-9). In

Mark her action is the immediate cause for the betrayal of Jesus by one of the Twelve (14:10f.) This contrast between the Twelve and the women disciples would suggest that in Mark's church women were considered to be the exemplary disciples of Jesus and had their place among the leaders of the community.[9] In Mark's theological perspective women are the functional successors of Jesus and they represent the true intention of Jesus and his mission within the messianic people of God.

It is debatable whether or not Acts 1:21f.[10] implicitly makes maleness a precondition for replacing a member of the Twelve. The position of Judas can be taken by "one of the men(*aner*) who have accompanied us during all the time that the Lord Jesus went in and out among us beginning from the baptism of John until the day when he was taken up." Only one of the original disciples of Jesus could become together with the Eleven a witness to the resurrection. It is not clear whether *aner* is used in 1:21 in a generic sense, since Luke often uses the address "men, brothers" (1:16; 2:29; 2:37; 7:2; 13:15; 13:26, 38; 15:7, 13; 22:1, 6; 28:17) in an inclusive sense to address the whole community, even when women are present (cf. 1:14 and 1:16). It could, however, also be argued that because of his theological understanding of the Twelve Luke maintains that only one of the male followers of Jesus is eligible to become one of the Twelve. Lk 8:1-3 clearly distinguishes between the women followers of Jesus and the Twelve. Differing from his Markan source, Luke has the women serve Jesus *and* the Twelve. He qualifies their *diakonein* insofar as he specifies that the women served them with their possessions. Just as wealthy women were strong supporters of the Jewish missionary endeavor, so according to Luke the Christian women support the ministry of Jesus and of the apostles. Luke therefore seems to limit the role of women in the Christian mission to that of benefactors.[11]

However, it must also be seen that Luke's theological concept and perspective have room for only a very limited function for the twelve apostles. The Twelve are mentioned for the last time in 6:2ff. and they disappear altogether after chapter 15. It is, moreover, curious that most passages speak only of the work of one man, Peter. Luke does not characterize the Twelve as missionaries, and there is little evidence in Acts that they were at all active outside Jerusalem. Luke knows likewise that the Twelve were not the official local ministers of the Jerusalem church or any other church. According to Paul and Acts the leadership of the Jerusalem church was clearly in the hands of James, the brother of the Lord, who was not one of the Twelve. Moreover, the Twelve were not replaced when they died (cf. Acts 12:2). The twelve apostles had no successors. Thus it is evident that Luke knows only of a very limited function for the Twelve in the primitive Church. Their significance appears to be limited to the very beginning of the Church and to its relationship to the chosen people of Israel. Luke seems to historicize their eschatological function vis-a-vis Israel in tradition. He limits their activity to the mission within Israel. After the Gentile mission is under way, the Twelve disappear from the historical scene. The elders and bishops in Acts are not understood as successors of the Twelve.[12] They are either appointed by Paul and Barnabas (14:23) or directly called by the Holy Spirit (Acts 20:28). Finally, Luke's requirements for becoming a member of the Twelve preclude the notion that the Twelve could have appointed successors.

In conclusion: The Declaration's argument that the Church, in faithfulness to the example of Jesus who did not choose women as members of the Twelve, cannot ordain women has no basis in the NT. The NT writers view the circle of the Twelve as belonging to the time of Jesus and to the very beginnings of the Christian movement. The Twelve's legitimization is rooted in their companionship with Jesus and in their witness to the resurrection. They have a special eschatological (Q) and historical (Acts) function vis-à-vis Israel.

It has to be stressed that according to the NT the Twelve's function was not continued in the ministries of the Church. Neither their symbolic-eschatological and historical-missionary function vis-à-vis Israel nor their function as eyewitnesses of the ministry and resurrection of Jesus is constitutive for the ministry of the Church. Luke's requirement that the replacement of Judas must be a male follower of the historical Jesus does not say anything about maleness as essential requirement for ordained ministry in the Church, since Luke does not envision any "apostolic succession" of the Twelve.

The theological issue at stake is therefore not whether or not women can be ordained even though Jesus did not call any woman to be a member of the Twelve-circle. The theological problem is whether the theological construct of "apostolic succession" can be maintained without any modification in view of the historical insight that the twelve apostles had no successors. The contention of the Declaration and the Commentary that women cannot be ordained because they were not members of the Twelve and therefore were not called to represent Jesus to the messianic people must therefore be judged as an attempt to solve modern critical problems on the basis of dogmatic statements phrased in a pre-critical era of Catholic biblical scholarship.[13]

Theologians more and more agree that the continuation of the function of the Twelve resides in the Church as a whole.[14] The Church can entrust the apostolic ministry and power to whomever it chooses without maintaining any historical-lineal connection with the Twelve. The Church's faithfulness to apostolic ministry and to the gospel of Jesus has to be expressed through service (*diakonia*). Together with the twelve apostles the Church must serve Jesus Christ who came to serve. According to Mark this apostolic witness of service was best exemplified by the women followers of Jesus.

Notes

1. For a general discussion of the problem cf. B. Rigaux, "The Twelve Apostles," *Concilium* Vol. 34 (1968), pp. 5-15; "Die 'Zwölf' in Geschichte und Kerygma," in Ristow-Matthiae, ed., *Der historische Jesus und der kerygmatische Christus* (Berlin, 2nd ed., 1961), pp. 468-486; G. Klein, *Die Zwölf*

Apostel. Ursprung und Gehalt einer Idee. Forschungen zur Religion und Literatur des Alten und Neuen Testaments, Vol. 59 (Göttingen: Vandenhoeck & Ruprecht, 1961); J. Roloff, *Apostolat—Verkündigung—Kirche* (Gütersloh: Mohn, 1965); R. Schnackenburg, "Apostolicity: the Present Position of Studies," *One in Christ* Vol. 6 (1970), pp. 243-73; V. Taylor, *The Gospel according to St. Mark* (London: Macmillan, 2nd ed., 1966), pp. 619-627; A. Vögtle in *Lexikon für Theologie und Kirche*, Vol. VX (Freiburg: Herder, 2nd ed., 1966), pp. 1443 ff.

2. For the extensive literature cf. H. Conzelmann, *1 Corinthians.* Hermeneia (Philadelphia: Fortress, 1975), pp. 251-254.

3. For an extensive discussion and literature cf. H. Merklein, *Das kirchliche Amt nach dem Epheserbrief.* Studia Antoniana (München: Kösel, 1973), pp. 273-278.

4. Cf. V. Taylor, *St. Mark*, p. 622; H. Schürmann, *Traditionsgeschichtliche Untersuchungen zu den Evangelien* (Düsseldorf: Patros, 1968), pp. 175f. maintains that the expression "twelve thrones" is found in Q.

5. Q is used to designate the source of the material that is common to Matthew and Luke but is not found in Mark. Since the material is almost wholly teaching material Q is often called "Sayings—source" or Logia source.

6. Cf. J. Coutts, "The Authority of Jesus and of the Twelve in St. Mark's Gospel," *Journal of Theological Studies*, Vol. 8 (1957), pp. 111-118; K. G. Reploh, *Markus—Lehrer der Gemeinde.* Stuttgarter biblische Monagraphien, Vol. 9 (Stuttgart: Katholisches Bibelwerk, 1969), pp. 43-58; K. Stock, *Boten aus dem Mit-Ihm-Sein. Das Verhältnis zwischen Jesus und den Zwölf nach Markus.* Analecta biblica, Vol. 70 (Rome: Biblical Institute Press, 1975), G. Schmahl, "Die Berufung der Zwölf im Markusevangelium," *Trierer theologische Zeitschrift*, Vol. 81 (1972), pp. 203-313; R. Pesch, *Das Markusevangelium. 1. Teil Herders theologischer Kommentar zum Neuen Testament*, II, 1 (Freiburg: Herder, 1976), pp. 202-209, 325-332 (literature).

7. Cf. K. Kertelge, "Die Funktion der 'Zwölf' im Markusevangelium," *Trierer theologische Zeitschritt*, Vol. 78 (1969), pp. 193-206.

8. Against K. Stock, *Boten aus dem Mit—Ihm—Sein*, who ascribes to the Twelve a special function, namely to represent Jesus and to continue his work. Cf. Hoever, K.G. Reploh, *Markus,* pp. 47f., who maintains that the Twelve are included among the disciples. They have no special function distinctive from the disciples but they are the origin and beginning of the whole Church.

9. Cf. P.J. Achtemeier, *Mark.* Proclamation Commentaries (Philadelphia: Fortress, 1975), pp. 92-100.

10. For Acts 1:15-26 cf. E. Haenchen, *The Acts of the Apostles* (Philadelphia: Westminster, 1971), pp. 157-165 (literature).

11. For a different interpretation cf. H. Conzelmann, *The Theology of Saint Luke* (London: Faber & Faber, 1961), p. 47 n. 1: "Features from the primitive community have naturally been projected back. Just as the male followers are turned into apostles, so the female followers are turned into deaconesses (v. 3)."

12. R.E. Brown, *Priest and Bishop* (New York: Paulist Press, 1970), pp. 51-59; R. Schnackenburg, "Lukas als Zeuge verschiedener Gemeindestrukturen," *Bibel und Leben*, Vol. 12 (1971), pp. 232-247.

13. Cf. the excellent article of R.E. Brown, "Difficulties in Using the New Testament in American Catholic Discussions," *Louvain Studies*, Vol. 6 (1976), pp. 144-158.

14. Cf. H. Küng, *The Church* (New York: Doubleday, 1976), pp. 443-461; R.E. Brown, *Priest*, pp. 73-86; K.H. Schelkle, "Dienste und Diener in den Kirchen der neutestamentlichen Zeit," *Concilium*, Vol. 5 (1969), pp. 158-164; K. Kertelge, "Die Funktion der 'Zwölf'," pp. 205f.

12
Ordination and the Ministry Willed by Jesus

Thomas P. Rausch

"In his itinerant ministry Jesus was accompanied not only by the Twelve but also by a group of women."[1] This sentence continues the argument of the Declaration in Chapter 2, that although Jesus deliberately broke with the attitude toward women of his milieu, nevertheless he "did not call any woman to become part of the Twelve."[2] The context for these references to the place of the Twelve in the historical ministry of Jesus appears earlier in the Declaration in what is really its fundamental thesis: ". . . the Sacred Congregation for the Doctrine of the Faith judges it necessary to recall that the Church, in fidelity to the example of the Lord, does not consider herself authorized to admit women to priestly ordination,"[3] or again, "the Church intends to remain faithful to the type of ordained ministry willed by the Lord Jesus Christ and carefully maintained by the Apostles."[4] Here is the crucial issue which the Declaration attempts to answer: what type of ordained ministry did the Lord intend for his Church? Several questions are in order: (1) What does the Declaration claim in respect to the type of ministry willed by Jesus? (2) Were "the Twelve" ordained? (3) What is the relationship between authoritative appointment to official ministry and the laying on of hands? (4) Did women share officially in the apostolic ministry? (5) What is the status of the Declaration?

(1) *The ministry willed by Jesus.* The Declaration could be read in such a way as to suggest that Jesus himself conferred ordination on men. However nowhere does the Declaration state that the historical Jesus ordained anyone. In interpreting these passages on the will of the Lord Jesus Christ, it is important to attend to the conventions of contemporary biblical language. {Many reputable Catholic and non-Catholic Scripture scholars presume that the primitive Church, confident of the guidance of the Holy Spirit, considered its own instructions and decisions as fulfilling the mind of the risen Lord} (cf. Eph 4:11; Acts 20:28). So also are the post-resurrection instructions of the Lord considered by some as coming from the primitive Church. Church documents follow this more "presumptive" school of interpretation, as Raymond Brown has noted:

> . . . in speaking of the will of *Christ* ecclesiologists are going beyond the ministry to the risen Lord who acts through the Spirit.

Classical church statements attribute the institution of sacraments and church order to Jesus Christ the Lord and not simply to what a modern scholar would call the Jesus of the ministry.[5]

Thus the Declaration should be interpreted as speaking not of the historical Jesus, but of the risen Lord acting through the Spirit in the early Church.

The ordained ministry in the Church is rooted in Jesus' call and appointment of the Twelve. The New Testament represents Jesus as calling the Twelve as a special group within his disciples during his historical ministry (Mk 3:14-19; Mt 10:1-4; Lk 6:2-16).[6] After the resurrection he gave them the apostolic mandate, sending them forth to preach the gospel to all nations (Mt 28:19ff.; Mk 16:15) and to be witnesses to his message (Lk 24:47). "As the Father has sent me, so I send you" (John 20:21). Such an appointment and commissioning of the Twelve implies and demands an enablement.[7] From the beginning of the Church the Twelve shared this ministry with others.[8] The Declaration therefore is correct in focusing not on ordination itself, but on the Twelve and the ministry of the apostles as the dominical institution from which the priestly ministry emerged.[9]

(2) *Were the Twelve "ordained"?* The New Testament does not picture Jesus as ordaining the Twelve by the laying on of hands. But one can ask what kind of a relation—if any—the New Testament writers perceived between the Twelve and the official Church ministers of the later New Testament. The Twelve are never called "priests" (*hierei*) in the New Testament, yet when Mark in 3:14 states that Jesus "appointed" (*espoiēsen*) Twelve, he chooses a verb used in the Septuagint for the appointment of priests for Israel.[10] This same verb, again with a ritual meaning, appears in the command of Jesus at the last supper to "do this (*touto poiēte*) as a remembrance of me" (Lk 22:19; 1 Cor 11:24-25). Joachim Jeremias argues that this command "is, as can be seen from a comparison with Ex 29:35; Num 15:11-13; Deut 25:9 . . . an established expression for the repetition of a rite."[11] According to Jeremias, "it is very probable that the command goes back to Jesus himself."[12] On the basis of Jeremias' research and from the usage of *poiein* in the Septuagint for the appointment of priests, Jerome Quinn argues that "the command of the historical Jesus at his last supper with the Twelve . . . was an appointment to a ritual function that must be understood against the background of Israel's priestly worship."[13]

Did then the command to repeat constitute an ordination? If by ordination is understood an authoritative appointment to an apostolic function, then all the elements are here: the command to the Twelve, phrased in established ritual language, to repeat the new covenant meal. The words of institution themselves are referred back to cultic and sacrificial formulae of the Old Testament.[14] The connection between the institution of the Eucharist, the command to repeat, and the ministry of the Church is strongly suggested in Luke's Gospel. In Luke, the synoptic narrative of the last supper events (prediction of the betrayal of Judas, eucharistic institution, departure for the garden, prediction of Peter's betrayal) is significantly altered. Luke places the prediction of the betrayal of Judas (22:21-23) immediately after the institution (22:15-20), while the prediction of Peter's betrayal (22:33-34) is situated within the context of the eucharistic meal, before the departure for the garden (22:39). What is especially significant is that after the institution of the Eucharist and between the two predictions of betrayal Luke rather abruptly inserts into this context of the institution a tradition on ministry and church order (22:24-32), expressed as an instruction of Jesus to the Twelve on their role of *diakonia*. The basic element in this ministry and church order tradition is the dispute over rank[15] which in Mark and Matthew appears in the context of the third prediction of the passion (Mk 10:35-45; Mt 20:20-28). But Luke has both transposed the tradition into the context of the institution of the Eucharist and expanded it, so that the reworked tradition includes a progression from the Church leader (*hēgoumenos*; cf. Heb 13:7, 17, 24) who must be like a servant (*hōs ho diakonōn:* 22:26), to the Twelve whom Jesus appoints to eat and drink at his *table* in the kingdom (22:30),[16] to Peter, for whom Jesus has prayed, that he may in turn strengthen his brothers (22:32).[17] It is fair then to conclude that in Luke's Gospel this insertion of a tradition on ministry and church order into the context of the Eucharist represents a specific effort on the part of the redactor to link the institution of the Eucharist with the ministry of Church leaders and that of the Twelve, who must serve as Jesus did.

(3) *Authoritative appointment and the laying on of hands.* It is not certain when the laying on of hands emerged as the sign of appointment or delegation to a share in the ministry of the apostles. It is clearly present in the later New Testament books (1 Tim 4:14; 5:22; 2 Tim 1:6; Acts 6:6; 13:3), though the roots of this rite lie in the Old Testament.[18]

Was appointment through the laying on of hands a practice inherited from Palestinian Judaism? Many scholars hold that it was. On the basis of the Talmudic literature they argue that the custom of a rabbi ordaining his disciple by the laying on of hands (*semikah*) was already established among Palestinian Jews in the first century of the Christian era. The first recorded case comes from the second half of the first century when Johanan ben Zakkai, the leader of the Pharisees at Jamnia, ordained his pupils Eliezer and Joshua (J Sanh 1, 3, 19a), though E. Lohse would argue that rabbinic ordination originated earlier with the development of the scribes as a specific group.[19] Hugo Mantel states that it was after the destruction of the Temple and thus with the ending of a unified Jewish state that "R. Johanan b. Zakkai, in pursuance of his general policy of making adjustments to a new situation, introduced the institution of ordination," in the sense of giving the individual teacher "the authority to declare a disciple a *hakam*" (an ordained scholar).[20] But there is evidence of an earlier practice. The Mishna (Sanh 4, 4), a collection of rabbinical traditions published in 200 A.D., describes a similar procedure for ordaining or appointing (*somekin*, the verb form of *semikah*) disciples as judges to the Jerusalem Sanhedrin, thus dating the practice prior to the destruction of Jerusalem in 70 A.D.[21]

What can be said about appointment to ministry in the Pauline churches? Since Paul mentions neither the laying on of hands nor any other ceremony for appointing a Church minister in those letters acknowledged today as authentically his, many reputable scholars would argue that the ministries in his churches were not "institutionalized," received through appointment. The ministries in the Pauline churches are described as "charismatic," that is, arising spontaneously in a community through the Spirit. It is in the latter sense that Küng speaks of Paul's churches as "associations of free charismatic ministries."[22] Yet since all ministries are charismatic gifts of the Spirit, it is as R. Fuller points out strictly speaking incorrect, even though convenient, to contrast charismatic and institutional. The real contrast is between spontaneous and institutional ministries.[23]

It is also true that in speaking of Paul's churches as associations of free charismatic ministries one runs the risk of over-simplification. There is a double principle of order evident within Paul's churches: "the self-regulation of the charismatic order in charity, and the ancillary apostolic direction"[24] for which Paul obviously knew himself to be responsible. The office of the apostles is constitutive for the primitive Church. But Paul's churches also had persons in recognized ministries of teaching and Church leadership. Though the functional ministerial vocabulary found in Paul's letters is still rather fluid and varies somewhat from church to church, still there is a certain order. There is first of all the office of the apostle, Paul himself, who exercised his authority over a number of churches. Ranked under the apostles at Corinth (1 Cor 12:28) are the prophets, teachers, and administrators (*kubernēseis*). Thessalonica has those "whose task it is (*kopiontas*) to exercise authority (*proistamenous*: cf. Rm 12:18; 16:2) in the Lord and admonish you" (1 Thes 5:12).[25] In Galatians the one "who catechizes" is entitled to material support for his ministry (Gal 6:6), as is the apostle himself (1 Cor 9:6-15). The Church at Philippi has its *episkopoi kai diakonoi* (Phil 1:1). The fact that these terms are almost always given in the plural suggests a collegial dimension to the ministry of church leadership.

Timothy and Titus have a special share in Paul's apostolic ministry, being sent as his delegates to those churches over which Paul exercised his own authority.[26] Their roles as apostolic delegates are much more explicitly developed in those later New Testament letters addressed to them where they are responsible for setting up and ordaining the local colleges of presbyters in the churches of Ephesus and Crete respectively.[27]

Thus Paul himself specifically associated others with him in his apostolic ministry, recognized the authority of those who already exercised it locally in communities he had not personally established (i.e., Rome), and most probably left behind church leaders in those communities he himself had founded (Thessalonica, Corinth, Philippi). There is then some evidence for more or less institutionalized ministries (i.e., authorized or delegated, not necessarily installed with the laying on of hands) even in his earliest letters.

The Acts of the Apostles, a later New Testament book, represents Paul and Barnabas as "ordaining" (*cheirotonēsantes*) presbyters in each Church established on their first missionary journey (Acts 14:23), but almost all scholars today see in this a highly idealized account of early Church history, colored by the later Lukan theology of the ministry. There is no proof that ordination by the laying on of hands was practiced from the earliest days. However, at least one case of authoritative appointment to ministry appears to be earlier than Paul. This example of authoritative appointment appears early in the history of the original Jerusalem community. Because of a dispute between the Hebrew Christians loyal to the Temple and the Hellenist Jewish Christians, it became necessary to provide the latter group with their own leaders. Luke describes this in the institution of the Seven (Acts 6:1-6). In a recent critical study of this text, Joseph Lienhard has argued that "the kernel of the narrative derives from a historical tradition," joined by the redactor of Acts to the Stephen episode.[28] What is significant here is that "the investigation has firmly established the fact that, early in the history of the primitive community in Jerusalem, certain members of that community were authoritatively appointed to an office," though it cannot be affirmed with the same certitude that the dispute was mediated by the Twelve.[29]

Lienhard bases his argument for the historical character of the narrative on the following points: (1) Though the first phrase of 6:1 reflects the hand of the redactor, the dissension reported within the community in the second phrase, with the Hellenists murmuring against the Hebrews, departs from the spirit of the Lukan summary sections. (2) The preservation of the names of the two contending groups, especially since the names are not self-explanatory, points to the tradition as the source. (3) The phrase "because their widows were being neglected in the daily distribution of food" contains no peculiarly Lukan vocabulary, but does include two New Testament *hapax legomena*. (4) Verse 6:5, containing the names of the Seven, can only be explained as Luke's reporting a tradition he received from the community; the very obscurity of the persons named suggests the basic historicity of the list.[30] (5) The obscurity in the established text of 6:6 as to who imposed hands, the community or the Twelve, is significant; a variant reading in the Western Text (D), clarifying that it was the apostles who laid on hands, "may indicate an early effort to fix a precedent for practices which were being established."[31] Lienhard affirms that 6:2-4, the speech of the Twelve, should be considered a redactional composition on the basis of its Lukan vocabulary, rhetorical structure, and theology.[32] But as with "6:1, 6:5-6 seem to be reporting a received tradition, and redactional elements do not have a significant role in the verses."[33]

This historical analysis of the institution of the Seven offers a concrete instance of an authoritative appointment to office early in the history of the primitive Church, presumably before the outbreak of the persecution which drove the Hellenist Christians (but not the apostles) from Jerusalem (Acts 8:1), before these refugees turned missionaries extended the gospel to Judea and Samaria (Acts 9:3), to Phoenicia, Cyprus, and Antioch (Acts 11:9), thus before Paul began his own missionary work and established his churches. If

Lienhard's analysis of Acts 6:1-6 is correct, his study should provide a caution against the statement that authoritative appointment to ministry was only a later development.

(4) *Women in the apostolic ministry?* There remains yet the historical question as to whether or not women received an official share in the apostolic ministry. No woman is ever identified explicitly as an apostle, with the problematic exception of Junias/Junia (Rm. 16:7),[34] though this question is beyond my task here. In this respect, it is interesting to note that the report of the Pontifical Biblical Commission and the Declaration of the Doctrinal Commission are in agreement on the historical question regarding women in the ministry of church leadership. Although the Biblical Commission acknowledges that "some women collaborated in the properly apostolic work,"[35] it points out that "all that we can know of those who held a role of leadership in the communities leads to the conclusion that this role was always held by men (in comformity with the Jewish custom)."[36] It continues, "the masculine character of the hierarchical order which has structured the church since its beginning thus seems attested to by scripture in an undeniable way."[37] The Declaration of the Doctrinal Congregation argues from ". . . the fact that Jesus did not entrust the apostolic charge to women."[38] Both documents seem to be in agreement that the question cannot be settled simply on the basis of the historical evidence. The Declaration states that "in order to reach the ultimate meaning of the mission of Jesus and the ultimate meaning of Scripture, a purely historical exegesis of the texts cannot suffice."[39] Where the two reports differ is not on the historical evidence but on the value that is to be given to the practice of the early Church as reflected in the New Testament. The Biblical Commission questions whether the rule of the early practice "must be valid forever in the church?"[40] and concludes:

> It does not seem that the New Testament by itself will permit us to settle in a clear way and once and for all the problem of the possible accession of women to the presbyterate.[41]

On the other hand, the Declaration of the Doctrinal Congregation bases its conclusion on what it discerns to be willed by the Lord Jesus Christ in respect to the type of ordained ministry in the Church.[42] As we saw earlier, this is not a simplistic attempt to read a definitive solution back into the mind of the historical Jesus. The Doctrinal Congregation does however give a far more definitive status to the practice of the early Church as witnessed to by the New Testament, judging this as coming from the action of the risen Lord through his Spirit in the Church. The type of ministry willed and that actually given are two different questions. Both are valid questions, but one is a question of historical evidence, while the other is more properly a theological question. In this respect, that is, in the properly theological question of the weight to be attached to the primitive practice, the Doctrinal Congregation differs with the Pontifical Biblical Commission.

(5) *The Status of the Declaration.* The Declaration, even though it

makes its appearance "in execution of a mandate received from the Holy Father,"[43] does not necessarily represent the *final* judgment of the Church itself. It may indeed represent a statement of the position of the Roman Catholic Church at the present time in regard to the question of the ordination of women.[44] But as the Letter to the Apostolic Delegate by the faculty of the Jesuit School of Theology at Berkeley suggests, this Roman Congregation has in the past committed itself to positions beyond which the Church has moved both practically and officially in its subsequent history. The Doctrinal Congregation has at one time condemned the Chinese Rites, the Copernican understanding of the solar system, and the modern biblical movement at the beginning of this century.[45] The declarations of the Doctrinal Congregation are not of themselves irreformable. Thus the Declaration of the Sacred Congregation for the Doctrine of the Faith on the ordination of women does not necessarily exclude a new evaluation of this question in the future.

Summary. Though the New Testament does not picture Jesus as ordaining with the laying on of hands, it can be argued that the redactor of Luke (c. 85 A.D.) sees a connection between the institution of the Eucharist and the ministry of the Church. If by ordination is understood authoritative appointment to an apostolic function, then all the elements are here. Many scholars today argue that appointment by the laying on of hands, possibly adopted from the Jewish practice of *semikah*, emerged only in the Church of the subapostolic age. The laying on of hands is evident in the Pastoral Letters, written according to most scholars in the 80s or 90s, though some would still hold for an earlier date. There is however some evidence for an authoritative appointment to office early in the history of the primitive Jerusalem community (Acts 6:1-6). If it can be proved that women did exercise the ministry of Church leadership in the earliest years of the Church, this would have an important bearing on the question of the ordination of women.

Notes

1. Declaration, par. 12.
2. *Ibid.*, par. 10.
3. *Ibid.*, par. 5.
4. *Ibid.*, par. 6.
5. Raymond E. Brown, *Biblical Reflections on Crises Facing the Church* (New York: Paulist Press, 1975), p. 58, n. 45.
6. Brown, in *Priest and Bishop: Biblical Reflections* (New York: Paulist Press, 1970), notes that "the majority of scholars still find persuasive the evidence that the Twelve disciples of Jesus were considered apostles of the Church from the beginning," p. 49.
7. See Jerome D. Quinn, "Ministry in the New Testament," in *Lutherans and Catholics in Dialogue IV: Eucharist and Ministry*, ed. Paul C. Empie and T. Austin Murphy (Washington: United States Catholic Conference, 1970), pp. 72ff.

8. *Ibid.*, pp. 69-100; "The sharing of apostolic Ministry is the historical matrix from which succession to the apostolic Ministry emerged," p. 100.

9. The Pontifical Biblical Commission Report also speaks of the ministry of the apostles as the *"urministerium* from which all the others derived," Part IV, 1. For a thorough analysis and a different conclusion see the essays by Elisabeth Fiorenza, pp. 114-122, 135-140.

10. 1 Sam 12:6; 1 Kgs 12:31; 13:33; cf., Heb 3:2. See Quinn, p. 77; also Vincent Taylor, *The Gospel According to St. Mark* (New York: St. Martin's Press, 2nd ed., 1966), p. 230.

11. Joachim Jeremias, *The Eucharist Words of Jesus*, trans. Norman Perrin (New York: Charles Scribner's Sons, 3rd ed., 1966), pp. 249-250.

12. *Ibid.*, p. 255. See also Quinn, p. 77.

13. Quinn, p. 77.

14. For the sacrificial and cultic elements of "body," "blood," "new covenant," "poured out," "for many" see Vincent Taylor, *Jesus and His Sacrifice: A Study of the Passion-Sayings in the Gospels* (New York: St. Martin's Press, 1965), pp. 125ff.; Taylor, *The Passion Narrative of St. Luke: A Critical and Historical Investigation*, ed. Owen E. Evans, Society for New Testament Studies (Cambridge [Eng.]: University Press, 1972), p. 78; Jeremias, *The Eucharistic Words*, pp. 220ff.; Joseph Ratzinger, "Ist die Eucharistie ein Opfer?" *Concilium*, Vol. III (1976), pp. 299-304.

15. John H. Elliott identifies the rank dispute as a tradition concerning ministry and church order in "Ministry and Church Order in the NT: A Traditio-Historical Analysis (1 Pt. 5, 1-5 & plls.)," *Catholic Biblical Quarterly*, Vol. XXXII (1970), pp. 374-375.

16. "I for my part assign to you the dominion my Father has assigned to me. In my kingdom you will eat and drink at my table and you will sit on thrones judging the twelve tribes of Israel," Luke 22:29-30.

17. Cf. Heinz Schürmann, *Der Abendmahlsbericht Lucas 22, 7-38 als Gottesdienstordnung-Gemeindeordnung Lebensordnung* (Paderborn: Ferdinand Schöningh, 1963).

18. See Eduard Lohse, *Die Ordination im Spätjudentum und im Neuen Testament* (Göttingen: Evangelische Verlagsanstalt, 1951).

19. E. Lohse, "Cheir," in *Theological Dictionary of the New Testament*, ed. Gerhard Friedrich, trans. and ed. Geoffrey W. Bromiley (Grand Rapids, Michigan: Wm. B. Eerdmans, 1974), p. 429. The struggle of the largely Jewish Christian community in Palestine or Syria to define itself against Jamnia Pharisaism is reflected in the anti-Pharisaism of Matthew's Gospel, written around the year 85. See Eugene A. LaVerdiere and William G. Thompson, "New Testament Communities in Transition: A Study of Matthew and Luke," *Theological Studies*, Vol. XXXVII (1976), pp. 571-582.

20. Hugo Mantel, *Studies in the History of the Sanhedrin* (Cambridge, Mass.: Harvard University Press, 1961), p. 139. On the meaning of "hakam," see pp. 132-135.

21. Mantel, pp. 206-207. The texts on rabbinic ordination can be found in Hermann Strack and Paul Billerbeck, *Kommentar zum Neuen Testament aus Talmud und Midrasch*, Vol. II (Munich: Beck, 1924), pp. 647ff.

22. Hans Küng, *Why Priests? A Proposal for a New Church Ministry*, trans. Robert C. Collins (Garden City, New York: Doubleday, 1972), p. 45. Küng writes that Paul "is evidently unacquainted with an institutionalized of-

fice in which one is installed and from which one then derives the obligation to be a minister."

23. Reginald H. Fuller, "The Ministry in the New Testament," in *Episcopalians and Roman Catholics: Can They Ever Get Together?* ed. Herbert J. Ryan and J. Robert Wright (Denville, New Jersey: Dimension Books, 1972), p. 99.

24. Heinz Schürmann, "Die geistlichen Gnadengaben," in *De Ecclesia: Beiträge zur Konstitution "Über die Kirche" des zweiten vatikanischen Konzils*, ed. G. Baruna (Freiburg: Herder, 1966), p. 515.

25. See Myles M. Bourke, "Reflections on Church Order in the New Testament," *Catholic Biblical Quarterly*, Vol. XXX (1968), p. 506 for an analysis of the functional continuity between the tasks of the *proistamenoi* of 1 Thess. and the presbyters of 1 Tim 5:17.

26. 1 Cor 4:17; 2 Cor 7:6; 13ff.; Phil 2:19ff.

27. John P. Meier, in *"Presbyteros* in the Pastoral Epistles," *Catholic Biblical Quarterly*, Vol. XXXV (1973), argues that at Ephesus Timothy finds an already existing Church with a well established college of presbyters, among whom some (1 Tim 5:17) have been assigned to the particular duties of teaching and preaching (as well as other tasks suggested by the list of qualities in 1 Tim 3:1-7). Only such a specialized presbyter would receive the title *episkopos*. In the more primitive situation of the Church on Crete, *presbyteros* and *episkopos* are still equivalent terms, pp. 337-345.

28. Joseph T. Lienhard, "Acts 6:1-6: A Redactional View," *Catholic Biblical Quarterly*, Vol. XXXVII (1975), p. 236.

29. *Ibid.*

30. *Ibid.*, pp. 230-235.

31. *Ibid.*, p. 236.

32. *Ibid.*, pp. 231-235.

33. *Ibid.*, p. 236.

34. See Bernadette Brooten's study, " 'Junia . . . Outstanding Among the Apostles' (Romans 16:7)," pp. 141-144 in this volume.

35. Pontifical Biblical Commission Report, Part III.

36. *Ibid.*, Part IV, I.

37. *Ibid.*

38. Declaration, par. 13.

39. *Ibid.*

40. Pontifical Biblical Commission Report, Part IV, 2.

41. *Ibid.*, Part V, 2.

42. Declaration, par. 6.

43. *Ibid.*, par. 5.

44. See the Commentary on the Declaration.

45. Letter to the Apostolic Delegate from the faculty of the Jesuit School of Theology at Berkeley, *Commonweal*, Vol. CIV, No. 7 (April 1, 1977), p. 205.

13
Women Leaders in the New Testament

J. Massyngberde Ford

The Declaration comments on the service of women during Jesus' itinerant ministry, but it overlooks the progressive attitude of Jesus and the early Church towards women.

One cannot emphasize sufficiently the role which women played in the early Church, a role which would not always be accepted by their contemporary culture. We find Phoebe, a deacon (not a deaconess), described in Rom 16:1-2 as an "authoritative leader." The Greek word (*prostatis*) is the feminine form of *prostatēs* which is found frequently in the LXX, e.g., 1 Chr 27:31; 29:6; 2 Chr 8:10; 24:11; 1 Esdras 2:12; Sir 45:24; and 2 Macc 3:4. These passages refer to stewards of the king's property, chief officers over the people and to priests. Most translations of Rom 16:1-2 are very weak, presenting Phoebe as a mere helper or friend of many, including Paul. Yet we know that Jewish sources[1] refer to women who were mothers of synagogues and rulers of synagogues and one woman who was given the privilege of *proedria*, that is, sitting on the foremost bench. We also find references to women Jewish elders.[2] Thus Jewish women who were prominent in the synagogue may well have retained that authority when they became Christians. Further, in Rom 16:7 we find the woman Junia who is an apostle.

Women deacons are mentioned several times in the New Testament (Rom 16:1-2; 1 Tim 3:11; and perhaps Phil 1:1); presumably they performed work similar to that of the male deacons but perhaps only with women and children. Gerhardsson[3] has found a linguistic parallel between Acts 6 (the choosing of the male deacons) and the pericope about Mary and Martha (Luke 10:38-42). He thinks that behind both texts lies the Jewish concept of one's lot, either a lot for the Torah or a lot for business. To Mary is assigned the lot of the Torah—to learn, pray and to teach—while Martha receives the lot of serving tables like the seven male deacons. Mary's lot is like that of the apostles for prayer and the Word (Acts 6).

Although women, minors and slaves were not permitted to be witnesses according to Jewish law (even witnesses concerning the new moon), the Gospel makes it quite clear that women were witnesses from the time of the ministry in Galilee (Luke 8:1-3) to the passion, death and resurrection of Jesus. As Conzelmann says: "Women have their share in the *anabasis* of Jesus, and later they witness the Crucifixion and the Resurrection." Even though Luke has a narrow interpretation of the concept of witness and apostles (the strict definition of Luke 6:13 is in fact adhered to in Acts 1:22), the "Galilean women and Mary seem to stand in a similar relation to one another as the Twelve and the Lord's Brethren."[4]

It is also appropriate to draw the readers' attention to the fact that in his Prologue Luke mentions "eyewitnesses and ministers of the word" and then continues by describing the functions of Elizabeth and Zachary, Mary and Elizabeth, Simeon and Annah. We notice the dual witness which is important for Luke, whose pairs often include both men and women. Moreover, the reference to the seventy or seventy-two sent out on their mission (Luke 10:1-12) does not, in contrast to the pericope about the lepers (Luke 17:11), tell us that all seventy disciples were men; they probably included husbands and wives like Priscilla and Aquila. Women are truly the disciples of the Lord because they follow him (*sunakoleutheō*—a technical word for a disciple following a master; cf. also Tabitha in Acts 9:36 who is described as a disciple). Even if Jesus did not choose women among the Twelve (and modern scholarship is beginning to question whether there were precisely twelve) perhaps if there originally were more than the symbolic number needed for the twelve tribes of Israel, they might have included women. At least we know they did not include Gentiles or Blacks. Moreover, women were permitted to read the Torah:

> Our Rabbis taught: All are qualified to be among the seven (we read), even a minor and a woman, only the Sages said that a woman should not read in the Torah out of respect for the congregation (Meg. 23a).

Swidler[5] finds a woman in Smyrna and one in Myndos who were called presidents of the synagogue and a woman proselyte who was named the mother of two synagogues. Swidler[6] also expounds on a famous woman scholar, Beruria, who was the wife of R. Meir, although she seems to be the exception to the general rule that women did not learn the Torah. In the light of this information one is able to understand why Priscilla and Aquila could teach even the famous biblical scholar, Apollos (Acts 18) and the prominence of such women as Lydia, Chloe and Phoebe and the other many women whom Paul greets as laborers in the vineyard of the Lord (in Rom 16 about eight women are mentioned, and in Phil 4:2-3 four women's names occur). 1 Tim 2:12 is no hindrance either to a woman teaching (because this is merely the opinion of the author, not of the Lord) or to having an authoritative position (because the word *authentein* which is usually translated "have authority" really means "play the tyrant" or "have supreme authority").

Whereas St. Paul may seem a misogynist, he is ahead of his times in many ways. For example, he sees marriage as mutual responsibility and authority (e.g., 1 Cor 7:4 and the whole of 1 Cor 7, where he deals first with the male side of the problems under discussion and then with the female). He certainly expects women to pray and prophesy in public (1 Cor 11) and never states that any of the spiritual gifts are for males only. 1 Cor 14:34-35 seems to be an interpolation, as it is found after v. 40 in some manuscripts. 1 Cor 14:36 is addressed to the entire Christian community. The "headship" of husbands over wives is difficult (1 Cor 11 and Eph 5) but *kephelē* is rarely used for headship in the New Testament or the Old, in which the references are mainly in Judges (where Deborah is leader, judge and war conductor) and in some manuscripts of Isaiah. In the Gospels there is absolutely no teaching about the headship of the male or the subordination of woman. Therefore the teaching and praxis is *not dominical.* On the whole the prominent women in the Bible are ones who use their own initiative and authority to fulfill God's will, e.g., Sarah, Rebecca, Tamar, Deborah, Huldah, Judith, Ruth and Esther, Priscilla, Lydia, Phoebe *et ceterae.* These are the women held up for our example.[7]

The Declaration asserts that Mary was not entrusted with the apostolic charge. Yet in fact when Jesus places Mary over the beloved disciple (and the Church) on the cross (John 19:26-27) he places her in a superior position over the apostle. Thus she should be regarded as Mother of the apostles, and in Judaism mothers received equal honor with father. Mary may be the Elect Lady addressed in 1 or 2 John 1.[8]

Notes

1. See *Jewish Encyclopaedia* under "diaspora."
2. Harry J. Leon, *The Jews of Ancient Rome* (Philadelphia: Jewish Publication Society, p. 181, n. 2.
3. B. Gerhardsson, *Memory and Manuscript* (Lund: C.W.K. Gleerup, pp. 234-245.
4. Hans Conzelmann, *The Theology of Luke* (New York: Harper & Row, pp. 46ff.
5. Leonard Swidler, "Women and Torah in Talmudic Judaism," *Conservative Judaism*, Vol. 30, No. 1 (Fall, 1975), p. 28.
6. *Ibid.*, p. 33.
7. For further details see my article "Biblical Material Relevant to the Ordination of Women," *Journal of Ecumenical Studies*, Vol. 10, No. 4 (Fall, 1973), pp. 669-699.
8. See the author's article "Our Lady and the Ministry of Women," *Marian Studies*, Vol. 23 (1972), pp. 69-112.

14
The Apostleship of Women in Early Christianity

Elisabeth Schüssler Fiorenza

The Vatican Declaration and Commentary appear to assume that the Twelve and the apostles were essentially one and the same group of people (cf. n. 10). Since no woman was called to be a member of the Twelve, no woman received the apostolic charge. This conclusion is, however, not cogent if initially the terms the Twelve and the apostles were not coextensive but designated different leadership circles in early Christianity which only partly overlapped. It must therefore be asked whether women might have received the apostolic charge even though they were not among the Twelve. In the following we must discuss more carefully how the NT writers understand the function and the office of apostle and whether or not, according to the NT, women were entrusted with the apostolic function and office in primitive Christianity.

From the outset we can say that the NT writings contain several different conceptions rather than a singular interpretation of apostleship. They give us neither a clear definition of apostolicity nor a simple definition of apostle. While non-specialists may feel certain who the apostles were, the numerous exegetical studies of the last twenty-five years[1] demonstrate that the case is not at all so clear. There is neither consensus on the origin and derivation of the Christian designation "apostle" nor agreement on who belonged to the circle of the apostles in early Christianity. The use of the designation in pre-Christian Hellenism and Judaism does not explain the meaning of the term and its origin in early Christianity. The majority of scholars would agree today that neither the function nor the self-understanding of the Christian apostle can strictly be derived from the use of the "ambassador" term in Rabbinic Judaism, since the Jewish missionaries were never called "apostles" and use of the term is not documented for pre-Christian Judaism. The use and meaning of the designation "apostle" has a peculiar Christian origin and emphasis.

On the other hand the majority of scholars studying the problem agree that the generally assumed, popular understanding of apostleship limiting the circle and function of the apostles to that of the Twelve does not stand at the beginning of the development of the apostle-concept but at the end. In the Pauline letters, the oldest NT sources available to us, the term is still very fluid and not clearly defined.[2] These letters give evidence that Paul had a dif-

135

ferent understanding of apostleship than Luke. Moreover, Paul did not introduce the term and function but had found it already given in his tradition.
Finally, the Pauline texts also indicate that many more apostles existed in
early Christianity than we now know by name.

The following does not intend to trace the origin and development of the
concept of apostle[3] in early Christianity but simply to list the different types
and understandings of apostleship encountered in the NT writings. Only then
can we raise the question of which criteria for apostleship the NT writers
propose and whether women fulfilled these criteria and functioned as apostles.

1. *Apostleship based on the resurrection appearance of Jesus Christ*

The references to the circle of apostles in 1 Cor 15:7 and Gal 1:17-19 understand the apostles to be a cohesive group that was in existence before Paul
and lived probably in or near Jerusalem. Its claim to apostleship appears to be
based on the resurrection appearances of Jesus. There is no way to decide definitely whether or not in the pre-Pauline tradition and Paul's own understanding
women were members of this circle of apostles in Jerusalem.[4] It is true that
the masculine form of the noun is used, but the masculine form also permits
a generic usage of the word. What speaks in favor of such a generic interpretation of the term is that the NT often uses masculine terminology in a generic sense to include and to address the female members of the community.
Otherwise we would have to assume that most letters, sayings, and admoni-
tions expressed in masculine terminology would not pertain to Christian
women. In other words, the NT preaching and the gospel message would be
inherently sexist, if we would insist that all masculine forms in the NT are restricted to males.

Since according to the canonical and apocryphal Gospels women are the
first eyewitnesses to the resurrection and are sent to the male disciples to
proclaim the Easter message,[5] women could have been members of this circle
of the Jerusalem apostles. This is suggested by the summary account of Acts
1:14. The germ-cell of the primitive Church consisted of the Eleven, the
women witnesses with Mary of Magdala,[6] and the mother and brothers of
Jesus. According to 1 Cor 15:5, 7 and according to Mark, Matthew and
John, it was the Eleven, the women witnesses, and James the brother of the
Lord who experienced a resurrection appearance and were witnesses to the
resurrection. The summary description of Acts reflects traditions in which
women were a part of the nucleus of the primitive Church. This is significant
because Luke attempts to play down the qualification of the women disciples
for apostleship (cf. Lk 24).

2. *Apostles—charismatic missionaries*

It appears that a second group of apostles did not so much base their apostolic claim on a resurrection appearance as derive it from their missionary
success. The apostles of the Hellenistic missionary field appear to have been
itinerant preachers whose proclamation was confirmed by mighty signs and

wonders. The so-called "super-apostles" or "false apostles" or the "other apostles" against whom Paul might be polemicizing in 1 Cor 9:5 and to whom he certainly refers in 2 Cor 10-13, probably understood themselves in such a way. They seem to have placed special emphasis upon missionary success as the legitimization of their apostleship. They travelled from city to city, relying on the communities for their support and for letters of recommendation. They appear to have travelled with women missionaries or as missionary couples (1 Cor 9:5).[7]

Paul does not dispute their claim to apostleship as itinerant missionaries, for he calls himself and other co-missionaries apostles in the same sense. Such missionary apostles were Barnabas (Acts 14:4, 14), Timothy and Silas (1 Thess 2:6f.) and Andronicus and Junia (Rm 16:7). Just as Paul emphasized in his dispute with the Jerusalem apostles that he too has seen the risen Lord, so he insists vis-a-vis the super-apostles that he can claim for himself the signs and visions of an apostle (1 Cor 2:4; Rm 15:19; 2 Cor 12:1-7). Paul acknowledges that the apostle has the right to refrain from working for a living. Yet he emphasizes that he himself consciously has not made use of his right.[8] For Paul apostleship is not proved by exclusive claims and rights but by the fruits of the missionary work (1 Cor 9:15-18). Its decisive mark does not consist in signs and mighty speech but in the conscious acceptance and endurance of the labors and sufferings connected with the missionary task (1 Cor 4:8-13; 2 Cor 11-12). Andronicus and Junia,[9] mentioned in Rm 16:7, fulfill these criteria of Pauline apostleship. They had become Christians even before Paul and they had suffered prison for their missionary activity. They probably were Hellenistic Jews who had become highly respected among the apostles and are fellow prisoners of Paul.

3. *Apostles of the Churches*

2 Cor 8:23 and Phil 2:25 mention "apostles of the churches," who appear to be most similar to the emissaries of the Jewish community.[10] They are the official messengers or delegates of the Christian churches of Macedonia (2 Cor 8:23) or of the church at Philippi (Phil 2:25); Paul recommends them highly. A woman appears to have had a similar role in the church at Cenchreae. In Rm 16:1 Phoebe is called the *diakonos* of the church at Cenchreae and she too is highly recommended by Paul. In NT Greek the title *diakonos* means not primarily "servant" or "deacon" but "herald" or official messenger.[11] The term, however, is almost never used for charitable service. 1 Cor 3:5, 9 indicates that Paul uses this term exchangeably with *synergos*[12] (i.e., missionary co-worker). Moreover, 2 Cor 11:13 documents that Paul uses the titles *apostolos* and *diakonos* interchangeably to address the same circle of persons. It can therefore be assumed that the *diakonos* title characterizes Phoebe as official messenger and missionary apostle of the church at Cenchreae. Since the *diakonos* title can be used interchangeably with the *apostolos* title she is characterized as fulfilling the function of an apostle of the Church. Like other missionaries and apostles she has received a letter of recommendation.

4. *The Lukan understanding of apostleship*

A very late stage in the development of the apostle-concept and function is found in the Lukan writings.[13] Luke not only identifies the apostles with the Twelve but also spells out criteria for apostleship. To become one of the twelve apostles it is necessary to have accompanied Jesus from his baptism to his ascension and to become a witness to his resurrection. According to Luke's traditions women have fulfilled these criteria and functions of apostleship. Women accompanied Jesus from Galilee to Jerusalem (Mk 15:40f.) and they were the first disciples to receive the resurrection message (Mk 16:7) and to have seen the Lord (Mt 28:9f.; Jn 20:18). Why then does Luke limit apostleship to men (Acts 1:21)? The answer might lie in his identification of the apostles with the Twelve. Luke was aware that women fulfilled the conditions for apostleship. However, he was also aware that according to tradition no women were members of the Twelve. Thus he felt compelled to give the women disciples a preeminent place equal to that of the Twelve (Lk 8:1-3), while not calling them apostles and deemphasizing their resurrection witness (24:11.34). It becomes apparent that Luke's theological redaction had to formulate maleness as an additional criterion for apostleship because of the peculiar Lukan understanding that the circle of the apostles was co-extensive with that of the Twelve. It is, however, extremely significant that in the Lukan writings the twelve apostles fade from the picture once the Gentile mission is under way. Moreover, Luke's theological conception of apostleship as limited to the Twelve has no historical foundation, since the Pauline letters indicate that the circle of apostles was much wider in early Christianity, and that even in Paul's time apostleship was not yet clearly defined and limited. Finally, later writings still know of apostles as itinerant missionaries (Rev 2:2; 18:20; Didache 11:6).

In summary: A careful study of the NT writings demonstrates that different types and understandings of apostleship were present in early Christianity. Whereas the Pauline writings attest to a wider circle of apostles, Luke considers the Twelve to be the apostles par excellence. The Pauline letters know of two types of apostles. Whereas the Jerusalem type bases its claim to apostleship upon a resurrection appearance of the risen Lord, the itinerant missionary type derives its claim from the success of missionary work. In connection with these different types of apostles the NT writers spell out the following criteria for apostleship.

1. Apostles must be witnesses of the resurrection.
2. Apostles must be witnesses to the life and ministry of Jesus.
3. Apostles must be sent to missionary work and exhibit the charisms necessary for this work.

In arguing with his opponents at Corinth and in Galatia, Paul stresses that on the one hand he experienced resurrection appearance and that on the other hand he was sent to do missionary work and has proven himself an outstanding missionary. The requirement of personal involvement with the earthly Jesus and his ministry seems not yet to have been a necessary criterion for apostleship in Paul's time, since in no way could Paul have fulfilled this criterion. The NT writings however indicate that women fulfilled all these criteria of apostleship. Women accompanied Jesus from Galilee to Jerusalem, they were the primary witnesses of the resurrection, and they were outstanding missionaries in the early Church. On biblical grounds it would be easier to prove that Paul was not entrusted with the "apostolic charge" than to demonstrate that women were excluded from apostleship.

Notes

1. For surveys of research cf. H. Mosbech, "Apostolos in the New Testament," *StTh*, Vol. 2 (1948), pp. 166-200; E.M. Kredel, "Der Apostelbegriff in der neueren Exegese," *ZKTh*, Vol. 78 (1956), pp. 169-193, 257-305; J. Roloff, *Apostolat, Verkündigung, Kirche* (Gütersloh: Mohn, 1965), pp. 9-37; R. Schnackenburg, "Apostles Before and During Paul's Time," in Gasque-Martin, *Apostolic History and the Gospels* (Grand Rapids: Eerdmans, 1970), pp. 287-303; R.E. Brown, *Priest and Bishop, Biblical Reflections* (New York: Paulist Press, 1970), pp. 47-86; C.K. Barrett, *The Signs of an Apostle* (Philadelphia: Fortress Press, 1972); J.A. Kirk, "Apostleship since Rengstorff," NTS, Vol. 21 (1975), pp. 249-264.

2. Cf. H. Greeven, "Propheten, Lehrer, Vorsteher bei Paulus," *ZNW*, Vol. 44 (1952/53), pp. 1-43; D. Georgi, *Die Gegner des Paulus im 2. Korintherbrief* (Neukirchen: Vluyn, 1964), pp. 42f.; R. Schnackenburg, "Apostles," p. 289.

3. K.H. Rengstorf, *TWNT*, Vol. I (1933), pp. 406-448 (=*TDNT* I, 407-447); L. Cerfaux, "Pour l'histoire du titre Apostolos dans le Nouveau Testament," *Rech SR*, Vol. 48 (1960), pp. 78-92 and J.A. Kirk.

4. On the basis of this text it should therefore not be argued that the NT writers give a secondary position to the appearance to a woman or to women and that women were not "official" witnesses of the resurrection. The distinction between "official" and "unofficial" witness to the resurrection appears to reflect our contemporary church institutions and to project our situation back into the first century.

5. According to the critical criteria of historical authenticity, women were the primary witnesses to the resurrection. The criterion of *distinctiveness* or *dissimilarity* maintains that those NT materials can be considered to be historically authentic that are *dissimilar* to well-known tendencies in Judaism or in early Christianity. In the Judaism of the time women probably were not admitted as official witnesses. Moreover, because of apologetic reasons the early church played down the Easter witness of the women disciples (cf. already Lk 24). The criterion of *distinctiveness* would indicate that the women's witness is probably historically authentic. Secondly, the criterion of *multiple attestation* also speaks for the historicity of the women's witness, since all four Gospels know that women disciples first received the message of the resurrection. This knowledge likewise can not be due to a widespread Church practice of the time. Finally, the criterion of *cohesiveness* supports the historicity of the women's witness, since this tradition about the

resurrection witness of women coheres with the information of the Gospels that in his itinerant ministry women disciples accompanied Jesus, contrary to the customs of the time.

6. The most prominent of the women must have been Mary of Magdala, since all four Gospels transmit her name while the names of the other women vary. The *Gospel of Thomas*, the *Gospel according to Mary* and the *Pistis Sophia* understand her leadership as co-equal to that of Peter, who sees her as a rival. The tradition calls her "apostle to the apostles." This title is accepted by the statement of the Pontifical Biblical Commission: Part III. In my writings I have consistently pointed out the importance of Mary of Magdala: cf. E. Schüssler, *Der vergessene Partner* (Düsseldorf: Patmos, 1964), pp. 57-59; E. Schüssler Fiorenza, "Feminist Theology as a Critical Theology of Liberation," in W. Burkhardt, ed., *Woman: New Dimensions* (New York: Paulist Press, 1977), pp. 48-50; "Die Rolle der Frau in der urchristlichen Bewegung," *Concilium*, Vol. 12 (1976), pp. 3-9.

7. Their self-understanding and ministry appears to have been patterned after the itinerant ministry of Jesus. Cf. G. Theissen, "Itinerant Radicalism. The Traditions of the Jesus Sayings from the Perspective of the Sociology of Literature," *Radical Religion Reader: The Bible and Liberation* (Berkeley, 1976), pp. 84-93.

8. Cf. G. Theissen, "Legitimation und Lebensunterhalt: Ein Beitrag zur Soziologie urchristlicher Missionäre," *NTS*, Vol. 21 (1975), pp. 192-221.

9. See essay by Bernadette Brooten on the woman apostle Junia, pp. 141-144.

10. Cf. Rengstorf, *op. cit.*

11. Cf. J. Gnilka, *Der Philipperbrief* (HThNT X, 3; Freiburg: Herder, 1968), p. 39.

12. See essay by Mary Ann Getty on *synergos*, pp. 176-182.

13. G. Klein, *Die Zwölf Apostel* (Göttingen: Vandenhoeck & Ruprecht, 1961), pp. 202ff. maintains that the apostleship of the Twelve had its origin in Lukan theology. J. Roloff, *op. cit.*, p. 232, argues that Luke used existing traditions to develop his theological concept.

15
"Junia . . . Outstanding among the Apostles" (Romans 16:7)[1]

Bernadette Brooten

"Greet Andronicus and Junia . . . who are outstanding among the apostles" (Romans 16:7): To be an apostle is something great. But to be outstanding among the apostles—just think what a wonderful song of praise that is! They were outstanding on the basis of their works and virtuous actions. Indeed, how great the wisdom of this woman must have been that she was even deemed worthy of the title of apostle.

John Chrysostom (344/54-407)[2]

Also notable is the case of Junias or Junio, placed in the rank of the apostles (Rom. 16, 7), with regard to whom one or another [exegete] raises the question of whether it is a man.

Pontifical Biblical Commission (1976)[3]

What a striking contrast! The exegesis of Romans 16:7 has practically reversed. Whereas for John Chrysostom the apostle addressed by Paul is a woman by the name of *Junia*, for almost all modern scholars it is a man, *Junias*, whom Paul is greeting. The Biblical Commission is quite right in saying that only "one or another" exegete questions the prevailing view that the person named is a man. Most Romans commentators do not seem to be even aware of the possibility that the person could be a woman, and virtually all modern biblical translations have *Junias* (m.) rather than *Junia* (f.).

It was not always this way. John Chrysostom was not alone in the ancient church in taking the name to be feminine. The earliest commentator on Romans 16:7, Origen of Alexandria (c. 185-253/54), took the name to be feminine (*Junia* or *Julia*, which is a textual variant),[4] as did Jerome (340/50-419/20),[5] Hatto of Vercelli (924-961),[6] Theophylact (c. 1050-c. 1108),[7] and Peter Abelard (1079-1142).[8] In fact, to the best of my knowledge, no commentator on the text until Aegidius of Rome (1245-1316) took the name to be masculine. Without commenting on his departure from previous commentators, Aegidius simply referred to the two persons mentioned in Romans 16:7 as "these honorable men" (*viri*).[9] Aegidius noted that there were two variant readings for the second name: *Juniam* and *Juliam* (accusative in the verse). He preferred the reading *Juliam* and took it to be masculine. Thus we see that even *Juliam*, which modern scholars would take to be clearly femi-

141

nine, has been considered masculine in the context of the title "apostle."

If Aegidius started the ball rolling, it really picked up momentum in the Reformation period. The commentary which Martin Luther heavily relied upon, that by Faber Stapulensis (Paris, 1512, p. 99b), took the accusative 'IOUNIAN to be *Junias* (m.). Luther's lecture on Romans (1515/1516: *Weimarer Ausgabe* 56, p. 150) followed Faber Stapulensis on this and other points. Through Luther the *Junias* interpretation was assured of a broad exposure for centuries to come. In each of the succeeding centuries the *Junias* hypothesis gained new adherents and the argument was expanded. To make the *Junias* interpretation more plausible, some commentators suggested that it was a "short form" of the Latin *Junianus, Junianius, Junilius* or even *Junius*. This "short form" hypothesis is the prevailing view in modern scholarship.

The proponents of the new *Junias* hypothesis were, however, by no means left unchallenged. In 1698, for example, Johannes Drusius (in the *Critici Sacri*, Amsterdam, 1698, Vol. VII, p. 930) patiently tried to remind his colleagues that *Junia* was the feminine counterpart of *Junius*, just as *Prisca* was of *Priscus*, and *Julia* was of *Julius*. Christian Wilhelm Bose, in his doctoral dissertation *Andronicum et Juniam* (Leipzig, 1742, p. 5), questioned that *Junia/s* is a short form of anything. If that be true, he pondered, then one might just as easily argue that *Andronicus* is a short form of *Andronicianus*! In our century, the most notable protester against the *Junias* hypothesis has been M.-J. Lagrange (Paris, 1916; sixth ed. 1950, p. 366). His reason is a conservative one: because the abbreviation *Junias* is unattested, it is "more prudent" to stick to the feminine *Junia*. Unlike many of his Protestant colleagues, Lagrange was aware of the Patristic exegesis on this point. Precisely because the Church Fathers took the name to be feminine, Catholic exegetes of the past were generally slower to accept the innovation of *Junias*. But by now commentators of all confessions take 'IOUNIAN to be *Junias*.

What reasons have commentators given for this change? The answer is simple: a woman could not have been an apostle. Because a woman could not have been an apostle, the woman who is here called apostle could not have been a woman.

What can a modern philologist say about *Junias*? Just this: it is unattested. To date not a single Latin or Greek inscription, not a single reference in ancient literature has been cited by any of the proponents of the *Junias* hypothesis. My own search for an attestation has also proved fruitless. This means that we do not have a single shred of evidence that the name *Junias* ever existed. Nor is it plausible to argue that it is just coincidental that *Junias* is unattested since the "long forms" *Junianus, Junianius, Junilius*, and *Junius* are common enough. It is true that Greek names could have abbreviated forms ending in *-as* (e.g., *Artemas* for *Artemidoros*); such names are called "hypocoristica" (terms of endearment or diminutives, e.g., Johnny for John, or Eddie for Edward). Latin hypocoristica, however, are usually formed by lengthening the name (e.g., *Priscilla* for *Prisca*) rather than by shortening it, as in Greek. The *Junias* hypothesis presupposes that Latin names were regularly abbreviated in the Greek fashion, which is not the case. The feminine *Junia*, by contrast, is a common name in both Greek and Latin inscriptions and literature. In short, literally all of the philological evidence points to the feminine *Junia*.

What does it mean that Junia and Andronicus were apostles? Was the apostolic charge not limited to the Twelve? New Testament usage varies on this point. Luke, for example, placed great emphasis on "the twelve apostles." In fact, with one exception (Acts 14:4, 14: both Paul and Barnabas are called "apostles"), Luke does not honor Paul with the title "apostle." Paul, on the other hand, never uses the term "the twelve apostles." He himself claimed to be an apostle, though he was not one of the Twelve, and he also called others, such as James the brother of the Lord (Galatians 1:19; cf. 1 Corinthians 15:7), "apostle." This does not mean that Paul used "apostle" in an unrestricted, loose sense. Precisely because of the seriousness with which he defends his own claim to apostleship (he says that he received his call from Christ himself: Galatians 1:1, 11f.; 1 Corinthians 9:1), we must assume that he recognized others as apostles only when he was convinced that their own apostolic charge had also come from the risen Lord (cf. 1 Corinthians 15; 7: the risen Lord was seen by all the apostles). For Paul the category "apostle" was perhaps of even greater import than for other New Testament writers, because it concerned authority in the church of his own day and did not refer to a closed circle of persons from the past, i.e., a restricted number which could not be repeated.

From this and from Paul's description of his own apostolic work in his letters, we can assume that the apostles Junia and Andronicus were persons of great authority in the early Christian community, that they were probably missionaries and founders of churches, and that, just as with Paul, their apostleship had begun with a vision of the risen Lord and the charge to become apostles of Christ.

In light of Romans 16:7 then, the assertion that "Jesus did not entrust the apostolic charge to women" must be revised. The implications for women priests should be self-evident. If the first century Junia could be an apostle, it is hard to see how her twentieth century counterpart should not be allowed to become even a priest.

Notes

1. The following comments summarize briefly the results of a comprehensive study of the history of interpretation of Romans 16:7 and of the inscriptional evidence for the name IOUNIAN. The reader interested in more complete documentation is referred to that study, which will be published in the near future.

2. *In Epistolam ad Romanos*, Homilia 31, 2 (J.P. Migne, *Patrologiae cursus completus, series Graeca* [=PG] 60, 669f.).

3. "Can Women Be Priests?" (Report of the Pontifical Biblical Commission), see below, p. 344.

4. *Commentaria in Epistolam ad Romanos* 10, 26 (PG 14, 1281B); 10, 39 (PG 14, 1289A). The text printed in Migne has *Junia* emended to *Junias*, but the manuscripts have *Junia* or *Julia*.

5. *Liber Interpretationis Hebraicorum Nominum* 72, 15 (J.P. Migne, *Patrologiae cursus completus, series Latina* [= PL] 23, 895).

6. *In Epistolam ad Romanos* 16, 7 (PL 134, 282A).

7. *Expositio In Epistolam ad Romanos* 114 (PG 124, 552D).

8. *Expositio in Epistolam ad Romanos* 5 (PL 178, 973C).

9. *Opera Exegetica. Opuscula I* (Facsimile reprint of the Rome, 1554/55 edition: Frankfurt, 1968), p. 97.

16
Innocent III and the Keys to the Kingdom of Heaven

E. Ann Matter

It should be noted first of all that this portion of the Declaration is not an argument based on Scripture, nor does it have much to do with the Blessed Virgin Mary. There is, of course, a biblical passage to which Innocent III here alludes: Matthew 16:19, the promise of the keys to the kingdom of heaven and the power of binding and loosing to Simon Peter, the disciple who first witnessed that Jesus was "the Christ, the Son of the Living God." But any reference in this verse to the priesthood as a whole is derivative—in the opinion of tradition—from the institution of the papacy through that one disciple, Peter.

The power of the Church in general, and of the papacy in particular, was a special concern of this thirteenth century occupant of the Holy See. The power was clearly understood to be political and temporal as well as spiritual and eternal, following Christ's promise "whatever you bind on earth shall be bound in heaven, and whatever you loose on earth shall be loosed in heaven." As one modern historian has pointed out, the pontificate of Innocent III stands at the apex of the quest for secular power among the popes of the medieval Church. Of a series of popes who claimed such power, "Innocent III alone made good the claim. He not only ruled the Church, but he was a greater force in the secular politics of Europe than either emperor or national king."[1]

But without any doubt Innocent III ruled the Church as well. In fact, the quotation in the Declaration is the concluding sentence of a letter written to two Spanish bishops regarding the behavior of abbesses in their region:

> Recently certain news has been intimated to us, about which we marvel greatly, that abbesses, namely those situated in the dioceses of Burgos and Palencia, give blessings to their own nuns, and they also hear confessions of sins, and, reading the Gospel, they presume to preach in public. This thing is inharmonious as well as absurd, and not to be tolerated by us. For that reason, by means of our discretion from apostolic writing, we order that it be done no longer, and by apostolic authority to check it more firmly, for, although the Blessed Virgin Mary surpassed in dignity and in excellence all the Apostles, nevertheless, it was not to her but to them that the Lord entrusted the keys to the kingdom of heaven.[2]

In short, Pope Innocent II is in this letter exercising the powers of binding and loosing to deny the privileges of preaching, reading the Gospel, hearing confession, and giving the blessing to abbesses in a certain area of Spain. An immediate question arises: what is the historical context of this prohibition?

The letter seems to be directed to a situation in which women were *already* exercising a significant degree of authority in their communities and beyond. The monastery for which this warning was evidently intended was Las Huelgas, a Cistercian house of women which was founded with royal and papal sanction, and which had a good deal of power. In fact, the abbess of Las Huelgas exercised civil jurisdiction over sixty-four villages and quasi-episcopal authority in a wide variety of circumstances.[3]

The difficulty an historian must have with Innocent III's claim that such practices are "inharmonious as well as absurd" centers around the fact (admitted by scholars on both sides of the debate about the ordination of women) that certain jurisdictional and liturgical roles were held by abbesses in more than one time and place in the medieval Church.[4] The Commentary on the Declaration admits the existence of such a tradition very grudgingly, claiming that "these customs have been more or less reproved by the Holy See at different periods."[5] This is certainly not universally true. The order of Fontevrault, founded in 1101 as a community of nuns and canons ruled by the women, was given the honor of a papal dedication for its church.[6] In an earlier period, the Venerable Bede goes into great detail in recounting the sanctity of two great contemporary English abbesses, Etheldreda and Hilda. Etheldreda is listed at Ely, where she was abbess, as the first bishop of the cathedral; Hilda presided over the Synod of Whitby in 664, at which the English church decided to follow Roman rather than Irish customs of liturgy and monastic order. Her right in this matter has not been questioned by the Holy See. Hilda's monastic community included men as well as women.[7]

It is also important to note that reading the Gospel and preaching, two of the duties which Innocent III was so desirous of taking away from these abbesses, were in the early Church assigned to deacons. Again, it is not totally novel for women to be performing some of these diaconal duties. In fact, a good deal of scholarly effort in recent years has gone into the recovery of the outlines of the position of women deacons who are mentioned in the New Testament and by the Fathers.[8] This order of deaconesses is far from a recreation of archaic church discipline. Although the order *per se* seems to have merged with the mainline monastic tradition for women by the eighth century, claims for special honor and responsibility to be given to women in the category of "widows" (once a term for deaconesses; in the Middle Ages, usually older women who entered the religious life after the death of husband or dissolution of a marriage and often became abbesses) are evident in both medieval theology and liturgy.[9]

The pontificate of Innocent III marks a significant point for the future of women in monasticism. From the mid-twelfth century on, the places available to women in the mainline monastic houses became fewer, and the attitudes of the major orders towards nuns deteriorated rapidly, leading for one thing to the flowering of a less hierarchical and hierarchically-controlled form of religious life for women, the Beguines.[10]

So, the intentions of Innocent III in this letter, when considered historically, can be seen to arise from disciplinary rather than theological concerns, and from a particular disciplinary question with a long history in the Church, one which was answered in a variety of ways in a variety of periods.

Still, Innocent III's answer is the one held up by our twentieth-century canon lawyers and theologians, who point to the prolific citation of this letter in the classical texts of canon law as evidence of its importance.[11] We must, therefore, examine this tradition.

The references cited in the Declaration itself give us our most important clues: the letter of Innocent III is quoted in its entirety in the *Decretals* of Pope Gregory IX, under the heading "An abbess cannot bless monastics, hear confessions, and preach in public."[12] The *glossa ordinaria* for this passage (the standard commentary which accompanied the text in the medieval manuscript tradition) refers the reader to another passage of the *Decretals* for the reason for these prohibitions.

This passage (also cited in the notes to the Declaration) is a letter of Pope Honorius III, dated 1222, forbidding abbesses in Germany to excommunicate their subject nuns and clerics.[13] The *glossa ordinaria* on this passage is extremely rich. Beyond the standard fleshing out of the argument, it offers a broad commentary on the role of women with regard to law. Crucial to this interpretation and to the subsequent use of this text is the statement that women do not have legal right of jurisdiction. Abbesses, therefore, even though they must preside over their own communities, do so with power granted from the chapter (the regular meeting of all the abbesses and prioresses of the order). They do not, therefore, have full legal powers, as men do.[14] Within the monastic world proper, we should note that the same prohibitions were extended here to *monks* as well as nuns, as the abbots also drew their power of jurisdiction from the chapter. To some extent, then, the issue can be seen in monastic/clerical terms as easily as in male/female terms.[15]

Further, the gloss links the letters of Innocent III and Honorius III, and offers an over-arching rationale for such prohibitions: "a woman should not have such power, since she is not made in the image of God, but man is the image and glory and God, and the woman should be subject to the man, and should be as his handmaid."[16] The reader is then referred to the major text of classical canon law, the *Decretum* of Gratian, which makes very clear the connection between the legal role of women and their inherent incompleteness. In a chapter entitled "There is no power in woman, but in all things she is under the dominion of man," Gratian quotes from Saint Ambrose to the effect that women are not to be allowed to teach, to give witness, to swear oaths, or to judge. This is because they have no authority (*auctoritas*), but must be under the rule of the man.[17]

The next few chapters of the *Decretum* give the case its biblical underpinnings: Adam was deceived by Eve, therefore women should cover their heads, since they are not in the image of God.[18] But the use of the word *auctoritas*, and the reference in the gloss to civil law,[19] give witness to another of Ambrose's sources here: the legal traditions of the late Roman Empire, codified in the *Corpus Iuris Civilis* of the Emperor Justinian. Here, women are stripped of all voice in legal matters, even to the point of being forbidden to legally represent the rights of their children before the court.[20]

As Joan Range has pointed out, the role of Gratian and the other canonists is essential to the tradition of denying orders to women.[21] She shows how his response to developing tradition was crystallized as the true voice of that tradition. The same can be said for the canonists' use of Ambrose (steeped as he was in Roman Law), and of Innocent III (who was responding to a particular situation at Las Huelgas)—these statements came to be regarded as normative, but at each step of the tradition, as now, there were dissenting voices within the Church.

Of course, a difference remains between these sources and modern theologians in the relationship of the prescribed place of women in the Church to the acknowledged view of the nature of women. As we have seen, the medieval theologians and canonists are firmly rooted in a biblical teaching that woman is not in God's image and in a convenient Roman legal tradition that denies women all voice. Our contemporary Sacred Congregation for the Doctrine of the Faith can hardly claim such presuppositions with any credibility.

Perhaps the greatest irony of all is the place of the Blessed Virgin Mary in this associative web. Perhaps one would better say her non-place—the concerns of Innocent III, Gregory IX, and Gratian were to do with temporal rather than spiritual power. Clearly, Christ gave no temporal power *per se* to his mother. But modern Catholic biblical scholarship is increasingly ready to admit that neither did he intend to give such temporal power to his disciples, nor to link such power to the celebration of the Eucharist.[22] Furthermore, if the Virgin *is* to represent woman's role in the Church as Christ does man's role, then surely no theological argument can be made for the exclusion of women on the basis of the Fall. If Christ is the new Adam, must not his mother be the *New* Eve? This is, in any case, the opinion of the Fathers, who from the time of Irenaeus (second century) expanded the Pauline description of Christ as the New Man ("For as by a man came death, by a man has come also the resurrection of the dead" 1 Corinthians 15:21) to include Mary, the mother of that salvation, as the New Woman who undid the first disobedience of Eve through her obedience.[23] By the fifth century, Mary, the mother of the Savior, was held to be the *Theotokos*—the God-bearer. At the council of Ephess in 431, and again at Chalcedon in 451, the Nestorian party was anathematized for attempting to down-play the role of that one woman in the drama of redemption.[24] If Mary is, in the words of the Declaration, "the example of Christ's will in this [priestly] domain," how can her example be used as the witness to women's sacramental inferiority?

The development of Marian piety in the Middle Ages, especially between the period of Charlemagne and the High Middle Ages, is acknowledged by scholars to be partly in response to the world in which the Church found itself.[25] It is recognized, then, that the cult of the Blessed Virgin Mary can only be properly seen through the parallel development of Christology and theology of the Eucharist. The cult of the mother is inextricably bound to that of her Son, each developing in response to the changing dynamic of revelation and tradition. Believers (even those who assent to the Marian implications of the Declaration) understand these changes as God working through history in a dialectic between the needs and the historical reality of the Christian community. Obviously, the historical reality and the needs change in relation to one another—John Henry Cardinal Newman described this process in a throughly Roman Catholic way.[26] The most disappointing aspects of the Declaration are its tone-deafness to the tension between the needs and the history of the Church in the twentieth century, and its implication that any desire for growth in the Church (even along the lines Newman described so well a century ago) should be taken only as disobedience. No place is left for loving critics of the *status quo*; no possibility is considered that such criticism may be given in the name of Christ.

The situation is complicated and the answers are not obvious. Reinstating the jurisdiction of the abbess of Las Huelgas would not necessarily constitute a step towards the ordination of women. No critic of the use of the letter of Innocent III in the Declaration could seriously advocate such an anachronism as a panacea for our dilemma. But neither must modern theologians base their estimation of the role of women in the Church on concern for ecclesiastical power and theories of human nature which are no longer accepted by the people of God who are the Church. In this regard, it is far easier to admit the canonists' use of the letter of Innocent III than it is to accept the Declaration's dependence on a questionable solution to an outdated problem of monastic discipline and privilege.

Notes

1. M. Deanesly, *A History of the Medieval Church 590-1500* (London: Methuen, 9th ed., 1972), p. 140, at the beginning of a chapter about Innocent III. J. A. Range also points to the Investiture Contest as an important factor in Gratian's synthesis: "Legal Exclusion of Women From Church Office," *The Jurist*, Vol. 34 (1974), p. 119.

2. Epistle 187 (11 December, 1210) *PL* 216: 356. Quoted in full in the *Decretals* of Gregory IX, *Corpus Iuris Canonici* Lib. V, tit. 38, *De Poenitent.* ch. 10, "Nova" ed. J. Friedberg (Leipzig: Bernhard Tauchnitz, 1928), Vol. 2, coll. 886-887.

3. That the letter of Innocent III was meant for Las Huelgas is suggested by the Commentary, par. 35., where the secular power of the abbess of Las Huelgas is mentioned. Las Huelgas was founded by Alfonso VIII of Castille and his wife Leonora in 1187. The jurisdiction of the abbess was confirmed by Pope Urban VIII. In spite of such concerns as that of Innocent

150 Commentaries

III, the jurisdiction of the abbess was not suspended until 1873, when Pope Pius IX voided all exempt jurisdictions in Spain. See J. M. Escrivá, *La abadesa de Las Huelgas* (Madrid: Editorial Luz, 1944).

4. M. de Fontette, *Les religieuses à l'age classique du droit canon* (Paris: J. Vrin, 1967) gives a discussion of the role of abbesses in six orders of the High Middle Ages. The best collection of data on the positions and functions of abbesses in medieval monasticism as a whole is J. Morris, *The Lady Was A Bishop* (New York: Macmillan, 1973), although the conclusions reached by this work are not always historically satisfactory. See also Range, pp. 122-127.

5. Commentary, par. 35.

6. By Pope Callistus in 1119. See L. Cottineau, *Répertoire topo-bibliographique des abbayes et prieurés* (Macon: Protat frères, 1939), Vol. I, pp. 1185-1188, and R. Niderst, *Robert d'Arbrissel et les origines de l'ordre de Fontevrault* (Rodez: G. Subervieu, 1952).

7. For Etheldreda, see Bede, *Ecclesiastical History of the English People*, Vol. IV, pp. 19-20 and C. W. Stubbs, *Historical Memorials of Ely Cathedral* (New York: C. Scribner's Sons, 1897), frontispiece, and pp. xvii, 70-87. For Hilda, see Bede, Vol. III, p. 25, and Vol. IV, pp. 23-24.

8. On women as deacons, see Sr. A.M. McGrath, *Women and the Church* (New York: Doubleday, 1972), and the impressive recent work by I. Raming, *The Exclusion of Women from the Priesthood: Divine Law or Sex Discrimination?* trans. N. R. Adams, with a preface by A. and L. Swidler (Metuchen, New Jersey: Scarecrow Press, 1976).

9. The great care with which Peter Abelard discussed the proximity of the role of abbess to the ancient order of deaconesses is discussed by M. McLaughlin, "Abelard and the Dignity of Women: Twelfth-Century 'Feminism' in Theory and Practice," *Pierre Abélard, Pierre Le Vénérable* (Abbaye de Cluny, 1972), pp. 288-334. Special rituals of the reception of widows (as opposed to virgins) into the cloister echo this heritage; see R. Metz, *La consécration des vièrges dans l'eglise romaine* (Strasbourg: Bibliothèque de l'Institut de Droit Canonique, 1954), p. 157. One such ordo, found in Paris, B.N. latin 2833, was analysed in my paper "A Twelfth-Century *Ordo* for the Veiling of Widows," presented at the Third Berkshire Conference, June, 1976.

10. On the sudden rise of the Beguines, see B. Bolton, "Mulieres Sanctae," in *Women in Medieval Society*, ed. S. M. Stuard (Philadelphia: University of Pennsylvania Press, 1976), pp. 141-158. For the resulting legislation of the mainline orders, see Fontette, *passim*. By the thirteenth century, the Cistercians and the Premonstratensians had been closed to women.

11. Declaration, par. 13, n. 11, cites Greory IX, the gloss on Gratian, Thomas Aquinas, and the Pseudo-Albert. As the Commentary (par. 15) places special emphasis on the role of the canonists and canon lawyers in transmitting this letter, I will concentrate on Gregory IX, Gratian and their glossators. I am indebted to Van Edwards, of the University of Pennsylvania, for his help in dealing with the canon law material.

12. Gregory IX, *Decretals* Lib. 5, tit. 38, *De Poenitent.* Ch. 10, "Nova" *Corpus Iuris Canonici*, ed. Friedberg, vol. 2, coll. 886-887; Bernard of Parma, *Glossa in Decretal.*, Lib. I tit. 38, ch. 10, ed. A. Nardi (Lyons: Huegeton et Barbier, 1671), vol. 2, col. 1869.

13. Gregory IX, *Decretals*, Lib. I, tit. 33, *De Maioritate et Obed.* c. 12,

"Dilecta," ed. Friedberg, vol. 2, col. 201, to the abbesses of the diocese of Halberstadt.

14. "Dicas quod abbatissa habet iurisdictionem talem qualem, non ita plenam, sicut vir habet," Bernard of Parma, *Glossa* Lib. I, tit. 33, Cap. 12, "Dilecta," no. C, "Iurisdictione," ed. Nardi, vol. 2, col. 431.

15. *Ibid.*, col. 431.

16. *Ibid.*, col. 432.

17. Gratian, *Decretum*, Causa 33, quaest. 5, ch. 17, "Nulla est," *Corpus Iuris Canonici*, ed. Friedberg, vol. 1, col. 1255.

18. *Ibid.*, ch. 18, 19, ed. Friedberg, vol. 1, col. 1255.

19. Joannes Teutonicus and Bartholomew of Brescia, *Glossa in Decret.*, Causa 33, quaest. 5, ch. 17, "Nulla est," no. C, "Nunc testis": "in causa criminali, nisi in illis casibus in quibus infames admittuntur, nec in testamento." ed. Nardi, vol. 1, col. 1827.

20. *Corpus Iuris Civilis, Codex Iustinianus*, Code 2, tite. 12, law 18, ed. P. Kruegen (Berlin: Weidmann, 1954), p. 104.

21. Range, p. 126.

22. Biblical Commission Report, part II.

23. Irenaeus of Lyons, *Proof of the Apostolic Preaching*, 33. See the references in n. 25 below for the medieval development of this image and its importance for the developing cult of the Blessed Virgin Mary.

24. Denzinger, *Enchiridion Symbolorum*, 30th ed. (Freiburg: Herder, 1955), p. 143.

25. For further information on the cult of Mary, see H. Graef, *Mary: A History of Doctrine and Devotion* (London: Sheed and Ward, 1963); and L. Scheffczyk, *Das Mariengeheimnis in Frömmigkeit und Lehre der Karolingerzeit* (Leipzig: St. Benno-Verlag, 1959). The recent book by M. Warner, *Alone of All Her Sex: The Myth and Cult of the Virgin Mary* (New York: Alfred A. Knopf, 1976) also has much interesting information, although its radical-feminist bias is evident throughout.

26. J. H. Newman, *An Essay on the Development of Christian Doctrine*, edition of 1878. (New York: Doubleday, 1960), especially Chapter I, "The Development of Ideas," and Chapter VIII, "Assimilative Power."

17
Women and the Apostolic Community

Madeleine I. Boucher

The Declaration introduces the section on the apostolic age, the first generation of Christians, with this sentence: "The apostolic community remained faithful to the attitude of Jesus towards women." The statement makes two points. It refers back to the Declaration's earlier argument that Jesus, who broke through cultural boundaries by his positive attitude toward women, nevertheless showed by choosing only men for membership in the Twelve that he "willed" to exclude women from ordination. It also implies that the apostles consciously intended to follow in their teaching and practice what they understood to be the mind of Jesus regarding the place of women in the Church. Neither of these assertions can be derived from the New Testament. Both stages of the argument read far more into the biblical passages than can be learned from them by careful historical-critical analysis. We have here an example of eisegesis, not exegesis—of reading into, not out of the text.

The line of argument of the Declaration requires that a proper response begin by stating what might seem obvious, that Jesus was a first-century Palestinian Jew who was by and large bound by both the religious and the social limitations of that historical situation. He attended the synagogue, regarded the Temple as the center of Jewish worship, understood the Scriptures as expressing God's will, adopted as his own the eschatological perspective current at the time, that is, the view that the end of history was near and that a new era, the reign of God, would soon be inaugurated. He also lived for the most part within the accepted social norms of his culture.

Jesus dared to shatter these limitations in one respect: he sharply criticized the repressive legalism of the Jewish authorities, especially the scribes and the Pharisees and Sadducees. The Gospels tell us that their system could not break out of a sterile ritual to serve the sick (Mk 2:1-12; 3:1-6), the sinners (Mk 2:15-17), the hungry (Mk 2:23-28), even one's father and mother (Mk 7:9-13). Because of this, according to Mark, Jesus leveled at them the accusation, "You have a fine way of rejecting the commandment of God, in order to keep your tradition!" (Mk 7:9). His teaching placed Jesus in line with the great Israelite prophets, who spoke out against a mere external fulfillment of ceremonial commandments that was not based on justice and mercy (Am 5:21-27; Hos 6:6; Isa 1:11-17; 58; Jer 7:21-26). Jesus' message concerning the requirements of the law was to stress the ethical over against the cultic-ritual. He taught above all the unsurpassed importance of the double commandment to love God and neighbor (Mk 12:28-34).

It is in this context that Jesus' attitude toward women is to be interpreted. He disregarded whatever conventions might have interfered with his ministering to any class of people. He worked miracles for women (Mk 1:29-31; 7:24-30) and accepted them as friends and disciples (see Mk 15:40-41, which says that women followed Jesus in Galilee and on the way to Jerusalem). Jesus preached and worked among the poor, the outcast, the weak. He violated rabbinic regulations in this as in other matters (the Sabbath, ritual cleanliness, food laws). It is essential to understand that Jesus was not carrying out a program to bring about social equality by these deeds. Jesus' role was as the agent of eschatological redemption; his mission was to bring to the simple people of the land—to all classes, bar none—God's final forgiveness and salvation.

Jesus remained within the boundaries of the social mores of his time. It is for this reason that he chose only men for the Twelve, the future rulers of Israel in the new age. Jesus acted according to the social norm he knew, that positions of authority were reserved to men. To say that he "willed" thereby to exclude women from an ordained ministry in the Church that was to develop after his death and resurrection is to attribute more to Jesus than the evidence of the Gospels allows.

The early Church, apostolic and post-apostolic, can be described in much the same way, as we know from the epistles and the Acts of the Apostles. There are no texts which address the specific subject of women's ordination (a question which no doubt did not arise in the earliest Church), but there are passages which shed some light on women's status in general in the New Testament period. Women enjoyed full membership in the Church. They taught and took part in the spread of Christianity (Phil 4:2; Rom 16:3-4; Acts 18:24-26). They could prophesy at worship (1 Cor 11:5). One woman, a co-worker of Paul, was called a deacon (Rom 16:1-2). Still, positions of authority in the churches seem to have been held exclusively by men in both the Jewish and Hellenistic environments.

New Testament texts that speak explicitly on the role of women give us a qualified picture. Paul stated that "in Christ there is neither Jew nor Greek, there is neither slave nor free, there is neither male nor female" (Gal 3:28), teaching that in the "new creation" national, social, and sexual barriers were transcended. He enjoined woman's subordination in 1 Corinthians, but then toned down its absoluteness with the addition: "Nevertheless, in the Lord woman is not independent of man nor man of woman; for as woman was made from man, so man is now born of woman. And all things are from God" (1 Cor 11:11-12). Similarly the author of 1 Peter, after telling wives to be subject to their husbands, concluded by referring to the two as "joint heirs of the grace of life" (1 Pet 3:7). What this means is that the early Christians held a concept of equality *coram Deo,* before God.

The early Church did not, however, feel any compulsion to implement this religious equality in social structures. In marriage, wives were to be subject to their husbands (Col 3:18; 1 Pet 3:1-6; Tit 2:4-5; Eph 5:22-24). In the congregation, women must wear veils when praying or prophesying (1 Cor

11:3-6) and must remain silent (1 Cor 14:33-35, probably an addition by a later hand; 1 Tim 2:11-15), because they were subordinate. It is clear that these Christian writers (perhaps like their Jewish predecessors) maintained a dichotomy between the religious and social domains, and had no difficulty in holding together the recognition of equality before God and the practice of inequality in society.

The first Christians, like Jesus, hardly envisioned a program to change the established social structure. For Paul and the other apostles slavery was a legitimate institution. The subordination of woman was taken for granted as part of the created order. Even had their cultural background not been a limitation, the apostles would scarcely have thought in terms of social reform because of their belief that the end of the world was fast approaching. "The appointed time has grown very short," Paul reminded the Corinthians (1 Cor 7:29). In view of this he told these converts, Jews and Gentiles, slaves and freedmen, to remain in their present state of life: "Every one should remain in the state in which he was called" (1 Cor 7:20). It is evident from this passage that Paul did not preach social revolution. It is also evident that he saw a dichotomy between one's social state and life in Christ, for he said that the slave is "a freedman of the Lord" and the freedman "a slave of Christ" (1 Cor 7:22).

Paul did, however, call for one change of great consequence: this was the admission of Gentiles into the Church without the imposition of the Mosaic law (especially circumcision and dietary prescriptions). Just as Jesus' concern was to cut through legalism to the will of God, so Paul's desire was to win membership for Gentiles, law-free, in the Church. This is probably the real thrust of Gal 3:28, and of the other passages where Paul employs the pairs Jew/Greek and slave/free (1 Cor 12:13; Col 3:11): persons of all stations in life can be brought together in the Church. The statement is a baptismal-ecclesial one, and Paul is speaking not so much of equality as of *unity* in the Church: "we were all baptized into one body" (1 Cor 12:13; cf. Gal 3:28). Yet the revolutionary character of Paul's position can hardly be overestimated. He challenged centuries of tradition based on the Scriptures, and indeed the position of the first church in Jerusalem and the Twelve, in declaring the Mosaic law null and void.

The epistolary literature does not provide any theoretical discussion of either slavery or the role of women. Such references as there are to either are brief and directed to specific and limited situations. At 1 Cor 11:2-16, for example, in telling the women to wear veils Paul is simply instructing them to act with decorum and in conformity with social conventions so that the new converts will not appear conspicuous and eccentric in the eyes of the world. If the apostles did not call for the abolition of slavery or woman's subordination, neither did they set down social principles to be permanently normative. There is here no blueprint for society in an on-going history.

It is important to inquire into the rationale which the New Testament writers give for their views on women. *Nowhere in any epistle does the author give as the ground for the subordination of woman the will of Jesus.* This is all the more striking since Paul cites a command of the Lord in connection with several other issues, one of which is divorce (1 Cor 7:10, 25; 9:14; 11:23, 25; 14:37). Had his teaching on women come from Jesus, he would undoubtedly have said so. There is no evidence that the apostolic community knew of any tradition about the "will" of Jesus in this regard.

When exhorting women to behave in a submissive manner, the New Testament writers sometimes appealed simply to what was fitting (Col 3:18) or customary in the churches (1 Cor 11:16) or "natural" (1 Cor 11:14). The only text where Paul attempted to give his statement on women's subjection a *theological* grounding is 1 Cor 11:8-9, and there it is not the teaching of Jesus to which he appealed; it is the notion that woman is subordinate in the order of creation, an idea which he derived (correctly or incorrectly) from the second creation account (Gen 2:4-3:24). (The same argument appears in 1 Tim 2:13-14; cf. 1 Cor 14:34.) Any attempt to put forward the New Testament texts on women's subjection as normative will therefore have to deal with that notion. The question cannot be evaded: Can the idea that woman is subordinate in the created order still be entertained as serious and valid? In light of the empirical evidence of women's equality in so many areas of achievement, it is extremely doubtful that we can continue to take that view as "revelation"; the evidence fairly compels us to attribute it to the cultural limitations of the biblical writers.

New questions are asked by each generation from its own perspective. History, despite the apostles' expectation of the imminent end, goes on. Social issues have arisen which they did not foresee. We, unlike the ancients, simply cannot regard as compatible a belief in equality before God on the one hand and the practice of inequality in Church and society on the other. The Bible does not fail to give us pointers toward solutions to these problems. What we *can* know about the intention of Jesus and Paul is that both taught the centrality of love of God and neighbor and freedom from convention, tradition, law. It is this ethos that turns out to be sound and enduring in Christianity. The ultimate question is whether the Church's practice of keeping women in a second-class status can any longer be reconciled with such basic ethical guidelines as the principle of love and liberation from the constraints of tradition.

18
Peter's Pentecost Sermon: A Limitation on Who May Minister . . . ?

Pheme Perkins

Methodological Prolegomenon

When he faced the question of how Scripture was to be used in theological arguments, St. Thomas Aquinas argued that the true sense of Scripture, *quem auctor intendit*, is the literal sense, not the spiritual.[1] He goes on to insist that nothing necessary for salvation is contained *only* in the spiritual sense: *nihil sub spirituali sensu continetur fidei necessarium quod scriptura per litteralem sensum alicubi manifeste non tradit.*[2] In short, the *intentio auctoris* is to be discovered through literal interpretation of Scripture and is the controlling norm for theological use of Scripture.[3]

From a modern, literary perspective, E. Hirsch argues that the intention of the author is the only hermeneutical principle which can give us the meaning of any text. Unless we agree that the author's intention controls the meaning of a text, interpretation is subject to the individual whims and peculiarities of the various modern "relativisms."[4] The only reliable way of arriving at an author's meaning is to do the kind of patient, historical-critical and literary analysis which has characterized the best modern biblical scholarship. Hirsch points out that our clues to an author's intention are found in the use made of the linguistic and literary conventions of that time.[5] One cannot include unconscious or socio-cultural motivations as part of an author's meaning if there is no evidence in the work that he or she was aware of them.[6] These principles apply to biblical interpretation as much as to that of any other text. Any claim to present the literal—and hence theologically normative—meaning of Scripture must meet them.

The Declaration's Use of Acts 2:14

The Declaration refers to Acts 2:14 as evidence that ministerial priesthood should be restricted to men: "the proclamation of the fulfillment of the prophecies in Jesus was made only by Peter and the Eleven (Acts 2:14)."[7] It implies that the intent of Luke is to limit proclamation to men. But the criteria for the use of Scripture in theological argument require that one show that such a limitation is the conscious intent of the author. Unconscious assumptions do not qualify. A very literal reading of Acts 2:14 would hardly give such an impression. One might argue that since Peter is the only one of

156

the Twelve to speak, he alone can authorize proclamation. Or one might claim that Luke mentions the other Eleven because he does not wish to exclude them. In either case, the rest of Acts shows such an interpretation to be a dubious reading of Luke's intent. The Twelve and those directly commissioned by them are not the only ones to take up proclamation, as the cases of Barnabas, Paul and their many associates show. Although Paul does not belong to the Twelve, his ministry is just as legitimate as theirs.

Commentators have found it impossible to identify from Acts the basis for those who succeeded to Peter's tasks within the Jerusalem church.[8] That difficulty suggests that Luke did not intend to address himself to the question of ministerial succession. Rather—as all exegetes recognize—he focuses on Peter and Paul as the key figures in the divinely ordained spread of Christianity from Jerusalem to Rome.[9] The Twelve have a special eschatological role corresponding to the twelve patriarchs. No one succeeds to that office.[10] In Acts 2:14, Luke is simply presenting Peter as spokesman and preacher in the Jerusalem church.[11] Nothing is implied about ministerial succession or fitness for ministerial office. Nor does the passage place limits on who may preach the gospel, as the later descriptions of Barnabas and Paul make clear.

Conclusion

We can only deplore such lax methodology in an important document. St. Thomas is surely right to insist that theologians respect the intent of the sacred author. Luke did not intend to settle questions of ministerial succession. Indeed, the Biblical Commission report amply demonstrates the difficulties inherent in any claim that the New Testament can be invoked to decide the issue. It should be clear that just as one cannot presume that an author who does not address the question would be against the admission of women to the ministerial priesthood, so one cannot take the author's silence to imply consent. What the lack of clear biblical evidence does imply—as Aquinas has made clear—is that the issue does not involve "truth necessary for salvation." It is open for reflection and revision as the Spirit may direct the Church.

Notes

1. *S.T.* I^a 1, 10.
2. *S.T.* I^a 1, 10 ad 1.
3. See the discussion of Aquinas in M.D. Chenu, *Toward Understanding St. Thomas* (Chicago: Regnery, 1964), pp. 153f.; P. E. Persson, *Sacra Doctrina: Reason and Revelation in Aquinas* (Philadelphia: Fortress Press, 1970), pp. 41-90; B. Smalley, *Study of the Bible in the Middle Ages* (Notre Dame: University of Notre Dame, 1964), pp. 236-42.
4. See E. D. Hirsch, *Validity in Interpretation* (New Haven: Yale, 1967), pp. 1-31; *idem, The Aims of Interpretation* (Chicago: University of Chicago, 1976), pp. 74-92.

5. Hirsch, *Validity*, pp. 68-126.

6. *Ibid.*, pp. 51-61.

7. Declaration, par. 15.

8. See R. Brown, K. Donfried, & J. Reumann, eds., *Peter in the New Testament* (New York: Augsburg/Paulist, 1973), pp. 55f.

9. *Ibid.*, pp. 40-54.

10. *Ibid.*, p. 40, n. 91.

11. *Ibid.*, p. 41.

19
The Ministry of Women in the Apostolic Generation

Adela Yarbro Collins

Taking the literary context into account, the argument of the opening sentences of the Declaration's paragraph sixteen may be restated as follows: In the apostolic mission to the Gentiles, two factors were conducive to the introduction of the practice of ordaining women: (1) the decision that Mosaic practices were not necessarily binding and (2) the contemporary movement in Greco-Roman civilization for the advancement of women; since the apostles did not ordain women in spite of these two factors, they must have explicitly considered the possibility of ordaining women and rejected it in conscious conformity to what they believed was the will of Jesus Christ on the matter. This argument is not persuasive for two basic reasons. First of all, it ignores a number of historical and exegetical problems which bear directly on the validity of the argument. One such problem is whether the concept "ordination" is an appropriate category for the thought and practice of the apostolic generation. Second, it proposes inadequate justification for its position that the practice of the apostolic generation ought to be normative for the Church today. The reason given is that the leaders of this generation were conforming their practice to the will of Christ. Conformity to the will of Christ is never stated, however, in the passages to which the Declaration refers as a motivation for action. Even if it were, the legitimacy of such a claim would still need to be questioned.

The Attitude and Practice of the Twelve

The Declaration's conclusion that the Twelve did not ordain women is based on two passages in Acts. The nomination of two men as candidates to replace Judas Iscariot is interpreted as a passing over of Mary, the mother of Jesus, as a candidate (Acts 1:14-26). It is implied that this passing over of Mary was a conscious rejection of the possibility of ordaining women. The second passage is the account of Pentecost (Acts 2). Although the women also received the Spirit (2:1), only Peter standing with the eleven (2:14) made the public proclamation of the event. The implied conclusion is that women may have the Spirit, but are not authorized to exercise the official teaching function of the Church.

With regard to the first passage (Acts 1:14-26), it is not immediately apparent that the selection of Matthias involved his "ordination." He was chosen by lot and thereafter "he was reckoned along with the eleven apostles." There is no mention of the laying on of hands or other rite which was associated later on with ordination. The act of laying on of hands does occur elsewhere in the book of Acts. According to Acts 6, the whole body of the disciples in Jerusalem chose seven Hellenists "to serve tables" (vs. 2). The apostles prayed and laid their hands upon them (vs. 6). By analogy with later texts (for example, Book VIII of the *Apostolic Constitutions*, compiled in the late fourth century) this passage might be read as an ordination ceremony of deacons (literally "servants"). This interpretation probably does not correspond to the original intent of the passage, since the laying on of hands, even by the apostles themselves, is not confined in the book of Acts to situations in which persons are commissioned to a special ministry. In 8:17 the apostles lay hands on the Samaritan converts in order that they might receive the Spirit, a gift linked to Baptism. There is no indication that a particular ministry or office is involved. Similarly, in 19:6, Paul lays hands on disciples at Ephesus that they might receive the Spirit. Here also, it is a matter of proper Baptism and not ordination to an office. In 28:8 Paul lays his hands on the father of Publius and heals him. In 9:17, Ananias' laying of hands on Paul is associated both with the gift of the Spirit (related to Baptism—vs. 18) and with the healing of his blindness. The one who lays on hands here is not an apostle (at least according to Acts) and the gesture is not directly related to Paul's commission. In 13:3 Barnabas and Saul receive the laying on of hands from members of the Church at Antioch (including at least Simeon Niger, Lucius of Cyrene and Manaen—vs. 1). Here a special ministry is indeed involved, missionary work. The ones who lay on hands, however, are not the Twelve, and Barnabas and Saul are not given any special titles. The book of Acts then does not support the theory that there was a fixed ordination ceremony during the apostolic generation. It is thus questionable whether the idea of ordination to a particular office had yet developed. What we seem to have is rather a more fluid conception of particular functions in the community (for example, serving tables and missionary work). Those designated for such tasks might be prayed over and receive the laying on of hands, but there is no indication that these confirming activities had to be performed by the apostles or by people designated by them.

The selection of Matthias by lot to replace Judas is a special case, and its relationship to the various forms of ministry in the apostolic period is not clarified by the book of Acts.

The second passage of Acts referred to by this section of the Declaration is Acts 2, the event of Pentecost and the proclamation of Peter which followed. The Declaration implies that mention of Peter, standing with the eleven (2:14), as the author of the speech is a deliberate indication of the apostles' exclusion of women from official ministry. There is no indication that the exclusion was deliberate. Furthermore, the Pentecost proclamation is a special situation, like the election of Matthias. The book of Acts does not indicate how this event was related to the other ministerial activities performed during the apostolic generation.

The picture of the apostolic period given by Acts, however, does imply that the leadership was predominantly male. It is assumed that Judas' replacement would be a man (1:21) and that the seven ministers to the Hellenists would be men (6:3). The emissaries selected by the Jerusalem Church to accompany Paul and Barnabas to Antioch were men (15:22). The point the Declaration intends to make is that there must be a deeper reason for this fact than cultural conditioning, given (1) the break in principle with Mosaic practices, and (2) the greater freedom of women in Greco-Roman civilization relative to Jewish culture. There are several problems with this argument. First of all, the book of Acts represents a mediating position on the question of the break with Mosaic practices. Paul's thought exemplifies one pole; the opposite position was taken by those referred to in Acts as "believers who belonged to the party of the Pharisees" (15:5). The difference between Paul's position and the position approved of by the book of Acts may be seen by a comparison of Acts 15 with Galatians 2:1-10. The current scholarly consensus is that the same event is described in both passages—the consultation in Jerusalem on the Gentile mission.[1] In Gal 2:4, Paul refers to "our freedom which we have in Christ Jesus." It is clear from 1 Cor 8-10 and Romans 14 that this freedom included the rejection in principle of the Jewish dietary laws. According to Galatians 2, the Jerusalem leaders added nothing to Paul's message except the request to "remember the poor." According to Acts 15:20, 29, however, the consultation ended with an agreement which would require Gentiles to observe certain Jewish dietary laws. Since the book of Acts reflects only a partial break from Mosaic food laws, it is not surprising that there is little evidence in Acts for an increase in the leadership of women relative to current Jewish practice. The book of Acts reflects a moderate position on the issue of food laws in spite of the significant movement, exemplified by Paul, to abolish their binding character. We have far less evidence that the leadership of women was a controversial issue during the apostolic generation.

The second problem with the argument mentioned above is the implication that the movement for the emancipation of women in Greco-Roman civilization was so strong that there would be significant pressure on the leaders of the early Church in the Greco-Roman milieu to allow women to exercise leadership within the Church as they were doing outside. In fact, the movement for the advancement of women was by no means so strong and widespread. Since the time of Alexander the Great, women in regions dominated by Hellenistic civilization gradually attained more extensive education; greater legal rights, especially in relation to marriage and divorce; and some increase in economic rights. Analogous trends can be traced in the late Republic and early empire in Rome. However, even among the most aristocratic and wealthy families in Greco-Roman culture, the leadership of women in the public realm was extremely rare.[2] Women were thought of primarily as wives and daughters and exercised their influence on politics and society only indirectly—through their men. While women had greater flexibility of lifestyle in Greco-Roman culture than most Jewish women, their emancipation had hardly progressed to such a point that the issue of the leadership of women would have been forced upon the apostles as they preached the gospel in the Greco-Roman milieu.

As noted above, the Declaration's conclusions regarding the practice of the Twelve on the issue of the leadership of women are based solely on the book of Acts. It should be noted that there is no statement in Acts which excludes women in principle from any ministerial role. No rationale whatever is given for the *de facto* exclusion of women from the more prominent leadership roles mentioned in Acts. The Declaration's conclusion that this *de facto* exclusion resulted from an attempt to follow the will of Christ is completely unfounded. Since the issue of the leadership of women is in large part a social issue, the social attitudes and practices of the time were undoubtedly contributing factors in this *de facto* exclusion. If the book of Acts did contain statements excluding women in principle from some form of ministry, thoughtful Christians today would be moved to examine the validity of the arguments presented in support of those statements. The argument of conformity to the will of Christ is certainly not a persuasive one. The Gospels tell us very little about the inner life of Jesus. The exclusion of women from the Twelve in the Gospels is a *de facto* exclusion without explicit rationale. There is no evidence that this exclusion reflects a conscious decision by Jesus that women ought to be excluded from the forms of ministry which developed later on in the early Church.

The Attitude and Practice of Paul

Section three of the Declaration, "The Practice of the Apostles," concludes that Paul made a deliberate decision against "conferring ordination" on women (par. 16) and against extending the collaboration of women "to the official and public proclamation of the message, since this proclamation belongs exclusively to the apostolic mission" (par. 17). The first difficulty in these conclusions is the appropriateness of the term "ordination" for Paul's understanding of ministry. His starting point is the universal Christian experience of Baptism which involves the reception of the Spirit (1 Cor 12:13). With regard to ministry, the result of the universal experience of the Spirit is that each person is given a ministerial gift to exercise for the benefit of the community (1 Cor 12:4-7). The image of the body used by Paul in this chapter makes it clear that he is not presenting an egalitarian model in which individual differences are to be leveled. He explicitly rejects the idea that the gifts (and thus ministerial functions) are universally interchangeable (12:29-30). A certain hierarchy is implied: The apostles were appointed "first," the prophets "second," and so forth (vs. 28) and Paul can speak of "higher gifts" (vs. 31). At the same time the understanding of ministry expressed in 1 Corinthians 12 is based on interdependence and mutual concern rather than on authority. There is little in this chapter which suggests the concept or practice of ordination. People are appointed to the various ministerial functions by God, not by leaders of the community passing on powers which they had previously received (vs. 28). Paul describes his own apostolic commission as a divine call "through a revelation of Jesus Christ" (Gal 1:12, 15-16). He does not give us much information about the appointment of others to their functions, but it is likely that a transcendent experience was involved in many cases. There is evidence that some functions, apparently those involving communication between local churches, were assigned by an election held in one or more local churches (2 Cor 8:19, 23). This practice is also attested by Ignatius (*Phld.* 10:1, *Smyr.* 11:2 and possibly *Pol.* 7:2). According to the *Didache* (15:1), bishops and deacons (literally, "overseers" and "servants") were elected by the local congregations.[3]

There is no evidence in the undisputedly authentic Pauline letters for a special ceremony linked with the appointment to a ministerial office. For example, the term "laying on of hands" does not occur in these letters. In the Pastoral Epistles, however, whose authorship is disputed, we do find a particular ceremony associated with the appointment of Timothy to a particular form of ministry, the laying on of hands (1 Tim 4:14 and 2 Tim 1:6). It is not obvious that Timothy's duties are associated in the Pastoral Epistles with a particular office. His work is described as the work of an evangelist on one occasion (2 Tim 4:5), but elsewhere his duties are simply described (for example, 1 Tim 4:11-14). Timothy's ministry is based on a gift of God (2 Tim 1:6) which he received through prophecy (1 Tim 4:14). Like Paul's commission, Timothy's is rooted in a transcendent experience understood as a divine call. The transcendent sign is combined with community approval, expressed by the laying on of hands by the council of elders (1 Tim 4:14) and with the approval of the apostle Paul (2 Tim 1:6). Timothy, as noted above, is not called a bishop, presbyter or deacon. Thus, the ceremony ascribed to him does not necessarily apply to the installation of others into those forms of ministry. The only other reference to the laying on of hands in the Pastoral Epistles is 1 Tim 5:22. The allusion is vague and thus difficult to interpret. The association of this laying on of hands with the forgiveness of sins is as plausible as its association with installation into a special ministry.[4] It is thus not clear that the concept and practice of ordination as evidenced in later times are reflected even in the Pastoral Epistles, which are generally agreed to be the latest letters in the Pauline corpus.[5]

The assertion that Paul refused ordination to women is not a meaningful one, since the category "ordination" is problematic for the Pauline letters. The question should thus be rephrased in terms of the participation of women in what Paul considered the primary forms of ministry. With regard to the apostolic ministry, it must be noted first of all that Paul did not consider apostolic ministry or the title "apostle" to be limited to the Twelve. His broader understanding of the title "apostle" is obvious in 1 Cor 15:3-11. In Romans 16:7, Paul greeted two apostles by name. One is clearly a man, Andronicus. It is very probable that the other name is a woman's name and should be translated "Junia" rather than as a man's name ("Junias").[6] In his list of ministerial functions in 1 Cor 12:28, Paul lists apostles as appointed "first." The evidence bearing on the translation and interpretation of Rom 16:7 supports the conclusion that Paul did not exclude women from the exercise of what he considered the primary form of ministry.

It is clear from 1 Cor 12:31-13:13 that Paul considered the highest gift of the Spirit to be love. The other gift which he singles out for special praise is prophecy (1 Corinthians 14). In the list of ministries (12:28), Paul names prophets "second" after apostles. In 1 Cor 11:2-16 he explicitly acknowledges prophesying by women. Paul restricts only their manner of dress and does not limit their prophetic activity itself in any way. He thus explicitly affirmed the exercise by women of the prophetic ministry which he called the "second." It would seem then that Paul did not exclude women from the forms of ministry which should be considered the equivalents of the later ordained ministry.

The second conclusion in the third section of the Declaration regarding Paul is that he refused to allow women to engage in the official and public proclamation of the message. The first argument given in support of this conclusion is that Paul refers to women as "my fellow workers," but reserves the title "God's fellow workers" for men. The weakness of this argument has already been pointed out.[7] The second argument is given in section four, "Permanent Value of the Attitude of Jesus and the Apostles" (par. 20). This argument is that 1 Cor 14:34-35 and 1 Tim 2:12 show that Paul prohibited women from exercising the official function of teaching in the Christian assembly.[8] There are several flaws in this argument. First of all, there is no indication whatsoever in 1 Cor 14:34-35 that the issue is teaching by women in the assembly. On the contrary, vs. 35 implies that the issue is whether women ought to ask questions in the assemblies, that is, whether they should actively seek to be taught. Many exegetes take the position that these verses are not by Paul but are a later interpolation. There are strong arguments in favor of this position.[9] Even if this passage was written by Paul, it cannot be understood as excluding women from "official" teaching (if "official" means "authoritative"). Besides the reason mentioned above (the issue is women's questions, not their teaching), the passage cannot be so understood because Paul affirms the prophesying by women in 1 Cor 11:2-16. Chapter 14 makes clear that prophesying for Paul means in part authoritative teaching. The one who prophesies speaks to the members of the congregation, apparently during the worship service, "for their upbuilding and encouragement and consolation" (14:3). The purpose of prophesying is "that all might learn and all might be encouraged" (14:31).

The other passage referred to in support of this argument is 1 Tim 2:11-15. There is no explicit indication that this passage refers to the conduct of women in the Christian assembly. Rather, it seems to refer to the conduct of women in general. This impression is reinforced by the phrase "in every place" which modifies the preceding instructions on how men ought to pray. The prohibitions of teaching and of the exercise of authority by women over men (vs. 12) thus appear to be absolute. These prohibitions are in real tension with 1 Corinthians 11 and 14. As noted above, many exegetes question whether the Pastoral Epistles were written by Paul (for reasons other than this particular tension).[10] In any case, whether this passage was written by

Paul or not, the Catholic Church has long since acted in a way which denies the normative character of the straightforward meaning of this text. The active role of women in teaching at various levels in Catholic education is contrary to the simple prohibition of teaching by women in 1 Tim 2:12. The next part of this verse does not deny only a particular kind of authority to women, but simply denies any authority of women over men whatsoever. The Declaration itself mentions two events in the Church which go against both prohibitions of that verse: the naming of Saint Teresa of Avila and Saint Catherine of Siena as Doctors of the Church (par. 2) and the inclusion of women in some of the working bodies of the Apostolic See (par. 3).

The rationale given in 1 Tim 2:11-15 for the exclusion of women from teaching and from the exercise of authority over men is not conformity to the will of Christ. According to section three of the Declaration, such conformity was Paul's reason for not allowing women to proclaim the Christian message publicly and officially (pars. 16-17). The stated rationale in 1 Timothy 2 is an interpretation of Genesis 2-3 which implies the subordination and moral inferiority of women (vss. 13-14). In 1 Corinthians 11, Paul alludes to Genesis 2 in a way which seems to support the idea of the subordination of women to men (vss. 3, 7-8). But in the same passage Paul qualifies this traditional Jewish exegesis of Genesis 2 by saying that in the Lord men and women are interdependent (vss. 11-12). He thus explicitly undercuts the normative character of the traditional interpretation of Genesis 2 for the Christian community. This qualification, as well as the fact that he did not forbid women to prophesy, show that there was indeed a tendency in the apostolic generation to increase the participation of women in ministry. The revival of the traditional Jewish, normative use of the Adam and Eve narrative in 1 Timothy must be understood in the context of the difficult circumstances in which the letter was written.[11] It is questionable that the teaching of 1 Tim 2:11-15 ought to be normative in other historical circumstances.

The third section of the Declaration embodies an attempt to close debate concerning the ordination of women on historical and exegetical grounds. It is clear that this attempt has failed because of faulty exegesis and inaccurate historical interpretation. In any case, as the Biblical Commission has pointed out, it does not seem that the issue can be decided on Scriptural grounds alone. Further discussion should take up the question whether exegetical considerations ought to be the main ones.

Notes

1. Günther Bornkamm, *Paul*, trans. D.M.G. Stalker (New York: Harper & Row, Publishers, Inc., 1971), p. 31.

2. Sarah B. Pomeroy, *Goddesses, Whores, Wives and Slaves: Women in Classical Antiquity* (New York: Schocken Books, 1975), pp. 125-26, 189.

3. Eduard Lohse, "Cheirotoneō," *Theological Dictionary of the New*

Testament, Vol. IX, ed. Gerhard Friedrich, tr. and ed. by Geoffrey W. Bromiley (Grand Rapids, Michigan: Wm. B. Eerdmans Publishing Company, 1974), p. 437.

4. Martin Dibelius and Hans Conzelmann, *The Pastoral Epistles*, trans. Philip Buttolph and Adela Yarbro, ed. Helmut Koester (Hermeneia; Philadelphia: Fortress Press, 1972), p. 71.

5. Paul Feine, Johannes Behm and Werner Georg Kümmel, *Introduction to the New Testament*, 14th ed., trans. A.J. Mattill, Jr. (Nashville: Abingdon Press, 1966), pp. 261-72.

6. For a fuller discussion of this point, see the essay by Bernadette Brooten, pp. 141-144.

7. John R. Donahue, "Women, Priesthood and the Vatican," *America*, Vol. 136 (April 2, 1977), pp. 286-87; see also the essay by Mary Ann Getty, pp. 176-182.

8. For a detailed discussion of this second argument, see the essay by Robert Karris, pp. 205-208.

9. Hans Conzelmann, *1 Corinthians*, trans. James W. Leitch, ed. George W. MacRae, S.J. (Hermeneia; Philadelphia: Fortress Press, 1975), p. 246.

10. Feine, Behm and Kümmel, *Introduction to the New Testament*, pp. 261-72; Dibelius and Conzelmann, *The Pastoral Epistles*, pp. 1-5.

11. Dibelius and Conzelmann, *The Pastoral Epistles*, pp. 65-67.

20
Goddess Worship and Women Priests

Leonard Swidler

The Declaration states that the presence of women priests in various religions and cults in the Hellenistic world would have suggested to the Christian evangelizers the idea of having women priests in the Christian tradition. There are several difficulties with such a notion. One is the assumption that there were in fact, or even in thought, priests (*hiereîs*) during the early decades in Christianity. In fact, Jesus is the only "Christian" priest (*hiereus*) spoken of in the New Testament (Hebrews 8 and 9). However, even if the Declaration authors meant priests in a very extended sense so as to include the Christian presiders at communal prayer and specifically the Eucharist (and we have no evidence of who did and who did not fulfill this function for the early decades of Christianity), the presence of women priests of cults in the Hellenistic world would have had precisely the opposite effect, because of the centuries-long fierce battle of patriarchal Jewish Yahwism against the cult of the Goddess, and the women priests associated with it, and the consequent placing of women in a denigrated and even feared position. This point is worth dwelling on not only because it will set aright a misunderstanding in the Declaration, but also, and perhaps more importantly, because it will elucidatate a very important dimension of what is a basic underlying reason for both the Jewish and Christian opposition to women's religious leadership, especially cultic.

The earliest evidence we have of human religious activity in the Old World points strongly and unambiguously to the worship of the Goddess— the divine was first worshiped as female. The archeological excavations at the upper paleolitic levels have produced innumerable female statuettes that are either figurines of the Goddess or at least are attempts at sympathetic magic, endeavoring to induce the fertility that all life depended on.[1] There is no male God at this early period.[2] As the paleolithic period gave way to the neolithic the worship of the Goddess became even more vigorous and explicit. All of the Old World areas that developed major civilizations, i.e., complex societies in which towns and cities and the differentiation of culture that accompanies them, show massive evidence of having initially been Goddess worshiping. That includes the Indus valley, the Near East, Old Europe, i.e., the Balkans, Asia Minor and the Eastern Mediterranean islands, and Egypt.[3]

The gradual shift away from the total dominance of the Goddess (except

167

perhaps with Egypt, whose history is even more complex than the others) to the participation of a clearly subordinate male God was connected with the development of animal husbandry, whence the role of paternity became apparent. There never was any question about the female's essential role in bringing new life into the world; but the role of the male and sex were not always so obvious. Still, even at this stage the male God played a vastly subordinate role vis a vis the Goddess.[4]

The role of the God however in a number of instances advanced to that of an equal and even that of a superior of the Goddess, apparently under the impact of waves of attacks of patriarchal, male-God worshiping, animal-herding Indo-Europeans who came down out of the northern mountains, perhaps originally from around the Caspian sea[5] (the Goddess worshipers were at least matrilineal and perhaps at one time even matriarchal in societal structure[6]). They appear as Hittite conquerors of Anatolia sometime before 2000 B.C., ranging eventually down into Palestine.[7] In the second millenium B.C. the patriarchal Father-God worshipers swept into almost all the Goddess-worshiping civilizations, from the Indus valley on the East through the Mesopotamian and Asia Minor areas to the Old European on the West.[8] Perhaps only Egypt was unconquered by the patriarchal Indo-Europeans, though even it was dominated at times by Asian nations that were probably "carriers" of Indo-European patriarchal ideas, e.g., the Hyksos in the seventeenth and sixteenth centuries B.C. Marija Gimbutas describes in detail the world of the early Goddess worshipers in Old Europe and notes that "it is then replaced by the patriarchal world with its different symbolism and its different values. This masculine world is that of the Indo-Europeans, which did not develop in Old Europe but was superimposed upon it. Two entirely different sets of mythical images met. . . . The earliest European civilization was savagely destroyed by the patriarchal element and it never recovered, but its legacy lingered in the substratum."[9]

Thus there was an intense struggle between the forces promoting the worship of the Goddess and the worship of the God. The tendency was for the God worshipers more or less gradually to become dominant. But there were occasions when the Goddess forces not only manifested themselves—as, e.g., in the Christian tradition of *Mater ecclesia* and devotion to the Virgin[10] and in Jewish Cabbalah[11]—but even again became dominant, as in the worship of Isis in the Roman Empire and the *Magna Mater* especially in Asia Minor around the beginning of the Christian era. In fact the resurgence of the worship of the Goddess in the Hellenistic world, coupled with its general subterranean persistence in the Semitic world, was the setting in which Christian missionary work began and developed. But to appreciate the Jewish, and therefore first Christian, reaction to the presence of Goddess worship and its women priests (there often were many male priests as well), one must recall the vigorous patriarchal male-God imagery of the Hebraic tradition and its long, fierce battle against Goddess worship.

No one questions the fact that the dominant imagery of the Hebrew divinity is masculine; it is that of a Father-God, a warrior-God, a God who refers to his people Israel as his bride, etc. The personal name of this God is Yahweh and his devotees are most zealous about the elimination of the veneration of any other divinities. Nevertheless female imagery of the divinity persists throughout large portions of the Bible, perhaps starting with the plural form of the name of the divinity in Genesis one, *Elohim*, which is probably derived from the feminine form of the name for divinity, *Eloah*, also often used in the Old Testament,[12] through the latest book in the Catholic canon of the Old Testament, the Book of Wisdom, wherein the feminine dimension of the divinity, *Sophia*, is so hypostatized it becomes almost the Goddess as the consort of God (*Theos*).[13]

But the Yahwists struggled for hundreds of years to suppress the worship of the Goddess among the Hebrews. In tracing the history of this struggle it should be noted first that in the land of Canaan the Goddess worship had already declined by biblical times so that there were at least three names of the Goddess, Anath, Astarte, and Asherah (probably originally one[14]) who were subordinate to the male God Baal.[15] There have been hundreds of Goddess figurines dug up all over Palestine at pre-, early, and middle biblical levels,[16] though little in the way of male God figurines. Biblical texts give us only a glimpse of the pervasiveness of the Goddess worship among all the Hebrews, mostly by way of condemnations of it by Yahwist prophets and destruction of Goddess images etc. by reforming Yahwist kings. It is worth outlining this history briefly to gain some sense of the implacable fury vented by the Yahwists on the Goddess worshipers.

In the time of Judges (before 1000 B.C.) "the people of Israel . . . stopped worshiping Yahweh and served the Baals and the Astartes" (Jg 6:25f.). Later Solomon (961-922) "worshiped Astarte, the Goddess of Sidon" (1 Kg 11:5). Then the prophet Ahijah said: "Yahweh the God of Israel says to you, 'I am going to take the kingdom away from Solomon. . . . I am going to do this because they have rejected me and have worshiped foreign Gods: Astarte, the Goddess of Sidon' " (1 Kg 11:31-33). In the next generation Ahijah said to the wife of Jeroboam, King of Israel (922-901), that, "Yahweh will punish Israel . . . because they have aroused his anger by making idols of the Goddess Asherah" (1 Kg 14:15). Meanwhile in Judah the people "put up stone pillars and symbols of Asherah to worship on the hills and under shady trees. Worst of all there were cult prostitutes (*qadesh*) in the land. And they imitated all the abominations of the people Yahweh had thrown out before the Israelites came" (1 Kg 23f.). Then in Judah the next king, Asa (913-873), "expelled from the country all Temple prostitutes (*qedeshim*) from the land and removed all the idols his fathers had made. He removed his grandmother Maacah from her position as queen mother, because she had made an obscene idol of the Goddess Asherah. Asa cut down the idol and burned it in the Kidron valley" (1 Kg 15:12f.). In the next generation King Ahab (869-850) of Israel "put up an image of the Goddess Asherah" (1 Kg 16:33). At that time there were at least "four hundred prophets of Asherah" (1 Kg 18:19) in Israel. Under King Jehoahaz (815-801) the people of Israel "still did not give up the sins into which King Jeroboam had led Israel, but kept on committing them; and the image of the Goddess Asherah remained in Samaria" (2 Kg 13:6). The Goddess cult in the North apparently continued, for in 721 when Israel fell to the Assyrians it was recorded that it fell "because the Israelites sinned against Yahweh their God. . . . They worshiped other Gods. . . . On all the hills they put up stone pillars and images of the Goddess Asherah" (2 Kg 17:7, 10).

The Bible redactors report somewhat more favorably on the attempts at reform led by some of the kings of Judah, but in the process indicate the pervasiveness and persistence of the Goddess worship among the Hebrews. After early reforms under King Joash (837-800) of Judah it was said that the "people stopped worshiping in the temple of Yahweh, the God of their ancestors, and began to worship idols and the images of the Goddess Asherah" (2 Ch 24:18). Goddess worship obviously continued until King Hezekiah (715-687) of Judah "broke the stone pillars and cut down the image of the Goddess Asherah" (1 Kg 18:4). But his own son Manasseh followed as king and "made an image of the Goddess Asherah" (2 Kg 21:3). Then came the last great reform efforts before the Exile under King Josiah (640-609) of Judah, who "removed from the Temple the symbol of the Goddess Asherah, took it out of the city to Kidron valley, burned it, pounded it ashes to dust. . . . He destroyed the living quarters in the Temple occupied by the temple prostitutes. It was there that women wove robes for the Asherah" (2 Kg 23:6f.).

All three of the greater prophets mention the worship of the Goddess. The oldest, Isaiah, predicts around 735 B.C. that when Yahweh punishes Israel the people "will no longer rely on altars they made with their own hands, or trust in their own handiwork—symbols of the Goddess Asherah" (Is 17:8). At another place he adds that, "Israel's sins will be forgiven only when the stones of pagan altars are ground up like chalk, and no more symbols of the Goddess Asherah or incense altars are left" (Is 27:9). Ezekiel, who traditionally is said to have been active around the time of the fall of Jerusalem a generation after King Josiah in 586, reported being shown "at the inner entrance of the north gate of the Temple an idol that was an outrage to God" (Ez 8:3). In line with most scholarship the New American Bible notes here that "this was probably the statue of the Asherah erected by the wicked King Manasseh—cf. 2 Kg 21:7; 2 Ch 33:7, 15. Though it had been removed by King Josiah—2 Kg 23:6—it had no doubt been set up again . . . ." In the same vision Ezekiel reported on a sight three times more abominable, namely, at the north gate of the Temple were "women weeping over the death of the God Tammuz" (Ez 8:14—a part of a seasonal ritual in which the death of plants in Fall was likened to the descent into the nether world by the subordinate male God Tammuz, to be triumphantly restored to life in Spring by the source of life, the Goddess Astarte—or Ishtar in Babylonian or Inanna in Sumerian traditions).

Some years before, Jeremiah complained that the people of Judah "worship at the altars and the symbols that have been set up for the Goddess Asherah by every green tree and on the hill tops and on the mountains in the open country" (Jer 17:2-3). Later the same prophet Jeremiah was taken with the remnant of Judeans, after the Babylonian destruction of Jerusalem in 586, into Egypt. He berated the people for having brought on the disaster by worshiping other Gods. Who the "other God" was is made clear by the people's response: "Then all the men who knew that their wives offered sacrifices to other Gods and all the women in the crowd . . . said to me, 'We refuse to listen to what you have told us in the name of Yahweh. We will do everything that we said we would. We will offer sacrifices to our Goddess, the Queen of Heaven [Anath-Astarte was addressed as Queen of Heaven in Egypt[17]], and we will pour out wine offerings to her, just as we and our ancestors, our king and our leaders, used to do in the towns of Judah and in the streets of Jerusalem. Then we had plenty of food, we were prosperous, and had no troubles. But ever since we stopped sacrificing to the Queen of Heaven and stopped pouring out wine offerings to her, we have had nothing, and our people have died in war and starvation.'

"And the women added, 'When we baked cakes shaped like the Queen of Heaven, offered sacrifices to her, and poured out wine offerings to her, our husbands approved of what we were doing' " (Jer 44:15-19). It is clear from this that the women too were "priests" in this cult.

Probably from around this time onward a colony of Jews lived at Elephantine, Egypt. From their papyrus letters and documents of the late fifth century we know that not only did the Jewish women as well as the men contribute money to the Temple and that the women could divorce their spouses as well as the men could, but also that in the Temple along with Yahu (as Yahweh was addressed there) the Goddess Anathbethel was also worshiped.[18] In another Elephantine document the Goddess Anath is apparently referred to as the consort of Yahweh: "He swore to Meshullam b. Nathan by Yahu the God, by the Temple and by Anathyahu."[19]

After the return of the Jewish people to Jerusalem from the Babylonian exile the public worship of the Goddess seems to have been successfully suppressed, being relegated largely to feminine manifestations of God as in the post-exilic wisdom books' praise of the feminine *Hokmah* or *Sophia,* Wisdom, and the growing reference to God's feminine Presence, *Shekinah,* an Aramaic term first found after the beginning of the Christian era in Rabbinic and Targumic writings. One of the high-cost ways this was accomplished was by the banning of intermarriage. By this time Jewish women in any case could not marry non-Jews; Jewish men also were not supposed to marry non-Jewish women, though in fact they did. The reason foreign wives were not to be taken is that they were seen as the source of corrupting Goddess worship, e.g., Jezebel and her worship of Asherah. This enforcement of the Deuteronomic prohibition (Dt 7:1-4) took the drastic form of the divorce and driving out by the Jewish men of their non-Jewish wives and children![20]

The post-exilic Jewish literature, wisdom, apocalyptic and rabbinic, exhibits a growing restriction of women, a hostility toward them and a preoccupation with illegitimate sex as the source of all evil. E.g., the third century Ecclesiastes says "I find woman more bitter than death; she is a snare, her heart a net, her arms are chains" (Eccles 7:26). Second-century Ben Sira has much negative to say about women; the following is a small sampling: "For a moth comes out of clothes, and woman's spite out of woman" (Ecclus 25:26); "Any spite rather than the spite of a woman" (25:13); "A man's spite is preferable to a woman's kindness; women give rise to shame and reproach" (42:13f.); "No wickedness comes anywhere near the wickedness of a woman, may a sinner's lot be hers" (25:19); "Sin began with a woman, and thanks to her we all must die" (25:24). Around the year 100 B.C. Jewish apocalyptic literature flourished; it was decidedly negative toward women and sex. The Book of Jubilees, for example, suggested that every woman is a nymphomaniac: "For all their deeds are fornication and lust, and there is no righteousness with them, for their deeds are evil" (25:1). The Testament of the Twelve Patriarchs reflects the same attitude: "For women are evil, my children; and since they have no power or strength over man, they use wiles by outward attractions, that they may draw him to themselves. And whom they cannot bewitch by outward attractions, him they overcome by craft" (Testament of Reuben 5:1f.). The Essenes are said by Philo to refuse marriage "because a woman is a selfish creature, excessively jealous and an adept at beguiling the morals of her husband and seducing him by her continued impostures."[21]

The early rabbis continued the hostile attitude toward women. Their few positive statements about good wives are massively outweighed by their negative comments,[22] of which the following is a tiny example: "A woman is a pitcher full of filth with its mouth full of blood, yet all run after her";[23] "The most virtuous of women is a witch";[24] "Women are light-headed";[25] the daily prayer: "Praised be God that he has not created me a woman";[26] already in 150 B.C. Rabbi Jose b. Johanan said ". . . talk not much with womankind. This they said of a man's own wife: how much more of his fellow's wife! Hence the Sages have said: He that talks much with womankind brings evil upon himself and neglects the study of Torah and at last will inherit Gehenna";[27] women automatically lead to sex and hence to sin: "He who gazes at a woman eventually comes to sin";[28] "A woman's leg is a sexual incitement. . . . A woman's voice is a sexual incitement. . . . If one gazes at the little finger of a woman it is as if he gazed at her secret part";[29] "Rabbi Akiba (50-132 A.D.) said: "Whence do we learn of an idol that like a menstruous woman it conveys uncleanness by carrying? Because it is written, Thou shalt cast them away like a menstruous thing: thou shalt say unto it, Get thee hence. Like as a menstruous woman conveys uncleanness by carrying, so does an idol convey uncleanness by carrying."[30]

It is with this centuries-long Hebrew-Jewish hostility toward Goddess worship, the women priests associated with it (especially as it often included "sacred sex" between at least a king or leader or perhaps other devotees and a woman priest—*qadesh*), and the greater freedom for women accompanying it, that the first Christians (the Apostles, Paul, etc.) entered the Hellenistic world with the Christian gospel. Moreover, it was first to the diaspora Jewish synagogues where these attitudes would also have been strongly present that they went.

In that Hellenistic world these Jewish Christians faced the worship of the Goddess in strong resurgence, from the worship of the Phrygian *Mater Magna* or Kybele throughout Asia Minor and even in Rome, to the cult of Isis and her veneration under many other names—Demeter, Athena, Venus, Ceres, Ma Bellona, etc. The worship of *Mater Magna* or Kybele in Asia Minor was not only extremely influential, but also often included ecstatic passion, self-mutilation, even self-castration by male devotees so as to attain complete identity with the Goddess.[31] Although in fact the most pervasive Goddess worship at the beginning of the Christian era, the Isis cult, did not promote sexual excesses or promiscuity,[32] it was widely rumored to do so, and thus the effect of seeing women priests of Isis on the early Christians was just as negative as if it were true. E.O. James notes that "her cultus was the most effective rival to Christianity from the second century onwards, and during the temporary revival of classical paganism in Rome in A.D. 394, it was her festival that was celebrated with great magnificence."[33] He further notes that, "the unprecedented victory of the cultus [Isis] over official opposition and its persistence during the first three centuries of the Christian era are a testimony to the deep and genuine religious emotion aroused in the initiates by the ritual."[34] In fact, her public worship was brought to an end only by Emperor Justinian in 560. Moreover, throughout the Hellenistic world one can speak of a growing "women's liberation movement" increasing in effect from the time of Alexander through the time of the Roman Empire until the triumph of Christianity in the fourth century[35]—paralleling the resurgence of the Goddess worship.

Given the Hebrew-Jewish-early Christian attitude toward Goddesses, and women, the context of the Hellenist world with its swelling Goddess worship, priestesses and relative freedom for women was well calculated to intensify the Jewish-Christian emphasis on a male God, male priests, and male dominance. The ages-long struggle of the devotees of a Father-God against a Mother-God, priest against priestess, patriarchy against matriarchy lay behind the early Christian (not Jesus's or even authentic Paul's) failure to make women priests when that role became established, and the corresponding un-Jesus-like subordination of women.

With that knowledge and with a proper stress on the core Judeo-Christian tradition of the transcendence of God beyond all sex, plus a recovery of the balancing feminine imagery of God in the Bible and Christian tradition and other "grace-full" traditions in the heritage of humanity, the Catholic Church can now move to the creative step of making the priesthood reflect more fully that God (*Elohim*) "in whose image we are made, male and female" (Genesis 1:27).

Notes

1. E.O. James, *Prehistoric Religion* (New York: Barnes & Noble, 1957, pp. 147, 153. Cf. J. Edgar Bruns, *God as Woman, Woman as God* (New York: Paulist Press, 1973), pp. 8-10.

2. E.O. James, *The Cult of the Mother-Goddess* (New York: Praeger, 1959), pp. 21f.

3. *Ibid.*, pp. 22-47.

4. *Ibid.*, pp. 47, 138.

5. *Ibid.*, p. 99.

6. *Ibid.*, p. 228.

7. The Hebrew Bible refers often to Hittites in Palestine, e.g., Uriah the Hittite, husband of Bathsheba, a soldier in King David's army (2 Sam 11:3).

8. H.R. Hays, *In the Beginnings* (New York: Putnam, 1963), pp. 209f.

9. Marija Gimbutas, *The Gods and Goddesses of Old Europe* (Berkeley: University of California Press, 1974), p. 238.

10. James, *Mother-Goddess*, pp. 192-227; Bruns, *God as Woman*, pp. 56-69.

11. Raphael Patai, *The Hebrew Goddess* (New York: KTAV, 1967), pp. 157-206.

12. *Elohim* is one of the three Hebrew variants, *El, Eloah, Elohim* (*Elah* in Aramaic portions of the Bible), which usually are used interchangeably (similar words are used in the rest of the ancient Semitic world for the deity, e.g., Akkadian *ilu*, Arabic *'ilah*). Of special interest is that *Elohim* is plural (which is reflected in the occasional plural verb forms used, e.g., Genesis 1:26), probably coming from the singular feminine form of the word for God, *Eloah* (*ah* is a singular feminine suffix; *im* is a plural suffix that can be feminine or masculine). There is likely a residue of a very ancient Semitic female God, *Eloah*, a male God, *El*, and a court of female and male Gods, *Elohim*, reflected in this Hebrew biblical usage. This intermixing of masculine and feminine forms for God by the biblical writers indicates both a combining of sexual images in God, and a transcending of all sexuality. The combining of feminine and masculine forms seems to be the first phase, and the transcending of sexual forms the second phase.

13. Wisdom, *Sophia*, is said to possess omnipotence (7:23, 27), omnipresence (7:24), immutability (7:27), sanctity (7:22)—all clearly exclusively divine characteristics. Moreover, She participated in creation (7:12, 21), and is at present the sustainer and ruler of the world (8:1). Still further, *Sophia* is described as a breath of the power of God, a pure emanation of the glory of the Almighty (7:25).

14. James, *Mother-Goddess*, p. 69.

15. *Ibid.*, p. 74.

16. Patai, *Hebrew Goddess*, pp. 58-61.

17. *Ibid.*, p. 55.

18. Arthur E. Cowley, *Aramaic Papyri of the Fifth Century B.C.* (Oxford: Clarendon Press, 1923), p. 72.

19. *Ibid.*, p. 148.

20. Ezra 9 and 10; cf. Nehemiah 13:23-28.

21. Philo, *Hypothelica*, 11, 14-17.

22. Cf. Leonard Swidler, *Woman in Judaism* (Metuchen, N.J.: Scarecrow Press, 1976).

23. *Babylonian Talmud*, Shabbath 152 a. This teaching is attributed to a "Tanna," i.e., a rabbi of the early period, the time before the Mishnah was finally edited in the second century A.D.

24. Attributed to Rabbi Simon ben Jochai, around 150 A.D. *Mishnah,* Terum 15.

25. *Babylonian Talmud,* Shabbath 33 b.

26. *Ibid.,* Menachoth 43 b; *Palestinian Talmud,* Berakoth 13 b; *Toseph-ta,* Berakoth 7, 18.

27. *Mishnah,* Aboth 1, 5.

28. *Babylonian Talmud,* Nedarim 20 a.

29. *Ibid.,* Berakoth 24 a.

30. *Mishnah,* Shabbath 9, 1.

31. James, *Mother-Goddess,* p. 167.

32. Sharon K. Heyon, *The Cult of Isis Among Women in the Graeco-Roman World* (Leiden: E.J. Brill, 1975), pp. 111ff.

33. James, *Mother-Goddess,* p. 180.

34. *Ibid.,* p. 177.

35. Klaus Thraede, "Frau," *Reallexikon für Antike und Christentum* (Regensburg, 1970); Leonard Swidler, "Greco-Roman Feminism and the Reception of the Gospel," *Traditio-Krise-Renovatio aus theologischer Sicht,* Berndt Jaspert and Rudolf Mohr, eds. (Marburg: N.G. Elwert Verlag, 1976), pp. 41-54.

21

God's Fellow Worker
and Apostleship

Mary Ann Getty

Both the Vatican Declaration and the official Commentary on the Declaration refer to the fact that Paul includes women when he refers to the
ministers of the gospel.[1] The Declaration concedes that Paul mentions the
work of many women for whom he is particularly grateful; it further concurs
that certain women "worked with the Apostle" and had "important influence
on conversions."[2] Scholars have studied the implications of Paul's reference
to women as disciples, deacons, prophets and even apostles.[3] Therefore it
comes as a surprise that the Declaration and Commentary would single out
the unusual phrases "God's fellow worker" (*synergos Theou*) and "my fellow
worker" (*synergos moi*), and postulate a highly significant but obscure and
questionable distinction between these as providing the basis for "official"
apostolic ministry;[4] it is a further widening of a credibility gap that this distinction would be given gospel value. The expression "God's fellow worker"
appears for certain only once, twice at the most.[5] Emphasizing Paul's restriction of this phrase to men runs the risk of leading the reader to believe that a
deliberate attempt is being made to exclude women from accepting their apostolic responsibility.

A variety of terms are used in the New Testament to describe the ministers of the gospel. The Declaration contends that Paul did not portray women
as fulfilling a properly apostolic role, since he distinguishes between "God's"
and "my" fellow workers and in so doing refrains from extending women's
role to "the official and public proclamation of the [Resurrection] message,
since this proclamation belongs exclusively to the apostolic mission." Study
of the term "fellow worker" modified by "God's" or "my" does not support
such a contention; certainly it does not seem to be Paul's intent to make such
a rigid distinction. Further, it is not at all clear how such a firm distinction
can be made between "official and public proclamation" and the service of
the gospel rendered by women such as Paul does explicitly describe.[6] This is
particularly true in the early Church when there were no clear and distinct offices or ministries and where the concept of roles and functions was very
fluid. Further, when Paul speaks of the Resurrection appearances in 1 Cor
15:5-10, it is not certain that he excludes women; it is therefore questionable
that women did not and cannot "officially" proclaim the Resurrection. We
must therefore study the term "fellow worker" in order to ascertain what
possible bearing this term could have on defining the apostolic mission, or

176

what relationship this term has with the proclamation of the Resurrection. Further we will offer some reflections on Paul's description of the much more important role of the apostle.

It is important to realize that our present form of priestly ministry seeks to find its origins in the Scriptures, especially the New Testament. One problem in doing this is that no one office or title in the New Testament subsumes all the forms we have traditionally connected with the priesthood.[7] Only later did the Church try to collect all the functions described in the various New Testament terms under the general heading "Priest" (*hierus*). The term "priest" (*hierus*) is not used in the New Testament of any individual Christian, although it is used to describe the priesthood of all believers and the priesthood of Christ which replaces all human priesthoods.[8] This is not to say that the notion, practice and sacrament of priestly ministry are not present in the New Testament. It should, however, be emphasized that the notion of ministry and priesthood was expressed in a variety of terms, among which "God's fellow worker" is hardly the most significant.

The term "fellow worker" (*synergos*) is unusual in both the Septuagint Greek translation of the Old Testament and the New Testament. It appears in the Septuagint only in 2 Macc. 8:7 and 14:5, meaning "favorable opportunities." In the New Testament outside of Paul, the term occurs only in 3 Jn 8. In Paul it occurs ten times: with "God's" (1 Cor 3:9, but compare 1 Thess 3:2), with "my" (Rom 16:3, 21; Philem 24; Phil 4:3) or "our" (Rom 16:9; Philem 1; cf. 2 Cor 8:23) and with a thing (2 Cor 1:24; Col 4:11). The position adopted by the Declaration implies that Paul intended a substantial difference of function, office and authority by these different modifiers. It would not be possible to substantiate these differences, especially since the term itself is so rare.

The only certain instance of the use of "God's fellow worker" is in 1 Cor 3:9. The meaning of this phrase is best explained by its context. Paul is attacking the factions and party strife in Corinth. The community was being fragmented because some Christians were saying, "I belong to Paul," while others retorted, "I belong to Apollos," or "I belong to Cephas" or "I belong to Christ" (1:12). Jealousy and competition threatened to divide and destroy the community. In 3:1-15, Paul emphasizes the unity of purpose of his own and Apollos' work. Paul makes a friendly gesture toward Apollos since it appears that rivalry among their respective followers has put the work and the fruits of the work of them both in a doubtful light. In effect, Paul wants to stress it is God who calls all Christian ministers and all are doing God's, not human, works. The gospel is the power of God (1:8), and those entrusted to preach it are not to be thought of as competitors and rivals, but as bearers of a divine message charged with divine power. Paul uses the phrase "God's fellow worker" in order to give more authority to the common ministry shared by Apollos and himself, since this commonality is the aspect of the ministry that is under attack. Paul is obviously not trying to specify a title applicable only to Apollos and himself as men.

The nearest parallel to this expression in 1 Cor. 3:9 is found in 2 Cor. 6:1

where Paul refers to the whole Corinthian community who are "working together with God."[9] It is clear from this passage that in so referring to the Christians at Corinth, Paul is not trying to exclude the women. The authors of the Declaration seem to be aware of the questionable reading of 1 Thess 3:2, since they do not refer to it as a strict parallel to 1 Cor 3:9 but as a verse to be compared.[10] There Timothy is called Paul's brother and God's "servant" or "fellow worker," in a passage implying that, as Paul's messenger to the community, Timothy had the same authority as Paul claimed for himself. The context explains the expression; especially in the light of the questionable reading of this verse, it is hard to demonstrate that Paul uses any more of a technical, exclusive phrase than he does in 2 Cor 6:1.

The Declaration's distinction between "God's fellow workers" and "my fellow workers" cannot be substantiated. It can be noted that the phrase "my fellow workers" appears most frequently in the context of the general community, which undoubtedly was made up of men and women; it sometimes refers only to men and sometimes includes women who are named. There is no legitimate conclusion that can be drawn along sexual lines as to the meaning of the phrase. The expression represents Paul's more usual designation of his own and the community's respective roles in the ministry; "my fellow worker(s)" appears wherever there is not a more fundamental problem of jealousy or competition such as we see in first Corinthians.

Further, it is difficult to accept a firm and distinct connection between the phrase "God's fellow worker" and the "official and public proclamation" of the Resurrection, a connection suggested by the juxtaposition of sentences about these in the Declaration. Although Paul calls Apollos (1 Cor 3:9) and possibly Timothy (1 Thess 3:2) "God's fellow workers," he does not mention a Resurrection appearance to either of these men. In fact, if we are to assume that only those Paul designates as *synergos theou* bear the authority of the apostolic mission, then the ministers of the gospel are quite limited in numbers indeed.

It is true that Paul does not explicitly mention the Resurrection appearances to the women nor the important role the women played in announcing the Resurrection to the male disciples as all four gospels report. But we cannot conclude from this that Paul meant to exclude women's testimony from the "official and public proclamation" and consider it non-official and private. Paul's intention in 1 Cor 15:5-10 is not to give a narrative account nor an exhaustive listing of the Resurrection appearances. If it were, what could we say about John's reliability in the account of Thomas' absence (Jn 20:24) and Jesus' return for his sake, for example? Paul's concern in the very important chapter of 1 Corinthians 15 explains why he is selective in his references to the Lord's appearances; Paul is defending his own authority. It is the fact that he has seen the Lord himself that grounds his mission to preach, however officially and publicly. Since he does not dispute the gospels' testimony about the appearances to the women, but merely tries to justify his own right to proclaim the Resurrection, we have no basis for thinking that Paul meant to exclude the women's testimony as less than official. When Paul says that the Lord appeared to Cephas, then to the Twelve, then to more than five hundred, to James, to all the apostles and finally to Paul himself, he is not excluding anyone but identifying the source of his own authority. Since even before the other apostles, Paul considers himself an apostle, it is not likely that he would put himself in a separate category in 15:8 if his own authority were not the matter in question. Perhaps the appearances to the women were taken for granted and therefore it was not necessary to mention them! In any case, why exclude them from the categories of the "more than five hundred" and "all the apostles," since women count and one, at least, is called an apostle explicitly by Paul in Rom. 16:7?[11]

The term "apostle" is rightly considered one of the most significant New Testament terms that provides a basis and model for the Church's concept of priestly ministry. (It is certainly far more important than "God's fellow worker," for instance.) While the Gospels often use the term "disciple" to describe the role of Christ's followers, the epistles' frequent use of "apostle" provides us with one of the earliest and broadest understandings of the Christian ministers of the Gospel. We must therefore examine briefly this term "apostle" in Paul, who originally used it and most aptly described it in reference to his own work in proclaiming the gospel, in order to ascertain if women were excluded from this office by its nature or whether women could have been or actually were included in the apostolic ministry. This will enable us to determine whether there is anything in the attitude or practice of Paul which would be normative for either excluding or including women in the apostolic ministry or in the vocation we know today as the priesthood.

According to Paul, who was, of course, the first to use the term "apostle" and to vehemently defend his own right to be called an apostle, the missionary connotation is key to its understanding. After the model of Christ, the apostle leads a life of service for others. Although the Gospels hint that the disciples were sent forth during Jesus' earthly ministry (Mk 6:7ff.; Mt 10:17-18; Lk 9-10), the definitive "sending forth" that constituted apostleship came after the Resurrection.[12] The apostolic command is given after the Resurrection in the Gospels (Mt 28:19; Lk 24:47-48; Jn 20:21; Markan Appendix, 16:15). However, the New Testament is generally silent about the apostolate of the Twelve, and consequently the paradigm for the apostle is Paul, who was not one of the Twelve nor even a disciple of Jesus during his ministry. This distinction helps to show that the disciple, the Twelve and the apostle had separate roles in the early Church's understanding.

The Pauline definition of apostle does not indicate that women were not given the apostolic charge. Three main ideas surface in studying Paul's presentation of the role of the apostle: the apostle is called to preach, the apostle founds, forms and cares for the community, and the apostle is responsible for the church at large.[13]

The first characteristic of the apostle is service to Jesus Christ who sets the apostle apart to preach the gospel, especially the Resurrection. We have already tried to show that this function does not exclude women.

Secondly, the apostle is sent not to baptize but to establish, form and care for the local communities. In nurturing the communities and while describing himself as a "nurse" or a mother "feeding her young children milk" (1 Cor 3:1ff.) and experiencing labor pains until "Christ is formed in you" (Gal 4:19), Paul points out some of the less obvious but perhaps more provocative aspects of his apostolic ministry. These include the service of ordinary work, the service of prayer and the service of suffering;[14] none of these ministries is outside of women's actual experience.

Thirdly, the apostle is responsible for the pastoral care and nurturing not only of the local community but also of the Church at large. Paul's zeal for the conversion of the Gentiles did not put him out of touch with the Jewish-Christian Church in Jerusalem. This is one of the more pertinent dimensions of the apostleship that can enlighten our own dilemma today, one which the official Commentary on the Declaration itself admits. We are involved in a controversy over a question analogous to the one that existed in the Pauline churches. The Jewish-Christian leaders at Jerusalem wondered how and with what qualifications the Gentiles could receive Baptism. The Roman-Christian leaders at the Vatican now wonder how and with what qualifications women can receive Orders. The Gentiles' entrance into the Church perhaps presented an even more serious dilemma and conflict in the early Church than the problem of the ordination of women does today. It threatened the very existence and life of the Church and of every single Christian. It went way beyond a discussion between Peter and Paul. Further, Peter's followers could have claimed to have a "natural resemblance" to Jesus who was circumcized; the Gentiles were not. In fact, some of the major New Testament writings, especially Galatians and Romans, address this very question. Jesus had not, after all, given clear directions for the admission of the Gentiles; where did the Church receive its authority to interpret Jesus' mind on this subject and admit Gentiles with a minimum of requirements (Acts 15:1-29)?

Both the Declaration and its Commentary testify to the timeliness of addressing this question of the ordination of women which has become "pressing" only in our day. These documents admit that until now the Vatican has not been forced to address this matter. The fact that the Vatican now feels required to face the question demonstrates that, in fact, women are exercising responsibility to and for the Church at large by bringing the question before the authorities, a responsibility that properly belongs to the apostolic charge.

Conclusion

Our conclusion may be simply summarized. No clear or significant distinction can be made between "God's fellow workers" and "my fellow workers." In fact, it might seem to many that the more significant term for the apostolate of the Church is the term "my" (or "our") fellow workers, since this refers to the ministry of all the members rather than of a few individuals (three, to be exact).[15] In any case, the term had no longevity; it is not a significant one to represent ministry, and there is nothing to support the argument that only those who are designated "God's fellow workers" have the authority to officially and publicly proclaim the gospel. Further, this term has little bearing on the properly apostolic ministry which women indeed seem to have performed in the early Church and which they continue to perform today as they contribute to and enrich our understanding of the far more important notion of apostleship as a model for priestly ministry.

Notes

1. Declaration, par. 16; Commentary, par. 23.
2. Declaration, par. 16; Commentary, par. 23.
3. For example, see E. Fiorenza, "Women Apostles: The Testament of Scripture," in *Women and Catholic Priesthood: An Expanded Vision*. Proceedings of the Detroit Ordination Conference, ed. by A.M. Gardiner (New York: Paulist Press, 1976), p. 96; A. Lemaire, "The Ministries in the New Testament, Recent Research," *Theological Bulletin*, Vol. 3 (1973), pp. 133-166; D. Senior, *Jesus, A Gospel Portrait* (Dayton: Pflaum Publishing, 1975), pp. 51-82; R. Brown, "Roles of Women in the Fourth Gospel," *Theological Studies*, Vol. 36, No. 4 (Dec., 1975), pp. 688-699; E. Carroll, "Women and Ministry," *Theological Studies*, Vol. 36, No. 4 (Dec., 1975), pp. 660-688.
4. This distinction of dubious significance and even validity, is made by I. De la Potterie, *Titres missionaires du chretien dans le Nouveau Testament* (Rapports de la XXXIeme semaine de Missiologie, Louvain, 1966), Paris: Desclee de Brouwer, 1966), pp. 44-45.
5. 1 Cor 3:9; cf. 1 Thess 3:2.
6. The Declaration mentions the ministries of Priscilla, Lydia and Phoebe, noting that these show ". . . a considerable evolution vis-a-vis the customs of Judaism. Nevertheless, at no time was there a question of conferring ordination on these women" (par. 16). It would be hard to determine for certain that, in fact, no ordination was conferred, and even more difficult to ascertain that the question was never even raised. The Statement of the Biblical Commission that "some women collaborated in the properly apostolic work" seems to be more honest and to the point. The Commission further says that in speaking about women, Paul "insists on specifying that they have tired themselves for the community, using a Greek verb (*kopian*) most often used for the work of evangelization properly so called" (Part III).
7. Cf. R. Brown, *Priest and Bishop: Biblical Reflections* (New York: Paulist Press, 1970).
8. *Ibid.*, p. 13.
9. Cf. A. Robertson and A. Plummer, *A Critical and Exegetical Commentary on the First Epistle of Paul to the Corinthians*, International Critical Commentary (New York: Charles Scribners' Sons, 1912), p. 58.
10. The reading of 1 Thess 3:2 is disputed: the main questions are whether *synergon* or *diakonon* should be read and whether *tou theou* should be dropped. Some substitute *diakonon* for *synergon* while others have the conflated reading *kai diakonon tou theou kai synergon emon*.
11. There is no reason to substitute a masculine form for the feminine name Junia in Rom 16:7, as E. Fiorenza points out. This is one instance where a woman is explicitly called an apostle. Fiorenza, *op. cit.*, p. 96; see

also the Statement of the Biblical Commission, Part III; see also in this volume, pp. 141-144.

12. Brown, *Priest and Bishop*, p. 27.
13. *Ibid.*, pp. 26-34.
14. *Ibid.*, pp. 29-34.
15. I.e., Paul, Apollos, Timothy.

22
"The Permanent Value of Jesus and the Apostles"

J. Massyngberde Ford

The Declaration asks whether it would be possible for the Church to depart from the attitude of Jesus and the apostles. Without any doubt the New Testament shows that this is possible. Three examples will suffice. First, Jesus and the apostles in the Gospels do not have any organized mission to the Gentiles. Indeed, in Mt 10:5-6, Jesus charges the twelve apostles:

> Go nowhere among the Gentiles, and enter no town of the Samaritans, but go rather to the lost sheep of the house of Israel.

Yet Paul felt called to devote himself to a mission to the Gentiles and adopted the unprecedented custom of not requiring male circumcision. Secondly, Jesus, the apostles (both before the resurrection and afterwards) and Paul all attended the services and sacrifices at the Temple. Thirdly, the Epistle to the Hebrews breaks with all tradition and replaces the worship of the Temple and the traditional priesthood.

The most surprising omission from both the U.S. Bishops Statement on the Ordination of Women (1973)[1] and the Declaration is the complete absence of any reference to the Epistle to the Hebrews. One would, therefore, imagine, although this is not explicitly stated, that the hierarchy's concept of priesthood is based largely or exclusively upon the Old Testament levitical priesthood. Even from the days of Clement of Rome[2] the Christian Church seemed to model itself upon the Aaronic one. This is patent, for example, in the list of those who were precluded from the priesthood until a few (about 5-10) years ago. In Lev 21:17-21 we read:

> Say to Aaron, None of your descendants throughout their generations who has a blemish may approach to offer the bread of his God. For no one who has a blemish shall draw near, a man blind or lame, or one who has a mutilated face or limb too long, or a man who has an injured foot or an injured hand, or a hunchback, or a dwarf, or a man with a defect in his sight or a catching disease or scabs or crushed testicles; no man of the descendants of Aaron the priest who has a blemish shall come near to offer the Lord's offering by fire; since he has a blemish, he shall not come near to offer the bread of his God.

Canon 968 has been interpreted along these lines. To give a few examples of those precluded: those born out of wedlock; those having a bodily defect through mutilation, blindness, deafness, inability to speak, lameness which requires the use of a cane, the possession of a sixth finger, the adhesion of the three end fingers, epilepsy, judges who have imposed the sentence of death, members of a lynching party, slaves and *castrati*. It is possible to obtain a dispensation for many of these impediments nowadays. Yet would these people have a natural resemblance to the Jesus who did not join lynching parties but accepted Paul who was responsible for many deaths? He suffered, but did not impose, capital punishment. He conducted his priestly ministry on the cross as the most mutilated of all persons:[3] a handicapped person might well be a better image of Christ *qua* sacrificing priest than a healthy one.

It is, moreover, surprising that the Old Testament never specifically denies the priesthood to women although in surrounding cultures women did act in the capacity of priests and high priests.[4] At Mari near the Euphrates in Syria (mainly 1790-1945 B.C.) one finds women playing important roles in society and religion.[5] In Mesopotamia in the third millenium they could be chief priestesses in the Temple.[6] There was the Ugbabtum Priestess who could live either in a cloister or at home but could not marry or have children.[7] Such priestesses had to maintain a certain amount of dignity and even a certain distance from profane activities, e.g., they could not enter a tavern. Priestesses captured in war[8] were shown greater deference than were the other captives.[9] In the light of this kind of material it is quite remarkable that we find no statement in the Old Testament nor the New denying that a woman can be an elder or a priest. This is all the more surprising in that at Ephesus there was a college of virgin priestesses to worship the goddess Artemis: some of Paul's converts may have come from these ranks and perhaps this is why he does place some reserve on women although he never denies to them the priesthood or the presbyterate.[10]

Further, it is of utmost importance to state specifically that the words "priest" and "priesthood" are not used with reference to any individual Christian male or female (only Jesus) in the New Testament. The text mentions only Jewish priests who accepted the faith (Acts 6:7), the priesthood of the faithful who are baptised (Rev. 1:5 and 6; 5:10; 20:6; 22:3-5 and 1 Peter 2:5 and 9) and/or the priesthood (and kingship) of the whole community.[11] Jesus attended the Temple services and sacrifices until he died and his disciples appear to have continued this practice until the fall of the Temple to the Romans in 70 A.D. It is very interesting that Jesus and his followers did not imitate the practice of the Qumran covenanters or the Samaritans by refraining from worship in Jerusalem, which they deemed defiled. It appears that only after the destruction of the Temple did both Judaism and Christianity begin a religion without bloody sacrifice and without hereditary priesthood. Hereditary priesthood presupposes a married, not celibate, clergy; this marital regulation is deeply imbedded in the Scripture Tradition, but the Latin Church later saw fit to alter it.

Thus a study of priesthood must begin with a study of the priesthood of all the baptised whether male or female. Yet throughout the history of the Church, only males and hermaphrodites[12] (provided that the dominant sex is male) have been called to exercise this priesthood in liturgical and other functions.

However, to return to the New Testament. It is important to realise that in the eyes of his Jewish contemporaries Jesus was not a priest, either from the line of Aaron, Levi or Zadok, nor do we learn that any of the disciples were descended from the priestly families. The New Testament records no ordination of any followers of Christ to the priesthood, although women elders in Titus (2:2) are counseled to be *hieroprepeis* "priestly in their conduct." On the contrary the New Testament emphasizes strongly that the priesthood of Christ is not according to Levi but according to Melchizedek (Heb 5:6), and thus those who are in Christ, dead, buried and raised with him, share in this same priesthood. Melchizedek, as we now know from the Dead Sea Scrolls (11 Q Mel) and Gnostic literature, was a supernatural figure, without father or mother and presumably sexless if he were "angelic."

Fred L. Horton, Jr.,[13] cites James A. Sanders[14] who thinks that "Hebrews is a document relating to the revolt against Rome in the first century and was probably written in A.D. 69-70." Melchizedek appears in Genesis 14:17-20 in a pericope thought to be a later inserton into the text and considered an aetiological legend showing Abraham's submission to the Jerusalem (Salem) priesthood.[15] It is usually assigned to a date after the Priestly stratum of the Pentateuch.[16] Melchizedek appears in Ps 110:4, which some date in the Maccabean period when the rulers eventually combined the priesthood and kingship in one office.[17] But we have no evidence of a ruling dynasty in pre-Israelite Jerusalem, and Melchizedek in the Hebrew Bible is never unequivocally identified as king of Jerusalem.[18] Philo describes Melchizedek as "self-taught" and "instinctive," and he makes him a peaceable king.[19] For Philo, Melchizedek is a presentation of the Logos.[20] He possesses a unique, self-taught priesthood, and in *Leg. All.* 3:79 we find that "God did not prefigure any work of Melchizedek . . . but set him out from the very first as priest and king."[21]

In 11 Q Mel from Qumran Melchizedek is a supernatural figure who comes to inaugurate the Jubilee and to take vengeance on the sons of Belial. He is in the assembly of *El.* The anointed one is a prophet who announces the reign of Melchizedek.[22] Melchizedek's reign is a heavenly one but also an earthly one. However, we do not hear of an ascension. Sanders states, "In 11 Q Melch the great high priest of Gen 14 and Ps 110 is made not only a deity . . . in the heavenly court, but is set over all other *elohim* as king, judge, and redeemer, in the final great eschatological drama."[23]

The Christian interest in Melchizedek began to develop towards the end of the second century A.D. He was thought to be a divine or angelic figure.[24] Heretical sects, from which the majority of references came, made him a heavenly being[25] sometimes superior to Christ.[26] One writer identified him with the Holy Spirit[27] and others with the Logos and Son of God before entering the womb of Mary.[28] Gnostic sources also mention Melchizedek and

call him the "Great Receiver of Light."[29] Melchizedek takes the power he
has received from the archons and purifies it.[30] He is also said to "seal"
souls.[31]

Perhaps the mainstream of the Church did not accept the figure of
Melchizedek and relate it to the hierarchy of the Church because so many of
the writings about Melchizedek come from heretical sects and because of the
Qumran Supremacy of Melchizedek over the two Messiahs.

Yet in spite of the above exaggerations about Melchizedek he still remains the model priest both for Christ and all Christians. If he is an angel, he
is also sexless (he is also without father or mother). This is the image and
"natural resemblance" that must be projected at the altar, a priesthood according to Melchizedek and according to the Epistle to the Hebrews. The
qualities and requirements for such a priesthood are as follows.

Firstly, perfection is not through the levitical law (7:3), which, presumably would correspond to the Catholic ritual law and canon law,

> For when the priesthood is changed, of necessity there takes place a
> change of law also: There were no priests from Judah before Christ
> (7:14).

"Of necessity" seems to connote logical consequence, not external force.

Montefiore[32] says, "He [the author of Hebrews] first deals with Melchisedek, making the same kind of point as Paul did in connection with the
promise given to Abraham (Rom 4; Gal 3:1-22). Paul wished to show that the
Law had been abrogated, and in order to do this he had to go behind the Law
to the period before it was given, to prove that, although it was given by God,
it had only transitory authority and limited efficacy. Our author makes use of
Melchisedek, again going behind the Law to the period before it was given in
order to prove his point. But his application is necessarily different from that
of Paul. Levitical priests were appointed on hereditary principle; the mother
must be Israelite and the father a priest before him."[33] "It was a fleshly or-
dinance, though free from Pauline over-tones of sin, but it connotes the tran-
sitoriness and earthly nature of the commandment."[34] A priest-like Melchizedek could not be appointed because he did not conform to certain legal
requirements.

As Westcott says of Jesus, "He was made priest because of his inherent
nature."[35] "He was not in priestly succession: he simply *arises*, as it were, out
of the blue."[36] His divine nature, united to his humanity, conferred upon the
latter *the power of a life that nothing can destroy.*[37] This union of natures
took place when the Son became incarnate, for it was then that he was given
his priestly office (10:5). Thus an entirely new order (*taxis*)[38] of priesthood
arose, and as Héring observes:[39] "Le dynamisme s' oppose au legalisme juif
et l' auteur en a pris nettement conscience." *Kata dunamis zoēs* means full of
life or giving life.[40]

Buchanan remarks[41] that the Hasmoneans were levitical priests of the
line of Aaron but descended through Joarib; they were not sons of David or

of Zadok (Genisis Rabbah 97; 99:2). Simon was priest until a true prophet should arise (1 Macc 14:41). Simon's son John Hyrcanus I "was the only one to hold three offices [at once], rule of the nation, high priesthood, and prophecy" (Josephus *War* 1:68). "Hyrcanus' oldest son, Aristobulus I, was the first to assume the crown and openly claim to be both high priest and king" (*War* 1:70). The Hasmoneans associated themselves with Gen 14:18; they also identified themselves with Ps 110. However, Buchanan also says,[42] "Nonetheless the Hasmoneans had arisen from Judah and had become high priests. Jews in the author's [Josephus] time knew that very well, for the Hasmonean family continued to have a great deal of influence in Palestinian politics until the last of the fortresses had been captured in A.D. 73 and their memory never ceased." The intertestamental *Test. Lev.* 8:14 predicted that a new king would arise from Judah who would establish a new priesthood. This was probably intended to apply to Hasmoneans.

Moffatt[43] points out that "the positive contrast (v. 19) is introduced by the striking compound *epeisagogé*, a term used by Josephus for the replacing of Vashti by Esther (*Ant* 9:190)."

Michel[44] observes the speciality of Melchizedek's non-legal priesthood over against the levitical. It overthrows all priesthood and begins a new order (*taxis*). The distinct keywords: Melchizedek, *dekatē* (tithe), *taxis* (order), *nomos* (law), *horkōmosia* (oath), *eis ton aiōna* (for the age), and *archiereus* (high priest).

Intertestamental Judaism saw the Levitical priesthood as everlasting and definitive (*Jub.* 13:25ff.). Michel thinks that *Test. Lev.* 8:14(from Judah new kingship will arise which will create a new priesthood for the people) may be a Christian interpolation. *Test. Lev.* 18:1-8 points to an everlasting and eschatological priesthood.[45]

For the author of Hebrews the Christian hope is better than Jewish hope, first because the Jewish law was static while Christian hope is eschatological, and secondly because only Jewish *priests* can "draw near" to God (Ex 19:22), but *all* Christians share in the priesthood (1 Pet 2:5) and all can "draw near" to God.

Hence our concept of priesthood must not be based on sex or any physical requirement but upon the indwelling of indestructible life, that is, the Holy Spirit. The human nature of Jesus originates only from a woman.

The second quality of the new priesthood is participation in the New Covenant. Jesus was the guarantee of a better covenant (7:22), and in Hebrews this covenant is identified with the one mentioned in Jer 31:31 which says that there will be equality between all people, not one person teaching another but everyone knowing the Lord; surely knowing the Lord is an essential requisite for the priesthood (Hebr 8:8-11; cf. 10:16; 12:24).

The third qualification is to be holy, innocent, undefiled, separated from sinners and exalted above the heavens (7:26). According to Catholic teaching, Mary was so, and she has been portrayed as a priest dressed in the robes of Aaron since the fifth century. She is often portrayed by artists as close to the Eucharist.[46]

The fourth qualification is faithfulness. The women in the Gospels—and some contemporary women—are more faithful than men.

The fifth qualification is to be able to sympathize with weakness, to be tempted yet without sin, to be approachable in confidence (4:14-16) and to deal gently with the ignorant and misguided because they are beset with weakness (5:1-2).

The sixth is to make supplication and prayers with crying and tears (5:7); to be obedient in suffering; to make intercession continuously (7:25) and to be willing to do God's will (10:7). All these characteristics are found in a high degree in women. Hence Hebrews shows the way that women can contribute to the Church. See the excellent article by L. Swidler on Jesus' masculine and feminine characteristics in National Catholic Reporter, Vol. 13 (23 April, 1977), p. 15.

Notes

1. Printed in *Journal of Ecumenical Studies*, Vol. 10, No. 4 (Fall, 1973), pp. 695-99.

2. 1 Clem. 43, cf. 40-41.

3. There is a Rabbinic legend that Jesus was lame (*Sanh.* 106b).

4. For a study of priesthood in the Old Testament, see Aelred Cody, *A History of Old Testament Priesthood*, Analecta Biblica (Rome: Pontifical Biblical Institute, 1969). He gives only two scant references to Melchizedek pp. 92, 101f.

5. See Bernard Frank Batto, *Studies on Women at Mari* (Baltimore: John Hopkins University, 1972).

6. *Ibid.*, p. 9.

7. *Ibid.*, pp. 79-80.

8. *Ibid.*, pp. 82-83.

9. *Ibid.*, p. 86.

10. Markus Barth, *Anchor Bible on Ephesians* (New York: Doubleday, 1974), Vol. 2, p. 661.

11. Elisabeth Schüssler Fiorenza in *Priester für Gott* (Münster: Aschendorff, 1972), expounds these texts with precision. She avers that the New Testament develops the unified concept of the teaching of the priesthood of the faithful (p. 43). The priesthood is that of the community and closely associated with that of Christ. The redactor of Revelation used not only Ex 19:6; Is 61:6 and Dan 7, but the cult and sovereignty as it was found in his own time. The priesthood in Revelation is predicated of all Christians (p. 419).

12. It is most interesting that the Church will ordain hermaphrodites "Andragynoides cum certo sint viri, ordinum capaces existunt" (Heriberto Jones, *Commentarium in Codicem Iuris Canonici*, Paderborn, 1954, Vol. II, p. 182; cf. also Emmanuel Doronzo, O.M.M. *De Ordine*, Vol. 3, *De Subjecto*

1963. In the light of this it is difficult to maintain the concept of natural resemblances to Christ and also to preclude women from the priesthood for the bisexual person usually has a great many psychological problems to overcome and often commits suicide whereas women accept their sex.

13. Fred L. Horton, Jr., *The Melchizedek Tradition* (Cambridge: Cambridge University Press, 1976).

14. James A. Sanders, "Dissenting Deities and Phil. 2:1:11," *Journal of Biblical Literature*, Vol. 88 (Sept., 1969), pp. 279-90.

15. Horton, *op. cit.*, p. 17.

16. *Ibid.*, p. 18.

17. See George W. Buchanan, *To the Hebrews*, Anchor Bible Commentary (New York: Doubleday, 1972), pp. 94-95.

18. Horton, *op. cit.*, p. 45.

19. *Ibid.*, pp. 55-56. See Philo, *Leg. All.* 3:79-82; *De Congr.* 99 and *De Abrah.* 235.

20. Horton, *op. cit.*, p. 57.

21. *Ibid.*, p. 57.

22. *Ibid.*, p. 80.

23. Cited by Horton, *ibid.*, p. 80.

24. *Ibid.*, pp. 87-8.

25. *Ibid.*, p. 89.

26. For the Melchizedekians see *ibid.*, pp. 90-113.

27. *Ibid.*, p. 103.

28. *Ibid.*, p. 107.

29. *Ibid.*, p. 137.

30. *Ibid.*, p. 139.

31. *Ibid.*, p. 141.

32. H.W. Montefiore, *The Epistle to the Hebrews* (London: Adam and Charles Black, 1964), p. 123.

33. *Ibid.*, p. 125.

34. Buchanan, *op. cit.*, pp. 125-6, thinks that "fleshly" is used in disparaging ways; thus levitical priesthood "belonged to the classification of 'fleshly' which included all things that were ethically bad." Power of indestructible life may refer to Jesus' miraculous origin. As he had no end of days, his life was indestructible. The fleshly commandment was removed because it accomplished nothing. "In a similar way, Paul discredited the law, which he described as being 'of sin and death' (Rom. 8:2)"; it was "powerless . . . in that it was weak through the flesh" (Rom. 8:3).

35. Quoted by Montefiore, *op. cit.*, p. 125.

36. *Ibid.*, p. 125.

37. *Ibid.*, p. 126. Philo uses a very similar phrase in describing God's creation of Adam (*Leg. All.* 1, 32).

38. Otto Michel, *Der Brief an die Hebräer* (Göttingen: Vandenhoeck and Ruprecht, 1966), p. 269.

39. Jean Héring, *L'Epitre aux Hebreux* (Paris: Delachaux et Niestlé, 1954), p. 70.

40. *Ibid.*, p. 71.

41. Buchanan, *op. cit.*, pp. 94-100.

42. *Ibid.*, p. 124.

43. James Moffatt, *Hebrews*, I.C.C. Commentary (Edinburgh: T. and T. Clark), p. 98.

44. Michel, *op. cit.*, p. 268-9.

45. Michel (*ibid.*) compares the prophecy of Jer 31:31ff. to Hebr 8:8f.

46. Puy d'Amiens portrait. See the reproduction in *A Century of French Painting, 1400-1500*, ed. Grete Ring (London: Phaidon Press, 1949).

23
Women and the Earliest Church: Reflecting on the Problématique of Christ and Culture

Mary Rose D'Angelo

In attempting to use the "attitude of Jesus and the apostles" as a norm for theological decision,[1] the Declaration has raised the issue of Christ and culture, an issue fraught with theoretical and historical complexity. Denying the claim that social and cultural factors appear to have had more signifi-cance than theological demands in the exclusion of women from the Christian ministry, the Declaration makes the counter-claim that, since Jesus "broke with the prejudices of his time" and since the Hellenistic milieu would have enabled the apostles to shake off "Jewish" discriminatory attitudes toward women, the "attitude of Jesus and the apostles" cannot be explained by social and cultural factors.[2] Presumably, then, we must conclude that it is based on some positive theological demand. Both the denial and the counter-claim raise difficulties. Rather than attempting to defend the view of the un-named opponents, this essay will respond directly to the Declaration, point-ing out two major theoretical questions raised by the counter-claim and delineating the very complex problems of reconstructing the historical picture on which such claims must be based.

The Declaration begs the question of the attitude of Jesus by defining it as a *decision to exclude* women from the ministry, a decision which must be deduced from the absence of women from the Twelve and from the apostolic ministry of the earliest Church. The necessity of such a conclusion, is, howev-er, far from clear. First of all there are a variety of historical and exegetical problems involved. How are we to define the function of the Twelve? Is the Christian ministry defined by the pattern of the Twelve, and in what fashion? How do we regard the undoubted fact that the word *apostle* was applied to others? What was the function of an apostle? Can we be sure that no women filled this function? What functions did women fill in the earliest church? Other commentators will broach these problems, and the Report of the Pon-tifical Biblical Commission[3] touches upon most of them. I simply mention them as indications of the historical unclarity with which we are dealing. The real problem is, however, a problem of logic: we cannot be sure that a decision was made by which women were excluded from a clearly defined function in the church; we simply know that there were no women, Gentiles, or, it appears, slaves among the Twelve.[4]

191

The Declaration misrepresents the function of social/cultural factors in the formation of theology and practice by treating them as conscious elements of decision making, and by depicting its unnamed opponents as claiming that "by not calling women to enter the group of the apostles Jesus was simply letting himself be guided by reasons of expediency" and that "this attitude is inspired only by social and cultural reasons."[5]

Cultural conditioning, however, is primarily a matter of the limitation of decision at a level which is at least partially prior to reflection and decision, affecting decision less by causing one to choose between options than by limiting the options from which one can choose. Thus, the roles of women in the early church, insofar as we are able to know about them, cannot be explained without reference to the cultural and social possibilities of the period. The early Church's practice, and probably its theory of the status of women, was similar to that of its cultural milieu; more precisely, the range of roles for women within the early church was to a great extent determined by the cultural possibilities of the contemporary society and these possibilities were limited. We do not have clear evidence that women shared the apostolic ministry, and we do have unambiguous evidence of their increasing exclusion from ministerial roles. It is then unsafe to conclude that this reality sprang from a theological decision rather than from cultural limitation. Without such a conclusion, the interpreter is left without a clear scriptural imperative, and the necessity arises of making a theological decision which is consonant not only with tradition but also with what the Gospel demands in our cultural context.

Slavery gives us an example of a change in these cultural limitations and its effect upon the interpretation of the gospel imperative. The early church proclaimed at baptism that "in Christ there is neither Jew nor Greek, neither slave nor free, nor 'male and female' " (Gal. 3:28). The church received the slave as a brother or sister in the Lord, but did not quarrel with the institution of slavery. Hellenistic philosophers had already begun to question the institution[6] and Judaism had an inherent repugnance for the enslavement of a brother or sister (Israelite). Christianity shared these views and indeed extended them, but did not definitively come to see the owning of slaves and the sufferance of the institution of slavery as incompatible with the gospel until the late nineteenth century. Widening cultural consciousness (or perhaps conscience) made it possible for the baptismal declaration "in Christ there is neither slave nor free" to be recognized as a gospel imperative—but only gradually. The abolition of the distinction between slave and free attached to the new age; only gradually did it become clear how the eschatological reality which transforms the individual in Christ could be realized in the human condition as still tied to the old age.

The gradualness and complexity of this development underscores the problematic aspects of the Declaration's assertions that cultural influence on Jesus and the apostles can be discounted as a factor in the exclusion of women from ministerial functions. We can now turn our attention to the problems involved in the definition of the cultural attitude and deal with the

Declaration's arguments at that level. Different arguments are used with regard to the attitude of Jesus and that of Paul and the apostolic mission; as each involves its own set of historical and methodological problems, they are best treated separately.

The Attitude of Jesus and Its Relation
To His Cultural Context

The Declaration's monolithic view of the character and function of cultural influence leads it to the conclusion that Jesus was independent of such influence, that he "broke with the prejudices of his time by widely contravening the discriminations practiced with regard to women."[7] It sets forth (pars. 11-12) a series of examples of such contraventions on the part of Jesus; however; the suggestion that they represent Jesus' rejection of the social and cultural status of women in his time is open to attack on double grounds.

First, the problem of historicity arises in regard to each of the examples; it is not possible to ascribe any of these incidents to the historical Jesus with certainty, and most of them reflect the view, purposes or milieux of the individual evangelists who transmit them.[8] The Gospels of Mark and Luke in particular have been influenced by the concerns of the Roman empire, and many commentators upon these two Gospels would explain differences from Jewish or Palestinian views as evidence of such influence rather than as testimony to the unique attitudes of the historical Jesus.[9] While the attraction of grounding women's rights in the preaching of the Jesus of history is great, the attempt to do so is open to the same objections as the Declaration's somewhat naive attempt to ground the exclusion of women from the ministerial priesthood on a decision of the historical Jesus. Many scholars would maintain the historicity of these incidents, or of a clearly defined "counter-cultural" attitude of Jesus toward women.[10] Without denying the historicity of such an attitude of Jesus, we may avoid the vexed issue by making a more modest claim, speaking instead of the principles and attitudes communicated by the Gospel message and in the Gospels.[11] This approach has been taken with considerable profit by such scholars as Constance V. Parvey[12] and Raymond E. Brown,[13] in their studies of Luke-Acts and the Gospel of John respectively.

The historical problem underlines the second problematic aspect of the Declaration's contention; the authors claim these incidents as evidence of Jesus' rejection of or freedom from the attitudes of his time. But this assertion disregards the function of the stories in the Gospels, as well as their relation to their cultural milieu. Of none of the incidents cited by the Declaration can it be said that the Gospel writer intended to give Jesus' opinion on the social status of women; the focus in each case is quite different. The forgiveness Jesus extends to the adulterous woman is not intended by the author to teach "that one must not be more severe towards the fault of a woman than towards that of a man"; the legal penalty for adultery is the same for men and women, and disproportionate severity towards the "weaker sex" is not to be expected in Jewish law. In legal penalties in the strict sense, no distinction is made except in favor of the woman (this of course does not preclude a double standard in what falls under a penalty).[14] The message of the story is rather that a vengeful intent and inward sin, or sin that carries no social stigma, is no less sinful than adultery and murder.[15] That Mt 9:20-22 (and parallels) takes no notice of the woman's state of ritual impurity, if the omission is intentional, probably intends to speak only about Jesus' attitude to ritual law.[16] Jesus' contact with the woman in Luke 7 and with the Samaritan woman in John 4 and the presence of the women at the tomb are not intended as examples of Jesus' unusual attitude toward women, but rather as indications that the kingdom's need and reality transcend social conventions and human institutions and that God can use any instrument, however weak and despised, to establish the reign.[17]

The narratives of the empty tomb, however, point to the cultural limitations of this conviction: the evangelists and the early Church could conceive that God had chosen to reveal the mighty deed of Jesus to the women who were weak and foolish in human sight—but not that God's choice had given them the capacity to be witnesses in the sight of the law and the world.[18] This incapacity of women to be witnesses (which we now recognize as a social fact of the first century rather than an ontological defect of women) may well have been the factor which excluded them from the Twelve. At least the author of Luke-Acts defines the Twelve as witnesses of the ministry of Jesus from the baptism to the ascension. According to Acts 1:15-26, witness is the ministry (or office: *episcope*) of the Twelve. The inclusion of women at the empty tomb, then, does not constitute a direct confrontation with and rejection of the cultural restrictions placed upon women, but instead offers an extension of their role within cultural limits.[19] Likewise the attitude which the Gospels ascribe to Jesus should not be regarded as completely transcending the cultural boundaries of his milieu, but as belonging to, perhaps heading (at least in Palestine) the cultural evolution or counter-culture of his time, as being in the fore of a very complex process of expanding human horizons for women.[20] The evangelists' suggestions that Jesus upset convention for the sake of the kingdom fall within the range of cultural possibilities; the Jewish tradition also knows of stories about saints and Rabbis who outrage the convention of religion and even of decency for the sake of heaven and of compassion.[21] Although the rabbinical view of women is generally subordinationist,[22] there exist rabbinical opinions rejecting divorce and polygamy on the basis of an originally androgynous creation of humanity[23] affirming the equality of the sexes before the fall and at the end.[24] As for Jesus' women disciples, or followers, women were the mainstay of religion in the ancient world, and rabbis and philosophers alike relied upon the assistance of women and collected coteries of women followers like the ones attributed to Jesus, especially by Luke.[25]

Thus the primary function of these passages is never concerned with Jesus' attitude toward women. They do clearly distinguish the Jesus of the Gospels from the misogynists of the ancient world and indeed present him as deeply compassionate with the plight of women. Parvey even suggests that the inclusion and instruction of women in the Lucan community may be seen as a secondary function of many of the stories in Luke.[26] But it cannot be said on the basis of these stories that Jesus rejected or sought to change the cultural framework which assumed the subordination of women and indeed the institution of slavery. To suggest that Jesus could have included women in the Twelve if he had willed women to be priests and bishops has the same logical force as saying that he could have freed the centurion's slave if had he not willed the Church to support the institution of slavery.

What then can we say about the attitude of Jesus as the evangelists describe it? It is clear that they wish to declare on his authority that the Gospel and the Kingdom supersede normal human expectation and social convention. From this demand of the Gospel, and possibly from Jesus' prohibition of divorce, it is possible to conclude that: "The reign of God, inaugurated by his (Jesus') preaching, and in his presence, brings with it a full restoration of feminine dignity."[27] It may even be that the obliteration of sexual distinction in the resurrection which transcends and surpasses the equality of the creation is inaugurated before the resurrection in those who choose celibacy for the sake of the kingdom.[28] Within the possibilities of their cultural milieux, the evangelists also present Jesus as having a "good" practical attitude toward women, an attitude that is perhaps unusually favorable, if not unexampled. In other words, the Gospel writers give us a fairly radical principle about the equality of the sexes which is carried out by the Jesus of the Gospels to the extent which the decidedly limited cultural possibilities allowed. Surely the conclusion we should draw is that we also must implement this conviction of equality in Christ to the limits of our cultural experience, and perhaps also seek to broaden those limits.

The Attitude of Paul and the Apostolic Mission

Once the Christian community is extended beyond the borders of Palestinian Judaism, the cultural picture becomes still more complex. When the Declaration suggests that Paul and the other apostles of the Hellenistic mission would no longer be restricted by "social and cultural conditioning" because "in the Greek milieu . . . the same forms of discrimination did not exist,"[29] two difficulties are involved. First, we cannot assume that Paul, other Jewish apostles and those communities which were primarily Diaspora Jews could leave aside Jewish attitudes. Just the opposite seems to be true (cf. 1 Cor 11:2-16). Secondly, "the same forms of discrimination did not exist" in Hellenistic cultures, but the status of women was still problematic.

In fact the legal status and economic situation of women under Roman law was more independent than that of women under Jewish law. This was most notable in such areas of legislation as divorce and inheritance.[30] This should by no means be taken as applying equally throughout the empire, of course. Legislation before Justinian was very frequently determined by the ethnic character or history of the local population.

As the legal status of women varied throughout the Greco-Roman world, Hellenistic thought about women also varied. Among the moral philosophers, especially some of the Stoics, a view of men and women as equal in nature and the necessity of equal education were held.[31] More common and more influential in Christianity was that strain of moral philosophy, represented especially by the neo-Platonists, which used the adjective *female* as a derogatory term, the opposite of the cardinal virtue courage (*andreia*, or manliness) and a synonym for derivative, weak and secondary. This is especially well illustrated by Philo of Alexandria,[32] a very Hellenized Jewish philosopher, who typifies the cross-cultural atmosphere in which the earliest Christian missions must have been largely conducted. The usage derives from Plato[33] and pervades the thought of most of his interpreters.

This view of women leads to an observation about the place of women in the various Hellenistic religious groups of the era. The stigmatization of foreign religions by the satirists and critics like Juvenal focuses in particular upon their women adherents. The virulent attack upon women, especially women of means and independence, in Juvenal's *Satire* VI spares no foible of women worshippers.[34] It is unquestionable that the role of women in traditional religion was greatly extended in the Hellenistic era, particularly by the mystery cults which allowed women a more full role as worshippers than did traditional religion.[35] But the Declaration's suggestion that Hellenistic priestesses could have served as a model for Christian practice had the ontological necessities allowed women to be priests at all[36] fails on two counts. The first is the dearth of evidence that there really were priestesses who functioned in any roles similar to those of the male sacerdotal system. No feminine form of *pontifex* exists, and no instance of this word being applied to a woman has yet been found. Further, women named *sacerdos* appear to have been either mantic figures, like the sybils, or consorts of the male officiants or colleges, like the Vestal virgins, the wife of the *flamen dialis* and the priestess of Bona Dea, who presided over segregated rites of women.[37] Even the rites of the oriental goddesses had hierarchies either dominated by men or exclusively male.[38] Nonetheless, the real objection to the idea that the priestesses of Hellenistic religions could have served as a model is that no priest at all, male or female, could at the earliest period serve as a model for the Christian ministry. Minucius Felix can still boast that Christianity has no altars or temples and contrast to the bloody pagan sacrifices not the Christian liturgy but Christian moral action.[39] Even the Jewish priesthood does not initially serve as a model for the Christian ministry; the Christian liturgy is assimilated not to the temple service but to the lay (and male) service of the synagogue.[40]

Paul and the Hellenistic mission preached in a very complex cultural setting, one which had some incipient principles of equality and developing (but by no means extensive) areas of economic and legal independence, but also deep cultural resistance to such ideas and practices, greatly enhanced by a virulent backlash against them.[41] Juvenal, for instance, represents a protest essentially directed against "uppity women." This attitude differs from, but is no less strong than, the Jewish ideas of Paul and of those of his communities principally composed of Diaspora Jews.

What then can we conclude about Paul's relation to this cultural milieu? I would suggest that this relation is similar to the one between the attitude of Jesus as described by the evangelists and contemporary Judaism. According to the Gospels, Jesus appears to proclaim with the Kingdom a new situation in which the original equality of creation is restored and possibly even an anticipation of the eschaton in which sexual difference is superseded, at least in part. Paul has, and passes down, a baptismal tradition which does not merely re-establish the original equality but overturns the distinction of creation: "In Christ . . . there is no 'male and female' " (Gal 3:28; cf. Gen 1:27).[42] In both cases, the conviction is implemented only insofar as cultural possibilities admit. In the Pauline community, women have a role in the assembly: they may pray and prophesy.[43] But this is not entirely outside the cultural possibilities; prophecy at least was an accepted role for women in both Jewish and Greek milieux. And it is limited by the culturally acceptable, the "decent" (*to prepon*, 1 Cor 11:13) and the "custom" *(hē sunētheia,* 1 Cor 11:16). Paul permits women to pray and prophesy in the assembly—but they must be decently dressed. Although he abandons the attempt to ground the head-covering in a theological necessity and rejects its subordinationist import (1 Cor 11:11-12), he cannot allow the Corinthians to offend decency, or rather his own Jewish cultural conventions, which for Paul have assumed the guise of nature (1 Cor 11:14).[44]

The demand of decency, of that set of conventions by which a society elects to safeguard the sanctity of sexuality and human dignity, is precisely the strongest and most elusive factor of cultural conditioning.[45] As the Report of the Pontifical Biblical Commission remarks, the successors of Paul found it possible and apparently necessary to retrench the roles Paul had permitted to women.[46] That the sense of what is decent and fitting is a factor in this retrenchment can hardly be disallowed. As time went on and the Christian ministry developed into a priesthood, the roles allowed to women decreased. This may have been due in part to a fear of pagan goddesses and their cultic attendents, and certainly resulted in part from the understanding of the ministry as a fulfillment of the Jewish priesthood, and in part from Christian ascetic ideas.[47] But another factor must also have been the outraged sense of decency displayed in the pagan reaction to the relative permissiveness of Christianity toward women.[48] In its ambition to persuade the world by the purity of its life, the Christian church found it neessary to restrict the sphere of women within the assembly.

This concern of the early Church to live a life of exemplary morality might stand us in good stead in reflecting upon the norm that "the attitude of Jesus and the apostles" offers us in our attempt to make the theological tradition speak to the question of admission of women to the ministerial priesthood. Both Jesus and Paul seem to have found in the demand of the Kingdom and the Gospel an equality among humanity, even an abolition of sexual distinction that is at least incipiently recognized in the personal reality of the baptized. On the practical level, the Jesus of the Gospels and Paul both attempt some realization of this eschatological reality but are bound in both cases by cultural possibilities, as Paul says, by what is decent. The baptismal imperative remains, and the cultural context has so changed that admitting women to public and communal authority (pre-eminence in the community) no longer offends the sense of what is decent and human, and sequestering and subordinating women does offend the sense of human decency. In a Church in which the inhibiting cultural demands of earlier generations have been disguised as theology, the conviction of equality in Christ is obscured, and that which was once intended to secure and attest the moral probity of Christians becomes a sign of Christian moral obtuseness.

Notes

1. Declaration, par. 18. I recognize that the document does not attempt to use the New Testament as its sole theological norm; cf. III, 2.

2. Declaration, par. 19.

3. Report of the Pontifical Biblical Commission: "Can Women Be Priests?" II, 3, III, and IV.

4. The Commentary acknowledges the problem but cannot resolve it (III, 4). The logical problem is worked out at some length by Linwood Urban in "A Dialogue Concerning the Ordination of Women," *The Saint Luke's Journal of Theology*, Vol. XVIII, No. 4 (Sept., 1975), pp. 391-404.

5. Declaration, par. 19.

6. See E. Vernon Arnold, *Roman Stoicism* (New York: The Humanities Press, 1958), #309, p. 279, especially the reference to Philo in n. 44: *anthrōpos gar ek Physeos doulos oudeis* (*Sept. et fest. di.*, p. 283 M; *De Spec. Leg.* II.69, Cohn-Wendland). Seneca, *Epistolae Morales* 47 and Epictetus, *Discourses* Book IV provide representative Hellenistic discussions of slavery and freedom, in which freedom is seen as proper to the true philosopher; in many ways the discussion is similar to Paul's assertion of freedom in Christ (1 Cor 7:2-24; Gal 3:26-5.16).

7. Declaration, par. 19.

8. See Constance V. Parvey, "Women in the New Testament," in Rosemary Radford Ruether, *Religion and Sexism* (New York: Simon and Shuster, 1974), p. 138.

9. Krister Stendahl, *The Bible and the Role of Women* (Philadelphia: Fortress Press, 1966), p. 25.

10. Among them, Montefiore, *The Rabbinic Literature and Gospel Teachings* (London, 1930), pp. 46 ff., 217ff. Cf. *The Synoptic Gospels* (New York, 1927), Vol. I, pp. 281, 389; vol. II, pp. 67, 438. Also Leonard Swidler, "Jesus was a Feminist," *Catholic World* (Jan., 1971), pp. 177-183.

11. The hermeneutical problem of deriving principles upon which the Church acts from the New Testament has been carefully examined by Krister Stendahl in the study cited above (note 9) which is subtitled: "A Case Study in Hermeneutics."

12. Parvey, *op. cit.*, pp. 138-147.

13. "Women in the Fourth Gospel," *Theological Studies*, Vol. 36, No. 4 (Dec., 1975).

14. On this see Lev 20:8-21; cf. Dt 22:23-27. Sotah 3,8 summarizes the

legal distinctions between men and women, and they certainly do not include more severe penalties for women.

15. R.E. Brown in *The Gospel According to John*, Vol. I (Garden City, New York: Doubleday and Company, 1966), 388, gives a series of possible functions for the story, including some similar to the one I suggest, but not including the meaning suggested by the Declaration.

16. The story of course originates in Mark, and the legal question is not raised by the evangelists. However cf. Mark 7:1-23, a passage directly concerned with the attitude of Jesus to the law. The Commentary of D.E. Nineham, *The Gospel of Saint Mark* (Baltimore: Penguin, 1963), pp. 157-159 and 187-197 gives an adequate account of the function of both passages.

17. The function of Judith and that of Esther in the books that bear their names is similar. On John 4, see Brown's comments on 4:9 and 27 (*John*, Vol. I, pp. 170 and 172). Elsewhere, however, Brown has interpreted the later part of this chapter as commissioning the woman as apostle to the Samaritans ("Women," pp. 691-692).

18. Stendahl, *op. cit.*, p. 25.

19. Brown suggests that in the Johannine community women filled an apostolic or semi-apostolic function ("Women," p. 695). However, for the sake of argument, we shall allow the Declaration's contention that women held no apostolic office in the early Church.

20. On the variety of practice and theory with regard to women in the ancient world and the implications of that variety see Wayne Atherton Meeks, "Image of the Androgyne," *History of Religions*, Vol. 13 (1973-1974), p. 174: ". . . in practice the Jewish communities in the Roman empire seem to have reflected all the diversity and ambiguities that beset the sexual roles and attitudes of the dominant society." He would however admit that the roles of women are in general more circumscribed in Judaism, especially in Palestine (see esp. p. 199).

21. As an extreme example, see the story told about two saints in *Aboth de Rabbi Nathan* A 8; tr. Judah Goldin, *The Fathers According to Rabbi Nathan* (New Haven: Yale University Press, 1953), pp. 51-52. Also *Babylonian Talmud*, Kiddushin 81b.

22. See Leonard Swidler, *Women in Judaism* (Metuchen, New Jersey: The Scarecrow Press, 1976), esp. pp. 56-82.

23. David Daube, *The New Testament and Rabbinic Judaism* (London: The Athlone Press, 1956), pp. 71-83, gives the texts and explains the argument. He would assert the high antiquity of the teaching of the androgynous creation on the basis of Philo and Mekilta Pisha 146. On Platonic influence, see Meeks, pp. 185-186.

24. The tradition of the rabbinic interpretation of Gen 1:27 is very diverse. It includes doctrines of sexuality which assume an intention of equality in the creation which was not carried out in the reality, so that only the male was "*formed*," and the woman merely *builded* (*Babylonian Talmud*, Ber. 61 a,b; Er. 18 a). But *Genesis Rabbah* (Gen. R.), 14,2 insists on two formations, and 18,2 appears to be a polemic against this interpretation of *building*. Another interpretation proposes an androgynous creation (Gen. R. 8,1) and still another promises that the inequality will be remedied in the world to come (Gen. R. 9). These interpretations are for the most part credited to Amoraim, but Mark 10:2-10, Gal 3:28 and 1 Cor 11:2-12 are usually taken as witnesses to the antiquity of the discussion.

25. On women as followers and supporters of the Stoics and as Stoic philosophers, see Arnold, #300, p. 270. On their role among the Epicureans, see Meeks, p. 172 and notes. Wealthy and prominent Gentile women, including the emperor's daughter, appear throughout the Talmud and Midrashim as inquirers and patrons of rabbis (e.g., bSan 39a). Josephus frequently refers to the support of wealthy women proselytes and God-fearers; especially notable is the case of Helena, queen of Adiabene, *Ant.* xx,ii. On the role of women as disciples in Judaism, see Meeks, pp. 174-175; on its relation to early Christianity and its function in Luke-Acts, see Parvey, pp. 138-147.

26. Parvey, *op. cit.*, pp. 138-147.

27. Report of the Pontifical Biblical Commission, I,3. The Declaration appears to accept the assertion of the report on the basis of Mark 10:2-11: one assumes that an exegesis similar to that given by Daube (pp. 71-83) lies behind the conclusion. Stendahl insists that the passage must be taken to reflect "the given Jewish understanding of male and female," p. 27.

28. Mt 21:31 and 19:11-12; Report of the Pontifical Biblical Commission I.3, although I do not find this argument entirely clear. See also the Pauline baptismal tradition which supersedes the sexual distinction of Gen 1:27 (Gal 3:28). Note Meeks' comments on the cultural background, below, note 42.

29. Declaration, par. 19.

30. See, e.g., Inheritance, Law of, *Oxford Classical Dictionary*, ed. N.G.L. Hammond and H.H. Scullard (Oxford: Clarendon Press, 1970). But note that women do not inherit under Greek law.

31. Arnold, #300, p. 270; for Zeno, the conviction that men and women have the same nature extended to the idea that we should wear the same clothing, and only wear clothing for warmth (p. 288). Musonius Rufus, a Roman Stoic of the first century, expresses the conviction that woman can and must learn philosophy. Since virtue is the same in men and women, education should also be the same, and even work can be the same. See Cora E. Lutz, *Musonius Rufus, "The Roman Socrates"* (New Haven: Yale University Press, 1947), pp. 30, 38-43, 42-49. But it was the Epicureans who actually seem to have included women on an equal basis. See above n. 25.

32. E.g. Woman is contrasted with man as symbols of sense perception and mind respectively; *Qu.in Gen., passim*, esp. I 24-25: *Qu.in Ex.I.7*. Cf. Meeks, pp. 178-179.

33. E.g., *Symposium*, 181A-C; 191D-192A.

34. See especially lines 511-591.

35. See Klaus Thraede, "Frau," in *Realexikon für Antike und Christentum*, Vol. VIII (Regensburg, 1970), col. 207: also Günter Haufe, "die Mysterien," in J. Leipoldt and Walter Grundmann (eds.), *Umwelt der Urchristentums* (Berlin, 1965), pp. 101-126.

36. Declaration, par. 16.

37. Thraede speaks of "numerous priestesses" but without distinguishing their functions; both he and Haufe speak of a role of women in the initiation ceremonies of Eleusis, which role does not seem to be the equal of the dynastic priesthood of which Haufe also speaks (pp. 104-105). Evidence for women in high priestly offices is generally based upon iconographical rather than textual or epigraphical attestation, and is therefore highly ambiguous.

38. E.g., Lucian's account of the Syrian Goddess and Apuleius' account of the Isis cult in *The Golden Ass* give no evidence for priestesses, and epigraphical evidence is extremely scarce and ambiguous. The cult of Isis provides a possible exception, but here again, written evidence for the participation of women at high levels of priesthood is rare and ambiguous, but seems to be in keeping with the statements made above: see Sharon Kelly Heyob, *The Cult of Isis among Women of the Greco-Roman World* (Leiden: E.J. Brill, 1975), pp. 95-97, also 110. The iconographical evidence Heyob adduces for the priestess who represents Isis herself and for the participation of men and women on an equal basis seems to me particularly ambiguous in view of the frequent occurrence of the female orant in early Christian iconography.

39. Minucius Felix, *Octavius*, 32: note also 33 which assumes that the Jewish liturgy of sacrifice, which had used temples and altars, had never been acceptable to God.

40. Justin, who does apply the word *sacrifice (thysia)* to the Eucharist, likens it to the *prayers* offered by the "true Jews" of the captivity (*Dialogue with Trypho*, 117,2), making a careful distinction between this worship and the sacrificial liturgy of the temple. It is noteworthy that that part of the Eucharist to which the word *sacrifice* appears to apply here is the eucharistic prayer (117.3).

41. See Meeks, p. 179.

42. Robin Scroggs suggests that the formula rejects discrimination but admits distinction; "Paul and the Eschatological Woman: Revisited," *Journal of the American Academy of Religion,* Vol. 42, No. 3 (Sept., 1974), p. 533. But this idea cannot take into account the revision of Gen 1:27, which the formula cites, apparently according to the LXX, and rejects. See Krister Stendahl, *The Bible and the Role of Women* (Philadelphia: Fortress Press, 1966), p. 32. On the function of this formula in the baptismal liturgy and the function of re-unification formulae as a counter-cultural force in the ancient world, see W.A. Meeks, pp. 180-183 and 165-167, also p. 207, where he characterizes the idea as an expression of realized eschatology, amounting to "metaphysical rebellion" and "cosmic audacity."

43. Meeks would see the role of women in the communities of the Pauline school as broader still, indeed quite unusual in antiquity (p. 198, see also p. 199).

44. See Meeks p. 201. His resolution of what he calls the "apparent self-contradictions in Paul's response" into a decision to advocate *functional* equality but preserve *symbolic* distinction does not entirely convince me (pp. 201-202).

45. Note Meek's association of a threat to the male-female distinction with a threat to the ordered cosmos in the mind of antiquity (p. 179).

46. Biblical Commission Report II, 3, III.

47. Francine J. Cardman, "Women, Ordination and Tradition," *Commonweal*, Vol. CIII, No. 26 (Dec. 17, 1976), pp. 808-809.

48. See the comments of Porphyry, Julian, Libanius and Ammianua Marcellinus summarized in and/or quoted by Pierre de Labriolle, *La Réaction païenne* (Paris, 1942), pp. 284-285, 418, 432 (where Julian expresses scorn at Christians who are taught by their women!).

24
"Transitory Character" . . . Only in "Disciplinary Cases of Minor Importance"?

Juliana Casey

These two sentences refer to the "claim" that certain Pauline statements are of a "transitory character." The document says that these statements are "scarcely more than disciplinary practices of minor importance." It gives the example of the wearing of veils by women. Such requirements, it declares, "no longer have a normative value." While few would argue today that women must wear veils in the Christian assembly, the question is not quite so simple.

It is not clear that those Pauline statements which have been seen to be transitory or which have been corrected by later generations are simply "disciplinary practices of minor importance." Paul's attitude towards civil authority in statements such as those of Rom 13:1-7 where he says, "Let every person be subject to the governing authorities" (13:1), and that "He who resists the authorities resists what God has appointed" (13:2), or that everyone must pay taxes, "for the authorities are ministers of God," (13:6),[1] would find little acceptance among the world's oppressed, the political prisoners, the victims of torture or the families of those legions who have "disappeared" under totalitarian regimes. Further, the oft-repeated Pauline statement that slaves must "obey in everything those who are your earthly masters" (Col 4:22)[2] has been clearly contradicted by both the teaching and the actions of the Roman Catholic Church. While these statements were undoubtedly conditioned by the attitude toward authority prevailing in the first-century world, they nonetheless refer to something more fundamental than disciplinary practices and they have nonetheless subsequently been seen as having a transitory character.

The same is true of Paul's attitude concerning both women and marriage. While statements concerning the adornment of women (cf. 1 Tim 2:9) are clearly reflections of contemporary customs, those in which we are told that "man is the head of woman as Christ is the head of man" (1 Cor 11:2ff.; cf. also Eph 5:23) and that wives must be subject to husbands (Col 3:18; cf. Eph 5:22,24), or the later statements that women are to learn in silence (1 Tim 2:11), that no woman is to teach or to have authority over men (1 Tim

2:12) and that woman will be saved through bearing children (1 Tim 2:15) are hardly compatible with the present-day understanding of the dignity of each person, or with the document's own introductory statement that women have played a "decisive role and accomplished tasks of outstanding value" in the history of the Church. The last statement concerning salvation through the bearing of children is clearly in contradiction with the Church's unfailing encouragement of celibate women's religious communities. Further, the Pauline understanding of marriage as a concession to temptations of immorality as it is expressed in 1 Cor 7:1-9 is hardly the same understanding reflected in documents such as Vatican II's *Gaudium et Spes*. These statements, while clearly beyond the realm of "minor disciplinary practices," have generally come to be accepted as somewhat less than binding upon the consciences of the faithful, and their "transitory character" has subsequently been accepted as obvious.

There are, then, numerous teachings within the Pauline epistles which were written out of a particular cultural, sociological framework and which reflect the general opinion of the social milieu contemporaneous to the composition of the epistles. These statements deal with some very fundamental issues such as relationship to civil authorities, slavery and freedom, marriage, the dignity of woman. They are not all "scarcely more than minor disciplinary practices," yet they are all regarded today as less than normative.[3] The question of Paul's attitude toward women and toward their participation in the Church, then, cannot be answered by dismissing some statements as unimportant and preserving others which are seen as based upon firmer ground, such as Paul's idea of creation.[4]

The statements in these two sentences of the document, it appears to us, are based upon a limited and somewhat arbitrary view of those texts in the Pauline literature which have been generally accepted as no longer having a normative value. Further, the authors of the document introduce a false distinction between disciplinary practices and other, more important statements. Finally, they mistakenly limit the influence of the customs of the period to minor statements such as those concerning such things as the wearing of veils. Clearly, these customs—and the world-view which inspired them—are responsible for some rather profound and oft-repeated statements within the epistles. One need only think of the acceptance and practice of slavery for an example.

A final word should perhaps be added concerning the language of this particular section of the document. One would have wished that such an important and decidedly controversial document could have been written with more care and exactitude. The question of the normative value of certain scriptural passages is a serious one and demands more than a casual dismissal of certain texts as "scarcely more than disciplinary practices of minor importance." The debate concerning the meaning of these texts has been carried on by many serious and committed scholars. Expressions such as "one claims to see" do justice neither to those who have given of their effort and their science to correctly understand the word of God, nor to a declaration published by such an important body as the Sacred Congregation for the Doctrine of the Faith.

Notes

1. See also Tit 3:10.
2. This same idea is found in 1 Cor 7:21-24; Eph 6:5-8; 1 Tim 6:1-2; Tit 2:9-10.
3. It should be noted here that beyond those texts already mentioned, other statements, such as those concerning the marital status of bishops (1 Tim 3:1-7) and the dangers of younger widows who grow wanton against Christ (1 Tim 5:11), the reference to the Jews who killed the Lord Jesus (1 Thess 2:13-14), the prescription that Christians should not be "unequally yoked with unbelievers" (2 Cor 6:14), could be added to the list of those texts which are either ignored or considered as less than absolutely binding.
4. The following sentences in the document do this when they base the prescription concerning women speaking in the assembly upon Paul's understanding of the plan of creation. It should be noted, however, that the document contradicts itself here, for the text which it cites to support this position (1 Cor 11:7) is actually part of Paul's argument for the necessity of the wearing of veils—a prescription which it has dismissed as no longer having normative value.

25
Women in the Pauline Assembly:
To Prophesy, But Not To Speak?
Robert J. Karris

This sentence is the tip of an exegetical iceberg. The iceberg is the question of how 1 Cor 14:34-35 is related to 1 Cor 11:5. In 1 Cor 11:5 women pray and prophesy in the assembly; in 1 Cor 14:34-35 they are forbidden to speak in the assembly. Some scholars solve this apparent contradiction by arguing that 1 Cor 14:34-35 is a later interpolation and consequently non-Pauline.[1] The Declaration accepts the authenticity of 1 Cor 14:34-35 (and 1 Timothy) and solves the apparent contradiction by distinguishing between women's rights to prophesy and to teach in the assembly. It argues that the former right is granted whereas the latter is not.

Perhaps the contours of this exegetical iceberg will become more visible if we spell out the relevant Scripture passages:

1 Cor 11:5: "but any woman who prays or prophesies with her head unveiled dishonors her head—it is the same as if her head were shaven."

1 Cor 14:33b-36: "As in all the churches of the saints, [34]the women should keep silence in the churches. For they are not *permitted* to speak, but should be subordinate, as even the law says. [35]If there is anything they desire to know, let them ask their husbands at home. For it is shameful for a woman to speak in church. [36]What! Did the word of God originate with you, or are you the only ones it has reached?"

1 Tim 2:11-12: "Let a woman learn in silence with all submissiveness. I *permit* no woman to teach or to have authority over men; she is to keep silent."

Now that I have charted the waters we must traverse in commenting on this sentence from the Declaration, I will follow the Declaration's lead and focus on the verb "to speak," *lalein* in Greek.[2] It would seem that since 1 Cor 14:34-35 is genuinely Pauline and not interpolated, *lalein* might be interpreted via its context in chapter 14. Within that context *lalein* occurs in verses 2,3,4,5,6,9,11,13,18,19,21,23,27,28,29,39. With the exception of verses 3,11,28 and 29 *lalein* occurs with "in tongues" and means "to speak in tongues." Although William Orr/James Walther[3] suggest that *lalein* in 1 Cor 14:34-35 be interpreted as "speaking in tongues," I doubt whether that is the meaning. *Lalein* would seem to mean "to speak in tongues" only when "in tongues" accompanies and specifies it. In any case, the context of the passage gives no clear proof that *lalein* means to teach officially in the Christian assembly.

Besides context, the wording of the passage itself might help us understand the meaning of *lalein*. If we grant that both verses of 1 Cor 14:34-35 refer to the same situation, it seems that the occurrence of *lalein* in verse 35 helps one to interpret its occurrence in verse 34. In other words, *lalein* refers to the asking of questions within the assembly and does not refer to authoritative teaching.[4]

If one explores other passages in the Pauline correspondence where *lalein* occurs, one arrives at the following conclusion. *Lalein* only approximates "to speak" as the official function of teaching in the Christian assembly when it has an object which specifies it and gives it such a pregnant meaning. See, for example, 1 Thess 2:2: "but though we had already suffered and been shamefully treated at Philippi, as you know, we had courage in our God *to speak* to you the gospel of God in the face of great opposition." Contrast 1 Tim 5:13: "Besides that, they (young widows) learn to be idlers, gadding about from house to house, and not only idlers but gossips and busybodies, *speaking* what they should not." In 1 Cor 14:34-35 *lalein* has no object to specify it and consequently does not have the pregnant meaning of "to teach officially."[5]

In sum, it seems to me that in 1 Cor 14:34-35 *lalein* means to ask a question. Further, it does not seem patent that *lalein* in 1 Cor 14:34-35 refers to the official function of teaching in the Christian assembly. Consequently, it does not seem that this passage prohibits women from engaging in the official function of teaching in the Christian assembly.

Before concluding this essay, I would like to devote some space to 1 Tim 2:12, the third Pauline text to which the Declaration refers. Perhaps the Declaration viewed this passage as a sound parallel to help one interpret the difficult 1 Cor 14:34-35. But before 1 Tim 2:12 can qualify as an interpretive parallel to 1 Cor 14:34-35, two criteria have to be met: 1) the vocabulary and literary contexts should be similar; 2) the historical situations should be similar. Criterion one is not quite met. Although both passages contain exhortations, 1 Cor 14:34-35 uses the verb *lalein* whereas 1 Tim 2:12 uses *didaskein* ("to teach").[6] Let us see whether criterion two is met.

What is the situation behind 1 Tim 2:12? 1 Tim 2:8-15 seems to be instructions for men and women on conduct during worship. The injunctions for women in 1 Tim 2:9-12 have parallels in similar exhortatory materials in 1 Peter 3:1-6 and 1 Clement 1:3; 21:7.[7] An examination of these parallels shows that *didaskein* is unique to 1 Tim 2:12 and may have been introduced by the author into traditional exhortatory material because of his polemical situation. Further investigation of the author's situation would intimate that women had been won over to the heretics' side and were creating problems for the church.[8] Within this situation the prohibition of teaching may have

connotations of "false" teaching.[9] Briefly put, behind the prohibition of 1
Tim 2:12 seems to lie a problem created by female false teachers. To stamp
out this abuse, the author enjoins that women should not teach in the assembly.[10]

The situation behind 1 Tim 2:12 seems to be quite different from that of
1 Cor 14:34-35. Whatever the problems within the Corinthian community—
and there were many—it does not seem that female false teachers were one of
them. The two situations seem too disparate for one to use 1 Tim 2:12 as an
interpretive parallel to fathom the difficult 1 Cor 14:34-35. Moreover, as we
observed above, it seems that *lalein* in 1 Cor 14:34-35 bears the meaning of
"to ask a question" and cannot be construed to mean "to teach."

Notes

1. For a listing of scholars and the arguments which they marshall for
the non-Pauline character of 1 Cor 14:33b-36 (34-35), see Wm. O. Walker,
Jr., "1 Corinthians 11:2-16 and Paul's Views Regarding Women," *Journal of
Biblical Literature*, Vol. 94 (March, 1975), pp. 94-110 (95 n. 6). 1 Tim 2:12,
the other Pauline passage referred to here by the Declaration, fits into these
scholars' solution in this wise. The Pastoral Epistles, to which 1 Timothy
belongs, are not written by Paul and stem from the end of the first century
A.D. The rare verb "to permit" in 1 Cor 14:34 can be explained as derived
from 1 Tim 2:12 where "to permit" also occurs. This observation and others
lead scholars to date both passages from the same time—the end of the first
Christian century. In what follows I will not pursue further the thorny question of whether 1 Cor 14:34-35 and 1 Tim 2:12 are Pauline or not. For the
sake of this brief article, I will presuppose, along with the Declaration, that
Paul wrote both 1 Cor 14:34-35 and 1 Timothy.

2. The Declaration refers to "exegetes." Rather than align lists of exegetes against lists of exegetes, I have decided to provide a study of the term
lalein in 1 Cor 14:34-35 and in the Pauline corpus.

3. *1 Corinthians: A New Translation, Introduction with a Study of the
Life of Paul, Notes, and Commentary. Anchor Bible* (Garden City: Doubleday, 1976), p. 313.

4. See Herman Ridderbos, *Paul: An Outline of His Theology*, trans.
John Richard de Witt (Grand Rapids: Eerdmans, 1975), p. 462 n. 105. In
speaking of *lalein* in 1 Cor 14:34, Ridderbos remarks: "One can still consider
whether this is intended in the sense of 'to teach,' as in Tit. 2:1. But v. 35
points in another direction."

5. This conclusion is arrived at from a concordance study of the occurrences of *lalein* in the Pauline corpus. It does not seem necessary or advan-
tageous to list all those occurrences here. The samples given above are
deemed representative.

6. See note 1 above where the occurrence of the rare Greek word for
"to permit" in both passages was noticed.

7. For non-Christian parallels see Martin Dibelius/Hans Conzelmann,

The Pastoral Epistles: A Commentary on the Pastoral Epistles. Hermeneia, trans. Philip Buttolph and Adela Yarbro (Philadelphia: Fortress, 1972), pp. 46-47.

8. See 1 Tim 4:3; 5:11-15; 2 Tim 3:6-7.

9. On the methodology being employed here to argue for the author's insertion of *didaskein* into traditional material, see my article, "The Background and Significance of the Polemic of the Pastoral Epistles," *Journal of Biblical Literature*, Vol. 92 (December, 1973), pp. 549-564, esp. pp. 550,551 n. 10, and 563 n. 58. For a plausible setting for such female false teachers within the first century A.D., see J. Massyngberde Ford, *New Testament Studies*, Vol. 17 (1970/71), pp. 338-346, esp. pp. 343-344. For an argument similar to the one developed here, see David M. Scholer, "Exegesis: 1 Timothy 2:8-15," *Daughters of Sarah,* Vol. 1, No. 4 (May, 1975), pp. 7-8: ". . . the context of the Pastoral Epistles suggests that the heresy Paul is opposing here was centered on women in particular (see 1 Timothy 4:3; 5:11-15; 2 Timothy 3:6-7). I conclude that the admonition of 1 Timothy 2:11-12 is directed against the usurpation by women involved in false teaching" (p. 8).

10. It is characteristic of the author of the Pastorals that he most frequently argues by assertion and injunction. See my article cited above, "Background," esp. pp. 549-550.

26
The Divine Plan of Creation:
1 Cor 11:7 and Gen 2:18-24

Thomas L. Thompson

The Declaration's attempt to defend Paul's prohibition of women teaching in church (1 Cor 14:34-35) by stressing Paul's argument that such prohibition was derived from "the divine plan of creation" is a quite peculiar case of special pleading: it attempts to propose a distinction in Paul's disciplinary exhortations between commands which are "probably inspired by the customs of the period," and, as such, reversible (such as the obligation to wear veils), and other regulations which might be somehow understood as culturally transcendent, as part of a "divine plan," and consequently beyond the disciplinary power of the church to change.

This argument is peculiar in that the "divine plan" theory of Paul, which the Declaration has chosen to cite (1 Cor 11:7), is not directly related to Paul's prohibition of women speaking in the assemblies (1 Cor 14:34-35), which is based more simply on obedience, the law (v. 34), and by what Paul perceives as the shamefulness of it (v. 35). That is, Paul forbids women to teach for reasons which are most readily understood as culturally and historically susceptible. 1 Cor 11:7—the proof text cited by the Declaration—is directly related, however, to Paul's insistence that women be veiled (1 Cor 11:2-15)! The very prohibition which the Declaration considers to have been culturally determined, and therefore in theory reversible, is a prohibition which Paul understood as related to ecclesiological typology (1 Cor 11:3) and as based on what he understood as woman's subordinate place in creation.

Limited even to the categories of argument offered by the Declaration, one must conclude that the prohibition of teaching is both contingent and theoretically reversible, and that the requirement of veils has a somewhat more lasting character. However, the presuppositions from which the arguments of the Declaration proceed are hardly more sound than the arguments. If one accepts that Paul's discipline is in any way culturally and historically contingent, as the Declaration does—and one must—is it theologically legitimate to claim that the *criteria* for discerning the degree and actuality of contingency lie in what *Paul's historically influenced understanding and theology* propose as based in law, mores, or Scripture? Are not just such criteria profoundly determined by both Paul's individual personality and inclination, and, more globally, the thought world of the first century?

The historical limitations of this aspect of Paul's theology, and of the

Declaration's dependence on it, are very apparent in a comparison of 1 Cor 7 with what the Declaration proposes as a text relating to a "divine plan of creation" in Gen 2:18-24. The proposal of this text as somehow supporting in an ontological or theological way some essential subordination of the female to the male is ironic, since the basic literal meaning of the text centers itself around a narrative episode which stresses the complete likeness and equality of men and women(That *Paul* understood Genesis' priority as superiority, and that the priests of the Sacred Congregation understand Paul's superiority as irreversible hegemony, are merely a most obvious example of historically contingent changes in theology, caused by culturally inherent biases against women.)

It ought not be assumed that the cultural milieu of the author of Gen 2-3 was unbiased against women, though it is possible to argue that the author, whether a man or a woman, was sensitive to this kind of question. It is obvious that the narrator of the garden story saw more clearly than either Paul or the authors of the present Declaration, that the subordinate position of women in society was a fact illustrative of human alienation and hardly good or desirable. In terms of creation, however, both the biblical creation narrative (Gen 1) and the Garden Story (Gen 2-3) stress the unity of the sexes.

The author of Gen 1 has God cause the waters and the earth to develop vegetation, fish, fowl, and animals in their various forms and species (Gen 1:11,20,24), but humanity is created more directly, and not according to species or kinds, but in the form (or image) of God (Gen 1:26). It is not found in Genesis, as in Paul, that the male alone was made in the image of God, but it was humanity, male and female (Gen 1:27).

The Garden Story of Gen 2-3 allows a different manner of presenting this same understanding of the essential equality of men and women. That the author is fully aware of the male-centeredness of his or her contemporary society is clear from the aetiology of Gen 3:16 with its ironic perception of human alienation. Yet, the alienation and subordination of women is seen here precisely as a given which defines the evil of society and humanization. Not only is the creation of man and woman out of the original human in the Garden Story not understood as the cause of such subordination and alienation, but all of the elements which are used in this episode are arranged with the very opposite intention. The essential issue of the episode in Gen 2:18-24[1] is that the human *(ha-'adām)*, which has been placed in the garden, is lonely. God decides to overcome this lack by making another creature to help the human, a creature just like the human. In the vivid mode of the narrative, God then sets about forming other creatures in the same way that he had formed the human. Each of these creatures in turn God brings to the human, but with only incomplete success. The human names all of the animals and birds, but none of them were really like the human, nor fit to help it. Undaunted by this failure, God then tries a different way. If what is wanted is a creature like or equal to the human, then creation must proceed by separation, following the principle of like from like. God takes a bone from the human and out of that makes woman. When he takes the woman to the human to be identified, the human approves with a series of sayings which affirm the likeness and identity of men and women: like comes from like: bone from bone, flesh from flesh, woman *('issah)* from man *('iš)*. This identity is exemplified in marriage (here not understood as hierarchical as in Paul), where the two become one. The ultimate expression of equality is unity reestablished.

It is important to keep in mind, when comparing the narratives in Gen 1 and Gen 2-3, Paul's prohibitions, and the present Declaration, that all four are profoundly influenced by their historical and cultural contexts. All are written from a point of departure in male-centered societies. The culture of the authors of Genesis and of Paul might even be described as patriarchal, though misogyny is not as pervasive in early Israelite society as it is in Paul's or that of the authors of the present Declaration. In fact, it is this lack of misogyny in Gen 1 and Gen 2-3 which gives these narratives a sensitivity which is lacking in the others and ought to be instructive to the Church, if it is to reexamine its practice in a society and culture no longer patriarchal in order to rid itself of its inherited cultural burden of misogyny and prejudice. This burden, vast and still pervasive, had already been perceived as evil by our own tradition more than 2500 years ago.

Notes

1. For much of the following interpretation, I am indebted to Dr. Dorothy Irvin.

27
St. Paul's Attitude Toward Women

John L. McKenzie

I am asked to comment on the brief passage of the Declaration dealing with Paul's attitude toward women. The comment must certainly bear upon Galatians 3:28 and upon some apparent inconsistencies in Paul's attitude towards women.

The revolutionary force of Paul's language in Galatians 3:28 can hardly be appreciated without some knowledge of the background of the writer. Paul was reared as a Jew and professed Judaism until his adult life. One wonders sometimes how many modern Jews realize the degree of *machismo* there is in their religious heritage. Until Conservative Synagogues of the United States began to change their discipline in 1972 (not changed in Orthodox Synagogues, though Reform Synagogues eliminated the problem over a hundred years ago), the *minyan*, the minimum number of ten required for a synagogue service, meant ten male Jews; women do not count. One becomes a Jew by circumcision, and only by circumcision. Women are not obliged to the full *Torah*.[1] Jewish literature provides a generous measure of quotations expressing disrespect and contempt for women.[2] Josephus, whom not all Jews would admit as a witness, said flatly that woman is inferior to the male in every way. An ancient Jewish prayer preserved in modern Jewish prayer books expresses the Jew's thanks that God has not made him a *goy* or a slave or a woman.[3] It is of interest, although I am sure it is merely coincidental, that these three classes are precisely the three classes whose differential is annihilated in the unity of Christ Jesus.

In the world of Paul the difference between Jew and Gentile, slave and free, and male and female represented the deepest class divisions of society. I have spoken of the third class with reference to the Jewish world; in Hellenistic-Roman Society the social position of woman was higher than it was in Jewish society. A close examination of the social position of women makes one aware that the adjective "higher" is used in a qualified sense. The greater freedom of the Roman lady was the freedom to be promiscuous. Paul was not concerned with this. In a society in which women were not fully Jews he did say that in Christ the difference is unimportant.

In our ecumenical age perhaps it is not nice to resurrect the contempt of Gentiles, and especially of Christian Gentiles, exhibited in the sayings of Talmudic and medieval rabbis. If women were not fully human, Gentiles were brute beasts. If women were morally weak, Gentiles did not even know the difference between right and wrong. Gentiles in the Roman world were aware of Jewish contempt and they resented it.

Slavery none of us knows except by reading. In Roman law the slave was not a human person. You could kill a slave; you could not murder him. Humanity did emerge, for the emancipation of slaves was common; unlike the domestic animal, the slave could save money to purchase his freedom. But as long as he was a slave, he was a chattel in law. This difference also was annihilated in Christ. Yet slaves could become officers of the church; Gentiles could become officers of the church. But the unity of Christ which embraced Jews and Gentiles, slaves and free, did not quite encompass men and women. If Paul had meant this, it would have been easy for him to say so.

One cannot adduce any New Testament text in support of the ordination of women. One cannot adduce any New Testament text in support of the ordination of men. Officers named *hiereus*, priest, are not mentioned in the New Testament. The apostles were all men; the office expired with the first generation of the church. *Episkopoi*, overseers, and *diakonoi*, ministers, are mentioned. Both of these are obviously groups within the local church. We do not know their duties or powers. The number of offices, or what could be offices, in the apostolic church of the New Testament is so large it seems that almost every believer had an office. Very probably they did; for office was the working of the Spirit in the believer, and if the Spirit did not work in the believer something was seriously wrong. The office of priest (*hiereus* or *sacerdos* or *kohen*) was known in Greek and Roman religion and in Judaism; its absence in the apostolic church cannot be merely coincidental. I once suggested that the apostolic church rejected the whole category of the sacred as known in its predecessors and contemporaries—sacred places, persons, objects—and that the reintroduction of the sacred was an intrusion of a pagan element into Roman Catholicism.[4] Possibly I am arguing that women are not ordained and men should not be. Paul did fairly well with no consciousness of ordination but a great sense of mission.

We know little about the ministry of women in the apostolic church; and in a masculine-clerical tradition we have not tried to find out more. Phoebe is called a *diakonos* of the church of Cenchreae (Romans 16:1). This is surely an ecclesiastical office, however vague the definition of its responsibilities; I do not know why it is not an office in this passage except that Phoebe was a woman, and that begs the question. I doubt seriously that Phoebe was the only woman in the apostolic church who was a deacon. It is certainly unwarranted to assume that her service was limited to such things as the collection and distribution of old clothing. A saying of Jesus (Mark 10:43) exhorts whoever would be great among you to become your *diakonos*: that is, to be in the group of disciples what Phoebe was at Cenchreae. If one likes the kind of word games which are so highly regarded by the Congregation for the Doctrine of the Faith, one could project that the office of *diakonos* put Phoebe within reach of becoming great among the disciples.

Aquila and his wife Priscilla are always mentioned together. Paul counts them among his fellow workers, and they had a church in their house (Romans 16:3-5). They were obviously a husband-wife evangelical team, and the one thing we can be sure they did was to teach. The word "fellow worker" *(synergos)* is applied in the Pauline correspondence to Urbanus (Romans 16:9), Timothy (Romans 16:21; Philippians 3:2), Epaphroditus (Epaphras; Philippians 2:25; Philemon 24), Clement (Philippians 4:3), Philemon (Philemon 1), Demas and Luke (Philemon 24). These are men who were or could have been bearers of sacramental powers and jurisdiction, and no difference is made between them and Priscilla.[5]

Romans 16 is thought to be a list of Ephesian Christians. Besides Priscilla and Aquila, there are 24 personal names. Of these five are feminine, and two unnamed women appear also. Paul does not distinguish between services rendered by men and services rendered by women. The quarrel of Evodia and Syntyche (Philippians 4:2) must have been ecclesiastical; it is doubtful that anything less would have deserved mention in a letter to the whole church. Paul also says that they have struggled with him "in the gospel" (NAB "in promoting the gospel"). Clearly they were more than officers of the Altar Society; indeed, this mention by name suggests an important role in evangelization which scholars have not attended to. The context suggests that their importance may be compared with that of Clement (4:3).

Paul was not entirely consistent in his dealings with women. Few men are. The breadth of his statement in Galatians 3:28 and his practice, dim as our view of the details may be, clash rather sharply with his imposition of silence upon women in the assembly of worship (1 Corinthians 14:33-36) and the same prohibition amplified by some unnecessary anti-feminist rabbinical exegesis (1 Timothy 2:9-15). Modern scholars generally think that 1 Timothy is not from Paul himself; this, of course, does not close the question of how faithful the author was to the traditions of the Pauline school. In 1 Corinthians, which is surely from Paul, we hear the echoes of Jewish practice, in which women, according to some rabbis, should not even learn the *Torah*, let alone teach it.[6] Nevertheless, could Paul have addressed this to Priscilla? or to Phoebe? or to Evodia and Syntyche? Obviously he could not and did not. He wrote this to the church of Corinth about participation in charismatic worship such as speaking in tongues and in prophecy; and he seems to have forgotten in 14:33-36 what he said in 11:5. He does speak as the rabbi, as he does in many other passages. After all, he had been trained in rabbinical patterns of thought and speech. It appears that where we do not enshrine his rabbinical utterances and style as apostolic constitutions, we neither understand nor forgive him for going to a rabbinical school—and for learning his lessons so well.

Let me add a personal note. The contributors to this commentary were asked not to show in their tone the anger which they may feel. I wish to assure readers that the objective and dispassionate tone of this note does not disclose my whole mind about the Declaration. The Church is never served well by bad scholarship. I cannot think of any pontifical document which departed so far from the methods of sound learning as this document.

Notes

1. Hermann Strack-Paul Billerbeck, *Kommentar zum Neuen Testament aus Talmud und Midrasch* (Munich, 1928), III, pp. 558 f.
2. A. Oepke in Kittel, *Theologisches Wörterbuch zum Neuen Testament*, I (Stuttgart, 1933), pp. 781-784.
3. *Ibid.*, p. 777. The corresponding prayer to be said by a woman is: "Blessed art thou, Eternal One, our God, Lord of the world, who hast made me according to thy will."
4. *Did I say That?* (Chicago: Thomas More Press, 1973), 45-50.
5. This has some reference to the word game presented by the Congregation on "fellow workers," par. 17 of the Declaration.
6. Strack-Billerbeck, *Kommentar*, III, 468.

28
Substantive Changes in Sacraments?
Paul J. LeBlanc

It is on the quotation from the Council of Trent that this paragraph hinges. There are two issues which can be profitably explored: first, the context of this quotation, and second, the meaning of what comprises the substance of the sacraments.

Context

It's tough to live polemically. It is from within the controversy over communion under both species that this statement comes, and it is to this topic, and to the question of the communion of children under the age of reason, that the entire twenty-first session of the Council of Trent was devoted. Not that communion under both species was a central issue at the start of the Reformation, but it developed into an object of controversy. The bishops at this session were open to allowing communion under both species, and many were actively in favor of it.[1] But those who opposed it framed the question in such a way as to obscure the benefits of such a practice. They contended that no greater grace is given under two species than under one. As a result, there is no *necessity* to receive communion under two species. The next step in the argument has to be taken carefully. It could be, "therefore any request for communion under both species contains the seeds of heresy"; or "the discipline of the sacrament, i.e., whether communion is received under one species or the other or both, is a matter of indifference (doctrinally speaking),[2] and therefore only matters of scandal or doctrinal danger would dictate one or another of the methods."

Through the distinction which the Council made between the substance and the discipline of sacraments, the Council was able to face the doctrinal question alone and leave the disciplinary question in the hands of the pope (Pius IV, who was known to be personally in favor of communion under both species). The Council could affirm the historical facts that communion under both species was the original and general form of communion in the early Church, that gradually the usage of receiving communion from the cup fell into disuse, and that such a change did not entail a betrayal of the will of Christ.[3] The intensity of Counter-Reformation polemics, however, did not allow the openness of the Council to be pursued in later policy.[4] The Church has had to wait until our own times, for the Second Vatican Council and the revised *Order of Mass*, to see the gradual reintroduction of the practice of communion under both species.[5]

Such a context raises two important points for our concern over the ordination of women. First, the scope of the debate must not be unduly narrowed. There is more to priesthood than being a leader of cult. To confine the debate on the ordination of women exclusively to the cultic dimension of priesthood is analogous to confining the debate on the reception of communion under two species to the question of whether more grace is received under two species than under one. The activities of Jesus in the gospels are more often framed in terms of feeding, healing, teaching, preaching and exorcising than in terms of cultic presidency. Furthermore, the initial model for priests of the Christian dispensation was the presbyteral model, an institution of antiquity which was somewhat analogous to what we would call a city council—though it included religious jurisdiction too.[6] It would be important, then, for any discussion of women priests to include the wider, non-cultic dimensions of priesthood, as well as the cultic.

Second, the quality of the debate must not be allowed to take on the character of total warfare, for it is such a context which produces exaggerated claims. It would not be hard for the advocacy of the ordination of women to be presented in such urgent terms that it would be seen as the salvation of the Church (the Jesus-event lays first claim to that distinction). Nor would it be hard for the rejection of the ordination of women to be presented in such terms that the very orthodoxy of the Church depends upon it. The ordination of women is neither the greatest opportunity nor the worst heresy that the Church has ever encountered; yet if the debate gets out of hand, its effects could be felt far longer than the effects of the debate about communion under both species. The interpretation given by the Introduction to the *General Instruction of the Roman Missal* regarding the practice of communion under both species is instructive in this regard:

> Moved by the same spirit of pastoral concern, the Second Vatican Council was able to reconsider the norm laid down by Trent about communion under both kinds. The Church teaches that the full effect of communion is received under the one species of bread; *since that doctrine is rarely if ever challenged today*, the council gave permission for communion to be received sometimes under both kinds. . . . (Number 14, italics added)

The Substance of the Sacraments

This is certainly one of the more important issues raised by the Declaration. Although the Declaration stops short of saying that the maleness of the priest is a matter of substance, it correspondingly omits to say that it is simply a matter of discipline. It is obvious that if the matter is one which concerns the substance of the sacrament, the Church would have no authority over the matter, but if the matter were simply one of discipline, it could be changed by the Church at any time.

It is my impression that the substance of sacraments is rather more limited than we are accustomed to think. Let us look at several examples.

Eucharist. There is far more positive scriptural warrant for the reception of Eucharist under two species (Mt 26:26-28; Mk 14:22-24; Lk 22:19-20; 1 Cor 11:23-29; Jn 6:53-57) than there is positive scriptural warrant for the maleness of the priest of the Church, yet the reception of Eucharist under two species by anyone other than the priest celebrant is not considered part of the substance of the sacrament.[7] Can we then say that the maleness of the priest is sacramentally more substantive than these positive scriptural invitations to communicate under both species?

Anointing of the Sick. The scriptural basis of this sacrament is seen as being in Mk 6:13 and Js 5:14-15. In spite of the positive precept in James, the earliest implementation of this sacrament is in the episcopal consecration of the oil (and self-administration by the laity according to their needs). It is not until Carolingian times that the first organized ritual is produced with presbyteral anointing and laying on of hands. Even so, throughout this length of time, the sacrament is still destined to the sick. From the eighth century there is a gradual change of perception from the sacrament as being destined to the sick and for their healing, to a perception of the sacrament as being destined to the dying and for their purification (i.e., preparation for death). This change of perspective is accomplished by the twelfth century. It is only with the recent revision of the sacrament (1972) that some of the original perspective is restored.[8]

If such a change in the purpose of the sacrament is not regarded as pertaining to the substance of the sacrament, are we to regard the maleness of the priest as being any more sacramentally substantive?

Penance. The similarity between penance and baptism is striking. The calls of John the Baptist, Jesus, and the early Church to repentance and conversion led to baptism. It was the concern about the veracity of such a conversion that led the Church to allow the possibility of only one opportunity for reconciliation after the commission of serious post-baptismal sin. Reconciliation was granted only after the completion of severe penances (including, among other things, abstention from marriage relations with one's spouse) which were expected to be continued even after reconciliation was granted. Beginning in the sixth century, however, a new form of penance arrived on the scene, which was repeatable, and applicable to sins that were considered minor as well as major. Penances, while severe, did not continue after reconciliation. Then in the twelfth century another form—granting absolution *prior* to the performance of a usually minor penance—arose, along with a still different (and now defunct) form of pilgrimage penance (wherein laity with minor sins and clerics with grave and scandalous sins could confess their sins, be given a pilgrimage to undertake, and consider themselves absolved upon completion of their pilgrimage).[9]

These four widely differing forms of penance (our own familiar form—form one in the 1973 revision—arising only in the twelfth century) do not differ in substance from one another. Are we to regard the maleness of a priest as being any more sacramentally substantive?

Paul J. LeBlanc   219

Baptism-Confirmation. The earliest baptismal ritual we possess is that of the *Apostolic Tradition* of Hippolytus.[10] When the description of the baptismal ceremony is completed, the newly baptized is brought into the church where another imposition of hands and anointing takes place in front of the entire congregation. This is then followed by the sign of peace, some prayers (i.e., what we would call the general intercessions), and the presentation of the oblations.[11] The sense of this imposition and anointing, which is later separated from the entire ceremony as the sacrament we know as Confirmation, is that of a public affirmation of the fact that this person has now been baptized and is a full member of the Church. Such a public ceremony was needed because the baptism, for the sake of modesty because of the nakedness involved, was done privately and apart from the church.

Since the substance of neither of these two sacraments has changed in the course of later developments,[12] can we regard the maleness of the priest as being any more sacramentally substantive?

A final word. Even such a cursory outline would suggest that we are not talking about an issue pertaining to the substance of the sacrament of orders, but simply to its discipline. The more substantial issue is more likely to be the cultural one.

Notes

1. P. Richard, *Concile de Trente* in Hefele-LeClercq, *Histoire des conciles,* Vol. IX, Part 2 (Paris: Librairie Letouzey et Ané, 1931), p. 693.

2. It has aways been recognized that the sign value of receiving communion under two species is greater than that of one and for this reason is to be preferred. Today we would express it in terms of symbolism. Symbols are those things or actions which allow the human to enter into contact with the divine. As the quality of the symbol is enhanced, so too is human accessibility to the divine. The quality of the symbol does not increase grace, it simply facilitates our engagement in and orientation to the divine.

3. Cf. James J. Megivern, *Concomitance and Communion: A Study in Eucharistic Doctrine and Practice* (Fribourg: The University Press, 1963), pp. 252-254. A rather full discussion may be found in E. Dublanchy, "Communion sous les deux espèces," *Dictionnaire de théologie catholique,* Vol. III (Paris: Letouzey, 1908), cols. 552-572.

4. In 1564, Pius IV authorized some German bishops to permit communion under both species, but he had to suppress this concession the following year.

5. Cf. the Second Vatican Council's *Constitution on the Sacred Liturgy,* n. 55, the instruction *Eucharisticum Mysterium* (May 25, 1967), and the *General Instruction* to the revised (1969) *Order of Mass,* nos. 76 and 242.

6. André Lemaire, *Les ministères aux origines de l'Église* (Paris: Editions du Cerf, 1971), pp. 17-27.

7. Even the reception of communion under two species by a priest at

the Mass in which he is ordained is a matter of permission. Cf. the *General Instruction*, no. 242.

Such a vision is possible only in a context where in point of fact, although not in theory, the Mass is seen as the act of the priest and not of the Church. When a person acts in the name of the Church, whether or not the Church is there, he soon begins to conceive of himself, for all practical purposes, as the Church.

8. Antoine Chavasse, "L'Onction des infirmes dans l'église latine du IIIe siècle à la réforme carolingienne," *Revue des sciences religieuses*, Vol. XX (1940), pp. 64-122, 290-364; Claude Ortemann, *Le sacrement des malades: Histoire et signification* (Lyon: Editions du Chalet, 1971).

9. A handy summary of this development may be found in the two volumes by Cyrille Vogel, *Le pécheur et la pénitence dans l'Eglise ancienne* (Paris: Editions du Cerf, 1966) and *Le pécheur et la pénitence au Moyen-Age* (Paris: Editions du Cerf, 1969).

10. Bernard Botte. ed., *La Tradition Apostolique de saint Hippolyte; essai de reconstitution,* Liturgiewissenschaftliche Quellen und Forschungen, 39 (Münster: Westfalen, 1963).

11. *Ibid.*, no. 21, especially pp. 50-55.

12. For a thorough treatment of this development, cf. J. D. C. Fisher, *Christian Initiation: Baptism in the Medieval West,* Alciun Club, 47 (London: S.P.C.K., 1965), as well as the essays and bibliography in *Made, Not Born: New Perspectives on Christian Initiation and the Catechumenate* from the Murphy Center for Liturgical Research (Notre Dame: University of Notre Dame Press, 1976).

29
Authentic Theology
in Service of the Church
Anne Carr

This essay briefly examines the grounds on which the magisterium of the Church determines what can change and what must remain unchanged in the Church's doctrine and practice. The argument is that in the task of distinguishing and deciding, the Church is dependent on theology, and that theology, in the present historical context, is adequate insofar as it successfully draws on four major sources of reflection: Scripture, tradition, the human sciences, and contemporary experience. The theology of the Declaration is judged to be methodologically inadequate in relation to these sources, thus rendering the substance of its argumentation and its conclusions doubtful.

Discussing the limits of the Church's power over the sacraments and its need to distinguish the substance of the sacraments (over which the Church has "no power") from matters of mere historical practice or discipline, the Declaration asserts, "In the final analysis it is the Church, through the voice of her Magisterium, that, in these various domains, decides what can change and what must remain immutable."[1] It has been said that this is the really decisive argument of the Declaration, since "the argument attempted from Scripture, historical and systematic theology is not convincing."[2] Yet it is important to analyze as well the limits surrounding *this* recognized power of the magisterium itself. Such an analysis will enable us to answer the question of the ways in which the Church decides what can change and what must remain immutable. For the Declaration claims to have decided that the exclusion of women from pastoral office in the Church must not be changed. Are the grounds for such a decision present in the Declaration itself?

First it must be noted that this Declaration is not framed in an infallible form, even though the Pope "approved this Declaration, confirmed it and ordered it publication" (par. 41). Since its authority, as part of the ordinary magisterium, is fallible, it is clear that the matter of the ordination of women is *not* settled once for all. Appeal to the Holy Spirit, or the authority of God, in claiming that exclusion of women from the pastoral office is the mind of Christ or of divine revelation (to which in Scripture and tradition the magisterium is bound) in such a statement is not yet sufficient reason for eliciting the assent of the Church. For the very choice of a non-infallible form by the Congregation for the Doctrine of the Faith indicates that the statement's claim to truth is only as convincing as the reasons that are adduced in support of its conclusions.[3] "Logic and honesty suggest that statements of the [ordinary] *magisterium* are ultimately invitations to a dialogue in which the pros and cons can be sorted out."[4] Thus it is important to consider the grounds upon which the Church can decide for or against a change in its teaching or practice.

In its decision-making, the Church in its teaching office is, in fact, dependent on theology. While it is true that the magisterium ultimately decides or refrains from rendering a decision on the various positions offered by theology, nevertheless the teaching office of the Church depends on exegetes, historians of tradition and theologians to lay before the Church the results of their study and research.[5] Such dependence is clear in the Declaration, which offers several convergent arguments from Scripture and tradition, and a set of reasons from the analogy of faith, in support of its position. Theology in the Church, it has recently been suggested, can be understood as a "second magisterium" in the present post-juridical, post-authoritarian age. Pointing out that the pope and bishops today generally follow a model of authority developed by the Roman school theologians as recently as the latter part of the nineteenth century, Avery Dulles finds that an older tradition used the term "magisterium" primarily for licensed teachers of theology. Thomas Aquinas "make a sharp distinction between the *officium praelationis*, possessed by the bishop, and the *officium magisterii*, which belongs to the professional theologian.[6] Dulles argues for recognition of the proper competence of these two "complementary and mutually corrective" magisteria in order to insure that theology's goal as the pursuit of truth, in distinction from the pastoral role of the hierarchy, be clear.[7] The role of theology in its service to the Church is thus not an arm of the Church's pastoral authority but fidelity to truth in its reflection on revelation. Dulles' position is consonant with the long tradition of theology in the Church, with the spirit and letter of the Second Vatican Council,[8] and with the current self-understanding of theologians. Its general outlines of the intellectual integrity and independence of authentic theology are unexceptionable in a Church bound to the *truth* of God's revelation. "Theology must pursue the truth for its own sake, no matter who may be inconvenienced by the discovery."[9]

Given some such contemporary understanding of the relative independence of theology in its scholarly and truth-seeking role, and of the relative dependence of the Church's authoritative teaching function on theology, it is apparent why any theological position maintained by the ordinary magisterium is as authoritative as the power of the theological argumentation which supports it. How, then, can the Church decide what, in its doctrine and practice, must remain immutable? Clearly, it does so in dialogue with the findings and consensus of independent scholarship of contemporary theology in the Church.

The word "contemporary" here is crucial. Karl Rahner has shown that the historical character of the Church's theology as ongoing reflection on an historical revelation means that theology cannot be a closed system. "The spiritual, religious and secular situation in which the history of the revelation-event takes place functions as a stimulus to [its] growth."[10] Genuine theology must be in close contact with its historical situation and engage in continual dialogue with it in an open and critical way. It must also be recognized, Rahner adds, that theology can be sinful in failing to be rational enough, remaining complacent in the fortress of "ecclesiastical orthodoxy," believing it has an answer before it has really understood a genuinely new question.[11] Hence it can be argued further that the grounds and manner of the Church's decision-making in matters of doctrine and practice lies in the quality and fullness of its theological dialogue within its particular historical situation.

A brief indication of the components of adequate contemporary theological dialogue will indicate in a formal sense why the Declaration's theological argumentation fails to satisfy the requirements for an authentic and compelling decision of the ordinary magisterium in the case of the ordination of women.

Scripture

According to the Constitution on Divine Revelation of Vatican Council II, the Church and its theology are bound to the norm of Scripture, interpreted according to modern historical-critical methods of exegesis.[12] The failure of the Declaration to take into account the findings of the Pontifical Biblical Commission's recent report on the question of the ordination of women in relation to Scripture is well known. That report[13] indicates that the seventeen members present unanimously agreed that the New Testament alone does not settle the question of women's ordination, and a majority of members voted that the scriptural evidence alone is not enough to exclude the possibility of ordaining women. That the Declaration places such heavy weight on the attitude and practice of Jesus in its argumentation, and does not consider the findings of the Biblical Commission nor of recent scholarly publications on this complex question renders its scriptural argumentation and conclusions at least dubious.

Tradition

The same Constitution on Divine Revelation of Vatican II maintains that Scripture is to be interpreted within the context of the Church's tradition. While the Declaration affirms the importance of tradition, scholars have already noted a selective and partial reading of tradition and no reference to the findings of recent historical studies on the question of the exclusion of women from pastoral office. Such studies demonstrate that the reason for the traditional practice of excluding women from pastoral office rested not so much on an interpretation of the intention of Jesus with regard to the ordained ministry as on the belief in women's naturally inferior state in the order of creation, subordinate to the "headship" of the male.[14] The Declaration presents evidence of a tradition which rests on notions about the nature of woman which are false and which have been explicitly rejected by the human sciences, by common experience, by theology and by the magisterium itself.[15]

The Human Sciences

While no one disputes the central importance of Scripture and tradition in theology, there is certainly not full agreement about the relevance of the human sciences as dialogical partners in its contemporary reflection. For the Declaration asserts, "The human sciences, however valuable their contribution in their own domain, cannot suffice here, for they cannot grasp the realities of faith: the properly supernatural character of these realities is beyond their competence."[16] Following on this statement is an assertion of the radical distinction of the Church from other societies. While it is true that the human sciences cannot directly *judge* the realities of faith (or the structures of the Church as a society), the implications of the Declaration's assertion seem to be that the sciences are irrelevant to theological discussion. And the Declaration itself makes no use of the findings of contemporary biology, psychology, sociology, history and anthropology relevant to the question of the relation of the sexes or the nature of women, in its determination of "the respective roles of men and women," "a difference of fact on the levels of [their] functions and service," a difference which "is the effect of God's will from the beginning."[17]

This failure is contrary to the consonance and analogy between faith and reason affirmed in the Constitution on Faith of Vatican Council I[18] and implies a kind of "double truth" in which there can be a contradiction between human knowledge and revealed truth. It further appears to contradict the important statements of the Pastoral Constitution on the Church in the World of Vatican Council II about the appropriate use of the "findings of the secular sciences, especially psychology and sociology," and the blending of "modern science and its theories . . . with Christian morality and doctrine . . .[in order that] religious practice and morality can keep pace with . . . scientific knowledge and with an ever-advancing technology."[19] There is a large body of theological literature on the question of the ordination of women which makes use of the findings of the human sciences in its reflections but which does not appear to have been considered in the Declaration.[20]

Contemporary Experience

This final element in theological dialogue is difficult to define, but it is clearly implied by the historical character of theology. While much of contemporary experience is reflected in the human sciences and in current theological literature, the concern here is not simply with scholarship but with the everyday experience of people in the Church. It is to be noted that recent changes in the discipline of sacramental life (e.g., Confirmation, Penance, the permanent diaconate) have been made in relationship to contemporary pastoral and secular experience of Christians. In the Declaration, one finds little reference to any real understanding of the contemporary experience of lay people, and particularly of women. Added to the lack of open consultation with the broader theological community noted above is the striking lack of consultation with lay people, and especially with women, in a matter of direct concern to both.[21] The Declaration presents women, who are assured by the

Church of their equality and the desirability of their increased share in the Church's decision-making,[22] with the inequality of having their roles in the Church entirely determined by a male clergy.

We have outlined the dependence of the teaching function of the Church on the work of theology, considered as a relatively independent work of scholarship seeking the meaning and truth of Christian revelation in the contemporary situation. The adequacy of theology in turn is dependent on the quality and depth of its use of the sources of revelation in Scripture and tradition, in light of the present knowledge of the human sciences and the contemporary experience of all classes of persons in the Church. The Declaration has fallen far short of adequacy in its consideration of the results of contemporary theological studies of Scripture and tradition, and the relation of these to the human sciences and to contemporary experience. The result is a document which appears to have pre-determined conclusions, and which bears little evidence of open consultation with the wider theological and pastoral communities in the Church. As a fallible statement of the ordinary magisterium, its decision about what can change and what must remain immutable on the issue of the ordination of women to pastoral office in the Church is neither persuasive nor compelling, since the arguments are not sufficient evidence to support its conclusion. Only in the fullness of dialogue can an authentic decision about doctrine or practice occur in the Church.

Notes

1. Declaration, par. 23.

2. Edward Kilmartin, S.J., "Letters," *America*, Vol. 136, No. 9 (March 5, 1977), p. 178. Cf. also John R. Donahue, S.J., "Women, Priesthood and the Vatican," *America*, Vol. 136, No. 13 (April 2, 1977), pp. 285-289.

3. Englebert Gutwenger, S.J., "The Role of the Magisterium," *Dogma and Pluralism*, Concilium, Vol. 51, ed. Edward Schillebeeckx (New York: Herder and Herder, 1970), p. 53.

4. *Ibid.*, p. 52.

5. Karl Rahner, S.J., "Considerations on the Development of Dogma," *Theological Investigations*, Vol. IV, trans. Kevin Smyth (Baltimore: Helicon Press, 1966), pp. 15-16.

6. Avery Dulles, S.J., "The Theologian and the Magisterium," *Proceedings of the Catholic Theological Society of America*, Vol. 31, 1976, p. 242.

7. *Ibid.*, p. 243.

8. *Ibid.*, pp. 240-241.

9. *Ibid.*, p. 246.

10. Karl Rahner, "The Historicity of Theology," *Theological Investigations*, Vol. IX, trans. Graham Harrison (New York: Herder and Herder, 1972), p. 68.

11. *Ibid.*, p. 76. Cf. also Anglican/Roman Catholic Consultation,

"Statement on the Ordination of Women," *Origins,* Vol. 5, No. 22 (November 20, 1975), pp. 349-352.

12. *The Documents of Vatican II,* ed. by Walter Abbott, S.J. (New York: Guild Press, 1966), pp. 118-122.

13. Biblical Commission Report. Cf. also the bibliography in Anne E. Patrick, "Women and Religion," *Theological Studies,* Vol. 36, No. 4 (December, 1975), pp. 744-747.

14. Cf., e.g., Haye van der Meer, S.J., *Women Priests in the Catholic Church?,* trans. Arlene and Leonard Swidler (Philadelphia: Temple University Press, 1973); Roger Gryson, *The Ministry of Women in the Early Church,* trans. Jean Laporte and Mary Louise Hall (Collegeville: The Liturgical Press, 1976).

15. Cf., e.g., "Pastoral Constitution on the Church in the Modern World," *The Documents of Vatican II,* pp. 227-228; John XXIII, *Pacem in Terris* (New York: The America Press, 1963), No. 14, p. 14; Paul VI, "Address to the Committee for the International Women's Year," *Origins,* Vol. 4, No. 45 (May 1, 1975), pp. 718-719.

16. Declaration, par. 34.

17. *Ibid.,* pars. 5, 30, 31.

18. Denzinger #1797.

19. *The Documents of Vatican II,* p. 269.

20. Cf. the bibliographies in Anne E. Patrick, S.N.J.M., "Women and Religion," pp. 737-765; and *Women and Catholic Priesthood: An Expanded Vision,* ed. Anne Marie Gardiner, S.S.N.D. (New York: Paulist Press, 1976), pp. 199-208.

21. Cf. Third Synod of Bishops, *The Ministerial Priesthood and Justice in the World* (Washington: USCC, 1972), p. 44.

22. Cf. n. 15 above; Archbishop Joseph L. Bernardin, "Statement on Behalf of the Administrative Committee of the National Conference of Catholic Bishops," *Origins,* Vol. 5, No. 17 (October 16, 1975), pp. 257-260; Vatican Study Commission on Women in Society and in the Church, *International Women's Year 1975: Study Kit* (Washington: USCC, 1975), pp. 28-29; Vatican Study Commission on Women in Society and in the Church, "Recommendations on Women in Church and Society," *Crux Special* (September 20, 1976); cf. also *L'Osservatore Romano,* English ed. (August 12, 1976), pp. 4-5.

30
Did Jesus Exclude Women from Priesthood?

Sandra M. Schneiders

This sentence purports to give the principle upon which the fundamental affirmation of the Declaration rests, namely, "the Sacred Congregation for the Doctrine of the Faith judges it necessary to recall that the Church, *in fidelity to the example of the Lord*, does not consider herself authorized to admit women to priestly ordination"[1] (emphasis mine). Section 4 of the Declaration, and specifically the sentence being commented upon here, maintains that the reason why the Church is not only *unwilling* at this time to ordain women but is now, and will always remain, *unable* to ordain women to the priesthood is that Jesus acted in some way during his earthly life which divinely established the priesthood as exclusively male. This assertion raises two serious questions, one of theory and one of fact.

The Theoretical Question

The principle invoked by the Declaration is that in some cases of sacramental activity (obviously not in all)[2] some practice of Jesus is known to be directly and normatively relevant to later sacramental practice. In all (and presumably only) these cases the Church cannot alter the prevailing sacramental practice.

This raises the theoretical question of the *criterion* for determining in which cases the behavior of Jesus binds the Church. In respect to the issue of ordaining women the question becomes: on what grounds has the Sacred Congregation decided that Jesus' behavior in the matter of choosing the Twelve constitutes a norm binding the Church in the matter of ordaining priests? And on what grounds has it decided that the behavior of Jesus in the matter of choosing the Twelve is binding insofar as it touches on the sex of the Twelve but not insofar as it touches on their race, ethnic identity, age, or other characteristics?

Both the Declaration and the official Commentary imply that the operative criterion is the relationship that a certain symbolic activity of the Church manifests between the historical events of our salvation and the sacrament which realizes that salvation in our lives. In such cases, according to the Declaration and Commentary, a change in the practice of the Church would destroy the symbolic expressiveness of the sacrament because it would destroy or obscure the reference to the historical event.

The Commentary gives as an example of the application of this criterion the use of bread and wine in the Eucharist linking the sacrament to the Lord's Supper. The relationship between the Lord's Supper on the night before he died and the Eucharist is the clearest example (and perhaps the only clear example) of the relationship between a particular historical action of Jesus and a present sacramental activity of the Church. It is certainly clearer than the relationship between any known practice or action of Jesus and the present sacrament of ordination.[3] Furthermore, it is certain that Jesus' use of unleavened bread and wine at the Supper was not a mere historical accident or a culturally dictated choice, something which is not at all certain in regard to the choice of men only as members of the Twelve.[4] These elements were prescribed for the Jewish Passover of which the Christian Eucharist is a fulfillment. Therefore, unleavened bread and wine link the Eucharist with both the certain action and the explicit intention of Jesus in establishing the New Covenant in his blood.

Despite this clear connection between the historical action of Jesus and the sacramental practice of the Church the Sacred Congregation for the Doctrine of the Faith approved, under certain conditions, the use of grape juice rather than wine in the celebration of the Eucharist by alcoholic priests.[5] If, in this case in which Jesus' manner of acting and especially his intention in so acting is certain, and their relationship to the present sacramental practice is perfectly clear, the behavior of Jesus can be set aside for the good of the Church and/or some of its members, it is difficult to see why, in a case in which the actual behavior of Jesus, his intention, and the relationship of his behavior to the sacrament of ordination is not clear, and in which the pastoral reasons for a change in the sacramental practice are urgent,[6] the Church must consider itself unable to change. In other words, if the principle can be waived in a clear and certain case, it is not very convincing to argue that it must be applied absolutely in a much less clear and certain case.

In fact, the absence of any workable criterion for the application of the Declaration's principle seems to have been obvious to the Declaration's authors, for the final appeal in the Declaration is simply to the decision of the Magisterium in deciding when and how the principle is to be applied: "In the final analysis it is the Church, through the voice of her Magisterium, that, in these various domains, decides what can change and what must remain immutable. . . . The Church makes pronouncements in virtue of the Lord's promise and the presence of the Holy Spirit . . ." (par. 23).

This appeal of the Declaration to the Spirit's guidance of the Magisterium is, in the present case, more than a little suspect. It is a matter of record that the Magisterium, on this matter, is not expressing the faith of a very significant segment of the Church, especially in the United States.[7] Furthermore, the Magisterium, in this case, acted contrary to the growing consensus in the theological community that there is no theological obstacle to the ordination of women,[8] and in contradiction to the carefully studied and explicit conclusions of the Pontifical Biblical Commission. The Commission voted 12 to 5 that, should the Church decide to ordain women, it would not be acting contrary to the will of Christ.[9] In other words, the official biblical scholars at the service of the Sacred Congregation maintained that the major argument given in the Declaration cannot be defended on biblical grounds. The Congregation had this knowledge at hand before it published the Declaration, which nevertheless makes no reference whatever to the Commission's work or to its conclusions.[10]

In a case in which there is not a clear consensus among the faithful and in which the most competent available theological and biblical opinion run counter to the Congregation's position it is doubtful that the latter can legitimately claim to be guided by the Spirit unless it wishes to maintain that it is the sole and independent organ of the Spirit in the Church. Such a claim, which seems to be implicit in the way in which the Declaration was formulated, is contrary to the Church's traditional understanding of itself and especially to the renewed ecclesial self-consciousness since Vatican II.[11]

The Factual Question

The Declaration claims that in refusing to ordain women the Church is following a perpetually binding "manner of acting" of Christ. Even if there were some criterion for ascertaining which actions of Jesus were normative for the sacramental activity of the Church (and if such a criterion exists it is not clear from the Declaration or Church practice what it is or how it can be applied) it would still be necessary in the question of the ordination of women to *establish the fact* that Jesus acted in such a way as to indicate his intention to exclude women, for all time, from priestly ordination.

The Declaration maintains that the "manner of acting" of Jesus to which it appeals is Jesus' choice of males only as members of the Twelve. Implicit in this argument, and absolutely necessary for its validity, is a syllogism which is operative throughout the Declaration but which is never expressed:

Jesus ordained only the Twelve as priests.
But Jesus selected only males to be among the Twelve.
Therefore, Jesus selected only males to be ordained priests.

Let us leave aside completely the question of whether, in choosing only men to be among the Twelve, Jesus intended to exclude women as such, any more than by choosing only Jews he intended to exclude Gentiles as such, or in choosing only Caucasians he intended to exclude non-Caucasians as such, and so on.[12] A number of authors have already pointed out the invalidity of singling out sex as an object or as the only object of Jesus' intentionality in his choice of the Twelve. St. Paul's clear affirmation that the sexual distinction in matters salvific is abolished by Baptism into Christ (Gal 3:28) makes the Declaration's position on this point even more questionable on theological grounds than it already is because of its lack of foundation in the historical attitude of Jesus.

The most serious factual problem in the major premise of the Declaration's implicit syllogism is that Jesus did not ordain anyone, male or female, to the priesthood. The Twelve are not the unique or even the principal precursors of the later Church officials whom we call priests. And both men and women were among Jesus' immediate followers who were, in virtue of a commission from Jesus or subsequent activity in the early Church, the precursors of present day priests. The Declaration limits its argument to the Twelve for the obvious reason that this is the only group associated with Jesus which was composed exclusively of males and hence the only possible basis for the Declaration's conclusion regarding the exclusion of women from priestly ordination. But there is simply no historical grounds for regarding the Twelve as the first priests, for maintaining that Jesus ordained them, or for considering them as the exclusive precursors of that role in the Christian community which is later filled by ordained priests.

It is unnecessary to repeat here the careful scholarly work that has been done in recent years on the subject of ordained priesthood in the early Church.[13] Suffice it to say that there is wide consensus among reputable New Testament scholars that there were no Christian priests in New Testament times and therefore certainly none ordained or appointed by Jesus.[14] The priesthood does not emerge in the early Church until the end of the first century at the earliest and, even at that relatively late date, the evidence is scanty and unclear.[15]

The functions within the early Church which later came to be associated with ordained priesthood were never limited to the Twelve, and some were apparently never exercised by the Twelve. We have no clear evidence that any of the Twelve ever presided at the Eucharist and it is relatively clear that others, notably prophets, did so by some sort of official designation.[16] It is interesting to note that the role of prophet is one which we are certain women played.[17] The tasks of missionary proclamation, baptising, catechesis of new converts, administration and service of local communities, and the like, were functions that were certainly exercised by ministers who were not members of the Twelve and, in at least some (if not most) cases, not appointed by the Twelve.[18]

There is clear evidence that a number of these functions were exercised by women and no clear evidence that women were excluded from any of them as a universal practice or on principle. What we do know for certain is that there were women among the disciples who went about with Jesus during his public life (Lk 8:1-3), a woman who received an Easter appearance of Jesus and was directly commissioned by him to announce the kerygma (Jn 30:11-18),[19] women who were involved in the founding of early Christian communities (Acts 18 with Rom 16:3-5), women leaders in some early communities (Rom 16:1-2, 6, 12),[20] women involved in the catechesis of new converts (Acts 18:26) and in public liturgical functions (1 Cor 11:5). In short, there is no historical reason to maintain that women were certainly absent, much less intentionally excluded by Jesus and/or the early Church, from any of the functions which later came to be associated with the ordained priesthood.

The only group associated with Jesus to which it is certain that no women belonged was the Twelve. But the only role which belonged exclusively to the Twelve in the economy of salvation was that to which no one, male or female, is successor, namely, that of constituting together the foundation of the renewed Israel, the Christian community, as the twelve patriarchs constituted the foundation of the Chosen People.[21] Consequently, the all-male composition of the Twelve is irrelevant to the question of any future ministry in the Church, including ordained priesthood. The Twelve are immortalized as the foundation of the Church. As such they have no successors.[22] And as disciples, apostles, teachers, early Church leaders, etc., in which capacities they do have successors, they are members of a wider group which was never all male.

In summary, the principle invoked by the Declaration for the exclusion of women from the ordained priesthood, namely, that the practice of Jesus makes such exclusion mandatory for the Church, is *inapplicable in theory* because there is no criterion according to which it can be applied in this case, and *indefensible in fact* since Jesus did not ordain anyone to the priesthood and the functions in the later Church which were eventually associated with ordained priesthood were never restricted by Jesus to males.

Notes

1. Par. 5.
2. For example, we have no precedent in the behavior of Jesus for auricular confession, confirmation, anointing of the sick with oil, or most of the other sacramental activities of the Church, almost all of which have undergone change down through the centuries.
3. Contemporary sacramental theology has largely abandoned the search for specific "institution texts" for most of the sacraments.
4. Cf. John R. Donahue, "Women, Priesthood and the Vatican," *America*, Vol. 136 (April 2, 1977), pp. 285-289. See esp. pp. 285-286.
5. Letter of Cardinal Seper, Prefect of the Sacred Congregation for the Doctrine of the Faith, to Cardinal Krol, President of the National Conference of Catholic Bishops, dated May 2, 1974. The Letter was commented upon in a statement by Bishop J. S. Rausch, General Secretary of the NCCB, on May 23, 1974.
6. I am in no way minimizing the pastoral urgency of the decision in favor of alcoholic priests but wish merely to point out that the pastoral urgency of the ordination of women, if only because of the number of people negatively affected by the present exclusion of women from orders, is even greater.
7. The Detroit "Call to Action" Conference in Oct. of 1976 was an episcopally-originated consultation of the faithful in the United States. The participants gave the U.S. bishops a clear recommendation for the ordination of women to the priesthood.
8. The numerous responses criticizing the Declaration, e.g., that of the Faculty of the Jesuit School of Theology at Berkeley which was published in

the Los Angeles *Times* on March 18, 1977, bear witness to this growing consensus. A major objection to the Declaration is the failure of the Sacred Congregation to consult with theologians and theological faculties prior to publishing the Declaration.

9. The exact text of the questions (in English translation) on which the Commission voted during its plenary session in April, 1976, was published in the San Francisco *Monitor*, Vol. 118 (June 17, 1976), pp. 1-2.

10. For a comparison of the Declaration and the Biblical Commission Report see the essay by John R. Donahue, pp. 25-33.

11. See, e.g., *Lumen Gentium* II, 12 on the importance of the consensus of the faithful in doctrinal matters.

12. The Declaration's second section is entitled "The Attitude of Christ." It attempts to show that Jesus had every reason to select women as members of the Twelve, and, therefore, the fact that he did not do so indicates that he intended thereby to exclude women as such. The same argument, however, could be used regarding Gentiles. The Declaration, in its fifth section, maintains that sexual differences are much deeper and more significant than ethnic differences. It should be noted, however, that the early Church immediately admitted women to Baptism (cf., for example, Acts 17:4) even though Jewish law had no ritual initiation of women into the covenant community analogous to circumcision of males. Nevertheless, the admission of Gentiles to Baptism required a specific divine revelation (Acts 10:1-11:18). Evidently ethnic differences were more, not less, religiously significant in the early Church than sexual ones. The amazement of Jesus at the faith of Gentiles (e.g., Mt 8:10-12; Mk 7:24-30), which has no parallel in regard to women, suggests that this might also have been true of Jesus.

13. The bibliography on this topic is copious. The interested reader might consult R. E. Brown, *Priest and Bishop: Biblical Reflections* (New York: Paulist Press, 1970); Bernard Cooke, *Ministry to Word and Sacraments: History and Theology* (Philadelphia: Fortress Press, 1976), esp. pp. 525-536; André Lemaire, *Les ministères aux origines de l'Église* (Paris: Cerf, 1971), and a shorter, popularized version entitled *Les ministères dans l'Église* (Paris: Centurion, 1974).

14. Brown, *Priest and Bishop*, pp. 13-20.

15. There is some evidence of priestly activity by bishops in *1 Clement* 44:4 (c. 96 A.D.) and at least a suggestion of regulation of eucharistic presidence in the *Didache* (early 2nd century).

16. *Didache* 10:7.

17. Acts 21:9; 1 Cor 11:5.

18. Cf. Brown, *Priest and Bishop*, pp. 54-55.

19. For a fuller treatment of this crucial scriptural evidence regarding the apostolic role of women see my article "Apostleship of Women in John's Gospel," *Catholic Charismatic*, Vol. I, No. 6 (February/March 1977), pp. 16-20.

20. See Donahue, "Women, Priesthood and the Vatican," pp. 286-287.

21. This interpretation is rejected by the Declaration in note 10. The note takes the strange position that the Markan explanation (Mk 3:14) of the task of the Twelve, which is never attributed to Jesus, is to be preferred to the only logion on the function of the Twelve attributed to Jesus (Mt 19:28; Lk 22:30). Since it seems hardly tenable that Jesus had or claimed to have de-

tailed knowledge about the events of the eschaton (cf. Mk 10:40; 13:32) it is difficult to understand the note's assertion that Jesus' explanation of the function of the Twelve as judges of the twelve tribes refers only to "their participation in the eschatological judgment."

22. On this point see Brown, *Priest and Bishop*, p. 55.

31
Women Priests and Church Tradition
Rosemary Radford Ruether

This section of the Declaration states unequivocally that there has been an unbroken tradition throughout the history of the Church, universal in the East and the West, of excluding women from priestly ordination. This unbroken tradition is then given a normative character, on the assumption that what "has always and everywhere been the custom" of the Church must reflect the guidance of the Holy Spirit and is *de facto* infallible and unchangeable. This unbroken tradition as norm is further pronounced to be based on "Christ's example." It is said to be still normative today. Presumably this means that it is still normative everywhere, East and West, in the whole Church. This norm is then stated to be "God's plan for his Church."

This argument from unbroken tradition as binding norm is undoubtedly the central argument of the whole document, superseding and, in effect, dictating the arguments from Scripture and theology. Most critics of the document have regarded this statement of unbroken tradition as unassailable, at least as a fact, although not necessarily as a norm. In this one area the Declaration unquestionably states a fact: that the Church has never conferred priestly ordination on women. One cannot question this fact, although one might question the extrapolation from it of a norm and the assignment of this tradition to dominical intent and practice.

However, when the question of unbroken tradition is looked at more deeply and more broadly, it becomes clear that it crumbles at both ends: both in the argument from dominical foundations and in the maintenance of contemporary continuity. Moreover, it should be obvious that the Declaration was called into being precisely because the tradition is *no longer unbroken* and the dominical foundations of this historical tradition are *no longer unquestioned*! Thus the statement on the historical continuity of this tradition in the Church is first of all called into question because the very circumstances which occasioned this Declaration testify to the opposite case!

Let us examine three aspects of this statement on the normativeness of the tradition: 1) the origins of the tradition in dominical injunction and New Testament practice; 2) unbroken continuity in the practice of the Church, both East and West, and everywhere continuing unquestioned to today; and 3) the extrapolation from long-established practice into theological norm.

Without duplication of materials that will be covered in other comments, it is evident that the weakest link in the chain of tradition lies precisely in its foundations in Jesus Christ. Without this foundation assured, the rest of the

chain of tradition falls to the ground. The question of the dominical foundations of this tradition of excluding women from ministerial priesthood lies
precisely in the definition of priesthood assumed throughout the document. It
is assumed that the concept of priesthood of traditional Roman Catholicism
was, in fact, founded by Christ, conferred by him on an exclusive group of
twelve male apostles who, in turn, became the foundation of the line of episcopal apostolic succession from which priestly ordination flows; and that
women were, from the beginning, excluded from this line of apostolic sacerdotal ordination.

But it is evident to anyone with even an introductory knowledge of
Church history that the concept of priesthood of traditional Roman Catholicism is a historical construct that emerged gradually in the history of the
Church. There is not a trace of such a concept of priestly ordination in the
practice of Jesus himself. Jesus himself was not a *priest* in the meaning of
that term in his own day. The title more properly used for him in the context
of the religious organization of his own day was rabbi, not priest. Rabbinical
ordination was not clearly established in Jesus' time, and there is no evidence
that Jesus was ordained as a rabbi. The role of rabbi was still seen as something that arose somewhat freely and was acclaimed by groups of followers.[1]
It is in this sense that Jesus is a rabbi and functions as preacher, teacher and
exegete in his hometown synagogue (Lk 4:15 ff). But Jesus did not belong to
a priestly family. Thus he could not have been a priest in the context of
Judaism and is never shown functioning as a priest in the temple cultus.

Insofar as Jesus is seen as establishing a new priesthood in the New Testament, this is never described as a new priestly caste similar to the old temple priesthood. The term "priest" (sacerdos; hiereus) is used in the New Testament either for the whole "priestly people" of God (1 Pet 2:5) or for Christ
alone (Heb 7:15). The book of Hebrews, traditionally used as the foundation
of the idea of priestly ordination in Catholicism, in fact specifically excludes
the idea that the new eternal priesthood of Christ could be the basis of a new
priestly caste who are "many in number" (Heb 7:23-28).

There is a variety of leadership and ministerial roles and functions mentioned in the New Testament: followers and disciples of Christ, witnesses of
the resurrection, members of the pentecostal community, apostles, prophets
and teachers, workers of miracles, healers, helpers, administrators, speakers
in tongues, deacons, elders and bishops. Women, in fact, were included in
most of these categories. In the ministry of Jesus they are a part of the inner
circle of followers, are sent as witnesses of the resurrection and are named
among those in the pentecostal community upon whom the Spirit of prophecy is conferred. They appear as apostles and traveling evangelists, prophets
and teachers. Stories, such as the Acts of Paul and Thecla, in the early
Church clearly see them as healers, miracle workers and capable of conferring baptism. Paul specifically names one woman, Phoebe, a deacon (not a
deaconess) (Rom 16:1), a fact deliberately obscured in the Declaration. The
inclusion of women in the diaconate is clearly continued in the period of the

Pastoral epistles (1 Tim 3:11) despite their negative injunctions against women's leadership.

Women appear to be excluded in the Pastoral epistles from two types of emerging ministry: bishops and elders (both thought of as teaching ministry, rather than sacerdotum). It should be evident, therefore, that priesthood is not a concept that defines ministry in the time of Jesus or the apostolic Church, that there were a plurality of types of ministerial functions, and that women are included in those types of ministry that are earliest in the Church (disciple, witness, evangelist, apostle, prophet and teacher, charismatic healer and miracle worker) and become excluded only as another line of ministerial function not prominent in the earlier Church of Jesus, Acts or Paul, becomes dominant: the ministry of bishop, elder, and deacon. But even here they are included in the diaconate throughout the New Testament and into the first four centuries of the Church. Moreover, this second line of ministry—bishop, elder and deacon—is not modeled on priesthood, but on synagogue leadership which, at this time, rigidly excluded women from learning and teaching, contrary to the earliest practice of Jesus and the Church.[2]

The sacerdotal concept of ministry emerged gradually in the Church. Even at the end of the second century, when the concept of apostolic succession becomes prominent, the succession discussed is not that of priestly power, but of teaching tradition:[3] i.e., rabbinical succession of teaching, not sacerdotal succession of sacramental power. The priestly and sacramental concept of ministry in Christianity comes to predominate in the late third and fourth centuries and is closely associated with the elevation of the Christian ministry to the status of a sacred caste within the established Church of a Christianized Roman empire.[4] Cultic priesthood is now seen as a clearly separate caste, socially as well as ecclesiastically, and enjoys special privileges of social caste conferred by the Roman emperor.

It is during this period (the fourth century) that there is a distinct revival of the Old Testament concept of temple priesthood and an identification of it with the Christian ministry. With this identification comes the revival of purity laws which strictly exclude women from priesthood and even from proximity to the sanctuary. It is this concept of cultic priesthood that becomes most strictly exclusive of women. But it should be evident that this concept of priesthood is not of dominical foundation, is not normative in the apostolic period, and evolves gradually in the Church through changing historical circumstances.

Even with this more priestly concept of ministry we cannot say that there is a totally unbroken tradition of exclusion of women. Some Christians in the fourth century clearly did ordain women as presbyters, as well as deacons.[5] In the Medieval period not all traditions regarded women as necessarily excluded from priesthood. Both queens and abbesses received investment with the insignia of episcopal jurisdiction.[6] Moreover it became traditional in Mariology to speak of Mary at the foot of the cross as exercising a eucharistic priestly function.[7]

But the clearest break in the tradition of excluding women from ordination has arisen in the last century in the Western Churches. In 1852 the Congregational Church ordained the first woman seminary graduate, Antoinette Brown. Since that time there has been a steady change in the practice of excluding women from ordained ministry in branches of Western Christianity. Nor does this change remain limited to those who have the non-priestly concepts of ministry, but it has steadily moved into the more traditional Churches which value ideas such as priesthood, eucharistic cultus, and apostolic succession. In the 1930s Methodism moved to grant ordination of women and in 1956 full ministerial status (conference membership). Since that time, Presbyterians, Lutherans, and Episcopalians have also made the change to admit women to ordained ministry.

All these changes were made with the most careful consideration of Scripture, theology and the status of the tradition as norm for exclusion of women. The fact that all these branches of the Church, after such careful deliberation, have uniformly moved to reject the normative status of the tradition of exclusion of women from ordination clearly represents today a contrary body, not only of opinion, but of *tradition*, against the normative status of this tradition. Nor is it accidental that these changes have happened in those bodies of Christianity most open to historical criticism of Scripture and tradition and thus most sensitive to the distinction between binding theological norm and historical practice, which, however long-lived, may not be theologically binding.

Finally one must ask whether the mere longevity of a practice counts absolutely as norm, especially when its dominical foundations are in doubt. A parallel can be given for the justification of slavery. Historically the justification of slavery and of the subordination of women were closely linked. Both groups were seen as dependents within the patriarchal family and both excluded, as dependent and non-free persons, from ordination. Although earliest Christianity appears to reject slavery theologically (Gal 3:28), the justification of slavery as a legitimate institution parallels the justification of the subordination of women in the New Testament (Eph 6:5-9; Col 3:22-25; 4:1; 1 Tim 6:1-2; Titus 2:9-10; 1 Pet 2:19). The Church Fathers and scholastic theologians continue to justify slavery as a legitimate institution within the "fallen order of nature."[8]

It is only at the end of the 18th century and among the left wing groups of the Church, such as Quakers (who also pioneered the inclusion of women in ministry), that we find this tradition challenged. Only grudgingly was the tradition in favor of slavery abandoned by the Churches in the mid-19th century following the civil abolition of slavery. Today virtually all Christians would consider this tradition abhorrent. Yet it is evident that it has as much claim to being an "unbroken tradition of the Church" as has the tradition of exclusion of women from ministerial ordination. And, historically, the two issues were, in fact, closely intertwined in their rationales.

Long-established practice cannot be considered *ipso facto* normative for the simple reason that humanity, including the humanity of the Church, is sinful. The gospel does not establish perfection in the Church at the beginning, but establishes a vision of total redemption that is largely still unrealized in society. The history of the Church is one of gradual unfolding of further implications of this full realization of the gospel, especially for categories of persons—slaves, women, other races—not at first fully accepted. The norm of the gospel is not something established already in the past to be merely imitated from past practice. But it is an ideal that is ahead of us, symbolized as the Reign of God, which we strive to more and more completely realize. Thus, in dealing with any past tradition, one cannot assume normativeness merely from the fact of past practice. But one must examine it theologically and critically to see whether it does, in fact, conform to the full norm of the Reign of God, which is the true norm of the gospel.

Notes

1. The basic study on this is Eduard Lohse, *Die Ordination im Spätjudentum und im Neuen Testament* (Berlin: Evangelische Verlagsanstalt, 1951).

2. H.R. Niebuhr and D.D. Williams, *The Ministry in Historical Perspective* (New York: Harper and Row, 1956), pp. 14-23.

3. Tertullian, *Praes. Adv. Haer.* XXI; Irenaeus, *Adv. Haer.* III, 3.

4. Niebuhr and Williams, *op. cit.,* pp. 58-79.

5. Clara Maria Henning, in *Religion and Sexism: Images of Women in the Jewish and Christian Traditions* (New York: Simon and Schuster, 1974), p. 279.

6. Joan Morris, *The Lady Was a Bishop* (New York: Macmillan, 1973), pp. 16-23 and *passim.*

7. J.B. Carol, *Mariology* (Milwaukee: Bruce, 1959), Vol. II, pp. 377ff.

8. David B. Davis, *The Problem of Slavery in Western Culture* (Ithaca, New York: Cornell, 1966), pp. 62-90. See, for example, Augustine, *City of God* XIX, 15.

32
Important Clarifications on Argument and Authority

Mary Ellen Sheehan

· After a short introduction on the role of women in modern society and the church, the content of the Declaration is divided into six parts. From a simple listing of their titles, the parts appear to signal six areas from which arguments against the admission of women to the presbyteral ministry[1] are drawn equally. From a careful reading of the text, however, it is evident that this is not really the case. Paragraph 25 points clearly to this fact. Short as it is, it is the key to interpreting where the real "argument" of the Declaration is located and thus where the real debate should be centered.

This paragraph puts forth a basic distinction that points to at least two kinds of "arguments" used in the Declaration. There is first the Church's *normative* practice (and its "basis thereof") of excluding women from the presbyteral ministry; there is secondly the *illustration* of this norm in arguments of "profound fittingness" drawn from theological reflection. The first kind of argument—constant practice as normative—is developed in parts one through four. The second kind—illustrations of fittingness—is put forth in parts five and six. Our paragraph is clearly a transitional one, pointing both backwards to parts one through four and forwards to parts five and six.

On the Declaration's own admission, the real argument is the Church's constant practice of excluding women from presbyteral ministry, a practice which the Doctrinal Congregation believes is both *normative* and sufficiently explained and *justified* in the document. This argument is forcefully concluded in the last two paragraphs of part four:

> In the final analysis it is the Church, through the voice of her Magisterium, that, in these various domains, decides what can change and what must remain immutable. . . .

> This practice of the Church therefore has a normative character: in the fact of conferring priestly ordination only on men, it is a question of an unbroken tradition. . . .[2]

After taking up many arguments of various sorts as "basis" in the preceding four parts of the document, the issue is thus summarily boiled down to the

239

constant practice as normative. Why, then, the addition of two more parts explaining the "fittingness" of this practice?

The Declaration is clear on this point: it is not to argue demonstratively but to "illustrate this norm" and to "clarify this teaching" by showing the fittingness of exclusively male presbyteral ministers.[3] Interestingly, the Doctrinal Congregation admits to some reservation regarding this procedure in the Commentary: "In itself, such a quest is not without risk." But in a rather quick and facile manner, the Congregation dispels its hesitancy: "However, it does not involve the Magisterium. It is well known that in solemn teaching infallibility affects the doctrinal affirmation, not the arguments intended to explain it."[4]

Several important points from this paragraph and its parallels in the Commentary need to be made more evident. They provide the basis for ordering reactions to the documents and for clarifying both the nature of the Declaration and the nature of the real argument it proposes against the admission of women to the presbyteral ministry. In short, they offer a basis for internal critique of the document itself.

1. Arguments of fittingness are no real arguments at all. They are theological opinions—perhaps well formed and to be revered and even formative of religious attitudes and convictions—but they are not firm and definitive positions on the question.

The Doctrinal Congregation certainly alludes to this understanding of "fittingness" arguments,[5] but in style and content it does not persist in this understanding. It is selective in its choice of arguments of fittingness—accenting the natural resemblance model and avoiding, for example, an equally possible argument of fittingness based on the eschatological dimension of Eucharistic celebration. This argument also enjoys a long tradition in the Church, but it would lead to the possibility—indeed perhaps even the necessity—of including women as sacramental ministers since it is the Risen Lord, and not exclusively the male, human Jesus, that is signed and celebrated in the sacrament of the Eucharist. Further, the Congregation draws conclusions that are too literal, that claim too much, from its selected arguments of fittingness and then by its style accents these overdrawn and overstated conclusions.[6]

Some current reactions to the Declaration also fail to focus sharply the nature of arguments from fittingness. While some thinkers accept some arguments of fittingness as more compelling than others[7] and other thinkers do not accept them at all,[8] both groups should clearly identify their reflection task in terms of the nature of the fittingness argument itself, and be careful not to claim too much.

This is not to say that arguments of fittingness should not be attacked for faulty presuppositions or for incorrect understandings of such key concepts as symbol and myth (whether they be taken too literally or too historically, too absolutely or too relatively). But many and varied arguments of fittingness should be developed, and developed properly from their historical roots and evolution. It is simply too facile to jump to the universal truth and application of a symbol without this historical and cultural study.

In so doing, the limits as well as the legitimate insights from fittingness arguments will emerge and the theological reflection process will be clarified accordingly. This process is indispensable to a proper and traditional understanding of Magisterium as a characteristic of the Church. While the Declaration seems to acknowledge the limits of arguments from fittingness, it nevertheless over-exaggerates the importance of one such argument, the argument of natural resemblance. In the long run, this procedure distorts the real issue.

2. The real argument of the Declaration, on its own admission, is that the Church's constant practice of excluding women from the presbyteral ministry is taught with authority.[9] The Doctrinal Congregation regards this fact ("datum," as it is called in the Commentary)[10] as normative and as established and explained by the arguments it proposes from scripture, the attitude of Christ, and the practice of the Apostles in parts one through three. The Congregation believes that it has adequately and correctly discerned the attitude of Jesus and the Apostles on the question and that this attitude as presented in the Declaration is of "permanent value," as indicated by the title of part four.

But several questions emerge here that have not been satisfactorily answered by the Declaration. There is little dispute with the fact that the constant practice has been the exclusion of women from the presbyteral ministry. But is this practice *normative* and in a *permanent* way? Has the document really established this beyond any doubt? Silence on the question until relatively recent times cannot be used as a positive and definitive argument to uphold the practice. Too much of the Church's "constant practice" in other areas of its life and teaching have changed in the course of history to give absolute adherence to the normative nature of this practice.

Neither is it sufficient to assert that this issue is different because it "impinges too directly on the nature of ministerial priesthood. . . ."[11] The authors of the Declaration seem to argue that the truth of the Eucharist is dependent on a male minister as sign and that this is an absolute that is given to us by God in Jesus. But is this the case? By the Declaration's own admission, this is an argument of fittingness and therefore not finally compelling. What happens to this approach (not argument) when it is complemented with other elements of Eucharistic theology—that it is the Risen Lord who effects the sign, for instance, or that the Eucharist signs an eschatological reality as well as a literal meaning centered on the *memoria* of the historical Jesus as man?

But even more importantly, is the normative character of the constant practice of excluding women from the presbyteral ministry established by "recalling the Church's norm and the basis thereof . . ."? The Congregation is convinced that it has established the permanent truth of the practice by the arguments it has set forth from Scripture and Church practice in parts one through four. But has it? The exclusion of any reference to the findings of the Biblical Commission's Report (whose work here was commissioned by the

Doctrinal Congregation) is telling here. This action alone raises serious doubts regarding the Doctrinal Congregation openness to the *data* fully and adequately considered, i.e., the fact (the constant practice) and the possible interpretations (scriptural, historical, and symbolical) of that fact. It is simply not convincing—in fact, it introduces suspicion of the Doctrinal Congregation's credibility—to assert, "In the final analysis it is the Church, through the voice of her Magisterium, that, in these various domains, decides what can change and what must remain immutable."[12] What is meant by *Church*, by *Magisterium*, by *various domains* in this sentence?

The real battleground is in the area of the normative nature of the Church's constant practice regarding this issue. The Declaration is not unquestionably convincing here. It does, however, center and sort out some of the arguments. Scholars and practicing pastors (male and female) have the responsibility to criticize, put forth, and refine arguments centering on the normative value of practice. The history of the Church shows this to be a tension-filled but fruitful process that is part of the Magisterium itself.

3. There is a definite ambiguity in the Declaration, as well as the accompanying Commentary, regarding the understanding of Magisterium that is employed. On the one hand, it is clear that the Declaration is not infallible teaching, though it is not always reported as such. It is a declaration of a Sacred Congregation, and admittedly an important one. But it is not a solemn pronouncement of either an Ecumenical Council or the Pope acting *ex cathedra*. The Declaration, and the Commentary, generally respect this fact.[13]

On the other hand, there are some aspects of these documents that are at least in tension with the non-official pronouncement character of the Declaration. The Declaration is intended to be some kind of solemn and official teaching of the Church: 1) It is a Declaration of the Sacred Congregation for the Doctrine of the Faith; 2) It was approved, confirmed, and ordered to be published by the Pope; 3) It proposes to put forth the authoritative teaching of the Church;[14] 4) It proposes to do this in some kind of definitive way.[15]

With these kinds of tensions in the documents, what concept (or concepts) of Magisterium do they employ? What in fact is the real value of the Declaration? What is the nature of its teaching as authoritative?

In my opinion, based on some internal criticism of the Declaration itself, especially as crystallized in paragraph 25,[16] the Declaration and the accompanying Commentary are important theological documents. But they should never have been published under the authority of the Doctrinal Congregation and the Pope, however non-official this may be in the technical sense. Instead, the documents should have been published in a book or a journal, like any other theological work, as a position arguing in favor of maintaining the constant practice of the church and signed by those theologians of the Congregation who are committed to its claims.

The Declaration asserts too much about too many arguments, both those types of arguments put forth as the basis of the constant practice as normative (parts one through four) and those types identified as arguments of fittingness (parts five and six). On its own grounds, it is not a normative statement; it does not sufficiently identify or establish the nature of its teaching authority. This means that the question is still open. It simply clouds the issue to publish a Declaration of this sort in a semi-official way and to intend in tone and in several overdrawn conclusions that it be an authoritative teaching. The Doctrinal Congregation would have exercised its important task of safeguarding the Faith more truthfully and faithfully by being consistent with its own arguments and concluding that the question of admitting women to the presbyteral ministry is still open.

Notes

1. In my judgment, the phrase *presbyteral ministry* is to be preferred to the Declaration's wording of *Ministerial Priesthood*. The former makes *ministry* (as noun) central and specifies a type, *presbyteral* (as adjective). This is more in keeping with the New Testament development of ministry and ministries. The Declaration's phrasing accents *Priesthood* (as noun) and suggests that *ministry* is the qualifier. The contrast intended is perhaps with the priesthood of the laity, a valid but much later development.

2. Declaration, pars. 23 and 24.

3. *Ibid.*, par. 25.

4. Commentary, par. 37.

5. Declaration, par. 25; Commentary, par. 37.

6. Later commentators in this book will support this assertion. An example is the statement: "Christ is the Bridegroom; the Church is the Bride." While this is a rich and important biblical symbol, the declaration errs in reducing it to a literal meaning. If the Church is Bride, then in what way is it also Christ, if Christ is Bridegroom? If the Church is Bride, then can only women be the Church? Obviously, more nuance is needed to interpret this bridal symbolism and many other symbols must be introduced into the discussion in order to criticize and correct the deficiencies of any one symbol taken too exclusively or too literally.

7. A. M. Henry and Ph. Delhaye as quoted by Herve-Marie Legrand, O.P., "State of the Question: Views on the Ordination of Women," *Origins*, Vol. VI (Jan. 6, 1977), p. 466; David Burrell, "The Vatican Declaration: Another View," *America*, Vol. 136 (April 2, 1977), pp. 289-292.

8. Examples would be those who do not accept any symbol as absolute.

9. Declaration, pars. 23, 24 and 25; Commentary, par. 37.

10. Commentary, par. 37.

11. Commentary, par. 36.

12. Declaration, par. 23.

13. See especially the nuance offered in the Commentary, par. 37.

14. References as in note 9 above.

15. In addition to the references just cited, this point is reinforced by the wording of the title of part four, "The Permanent Value of the Attitude of Jesus and the Apostles."

16. See also pars. 23 and 24 and the parallel sections in the Commentary.

33
Diversity of Roles and Solidarity in Christ

Helen M. Wright

The Eucharist is "the source and center of the Church's unity," states the Declaration. In this context, it is ironic that the celebration of the Eucharist should be the moment in the life of the Christian community when the members are assigned roles according to maleness and femaleness. Yet, such is the position of the document when it requires that the priest possess maleness to act truly in the person of Christ at the celebration. Such an enforced division of roles on the basis of sex fosters a radical duality in the community worship.

The religious experience of women and men does not bear out this dichotomy. Contemporary Christians find the gracious presence of God in mutuality, so that friendship and equality become distinguishing marks of the Church. Even though gender, power and class may be used to distinguish people in society, Christians look for an expression of community that transcends these categories in the Church. The Judaic-Christian tradition offers a firm foundation for this aspiration in the belief that every woman and man is made to God's image (Gen 1:26; Wis 2:23). In that image they possess a mysterious presence of God, a presence charged with the power of the Creator, a presence that recognizes no dichotomy, that envelops the whole human person.[1]

The communitarian character of God's people developed and reached its fulfillment in Jesus Christ and his Church. The Pastoral Constitution describes it thus:

> For the very Word made flesh willed to share in human partnership. . . . In his preaching, he clearly taught the people of God to treat one another as brothers and sisters. In his prayers he pleaded that all his disciples might be one. . . . As the first born of many and through the gift of his Spirit, he founded after his death and resurrection a new community composed of all those who received him in faith and love. This he did through his Body which is the Church. There everyone, as members of one another, would render mutual service according to the different gifts bestowed on each. (*Gaudium et Spes*, art. 32)

Through the energy of his Spirit, Christ is still at work in the hearts of men and women. The gifts of the Spirit are diverse, but each gift empowers the recipient to continue Christ's saving action that God's reign may come on earth as in heaven. The freeing action of the Spirit enables each person to put aside selfish love and to work at bringing all earthly resources to the service of human life (*GS*, art. 38).

Paul spells out the roles that the early Christians played in this task thus: "And his gifts were that some should be apostles, some prophets, some evangelists, some pastors, some teachers" (Eph 4:11; Rom 12:6-8). He speaks too of those who would bring gifts of healing and interpretation of tongues (1 Cor 12:8-11). According to the New Testament witness, especially in the Pauline epistles, women are associated with the different charismatic ministries *(diakonias)* of the Church (1 Cor 12:4; 1 Tim 3:11, cf. 3:8): prophecy, service, probably even apostolate—without nevertheless, being of the Twelve. They had a place in the liturgy at least as prophets (1 Cor 11:4).[2]

Through the course of the centuries, it has come to be recognized that God gathers a people and fashions a Church by grace that is in some way institutionalized so that Christ's saving action is expressed through institutional roles. At the same time, the Spirit continues to create all sorts of gifts, initiatives and services for the benefit of the building of the kingdom. Theologically and pastorally, this leads to the gradual awareness that the priest is not the sole director of the assembly of the faithful, nor the only member in the community to act in the person of Christ.

The various ways that the People of God strive to take on the role of Christ and to realize his saving action today may be divided into three groupings.[3] First, there is the broad unstructured grouping. If the Church of tomorrow looks for its existence not only within its structures but in the structures of the global society, then the emerging signs of Christ's action in the first grouping are manifold. Some are occasional, some spontaneous, some conscious, some dictated by circumstances quite beyond the control of the people involved. In the latter category are to be found the millions of "anawin" of the world with whom Jesus identified in his description of the last judgment. They cut across lines of sex and race. They live out the *kenosis* of his Incarnation is a special way:

> . . . I was hungry and you gave me food,
> I was thirsty and you gave me to drink,
> I was a stranger and you welcomed me,
> I was naked and you clothed me,
> I was sick and you visited me,
> I was in prison and you came to me.
>
> (Mt 25:35-36)

In this grouping too are all those who strive in one way or another to minister to them as well as those who challenge the structures of society which cause such violations of human life.[4]

Group Two contains analogous ways of taking on the role of Christ, but the activities are more formally related to the Institutional Church. They too flow from the nature of the Church to be a community of faith, of cult, of caritative service and of apostolic witness. But, in contrast to Group One, they are more organized; they are publicly recognized by the official Church implicitly or explicitly. They comprise the liturgists, the lectors, the cantors, the preachers and catechists and teachers, the spiritual directors, the pastoral counselors and others. Pope Paul's Apostolic Letter *Ministeria quaedam* opens the way for each episcopal conference to recognize these ways of living out the baptismal commitment in the Christian community as well as to recognize new charisms as they emerge in the power of the Spirit.[5] It is difficult to reconcile this openness with the directive in the same document to restrict to men the institution into the ministry of reader and acolyte. Missing is Paul's understanding of the fundamental equality of all those who put on Christ in baptism: "There is neither slave nor free, there is neither male nor female; for you are all one in Christ Jesus" (Gal 3:27-29). The question must be raised as to how the Christian community, as community, can join Christ's prayer to the Father for unity when so many members of that community are excluded from sharing in even the most insignificant roles of leadership in the celebration of the sacrament of unity, the Eucharist.

Women have no official role in the Third Grouping of those who represent Christ in the Church. These are the ordained ministers, the deacons, the presbyters, the bishops. Essentially, they are called to express the leadership role of Christ. Through ordination, they are called, "ordered," to occupy a certain function, "ordo," in the community and to serve it. The members of the community ordained to the service of leadership become the converging point of the diverse charisms of Group One and Group Two in the Christian community. In this capacity, they can be called "the presiders over the building up of the Church." If one remembers that this role is functional, it becomes possible to express at the same time the equal dignity of all charisms, their common responsibility, and the special character of ordained ministry.[6]

According to the Declaration, it is the special kind of presiding at the Eucharistic celebration that prevents women from participating in ordained leadership in the Church. Because the priest acts *in persona Christi*, "taking the role of Christ to the point of being his very image when he pronounces the words of consecration," only males may do so.[7] The Dogmatic Constitution on the Church places the action of the priest in a context that allows for a better explication of *in persona Christi*. It states:

Acting in the person of Christ, he [the priest] brings about the Eucharistic sacrifice and offers it to God in the name of the people. (*Lumen Gentium*, art. 10)

Here it seems clear that the priest represents Christ as he offered himself to God for the people. So it is Christ, redeemer, representative of the human race who is present here. All peoples were redeemed insofar as Christ offered his total humanity, not just his maleness.[8] Instead of raising the question about a woman's capacity to express the image of God, the Church needs to ask how an exclusively male-dominated priesthood can be an authentic sign of Christ as he offers his saving action in the sacramental celebration.

The Risen Christ left behind a pledge of hope and strength for the pilgrim People of God in the sacrament of his love, the Eucharist. It was intended to provide a meal where people experienced diversity and solidarity. The gathering of Christians to celebrate the paschal mystery was to be a time when the community would recognize and experience the richness and variety of the gifts of the Spirit in their midst. It was to be a time when all barriers of race and sex and class would break down and allow for the oneness that being "in Christ" meant. But for more and more women, the Eucharistic celebration is becoming an experience of segregation and alienation.

Notes

1. In the context of the ancient understanding of "image," the meaning is not merely metaphorical but is used in a more literal sense; an image is the appearance in relief of the essence of the thing; it renders someone present. G. Kittel, "Image of God," *Theological Dictionary of the New Testament* (Grand Rapids, Michigan: Wm. B. Eerdmans Publishing Co., 1964), Vol. II, p. 389.

Schnackenburg insists that it is every human person, in his or her entirety, even with the human body in its present state, that is made to God's image. This contradicts Augustine's contention that the male alone is the full image of God (*De Trinitate*, 7.7, 10). Rudolf Schnackenburg, "Toward a Biblical Image of Man," in Juan Alffaro et al., *Man Before God* (New York: Kenedy, 1966), p. 5.

Gaudium et Spes makes it clear that the primary form of interpersonal communion produced by the companionship of man and woman is constitutive of "the image of God" dimension of a Christian anthropology (art. 12).

2. The Report of the Pontifical Biblical Commission on Women in the Bible, 1976, Part II, No. III.

3. Yves Congar, *Ministères et communion ecclésiale* (Paris: Les Editions du Cerf, 1971), pp. 46-48.

4. "Action on behalf of justice and participation in the transformation of the world fully appear to us as a constitutive dimension of the preaching of the Gospel. . . ." *The Synodal Document on Justice in the World*, 1971, Introduction.

5. "Besides the offices common to the Latin Church, there is nothing to prevent episcopal conferences from requesting others of the Apostolic See, if they judge the establishment of such offices in their region to be necessary or useful because of special reasons. To these, for example, belong the offices of porter, exorcist and catechist, as well as other offices to be conferred upon those who are dedicated to works of charity, where this service has not been given to deacons." Apostolic Letter, *Ministeria quaedam*, 1973.

6. Hervé Legrand, O.P., "Ministries: Main Lines of Research in Catholic Theology," *Pro Mundi Vita*, No. 50, 1974, p. 11.

7. St. Thomas qualified the notion that the priest is "the very image of Christ": ". . . the priest also bears Christ's image in whose person and by whose power he pronounces the words of consecration. And so, *in a measure*, the priest and the victim are one." Thomas Aquinas, *Summa Theologica*, Q.83, Art 1, Ad 3. In the Declaration, this citation from the *Summa* omits the qualifying statement that I have underscored.

8. If one understands "person of Christ" as it was defined at Chalcedon, the insistence on encompassing the maleness of Christ into it seems quite irrelevant. As Rosemary Ruether points out: "Traditional Chalcedonian orthodoxy denied to Jesus a 'human person,' making his person that of the divine Logos." Rosemary Ruether, "Male Clericalism and the Dread of Women," *The Ecumenist*, No. 11 (July-August, 1973), p. 65.

34
Women In the Sacramental Priesthood
Bernard Cooke and Pauline Turner

While it is true that the liturgical celebrant's role is essentially a sacramental role, that he does function as *sign*, the presumption in this text needs to be appraised: namely, that the reality of Christian priesthood is legitimately appropriated by the liturgical celebrant, and therefore that it is the celebrant alone who sacramentalizes Jesus' priesthood during the eucharistic action.

Early Christianity avoids applying to any individual in the Church the term "priest." Only Jesus himself is designated this way, and the term is extended to the community (I Pet 2:4-6) because it is the body of the risen Christ. Christian priesthood is, therefore, a power and a function that Christians bear *corporately*, which they exercise corporately in the sacramental liturgies, and to which they give expression in the intrinsic sacramentality of their entire life as a community of faith (Vatican II, "Church," 31, 34).

In the context of such usage of "priest" (a usage that prevails throughout the New Testament literature), it is clear that both men and women symbolize and "translate" the priesthood of Christ, since men and women are equally members of the body of Christ which is the Church. To deny to women the ability to symbolize Christ as priest would be to deny them entry into the Christian community. It would be to deny to them a Christian spirituality that consists essentially in the *imitatio Christi*, since all Jesus' activity was an expression of his priesthood.

Historically, there was a shift away from early Christianity's communal understanding of "priest," an increasing application of the term to Church officials—by the third century "priest" is commonly used of bishops—and the emergence of a group of professional "priests" who acted *upon* rather than *with* the rest of the community. In many ways this was a return to Hebrew Bible views of priesthood, to the "cultic isolation" of the Jerusalem Temple liturgies, and an abandonment of the familial and egalitarian approach to Christian life and worship that marked the earliest generations of the Church. It is in this context that the pattern of all-masculine liturgical ministry was established, a pattern grounded in the inheritance of Jewish patriarchal culture rather than in the faith tradition of first-century Christianity.

Given the fact that the entire Christian community does the eucharistic action, that the entire community professes its faith prophetically in the eucharistic proclamation, that the entire community shares the eucharistic sacrificial meal, there is a special role played by the celebrant (Vatican II, "Liturgy," 7, 10, 14). Obviously, this is a complex role, a highly specialized instance of leadership; but the heart of this role—as the Declaration accurately indicates—consists in the celebrant's being a *sacrament within a sacrament*. The celebrant symbolizes the community that is celebrating Eucharist; the celebrant, as a publicly designated (i.e., ordained) member of the collegial group of bishops/presbyters, signifies the link of a particular celebration of Eucharist with the universal Church's celebration of the Christ-mystery; the celebrant, because ordained, points to the centuries-long history of eucharistic celebration that stretches back to Jesus' own Passover meal with his disciples. This the celebrant does by profession of a personal faith that is shared with and reflects the faith of the present community, of the worldwide Church, and of the Church throughout history.

There seems to be no intrinsic impossibility of women acting in this "sacrament within sacrament" role. Since both men and women share a common faith, a woman's public profession of faith inevitably sacramentalizes the faith of the entire community. For the moment, the faith profession of Catholic women does not point directly to the faith witness of the presbyterial/episcopal *collegium*; but this is because they have been denied membership in this group. Since such specialized witness flows directly from membership in this group, admission to "Ordination" will automatically provide women with the ability to sacramentalize the historic apostolic witness.

35
Recognizing Christ in Women Priests
Robert W. Hovda

If one uses the verb "recognize" to indicate a larger than merely rational process (symbolic communication is of a more fully human order), then one must agree that symbolic functions or actions must be "perceptible" and that the faithful must be able to recognize them "with ease." One of the major problems in liturgical renewal is the fact that in medieval and modern times church practice has failed to observe that principle—e.g., in the eucharistic sacrament of eating and drinking. That not unusual disparity between church theory and practice, although it may introduce a note of humor, does not diminish the force of the argument.

Prescinding from what might be a legitimate discussion of the contemporary use of the word "sign" in this connection, our purposes here are better served by attending to the quite appropriate notions of perceptibility and recognition. Since we are dealing with the church, the community of faith, and its sacramental actions, the reality which must be perceptible and recognizable in the ministry of presbyter or bishop must be a reality of faith.

Christian faith is concerned with Jesus as the Christ, as the Word of God incarnate, God-with-us. The "us" of God-with-us refers, according to scripture and the entire tradition of the church, to the whole of humanity. There is no need of repeating here the carefully reasoned and documented work of R. A. Norris, Jr., in an article entitled "The Ordination of Women and the 'Maleness' of Christ."[1] Norris shows why any argument which pretends to find or invoke a Christological or faith dimension in the human fact of Jesus' maleness is not only a novelty in terms of Catholic tradition but also extremely damaging to traditional Christology.

One must say, therefore, that even if it were possible to separate the head from the body and seek to make perceptible and recognizable in the ministry of bishop or presbyter only the head, the Incarnate Word, the male person is inadequate to the full reality which faith contemplates. The sacraments of initiation, Baptism-Confirmation-Eucharist (far more fundamental and decisive in our transformation in Christ, in our becoming "signs" of Christ, than ordination to the presbyterate or episcopate), are the most obvious indication of where faith stands on the issue of identification with Christ.

Even with such a truncated view of the meaning and role of these ministries, then, the argument for perceptibility and recognizability in sacramental functions and actions must concede that until *both* male and female persons are represented in these personal symbolic functions the universality of Christ and redemption is made less perceptible and less recognizable.

But one must go further, recognizing also that the relocation of all specific ministries within the ministering community is a major challenge if current reform and renewal of Church is not to be frustrated. It is not enough to consider merely the head of the body, for the body, too, is Christ.

Since the call to conversion and to the initiation process which culminates in Baptism-Confirmation-Eucharist is addressed to all humans without sexual discrimination, the community of faith is female as well as male in its identification with Christ. Only such a Christ and church can dare to make the gospel's claim on the hearts of people. And such a church must be free to call to any specific ministry or function within the community those whose membership has already been established and who possess relevant training and qualifications for the job to be done.

Although the ministries of presbyter and bishop are minor compared to the dignity of Baptism, they, too, at their best and fullest, must make perceptible and recognizable not merely a human characteristic of Jesus but the aching aspiration to universality of Christ and Church. When the ordination of presbyter and bishop again becomes a fully perceptible and recognizable sacrament of the Church, coming out of the bowels and the needs of the Church, then our cultural and current restriction of such ordination to the male of the species will be perceived and recognized as intolerable.

Notes

1. *Anglican Theological Review,* Supplementary Series, No. 6, June, 1976, pp. 69-80. (Abridged version, "The Ordination of Women and the 'Maleness' of Christ," *Living Worship,* Vol. 13, No. 3, March, 1977.)

36
Aquinas on Persons' Representation in Sacraments
Christopher Kiesling

The Declaration's extension of representation by natural resemblance to persons as well as things in sacramental signs is a step forward. The sacramental sign is no longer regarded impersonally as a few words, gestures, and perhaps objects constituting the "matter and form" of the sacrament. The broader view is in harmony with the perspective of the Fathers of the Church and the early Scholastics. Thomas Aquinas himself makes this extension to the celebrant of the Eucharist and to the recipient of Extreme Unction (as anointing of the sick was known in his day). He also takes it into account in considering woman as the minister of Baptism. We will be considering these instances in Thomas' writings and the implications for the possibility of women's ordination.

In the treatise on the Eucharist, Thomas proposes an objection that Christ cannot be immolated in the Eucharist because there the priest and the victim are not the same. In response, he supposes as obvious that Christ is present as victim and proceeds to argue that he is present also as priest in the celebrating priest: "the priest . . . bears Christ's image, in whose person and by whose power he pronounces the words of consecration" (*Summa theologiae*, III, q. 83, a. 1, ad 3).[1] The word *image* is significant here. In the previous response (*ibid.*, ad 2), Thomas says that the celebration of this sacrament is "an image representing Christ's passion" *(imago repraesentativa passionis Christi)* and the altar represents the cross *(est repraesentativum crucis ipsius)*. Noteworthy is that the altar is simply representative of the cross, not an image thereof. The priest and the celebration of the sacrament, on the other hand, are representative images of Christ and his passion respectively. What is implied in the notion of image? Is the priest an image of Christ because he is male?

In his treatise on the image of God in "man," Thomas notes that an image is more than similitude or resemblance; it includes resemblance but adds something, namely, being pressed or squeezed out of another *(quod sit ex alio expressum)* or, in more euphemistic language, put forth from another or proceeding from another (*ibid.*, I, q. 93, a. 1). Hence an egg, Thomas goes on to exemplify, is not the image of a second egg, however similar and equal it may be to the second, because it is not put forth from the second *(non est expressum ex illo)*. Therefore, one male is not the image of another male simply on the score of similarity in maleness. The first is an image of the second only if his maleness derives from the second, as a son's maleness is the image of his father's but not of his brothers'.

The priest is not the "representative image" of Christ because of his maleness. The priest does not derive his maleness from Christ, but from his own father and grandfathers. One might object by saying that the priest does derive his maleness from Christ, for Christ willed that only males be ordained to the priesthood. But that Christ so willed is precisely the point in question. Moreover, in that situation the maleness of the priest would not be proceeding from Christ's maleness but from his will. Therefore the maleness of the priest would not be the basis for constituting him Christ's representative image, but only a condition for receiving that which does come forth from Christ to establish another person as his image. The questions on hand, therefore, are what precisely constitutes the priest Christ's image and whether maleness is an absolutely necessary condition for receiving that constitutive element.

Thomas' statement that "the priest bears Christ's image" is complemented by the clause "in whose person and whose power he pronounces the words of consecration" (*ibid.*, III, q. 83, a. 1, ad 3). Is this complementary clause merely descriptive of additional facets of the priest's being or is it explanatory of why the priest is Christ's image? I submit that it is explanatory.

In response to the question whether consecration of the Eucharist is properly the duty of the priest, Thomas enunciates as a general principle that whoever performs an act in place of another person necessarily does so through power granted by another *(Quicumque autem aliquid agit in persona alterius, oportet hoc fieri per potestatem ab alio concessam)* (*ibid.*, III, q. 82, a. 1). He goes on to say that when the priest is ordained, the power to consecrate the Eucharist in the person of Christ is conferred on him. Precisely because he is enabled by power from Christ so that he can act in Christ's stead, the priest is constituted Christ's image.

Thomas saw this empowering as the sacramental character of orders. *Character*, it should be noted, means fundamentally a similitude impressed by another—an image. This meaning is exploited by the Church Fathers and theologians in reference to all the sacramental characters. Thomas conceived the characters as instrumental powers derived from Christ perfecting the practical intellect for the making of the sacramental signs (*ibid.*, III, q. 63, aa. 2, 4). By the character of Holy Orders, the priest is empowered to perform those actions in the sacramental rites which signify bestowing divine gifts (*ibid.*, aa. 3, 6). The character of Orders, then, truly constitutes the priest Christ's image. It is not a person's maleness which constitutes that person the representative image of Christ, but a person's having the sacerdotal character, the instrumental priestly power to perform those actions signifying the giving of divine gifts, a power deriving through ordination from Christ, *the* donor of God's grace.

But, according to Thomas, can a woman be the subject of that priestly power, in order to become the image of Christ bestowing divine blessings?

The answer appears to be No in his *Commentary on the Sentences of Peter Lombard* (*In IV Sent.*, dist. 25, q. 2, a. 1, q^a 1, sol. I; cf. *Summa theologiae*, suppl., q. 39, a. 1). This passage is relied on by the Declaration. The passage makes two points worth noting.

First, we have in this place another instance of an extension of the sacramental sign to cover a person involved in the sacrament, and an extension of the principle of natural resemblance required of persons as well as things in the sacramental signs. The recipient of the sacrament of Extreme Unction, Thomas asserts, must be a sick person, in order that the need of a cure be signified. Presumably he sees natural resemblances between ointment and divinely bestowed created grace, between application of the ointment in anointing and the divine act of bestowing interior grace, and between the physically sick person and the soul in need of God's spiritual healing.

Second, the immediate reason Thomas offers in this passage for woman's inability to receive the sacrament of Orders is that she cannot signify some degree of eminence or superiority *(Cum . . . in sexu femineo non possit significari aliqua eminentia gradus, . . . ideo non potest ordinis sacramentum suscipere)*. But why cannot woman signify some degree of eminence? Simply because she is woman, because her sex is feminine? The answer appears to be No. It is because woman is in a state of subjection *(quia mulier statum subjectionis habet)*. So it does not appear that femaleness, femininity, womanhood *as such* is the barrier to woman's receiving holy orders, but femaleness *in a state of subjection*. If woman were not in this state of subjection, then perhaps she could signify some degree of eminence and so be fit to receive the priesthood.

Unfortunately Thomas's idea of the female of the human species involves essentially subjection or inferiority. The state of subjection which Thomas attributes to woman is not extrinsic to her nature, a condition which could be removed from her essence. The subjection is the result of the way in which she is generated (*Summa theologiae*, I, q. 92, a. 1, ad 1) and the result of man's naturally having greater discretion of reason (*ibid.*, ad 2). This subjection precedes sin (*ibid.*). Given these premisses, there is no possibility of woman as woman ever signifying a degree of eminence and hence of ever being a fit subject for the sacrament of holy orders.

If Thomas had not considered woman inevitably conditioned by subjection in virtue of the way she is generated and by reason of her role in generating offspring, would he have said that woman cannot signify a degree of superiority requisite to be a subject of holy orders? In the same question of his *Commentary on the Sentences* which we have been considering, he uses a distinction of Peter Lombard's between "things" (*res*: realities which are taken just for what they are without reference to something else) and "signs" (*signa*: realities which are not considered for themselves but in reference to something else). When it comes to "things," woman does not differ from man in the realm of the soul, since sometimes woman is found better than many men in regard to the soul *(Quia secundum rem in his quae sunt animae mulier non differt a viro, cum quandoque mulier inveniatur melior quantum ad animam viris multis), (In IV Sent.*, dist. 25, q. 2, a. 1, q^a 1, sol. I, ad 1). Thomas uses this idea to justify women's being prophetesses, who, like prophets, are superior to priests, for they mediate between God and priests, as priests mediate between God and people.

The valuable notion here is that Thomas recognizes that a person who is woman can be superior to men. It could be rejoined that Thomas does not admit the superiority of the woman precisely as woman, that is, as of particular bodily constitution, but as possessing a human soul, in which she does not differ from man. But if woman's biology and psyche were seen as equal to man's and equally active, though in a complementary way—rather than as inferior, passive, and subject—then the difference between man and woman by reason of bodily constitution would be neutralized. The subject of Holy Orders would have to be discussed in terms of the radical subject, the hypostasis, suppositum, person (in the Scholastic sense). The question would then be whether the human person, male or female, is able to signify a degree of eminence and hence be an apt subject for Christ's image by ordination. In view of Thomas' admission that a person who happens to be a woman can be superior in matters of the human spirit to many other persons who are men, it would have to be admitted that the female person as well as the male person is an apt subject to bear Christ's image as priest through ordination.

Thomas deals with the natural resemblance of sacramental signs when he considers the legitimacy of woman's baptizing in the case of necessity (*Summa theologiae*, III, q. 67, a. 4). The third objection Thomas proposes to woman's baptizing is this: In the spiritual rebirth which is baptism, water seems to take the place of the maternal womb and the one who baptizes represents the father. Since it is not fitting that a woman represent a father, she cannot baptize.

In line with his biology and his theology of the minister of sacraments, Thomas answers (*ibid.*, ad 3) that in human generation a woman cannot be an active principle but only a passive one. In spiritual generation, however, neither man nor woman function in virtue of their own powers, active or passive, but only as instruments of the power of Christ. Therefore a man or a woman, in the same way, can baptize in the case of necessity. Should a woman baptize outside of necessity, she and any cooperators would be doing wrong, but the person baptized should not be rebaptized. The requirement of natural resemblance between the persons in sacramental signs and the mystery signified is not so absolute that it cannot give way in the case of necessity.

According to Thomas, natural resemblance is a condition for sacramental signs to signify, but it is not finally constitutive of a sacrament. Sensible things by their very nature have a certain aptitude to signify spiritual effects. But it is divine institution that determines this aptitude, restricting it to one special significance. God chooses certain things before others to convey the significance of the sacraments in order that these significances can be more suitably conveyed (*ibid.*, III, q. 64, a. 2, ad 2; cf. q. 60, a. 5, ad 1).

Care must be taken, then, in two directions. On the one hand, we must not overly emphasize natural resemblance for our understanding of sacramental signs. We could miss what is truly the divine choice of what is to be signified. This choice is constitutive of the sacraments and natural resemblances subordinated to it. This choice must be discerned in divine revelation. It may be that the oft-quoted passage of Galatians 3:28 ("There does not exist among you Jew or Greek, slave or freeman, male or female. All are one in Christ Jesus") tells us something about the subject of the sacrament of Orders which theories of natural resemblance do not. It took the Church some decades to see through the dichotomy of Jew and Greek, still more centuries to see through the division of slave and freeman. It is premature to say that we fully understand the Christian view of the male and female diversity.

On the other hand, we must acknowledge that God uses natural resemblances between sensible things and persons on the one side and, on the other, the mysteries of grace to be signified. One of the reasons Thomas offers for the necessity of sacraments is that by them human beings are led through sensible realities to spiritual realities in the manner appropriate to human nature, which proceeds from knowledge of the sensible world (*ibid.*, III, q. 61, a. 1). Without any natural resemblances, analogies, between sensible realities and the revealed mysteries, sacraments would lead us into a world of illusion. God chooses certain things and persons to be the content of the sacramental signs precisely in order to provide more suitable signification *(ut sit convenientior significatio)* (III, q. 64, a. 2. ad 2).

We must take seriously, therefore, all the implications in the psychological and sociological realms of male priests to represent Christ. We cannot too readily dismiss what has been done and thought in the past as merely cultural determinism. The final arbiter, however, must be the totality of revelation. We need to continue to explore that revelation and hence the male and female imagery of the Scriptures. That imagery must be taken seriously also. If we cannot trust it to be telling us accurately about the mystery of the human-divine relationship, where do we go for truth? But at this point in history, we can wonder if this imagery as we understand it exhausts the divine revelation with regard to the relationship of man and woman, woman's place in world and in Church, and in the ordained priesthood.

Note

1. English translation from St. Thomas Aquinas, *Summa Theologiae,* Vol. 56, trans. Thomas Gilbey, O.P. (New York: McGraw-Hill Book Company, 1975), p. 137.

37
Women Can Have a
Natural Resemblance to Christ
Pauline Turner and Bernard Cooke

The Declaration is correct in drawing attention to the matter of women's capacity to symbolize the action of Christ in Eucharist. If there is any theological reason that can be adduced as argument against the full ministerial function of women in sacraments, it must lie somehow in the area of symbolic causality, since this is the distinctive mode of sacramental effectiveness. The Declaration's reasoning, then, on this matter is crucial to the Vatican contention regarding the impossibility of ordaining women to the ministry of sacramental celebration.

The Declaration's argument from "natural similitude," if probative, must rest on the fundamental ability or inability of human persons and human actions to signify God's creative activity. Interestingly, the basic biblical text in this regard (Gen 1:27) states that the male/female duality is required for humans to be "the image of God." Moreover, as this Hebrew Bible text continues, it is clear that it is precisely the creative relationship between men and women that reflects and makes present (i.e., sacramentalizes) the continuing creative action of God in history. This inclusion of both men and women in "the image of God" continues in New Testament thought, where the Church as body that images forth the risen Jesus includes both. Nor is there any inequality or inappropriateness in Christian women's share in this imaging of Christ, for Paul himself (Gal 3:28) insists that "in Christ" there is no distinction between male and female.

But can women sacramentalize what Christ does in Eucharist?—a question whose response depends upon our understanding of what it is that Christ does do in Eucharist. The action of Christ in Eucharist is basically one of giving himself (his body) as source of life to his fellow humans. According to New Testament thought, the principal analogue of this in human experience, an analogue so fundamental and intrinsic that it is itself a key Christian sacrament, is the relation between man and woman in marriage. In marriage (indeed in all human friendships) each of the persons gives himself or herself to the other; and this gift of self is a profound communication of personal life. Thus, it is the personal dialectic between men and women that points to, signifies, and sacramentalizes the role that Christ plays in Eucharist.

This seems to indicate that Christian eucharistic symbolism has to some extent been truncated up to the present, because only the masculine element in the man/woman "image of God" has been publicly represented in the official sacramental celebrants. The "similitudo naturalis" that underlies the eucharistic sacramentality deals precisely with *human personhood*, which includes and transcends all male/female distinctions.[1] Admitting women to full sacramental ministry will, of course, force upon us a thorough reconsideration of the operative sacramentalities of the eucharistic liturgy; but this should prove to be an enrichment.

Perhaps this is the place where another line of reflection should be introduced: the ordination of women to liturgical ministry in other Christian Churches presents the Roman Catholic Church with a *fait accompli*—at least if one is going to base one's position (as the present papal document does) on the *impossibility* of ordaining women. After Vatican II's decree on ecumenism (especially #3), Catholic theology can no longer deny all reality to eucharistic ministry in other Christian groups. Consequently, women are really exercising such ministry, for example in the Episcopal Church. One might contend that this ministry by women is ill-advised, that it raises psychological barriers to Church reunion, that it is premature; but it is difficult to see how one can contend that it is impossible.

Note

1. In discussing the liturgical celebrant as image of Christ, and precisely in the distinctive act of consecration, the papal document appeals to Thomas Aquinas' statement in the *Summa Theologiae*, q. 83, a. 1, ad 3; ". . . the priest also enacts the image of Christ, in whose person and by whose power he pronounces the words of consecration." There seems to be no argument by St. Thomas at this point from "similitude"; rather he concentrates on "the power of consecration" which derives from ordination. In the previous question (III, q. 82, a. 1) it is quite clear that Thomas is grounding the power of consecration on ordination, without any reference to the symbolic aspects of the eucharistic action having an effect on the effectiveness of the celebrant's action.

38
In the Image of Christ
Sonya A. Quitslund

If woman is just as much in the image and likeness of God, why is she not also in the image of Christ? Is Christ somehow more than God or less than God? Is she not just as much the offspring of a parent as her brother or as Christ the Son of God, and just as fully human as any male, including the Christ as defined at Chalcedon? Femininity certainly expresses as well as masculinity the relationship of the second Person to the first, for it is a relationship of infinite mutuality that defines the three Persons of the Triune Godhead.[1] If at first glance it is difficult for woman to accept that she cannot image Christ because she lacks "natural resemblance," further reflection on the teaching of the Declaration falls far short of persuading her.[2]

Regarding the maleness of Christ and so of the priest: the argument of the Declaration "convinces" only if its premise is taken as of unquestionable validity, but it is precisely the premise that is at issue.[3] Actually when the Declaration claims "The Word was made flesh in the male sex," it concedes that Christ "certainly must not be understood in a material perspective" and that "priests do not become representatives of Christ because of their masculinity" because ordination is "of a spiritual nature." The so-called indelible character of the priesthood is "a sign in the sacramental sense," which coupled with the Commentary's reference to what it calls "the deep identity of man and woman" would seem to imply that the statement's premise based on the precedent of the appointment of male apostles only by Jesus is not valid in the Congregation's very own words. The Declaration certainly gives an untenable interpretation of the Creed by equating the God-man concept with "God-male," as it also does in its eucharistic theology: "There is no 'natural resemblance' in the Eucharist if Christ's role is not taken by a man. . . . For Christ himself was and remains a man."

Nevertheless a careful and close study of the document can prove extremely enlightening—as much for what it does not say as for what and how it says what it does. By its very inadequacies it calls attention to a host of theological issues which have never before been satisfactorily dealt with. Hopefully it will serve as a needed catalyst to much unfinished theological business. The crux of its argumentation for rejecting the very idea of ordaining women centers on a rather narrowly conceived notion of apostolic ministry, the necessity of "natural resemblance" for the eucharistic ministry and the Church's desire to remain faithful to a practice deemed the official will of

Christ, clearly grasped by the Twelve and so communicated down through the ages via unwritten tradition.

In exploring the problem of seeing a woman *in persona Christi*, some consideration of the impact of sexual identity on tradition as well as the meaning and symbolism of the Eucharist will be necessary. Pertinent comments, but by no means exhaustive or comprehensive on the concept of ministry or sacramental orders should shed additional light.

The examination of data will focus on personal reflections and recent statements and/or documents pertinent to the issue because, by general consensus, we are dealing with a new issue which has never before been systematically explored by the Church. For this reason, arguments culled from antiquity as well as recourse to unwritten tradition have a limited value in advancing the argument. The key issue in this regard is ". . . to discover if tradition is simply repetition or if it has no meaning other than to face the future, a future specifically eschatological where there will be neither male nor female."[4] The former point has already proven itself to be theologically untenable. Moreover, "formal unanimity is not the guarantee of tradition because tradition does not lie in the letter, but is guided by the Spirit of Christ."[5] Even Pope Paul VI in a letter to the dissident Archbishop Lefebvre of Oct. 11, 1976, specifically stated that "Tradition is not a petrified, dead reality" but must be interpreted "in adaptation to changing circumstances." The Berkeley theologians are thus in "safe" company when they fault the Declaration for its notion of tradition described as "the inflexible transmission of past practices, regardless of the cultures out of which they came and the needs to which they responded."[6] What is needed are new insights and a genuine openness to the Holy Spirit. Hopefully this essay will suggest some new avenues to explore or new ways of looking at the familiar.

Setting the Stage

Reflection on the image of woman and of God in the New Testament, even the Hebrew Bible for that matter, raises the serious possibility that we have inherited and even been guilty of passing on an image of God which is fundamentally at odds with that communicated by Christ in the Gospels as well as in Paul's letters. It is an image from our patriarchal culture that vests power primarily in the will which has traditionally viewed woman as belonging to the male, taking her identity from him, and being compliant and yielding to his will. As such she can be the ideal of purity and holiness; she may even be a Doctor of the Church, but she is not to impose her will on men or women.

Have we, however, perhaps mistaken society's way of perceiving and behaving with reality itself, and even taken the idolatrous step of forcing God into these unreal categories, or has the process been the reverse? From a faulty notion of God's relation to the world, have we structured a pattern of unhealthy social relations which we unwittingly justify as by divine decree? On the natural level we obey our fathers so as to remain in their love. The child fears parental rejection because it attacks his or her fragile sense of self-worth directly, so that fear often motivates love and obedience. Later in life it may be fear of the loss of an inheritance that will continue to motivate love and obedience. But is not this how God has often been presented to us? In masculine terms, as a being out there in a dominating relationship to us?[7] An oppressive force before which we must capitulate or else live in constant frustration and ultimately lose our inheritance?

When the priest is seen as the mediator between God and humankind, as the minister of Christ's saving grace, and as such an authority, a teacher, a ruler, a judge to whose will we must submit, as sign of our submission to the God represented by the priest, the very idea of a female priest becomes clearly unacceptable on the level of symbol, let alone "natural resemblance," but this natural resemblance in the final analysis is not so much a resemblance to Christ as savior or the Word of God as to a distorted view of masculinity, a masculinity with which increasing numbers of men can no longer identify.

Is this concept of the divine as a dominating power too harsh? Is it true a woman cannot be a priest because the priest symbolises God's relation to the world? So long as religion is conceived in terms of domination, of having power and having power over, it encourages and even obliges us to model human relations on this paradigm and to use woman as the archetypal submissive one. As such she certainly cannot function as an adequate symbol. If this is true, then, and if we do not reject the idea of a woman priest outright, we shall have to deal with a serious internal conflict and confusion over some very fundamental religious ideas and feelings.

In the Image of Christ

The mystery of the Incarnation offers another perspective from which to approach this problem. It offers the image of a God who participates in the wholeness of human existence, who chooses not to stand over against humankind in judgment, but rather to become so completely identified with the human situation as to take on human flesh—not as a fully developed person, not even as a child, but as an ovum in the womb of a woman. Paul himself offers us the image of God as a pregnant mother when he quotes Epimanander's "in God we live and move and have our being." Teresa's insight in her classic spiritual treatise *The Interior Castle* is also inward-oriented. But how often do we think of ourselves as being outside of God? It is almost inevitable when we use masculine images for God. The priestly vocation, however, is most properly a call to nurture the spark of divine life implanted in each human person, something men and women ought to do for themselves as well as for each other. It is what God does for us. When we limit ourselves to male symbols for God, we end up in the "out there, domination" syndrome. During his earthly ministry Jesus revealed his priestly role in non-dominating terms; he came to heal, to make whole, to affirm the human dignity of all whether male or female, tax collector or prostitute. He shied away from those attracted to a too narrowly conceived image of his function—who saw potential and power in terms of domination, rather than in terms of service, of nurturing.

We have arrived at a turning point in human history when even the secular world recognizes that international relations perceived in terms of domination are ultimately self-destructive. Nations must share, must serve one another, if we are to create a viable world.

In Persona Christi

What then does the phrase *in persona Christi* (2 Cor 2:10 actually mean? The Jerusalem Bible translates it as "in the presence of Christ," i.e., in his place or in his name, with his knowledge, approval and consent. Christ's presence in the priest is thus mystical, not contingent on sex; it can be shared by all irrespective of sex.[8] It means "Christ, not the priest, is the real celebrant of the sacraments. The priest does not represent Christ immediately but only because he represents the Church—first of all by the very fact of ordination. It is impossible to attribute a privileged role to sexuality in the hypostatic union. Besides, all sacraments are celebrated corporately with the Holy Spirit, the Church gathered together being itself the subject of celebration."[9]

If woman cannot image Christ although our spirituality teaches the "imitation of Christ," then being a man is clearly more desirable than being a human being. Rejecting the notion that only a male can act *in persona Christi*, the Berkeley Catholic theologians argue that "the presence of women as priests, as well as men, could be an abiding sign to the faithful that all Christians 'have put on Christ Jesus' and in this identification lies their hope for salvation. It is simply a matter of fact that the exclusion of women from priestly ordination in our day does not reinforce 'the image of Christ' for a growing number of people, but rather symbolizes sexual discrimination within the Church. . . . The effect of aligning priesthood with masculinity may identify the Church as regressive for millions of human beings in the future."[10]

In dealing with this issue, many recent commentators have pointed out the significance of the symbols of our Christian faith. Writing in 1975, Hervé-Marie Legrand observed: "In that area [of symbols], one is touching on extremely profound realities where personal and social psychology, sexuality, religious experience and symbols so affect one another and condition one another to such a point that any discussion speedily becomes emotional."[11] The response to the Declaration by the Leadership Conference of Women Religious echoed similar concerns: "Its most significant value may be that it actually identifies the basis for deeper study, the relationship between natural sign and symbology. By using words like 'image,' 'sign,' 'representative' and 'symbol' interchangeably, the text calls our attention to the need for continuing study and research into the nature of symbol and its use in a faith community. This focus on the crucial question gives real direction to ongoing exegesis and dialogue."[12]

These same views were reiterated even more strongly and positively by David Burrell when he urged the Declaration be given a theological rather than just a political response: "The heart of the argument is *in persona.* . . ." The arguments to support this are from fittingness "articulated in an arena where current theology is relatively tone-deaf: that of symbolic activity."[13]

Nowhere is the confusion women experience over their ability or inability to image Christ more concretely drawn than in Paul VI's twice-repeated panygeric on womanhood: "As We see her, Woman is a mirror of the ideal human being . . . in His own image and likeness. . . , a vision of virginal purity. . . . She is . . . the mysterious wellspring of life, through whom nature still receives the breath of God . . . she symbolizes mankind itself."[14] Having read this in 1966 and again in 1974, why should women not have been surprised to learn that Christ took on not humanity or human nature but masculinity, and thus, although woman may mirror the ideal human being, she may not image Christ?

Sexuality

In the area of sexuality the Declaration makes relative symbols absolute. But such an interpretation is far from achieving universal acceptance. "Our likeness to Christ is in no way based on sexual differences, for it is reflected in where our hearts are, in how much we live Christ's Gospel."[15] In asking why woman cannot image Christ we raise the fundamental question: are womanhood and manhood constructions that imperfectly fit man and woman? If so we can make a case, but not if they are seen as two distinct complementary ways of being human, because then we have support for the thesis of predetermined roles for man and woman.[16]

Kari E. Boressen argues that "the whole doctrine of the nature and role of woman has been evolved from an exclusively androcentric point of view. The foundation of this doctrine is in the equation, man equals human being. Man, that is the male, is the exemplar of human being and woman is considered as being different from him."[17] As will be seen shortly, this essentially is the starting point of canon law. Augustine and Thomas both accepted the subordination of woman as an *a priori* given "by the very fact that she is a woman, even though equivalent as human, and thus created after the image of God."[18] "The androcentric structure of their . . . civilization leads them to an interpretation of scripture, which identifies this relation of the sexes with the order of creation itself. This sociological element is found in the presuppositions on which they work. . . ."[19] Unfortunately, the Declaration refuses to acknowledge that the exclusion of women from the priesthood could be simply of socio-cultural origin.

Although Christian anthropology affirms the pre-eminence of mutuality between human persons, and the Declaration itself rejects the notion of subordination which Augustine and Thomas took for granted, the Canon Law Society of America has found that an anthropology which retains a conventional understanding of dichotomies (spirit/matter, etc.) underlies some perspectives on the question of women in Church law and is incompatible with the findings of the modern human sciences. In fact, it works a grave injustice by preventing access to mutual sharing in the religious dimension of life.[20] "A woman's juridical status is directly related to that of her husband, if she is married; or, in many instances, to her father if she is a minor child. A single adult woman enjoys status in law, but the married woman loses her status to acquire another based on necessary factors. No status is assigned directly by reason of sex, yet maleness and femaleness really determine a person's juridical standing."[21] The Declaration thus presupposes that women and men are essentially complementary in a way that suits men for ordained ministry and women for non-ordained ministry. This presumes that equality is in fact realized through sexually differentiated functions.

Too often it appears the issue of sexuality is used to camouflage the issue of power. At least for the Christian tradition, Jesus' power came not from asserting lordship or superiority or difference of roles, but from participating so fully in life as to be scorned by the religious purists of his day, and by causing others, the disenfranchised, especially women, to participate so fully in his ministry as to leave the early Church with a paradox it chose to ignore. Instead Christian women have been socialized to accept suffering and taught to offer it up, to identify with Christ the Victim rather than Christ the Priest. But even Christ's sufferings had limits and even he asked God whether in fact it was all necessary. The question remains whether the distance between Christ the Victim and Christ the Priest is as vast as we have been led to believe.

There is no doubt that the really crucial issue raised by the Declaration is the nature of the symbol of Christ's human nature. Is it simply a natural symbol which means we must seek some special significance in his maleness? Or must the real meaning be sought on a deeper level? Christ is a mystery and as such to limit the symbolism to the natural, to the obvious, is to risk diluting the very message of Christ, the very self-revelation of the Godhead in the humanity of Christ. The Hebrew scriptures should have given us a clue. The prophets, in whose tradition Jesus placed himself, never tired trying to raise the sights of the people above the literal, material expectations in the light of which popular imagination tended to interpret past promises made to their ancestors.

Traditionally the male symbol has stood for authority, power, but Christ deliberately eschewed this interpretation. He avoided displays of his power which would have overwhelmed people. He rejected those attracted solely by a chance view of his power. His was a participatory ethic: "Go sell what you have and give to the poor, then come follow me." The Gerasene begged to be allowed to follow Jesus but was told: "Go back home . . . and tell them everything God has done for you." When the mother of James and John tried to do a little promoting for her sons, Jesus asked them: "Can you drink of the same chalice?" These men all sought to be called, and Jesus in calling them indicated that wealth, special privilege, whether of closeness to Jesus or status positions, were foreign to his concept of call. Each call was a little different but each entailed giving up what meant the most to the individual so that the one called would be truly ready to hear God's word and respond without hesitation. The obedience of discipleship constituted the key to kinship with Christ as expressed so succinctly in the retort: "Who is my mother? Who are my brothers? Whoever does the will of God is my brother, my sister, my mother." The women in the Gospels are remarkable in that their response to Christ's call never stands in need of revision. Perhaps there is something to be said in favor of being socialized to serve, to do the will of another.

When the Declaration states then that women cannot be ordained because they are not apt representatives of Christ we MUST ask why. Why are women not apt representatives? Sexuality does not really seem the issue, because a close reading of the New Testament suggests quite another interpretation of the data. Women can be seen sharing essentially the full public life and ministry of Christ, except for being counted among the initial twelve and possibly working miracles or being present at the Last Supper. But the women share whatever they receive, and if they were absent at the anticipation of Christ's death and resurrection, they were present for the real events. The resolution of the dilemma clearly cannot be achieved without a re-examination of the whole concept of ordained ministry.

Ordained Ministry

There are those today who fear all women want is power. But what power do they seek? There is a power that seeks to dominate and one that seeks to serve, the power of love. Unfortunately there are those for whom power is important. Christ is appreciated in terms of his powers, and the Church has often been viewed as essentially a power structure, a force in the world, even a force to be reckoned with. For such people the male is the symbol of power—from the level of brute force to the level of intellectual accomplishment. Man asserts his physical dominance over woman by raping her; his intellectual, by excluding her for centuries from the academic world, from the very chance to meet him as an intellectual equal. Against such a background woman is the symbol of powerlessness, and it is for this reason she is inadequate to represent Christ, not because of her sexuality or because any of the actual priestly roles are foreign to her. For the priestly act of Christ was the communication of the message of divine love which culminated in his death on the cross, and woman has ever been the Christian educator or proclaimer of the Word and a symbol of love, of self-sacrifice.

Christ did not hesitate to compare God to a woman looking for a lost coin, nor himself to a mother hen (Mt 23:37). God contrasted his own love for us to that of a mother for her child, and added that even if a mother should forget her child, he would never forget us (Is 49:15). Normally it is from our mothers we learn our first lessons of love, forgiveness and self-sacrifice. Christ outdid himself in pointing out that the capabilities of women equalled those of men. But it takes time to effect a social revolution, time Christ did not have but knew his Church would have.

What do we know about the actual origin and nature of the sacrament of Order? A functional priesthood was unknown in the New Testament; the presbyter was but a supervisor of community. Sacramental orders were introduced only around 100-150.[22] In other words, not only are the apostles not associated with the daily pastoral care of the people or the ministry of the Eucharist; according to the criteria for the valid reception of a sacrament, it is hard to find evidence that they even received this sacrament, for one must intend to receive a sacrament in order to receive it. Historically the Church had ministries before it had a theory of ministry; it had laws before it had a theory of law. As theory developed, however, it had immense significance in determining actual practice, even though often based on non-historical assumptions.[23]

Because women are claiming a call to ministry, a call they maintain flows naturally enough from their own Baptism, the Declaration states specifically that "Baptism does not confer any personal title to public ministry in the Church," thus choosing to ignore the emphasis of Vatican II on the co-responsibility of the laity for the mission of the Church. It continues: "Vocation cannot be reduced to a mere personal attraction which can remain purely subjective. . . . Authentication by the Church is indispensable. . . , a constitutive part of the vocation." However, what it chooses to forget is that in the past the Church has even obliged some to accept orders.[24] Of course, in those instances, the Church operated out of the context of the people of God instead of exclusively the magisterium. Without denying that the force of orders is not simply declaratory but constitutive, cannot the call of a community for a ministry by women in some very real sense confer the charism for the proclamation of the Gospel and the collegial overseeing of and building up of the Church on a woman as well as a man?[25]

Moreover, although the Declaration denies any discrimination regarding the ministry of women, women remain excluded from the reception of certain ministries.[26] Since lay men and sometimes even women are admitted to many of these functions although women may not be formally installed, "it is evident that the discrimination is based exclusively on sexual differences, at least in those areas which at present do not require the power of Order."[27] The Canon Law Society of America Statement further cites "two contradictory developments in the Church on the relationship of Orders and Jurisdiction. Vatican II reinforced the theoretical tie of Jurisdiction and Orders. Yet the pastoral practices of granting jurisdiction to non-ordained has been officially sanctioned, cf. *Motu Proprio Causas Matrimoniales*. Thus this needs thorough study in order to resolve the contradiction."[28]

Therefore, we must ask what ecclesiology underlies the insistence that no baptized person has an automatic right to ordination? Can it provide an adequate theology of charism which would recognize God-given calls and obligations? The consensus statement concludes at this point that "the charismatic Church" and "the institutional Church" are one. The juridical consequences of charisms are such that they will probably lead us to an entirely new understanding of ministry in the Church.[29] Moreover, if the Church lacks the au-

thority to alter major forms of ministry, how is this compatible with historical facts of change? with a sound theology of the Holy Spirit? a theology of
the freedom of all persons? with the possibility that we may ultimately still
belong to the early formative period of the Church?[30]

The Eucharist

According to the Declaration, St. Paul considered this "ability to represent Christ . . . as characteristic of the apostolic function." The supreme
form of this representation is in the celebration of the Eucharist—to the point
of being Christ's very image when the priest pronounces the words of consecration.

But what is the meaning of the Eucharist? It symbolizes the spiritual
nourishment of the Christian under the natural symbolism of bread and wine,
which, for the Christian, "represent" the body and blood of Christ. If we
approach this from the external "out there-dominating" syndrome, we ultimately are forced to deal with very unpalatable, cannibalistic implications: a
man says we must eat his flesh and drink his blood. This is how the contemporaries of Jesus interpreted the symbol. His words ". . . led to a fierce
dispute among the Jews. . . . Many of his disciples withdrew and no longer
went about with him" (Jn 6:52,66).

Such a development is inevitable if we can approach God only through
masculine images. "But there are some dimensions of love and ministry
which can only be conveyed by feminine images."[31] If we are accustomed or
become accustomed to seeing God through both masculine and feminine imagery, then the Eucharist takes on new meaning in the light of the most fundamental symbol of life in human experience: that of the unborn child who
draws its very sustenance and life from the flesh and blood of its mother.[32] It
is thus only through Epimanander's image of the pregnant God and our own
understanding of the beginnings of human life that we can draw close to a
truly profound understanding of the nature of the Eucharist and the intimacy
of the relationship Christ sought to establish with his followers and offers to
us today when he says: "Whoever eats my flesh and drinks my blood dwells
continually in me and I dwell in him (her). As the living Father sent me, and
I live because of the Father, so he (she) who eats me shall live because of me"
(Jn 6:56-58).

How then can we agree that "in actions in which Christ himself . . . is
represented . . . in the highest degree the case of the Eucharist—his role (this
is the original sense of the word *persona*) must be taken by a man"? If Paul
and Christ could represent the feminine dimension, why cannot women represent the masculine? If Mary, through the power of her own *fiat* was the first
actively to cooperate with the divine Will and so to make divinity incarnate
in our midst, why has it ever since been the case that women have been and
must continue to be excluded from a ministry that is in so many ways similar? Filled with the Divine Fire, Mary immediately began her priestly ministry of the Word by bringing the Good News to Elizabeth and to her unborn
child. Mary "listened to the WORD of God and put it into practice." Can

her daughters be blamed for wanting to respond in like manner?

The Declaration magnanimously proclaims: "The greatest in the king-dom . . . are not the ministers but the saints." This is a particularly weak solution to the argument and hardly a strong note on which to end, for women seeking ordination are not looking for status in heaven but rather are driven by that same zeal that moved the Apostle Paul to cry out: "I would willingly be anathema and be cut off from Christ if it could help my brothers (and sisters) of Israel, my own flesh and blood" (Rom 9:3). Like Jesus, those who support the ordination of women are not half so concerned with what people might think about the company they are keeping as with the unmet pastoral needs of the people of God today.

Notes

1. Margaret Farley, "Moral Imperatives for the Ordination of Women", in *Women and Catholic Priesthood: An Expanded Vision*, ed. Anne Marie Gardiner (New York: Paulist Press, 1976), p. 44.

2. As Peter Ellis rather facetiously put it during a panel discussion of the Vatican Declaration at Fordham University on March 30, 1977: "Trying to understand the Declaration's argumentation is like trying to comb your hair in a 50-mile-an-hour gale while standing on your head." Cited in National Catholic Reporter, Vol. 13, No. 24 (April 15, 1977), p. 24.

3. Cf. Richard A. Norris, Jr., "The Ordination of Women and the 'Maleness' of Christ," *Anglican Theological Review*, No. 6 (June, 1976), pp. 69-80, reprinted in *Living Worship*, Vol. 13, No. 3 (March, 1977). Norris argues that to accept that Jesus' maleness is the crucial aspect imaged by the priest is to alter the meaning of tradition.

4. Hervé-Marie Legrand, "Views on the Ordination of Women," *Origins*, Vol. 6, No. 29 (Jan. 6, 1977), p. 467.

5. *Ibid.*

6. "An Open Letter to the Apostolic Delegate," *Commonweal* (April 1, 1977), p. 205.

7. I am particularly indebted to Dr. Beatrice Bruteau for this insight into God as dominating force which she has developed in several unpublished lectures.

8. Bishop Joseph L. Hogan, as quoted in the *Rochester Courier-Journal*, Feb. 9, 1977.

9. Legrand, *op. cit.*, p. 466. Farley, *op. cit.*, agrees with Tavard in attributing a "social origin" to the theological view of the *image* as applied to women but insists theology is quite capable of incorporating sociologically-based ideas into itself and so reinforcing what it might otherwise have served to correct, p. 59f. Tavard argues on p. 54f. that not the theology of the *imago dei* but its sociology has been detrimental to women. Cf. *La Liturgie après Vatican II: Bilans, Etudes, Prospective*, ed. J. P. Jossua and Y. Congar (Paris: Editions du Cerf, 1967), pp. 283-88.

10. *Commonweal* (April 1, 1977), p. 205.

11. Legrand, *op. cit.*, p. 465.

12. "Declaration on Women in Ministerial Priesthood," *Origins*, Vol. 6, No. 34 (Feb. 10, 1977).

13. David Burrell, "Men best symbolize Christ," National Catholic Reporter (April 1, 1977), pp. 9 & 13.

14. Address of Paul VI, Dec. 8, 1974, to the Italian Catholic Jurists, originally included in an address to the Italian Society of Obstetricians and Gynecologists on Oct. 29, 1966.

15. Hogan, *op. cit.*

16. Gardiner, *op. cit.*, p. 57. Cf. the four serious consequences Farley foresees if the Church continues to choose not to ordain women, pp. 46-48.

17. Kari E. Boressen, *Subordination et équivalence. Nature et rôle de la femme d'après Augustin et Thomas d'Aquin*, (Paris-Oslo: Mame, 1967), p. 251, as cited by Legrand, *op. cit.*, p. 464.

18. *Ibid.*

19. *Ibid.*, pp. 259-260, or pp 464f. in *Origins*.

20. "Consensus Statement" from the Symposium on Women and Church Law, Canon Law Society of America, Rosemont College, Oct. 9-11, 1976, Rosemont, Pa., p. 2. Published in *Sexism and Church Law*, ed. James Coriden (New York: Paulist Press, 1977).

21. *Ibid.*, p. 5. The CLSA thus proposes adoption of a "single juridical personality" so the male will no longer represent the norm, with special status assigned for the female, p. 7.

22. Rev. Josef Bommer, Professor of theology at Lucerne, in *Vaterland*, Feb. 12, 1977.

23. CLSA "Consensus Statement," p. 3.

24. Legrand, *op. cit.*, p. 468. Cf. Y. Congar, "Ordinations invitus, coactus, de l'Eglise ancienne au canon 214," in *Revue des Sciences Philosophiques et Théologiques*, Vol. 50 (1966), pp. 169-197.

25. Legrand, *op. cit.*, 462f.

26. *Motu Proprio Ministeria Quaedam*, norm 7, even though it earlier speaks of the rights and responsibilities of all the faithful.

27. CLSA "Consensus Statement," p. 5.

28. *Ibid.*, p. 10.

29. *Ibid.*, p. 9. The CLSA proposes yet another study of juridical effects of charisms among the baptised, including these points: a) the juridical development of the notion of charism as a gift from God for the building up of the community, b) the criteria and process for the recognition of charisms, c) the conditions for the exercise of charisms, d) the system to evaluate and up-date the above criteria and process.

30. *Ibid.*, p. 3. Richard McBrien, "Women's Ordination: Effective Symbol of the Church's Struggle," in Gardiner, *op. cit.*, p. 91.

31. Joseph A. Komonchak, "Appendix E: Theological Questions on the Ordination of Women," in Gardiner, *op. cit.*, p. 252. In this context he takes up the marriage symbol which would be fascinating to explore, but due to the limitations of space must wait for another time.

32. Original idea suggested in response to a homily preached by the author on March 25, 1977, by Sr. Kevin Bissell.

39
Omnis Analogia Claudet
Dorothy Irvin

This section of the Declaration argues that since the Old Testament compares the divine-human relationship to a marriage, in which God is the male partner and the people of ancient Israel and Judah the female partner, the person exercising the eucharistic ministry in modern times must be a man and not a woman. The point is that the priest at Mass necessarily acts within the framework of this particular Old Testament analogy (rather than any of the others) and that the comparison binds us to fulfill certain of its features literally. Old Testament texts called on for support are the Song of Songs, Hosea 1-3, and Jeremiah 2.

When we sit down to read verses from the Song of Songs out of a bound volume, we cannot understand them unless we are aware of the circumstances in which they had their original use. They may seem to us strange, or lovely, or whatever, but what we really need to know is how they seemed and what they meant to the people who composed and used them as live music before they underwent their re-use in church history—that re-use which introduced a new understanding of them as an analogy of Christ and the Church, and, lastly and most strangely, as an argument against ordaining women to the Catholic priesthood.

There is nothing in Canticles about the Catholic priesthood, or about the ordination of women, or about Christ or about the Church, or about the marriage-relationship of Christ and the Church. Also, there is nothing in this book of the Bible about a marriage relationship of God to his people, Judah and Israel. Canticles and Esther have been pointed out as the only books of the Hebrew Bible that do not mention God. This has a corollary; the other books *do* mention God. They mention him generically as Elohim, and by name as Yahweh, El Shaddai, Yahweh of the Armies, El the God of Israel, etc. In short, when they want to talk about God, they know how to do it, and respect for the text demands that we not suppose that they really mean to mention God when they don't. What the text does not say cannot be equated with what it says.

With this caution in mind, let us approach the question of the original use and significance of this remarkable collection of songs. Without at this point excluding the use of analogy in exegesis, we can at least try to ascertain to what extent later analogical re-understanding is in accord with the meaning of the text itself. It should scarcely be necessary to mention that analogies built from Scripture do not have the significance of Scripture itself.

There is, it should be briefly noted, a train of thought in the Old Testament which does not present Yahweh as specifically male. The masculine form of verbs is used with the divine proper name, because verbs in Hebrew have gender; still, the feminine or non-sexual images used to describe God's deeds, as well as the pronounced absence of a female consort, are points which speak in favor of there having been a vivid sense, in the Old Testament period, that the human categories of male and female were inappropriate for God. Over against this train of thought was the image that God was masculine and people feminine, and that their relationship could be thought of as a marriage relationship, this being one of the commonest and most easily understood examples of an unequal alliance for mutual benefit. But this is not the only such image used in the Old Testament to describe the relationship between God and people; others are the covenant or treaty image (principally in Genesis and Exodus, also elsewhere), the mother-child image (Is 66:12-13), the shepherd-sheep image (Ps 23 and elsewhere), and the farmer-vineyard image (Is 2 and elsewhere). An understanding of these relationships is necessary for understanding what sort of God-people relationship is being envisioned.

It has not escaped the notice of the vast majority of Scripture scholars throughout the ages that the songs of the book of Canticles are love-songs, picturing with beauty and detail the amorous relationships of a woman and a man. A certain embarrassment arising from this recognition has lain at the bottom of the brisk preference for an analogous, rather than a literal, understanding of the text, and has impeded the attempt to reach, before going onto further application, a good understanding of the text's first meaning. But the lack of understanding of this text is not to be blamed entirely on prudishness, for in fact only with modern historical and anthropological study has it become possible to be aware of the depth and seriousness of the cultural differences separating us from our Scriptures, and the Bible is very much a product of the ancient Near Eastern culture.

The discovery and translation of ancient law collections, as well as of the actual documents of many marriages in ancient Near Eastern lands, have clarified and explained much of the Old Testament information about marriage. Another aid has been the customs of the present Arab inhabitants of Bible lands. Whether Christian or Moslem, their culture remains in many respects similar to that of the Old Testament world.

Study of these sources has made it possible to describe marriage in Old Testament times as follows:

The basis of marriage was the use of land to provide a livelihood, either as farm or pasture. Men were the landowners and land inheritors; however, they needed to marry, in order to have someone to do their farm work (a man's status rose as he worked less: Prov. 31, especially verse 23) and in order to beget a male heir. Women did not ordinarily inherit, so that their only claim on the land which furnished them with sustenance was through a husband, or after his death, a son. Marriages were arranged by the parents of the bride and groom, who worked out the bride price, the status of the wife (whether as principal wife, second wife, concubine, etc.) and the status of her children (whether her son would be an heir or not). The marriage was celebrated at a large gathering of both families, and generally included the elements of final payment, new or best clothes, a gathering of women exclusively at which the bride was dressed and the women danced and sang certain traditional songs about love and marriage, then entry into the house of the groom's parents or groom, a feast, with the men eating first and the women separately later (compare the feast in Esther 1:9). Thereafter the bride was expected to do most of the work in her new household, under the direction of her mother-in-law, and to produce an heir. She also wanted to produce an heir, as this event would continue her claim to support after the death of her husband, and as otherwise she was in danger of being divorced. If divorced, she had no land to live on, no place for a house, no land to grow food on or pasture animals on, in fact no animals to pasture. She did not own grain or wool or any commodity, and she was cut off from the benefit of any improvement she might have made on her husband's property. At best she could go out as a day-laborer or sell herself as a bondservant, with no protection for sickness or old age, when she would be unable to work.

It is in this cruel and ugly context that the divorce threats of the prophets and the forbearance of Yahweh in Hosea and Jeremiah 2 are to be understood. The prophets want to point out how destitute the people will be if their God divorces them, how they will lack even the necessities of life. These passages were undoubtedly more effective arguments when they were first composed than they are today, because the utter destitution of the divorced woman has to some extent been ameliorated since. However, the prophets are simply using a sociological fact that everyone was familiar with to illustrate the patience of God; God's goodness is the point they want to make.

The dependence of the married woman on the good-will of her husband was a fact of life that the prophets could count on being common knowledge. Ancient Judaism never set up binding norms about the reasons for which men could divorce their wives, and as far as we can tell, it remained very much a matter of his personal wish, influenced at one end of the scale by his dissatisfaction if the wife were not pretty, did not produce an heir, or did not work hard enough, and at the other by his inability to purchase an addition or replacement.

Therefore the women's principal concern was to preserve the love of their husbands; thus they hoped to avoid starvation and destitution. The fact that most of the songs in Canticles are sung from a woman's point of view, praising her own beauty and describing the love she receives, has struck some commentators. The reason for this lies in the social setting of the Songs, that little-known feature of the wedding which was the women's gathering. Until recently, not much was known about the women's gathering, because men are strictly excluded from it. Modern anthropologists who are women have turned up much information about women's cultures which was hitherto unknown. The principal concern of a woman on her wedding day was that she be loved and able to maintain her place; this was her hope and the hope of other women for her, which was expressed in the songs sung among women at her wedding.

Old Testament references to women as creators and transmitters of the literary culture of that period are numerous (2 Sm 19:35; 2 Chr 35:25; Is 23:15; Eccl 2:8; Zeph 3:14; Zach 2:10). They are said to sing ballad-type songs (Ex 15:20; Jd 5:1;12) about important legendary events; religious songs are part of their repertory (Ezra 2:65 and the parallel passage Neh 7:67) and they preserve proverb-like songs (1 Sm 15:6-7) as well as carry on the tradition of prophetic oracle song (Is 5). We know little about authorship of ancient Near Eastern writings; most works are anonymous. There is one Sumerian hymn which we know to have been composed by a woman, and other examples of women's literacy are known. (The attribution to Solomon, Canticles 1:1, is not thought to be a serious claim to authorship, as such claims, when they occur, have a different form and appear, together with title of the work, in the colophon, at the end). The exclamations addressed in Canticles to other members of the group, "O daughters of Jerusalem," and the references to the mother-daughter relationship—not common in the rest of the Old Testament—both indicate the setting of these songs in a women's group and in a women's literary tradition.

The Palestine (formerly Rockefeller) Museum in Jerusalem exhibits several statuettes of women musicians dating from the Iron Age, the pre-exilic period of the Old Testament. One of these plays a double-flute; another plays a stringed instrument which looks a little like a guitar. Comparative material indicates that the stringed instrument was used to accompany not only singing from memory, but, more particularly, oral composition. Thus archaeological material may support textual material in pointing to women as composers and writers of portions of the Old Testament text.

In evaluating the *Sitz-im-Leben* of Canticles, we are up against the startling fact that it is extremely unlikely that men could have heard or recorded these songs, being excluded from the gathering in which they had their origin and purpose. Thus the Song of Songs is more likely than anything else already investigated to be women's written contribution to the Old Testament.

A further point should also be clear now; Canticles does not mention God, and is not about a marriage of God and people.

To return to the question of analogy, let us try to find the point at which every analogy, pushed and driven too hard, begins to limp. Two kinds of analogy related to Scripture study may be recognized: 1) the use of analogy within the text of the Old Testament itself, and 2) later attempts to understand Scripture by setting up an analogue to some passage or concept in the text, and using that analogue to get the meaning of the difficult passage.

The second type of analogy is not really a part of the Scriptures. It is a method of Scripture study, extremely popular in the Middle Ages in Europe, but going back, as far as we can name its sources, to Philo and the Jewish study of the Old Testament under the influence of the Hellenistic culture. It is not seriously used any longer as an attempt to understand the Bible, in part because its analogies are drawn in from outside the Bible and were not intended by the text itself, and in part because it has a tendency to let the analogy replace and predominate over the primary sense of Scripture; in fact, that is the purpose for which it was developed. However, in the many centuries in which people had nothing better to use than analogy, many of these secondary, extra-biblical comparisons became well known; sometimes it is hard to remember that they themselves are not really in the text of the Bible, so accustomed are we to calling them to mind at particular places.

The marriage relationship of God and people in Canticles is one example of an analogy that is not there.

But if these additions have become consecrated by usage, they have never become consecrated by inclusion in the text of the Bible. No Scripture scholar today would defend the allegorical method as a tool for beginning Scripture students, or anyone else, to use; however it can still turn up as a weapon.

The Declaration follows the idea of the God-people marriage from Hosea, Jeremiah (and Canticles!) through the New Testament, where, according to the Declaration, it is replaced by the image of Christ as the bridegroom and the Church as the bride. This is why the priest at Mass always has to be a male. Let us ask seriously, Is the Church spoken of as the Bride of Christ in the New Testament? The texts usually quoted in support of this idea are Mt 9:14-15 and parallel passages, Mt 25:1-13, Rev 19 and 21, 2 Cor 11:1-4, and perhaps John 3:25-30.

Although the Gospel passages referred to use the image of a wedding, the relationship spoken of is not that of the bride and groom. In Mt 9:14-15 (and the parallel passages Mk 2:18-20 and Lk 5:33-35) it is the relationship of the bridegroom and wedding guests which is used to explain why Jesus and his disciples do not fast. In Mt 25:1-3 the sudden coming of the end time is likened to the wise and foolish virgins whose job was to greet the bridegroom at the wedding. His relationship to the bride, or who the bride might be, is not spoken of. A proverb about a bride and groom, whose original meaning is not clear, is used in a discussion about purifying to describe the significance of John the Baptist after the public appearance of Jesus in John 3:25-30.

The idea that the Church is the bride of Christ can perhaps be traced to Rev 19 and 20, and 2 Cor 11:1-4. In the Revelation passages the Heavenly Jerusalem (not the Church) is pictured as the bride of God, and of the Lamb. In 2 Cor 11:1-4 the writer Paul speaks of himself as betrothing the Christians at Corinth to Christ rather than to another Jesus, or another spirit, or another gospel. He is rather dubious himself about whether this is a good image, and this may be the reason why he adds the idea of betrothal to a spirit or a gospel, to attenuate the idea of betrothal to Jesus, which he calls "a little bit of foolishness." Would that it had remained in that status, and not been taken up for re-use in accordance with the wishes of the re-users, in some respects literally (Jesus was a male) and in some respects thoroughly disregarding the author's intention. Paul wishes to urge the Corinthians to hold to orthodox belief; he is not here talking about the relative positions of men and women Christians in Church ministry.

The intention of the author is likewise important in the first type of anal-ogy mentioned above. In the five examples already referred to, the rela-tionship between God and people is described in terms of parties to a treaty, mother and child, husband and wife, shepherd and sheep, farmer and vine-yard. These analogies are found within Scripture; they are properly under-stood by examining their elements in the light of the significance of such ele-ments in the Old Testament culture (rather than in ours). Even within the Scriptures the analogy is built on. The possibility of God ceasing to fulfill his part of the obligation due to the people's misbehavior is described in the terms of the original comparison—the tablets broken, the sheep scattered, the husband and wife divorced, the vineyard torn down. The Old Testament, it seems to me, is rather careful to avoid extension of the analogy to its ridicu-lous aspects. It does not, for example, ever bring in the thought that the shep-herd's ultimate purpose may be to butcher his sheep and eat or sell them. That would be inappropriate to what the analogy is trying to illustrate, and would destroy the acceptability and meaning of the comparison. Through all the imagery of God as husband and people as wife, it avoids the question of their offspring (although this thought is primary in the ancient oriental family relationship, as well as in the somewhat mythological image behind the Old Testament analogy). It uses the analogy only insofar as it is meaningful, and it is perhaps the sobriety and restraint characterizing the composition of the Old Testament comparisons that makes it possible to use difficult images with memorable effectiveness.

The Declaration wishes to require the person playing the role of one of the parties in certain Old Testament analogies to possess certain, although of course not all, of the characteristics of the party whose role is being played, in particular, sex. In the Old Testament use of the analogies, is this require-ment met?

Not all of the analogies used to describe the God-people relationship in the old Testament relationship have sex. The people, for example, can be compared to a vineyard, or to a *group* of animals, such as sheep. In these cases it is not clear which aspects might be insisted upon as necessary. This is the point at which the analogy limps; it has been carried beyond the point at which its meaning is helpful; and one feels that the user is being silly to insist further. The Old Testament itself does not go to such extremes.

Then there are cases in which the God-people relationship is described by images which do have sex. In Isaiah 66:12-13 God's relationship to the people is compared to that of a mother with her child. God is pictured as car-rying her child (in the *persona* of the people) on her lap and offering it a com-forting suck. Must God's role, God's persona (to use the language of the Declaration), then be taken by a woman? In the Jeremiah marriage passages to which the declaration refers the husband is played by Yahweh and the wife by the priests, the rulers, and the prophets, as well as by group references with a decidedly masculine tendency, "your fathers," "house of Jacob," Israel as male slave, etc. Does this mean that only men can be Church members? To insist that the people playing the wife should be feminine might be more in line with the Declaration, but the Old Testament does not push the analogy that far.

To insist then that people in certain of these roles have the sex of the *persona* mentioned in the Bible is self-serving bias rather than respectful and attentive reading of the Scripture. This insistence is wrong as Scripture study. It is also wrong because it is intended to deceive those who are uninformed, (as is the Declaration's insistence that there has never been an ordained ministry for women in the Church). It is intended to make people say, "Oh well, if Scripture says men can be ordained and women can't, then of course we have nothing more to urge," whereas in fact Scripture says almost nothing about the ordination of anybody.

One important aspect of this Declaration is that it comes at a time when our improved knowledge of Church history and improved understanding of early sources have made it possible to begin a new evaluation of texts and other sources relating to all ministry in the history of the Church. The inadequate scholarship of the Declaration may act as a limitation to the historical study of men's as well as women's ministry.

40

Bridegroom: A Biblical Symbol of Union, Not Separation

Carroll Stuhlmueller

The biblical image of "the divine Bridegroom" is pursued in chapter five of the Roman Declaration as a strong argument against the priestly ordination of women. Because it is an important and continuous way of referring to Yahweh and to Jesus, this symbol would seem to exclude women from representing Jesus in a public or official way. A bridegroom evidently must be a man, not a woman.

Like other major symbols in the Bible, this one too turns out to be at once simple and complicated. Marriage, the most basic institution of human society, offers the easiest and most effective example for explaining any number of life experiences. Yet, marriage is rooted not just in the male and female anatomy, clearly distinguishable, but also in the masculine and feminine genders, mixed and shared in each person, whatever their sex. No aspect of human life is more mysterious, complex and labyrinthine than gender in its relation to sex.

This seemingly contradictory situation of every person is corroborated by the involved and almost convoluted history of the image of "divine bridegroom" in the books of Hosea and Jeremiah, cited by the Roman Declaration, as well as in later parts of the Bible influenced by these prophets. For this reason the application for today can be made only after carefully investigating the historical evolution of this type and drawing some clear principles for hermeneutics.

The difficulty is apparent at once. Hosea gives Yahweh the title "Spouse of Israel" (in Hos 2:18, Israel will address the Lord as "my husband"), even though God possesses neither a human form nor any sexual differentiation. Despite this lack of sex, God reveals supereminently the masculine and feminine qualities of gender. The perfect male and female are both created at once to the divine likeness (Gen 1:27). In continuation with the Old Testament tradition, Jesus referred to himself as bridegroom (Mk 2:19). Jesus never exercised any sexual activity as a husband in marriage. Such a "natural resemblance," to quote the Roman Declaration from a different context, is not to be found in Jesus. In him, nonetheless, masculine and feminine genders flowered magnificently.

The titles of bride and groom, as used of Yahweh, Jesus, or the Church, do not immediately signify male and female as they consecrate all people and

God in most intimate union. Marital union or the merging of the sexes, not their differentiation and separation, dominate the biblical symbol. We must look more closely at the origin and history of the image in the Old Testament.

Yahweh was first presented as "spouse" in a clear and emphatic way in the preaching of Hosea. The prophet was generally inspired by the book of Deuteronomy, but he drew the precise image from the fertility ceremonies of the Canaanites who worshipped male and female deities. Hosea's own marriage provided the final impulse and cut dark lines of tragedy and poignancy into the symbol. At once, however, Hosea broke the myth by transferring the context of the sacred marriage from "nature" to "history," taking it back to the days of Moses when God drew Israel out of Egypt to make a covenant, or as Hosea would say, an espousal, with this chosen people.

Hosea also repudiated the promiscuous sex sanctified as divine ritual among the Canaanites, and proceeded to call it by its right name, "whoredom" or "harlotry." Yet, the most degenerate act of all, as chapter 4 of this prophecy enunciates, was the whole battery of offenses against justice and compassion. These sins rightly deserved to be named "harlotry."

The image of bride and groom is quickly adapted then to reach beyond sexual forms and actions. In Hos 2:21-22 God addresses *all* the people Israel, be they men, women, girls or boys:

I espouse you to myself forever
. . . in love . . . in fidelity.
Then you shall know Yahweh.

The Hebrew word "to know" *(yada')* normally expresses the full sexual experience of marriage (Gen 4:1; 1 Kgs 1:4). Yet, this image is extended to the heavens and the earth and even performs the miracle of mercy, transforming the illegitimate child *lo-'ammi* into Hosea's and God's very own offspring.

Even though Israel appears under the image of a bride, Hosea refers most frequently to the male rulers, particularly to priests (4:4, 9; 5:1), princes (5:10) and kings (7:5-7) as guilty of violating the "marriage bond" with Yahweh and like an unfaithful spouse committing harlotry. Because of such evil leadership, all Israel is led into "whoredom" (4:6-19; 5:5; 7:1-2). Therefore, Hosea did not stress male and female sexuality as he emphasized intimate union and called its violation "whoredom."

Jeremiah, dependent upon Hosea in style, attitude and imagery, lays the blame principally upon "their kings and their princes, their priests and their [charismatic or cultic] prophets" as guilty of breaking the marriage bond with Yahweh (2:26). The prophet compares these men to "a frenzied she-camel, coursing near and far . . . snuffing the wind in her heat—who can restrain her lust?" (2:23-24). The image, somewhat crude when applied to human beings, underlines the cruel hideousness of Israel's breaking the covenant or marriage-bond with Yahweh. Marital union, not sexual differentiation of male and female, and its violation by male leadership are intended when Israel is described as Yahweh's spouse. Yahweh's intimate bond with

Israel and also the pain and obscenity of its rupture are the key ideas of Jeremiah.

The image is developed further. Even more emphatically than chapter 11 of Hosea, Jeremiah transformed the days of the exodus experience into an idyllic honeymoon:

> I remember your youthful devotion,
>   your bridal love,
> How you followed me through the desert. (Jer 2:2)

Yet, in this allusion to the exodus out of Egypt, Jeremiah and Hosea were thinking principally of a *new* exodus. The past was not so much a point of comparison with the present as a type of the future; as the past was being pondered, it was continually absorbing features of later existence into its evolving image. The return of the exiled people to their own homeland is presented not only along the lines of a new exodus but also as a return of a sinful, adulterous spouse to the moment of first espousal and initial virginity. The image, as earlier with Hosea, breaks natural bonds and performs a miraculous reversal.

In the important chapter 31 of Jeremiah, the covenant or marriage formula is first repeated, then the exodus, finally the rejoicing over the marriage of the "virgin" Israel:

> At that time, says the Lord,
>   I will be the God of all the tribes of Israel,
>   and they shall be my people [cf. 31:33].
>   Thus says the Lord:
> The people that escaped the sword
>   have found favor in the desert.
> As Israel comes forward to be given his rest,
>   the Lord appears to him from afar:
> With age-old love I have loved you,
>   so I have kept my mercy toward you.
> Again I will restore you, and you shall be rebuilt,
>   O virgin Israel;
> Carrying your festive tambourines,
>   you shall go forth dancing with the merrymakers.
> Again you shall plant vineyards
>   on the mountains of Samaria;
>   those who plant them shall enjoy the fruits. (Jer 31:1-5)

The marriage image undergoes a grand and wondrous reversal. Israel is transformed from an adulterous or sinful nation in exile to a virginal or saintly people at home! Again, sexual differences are not being emphasized but full marital union between Israel and their loving spouse Yahweh. Also to be noted in this passage is the easy movement back and forth between the mas-

culine and feminine gender. The first six lines speak of Israel in the masculine; lines 7 to 14 in the feminine; the last three lines again in the masculine.

Jeremiah's imagery nudged Israel's poets and preachers ever closer towards the ecstatic joy of the eschatological age. In this development the marriage symbol is combined with the image of the city Zion or the Jerusalem
temple. In fact, the passage just quoted from Jeremiah concluded with: "Rise
up! Let us go to *Zion*, to the Lord our God."

Zion becomes a dominant theme with the unknown prophet of the Babylonian exile, called Second or Deutero-Isaiah, author of the Book of Consolation (Is 40-55). He compares both Zion and God to a woman:

> But Zion said, "The Lord has forsaken me;
>   my Lord has forgotten me."
> Can a mother forget her infant,
>   be without tenderness for the child of her womb?
> Even should she forget [which is impossible],
>   I will never forget you. . . .
> Look about and see,
>   they are gathering and coming to you.
> As I live, says the Lord,
>   you shall be arrayed with them all as with adornments,
>   like a bride you shall fasten them on. (Is 49:14-18)

Second Isaiah combines the images of Zion-mother and Zion-virginal bride,
and quickly modulates the image of God from mother to that of bridegroom.
The symbolism is very complex—admittedly the case with the Bible and
Semitic literature—but a consistent note of intimate love and marital union
pervades the passage.

The entire second half, chapters 49 to 55, of the Book of Consolation is
dominated by the theme of Zion-Jerusalem, presently a woman barren, for-
saken and deprived of her children, and yet being summoned with the repeated
command, "Awake! Awake!" (51:9, 17; 52:1). In chapter 54 Zion-Jerusalem,
representative of all the people Israel, is told to "spread out your tent cloth
unsparingly" (always a nuptial symbol—cf., Ps 19:5-6; Ez 23). She is then
consoled by an oracle of

> Fear not! . . .
> The shame of your youth you shall forget,
>   the reproach of your widowhood no longer remember.
> Your maker is your husband. . . .
> The Lord calls you back,
>   like a wife forsaken and grieved in spirit.

What makes this passage so significant is not only Zion's passage from widowhood to a new virginity, from virginity to a new marriage, from barrenness
to fertility, but also the very subtle way that maternal love is attributed to

Yahweh. The prophet speaks of Yahweh first as "husband' but then alludes to the "tenderness" *(raham-im)* of the Lord "who has mercy on you" *(me-raham-ek)*. The Hebrew root *raham*, occurring in each case with emphatic position, means the maternal womb.

The Lord will so enhance the glory of Jerusalem that in chapter 60 it will be difficult to distinguish Jerusalem, normally addressed in the feminine form, from the Lord Yahweh:

> I will appoint peace your governor,
>   and justice your ruler. . . .
> You shall call your walls "Salvation"
>   and your gates "Praise."
> No longer shall the sun
>   be your light by day. . . .
> The Lord will be your light forever. (Is 60:17-19)

The same miraculous transitions rush upon us in chapter 62:

> No more shall people call you "Forsaken," . . .
> But you shall be called "My Delight"
>   and your land "Espoused." . . .
> As a young man marries a virgin,
>   your Builder shall marry you;
> And as a bridegroom rejoices in his bride
>   so shall your God rejoice in you. (Is 62:4-5)

Again the reverse movement from widowhood to virginity for a new marriage is miraculously achieved. Our attention, however, is not directed to sexual differentiation but to marital union, its joy and satisfaction. Male and female sexuality is not attributed to God, but intimacy, fidelity and joy are experienced in God's union with Zion-Jerusalem.

The union becomes all the more complete in the Zion psalms. In these pieces of exalted poetry, Zion is the throne of God and even a figure of the divine (Pss 46 & 48).

This same development continues as it repeats itself in the New Testament: Jesus is joyfully presented as bridegroom and then repudiated (Mk 2:19); Israel or the Church are changed from sin and adultery to a new and glorious status of virgin spouse (2 Cor 11:2; Rev 14:4). It is interesting to note that in Rev 14 the gender of the virgins has subtly modulated from female to male, the 144,000 elect who inhabit the heavenly Zion. The gender changes once more to the feminine in chapter 21 of Revelations, for the "new Jerusalem, the holy city, coming down out of heaven from God, [is] beautiful as a bride, prepared to meet her husband" (Rev 21:2).

Finally, the intricate overlapping of motifs and the dramatic turns in the evolution of symbols would be compounded all the more if our study would have also investigated the sub-theme of Zion-temple. It modulates: a) from a movable desert tent, leading or following the nomadic people (Lev 23:42-43;

Num 10:33-36), b) to a fixed and glorious temple to which the people come in pilgrimage (1 Kgs 8; Zech 14:16-19), c) to the person of Jesus, center of worship (Jn 2:21), and eventually, as we have seen, d) to the heavenly home of all the elect, Jewish and Gentile. As a symbol it does *not* maintain the natural resemblance of a city nor of its first form of desert tent.

We conclude from this study, especially from our investigation of Hosea, Jeremiah and Second Isaiah, that the Yahweh-Spouse or Jesus-Bridegroom image does not stress sexual differences but intimate, joyful and fruitful union of all persons; it rests in the psychological complexity of masculine and feminine genders in everyone, including God and Jesus. We also note that biblical symbols modulate with amazing versatility and at key moments break natural laws and resemblances.

This fact must be clear in the case of the bridegroom Yahweh to whom the Old Testament never attributes human or sexual anatomy. In both Hosea and Jeremiah the unfaithful wife is seen at once in the person of male individuals, the civil and religious leaders, as well as in the entire people Israel, men and women. The nuptial imagery turns out to be more complex in that the widow becomes the virgin prepared for first espousal in the eschatological Zion or Jerusalem. Zion as bride and mother is thus seen as the embodiment of God, the bridegroom, in Is 60 and 62 as well as in Pss 46 and 48.

The image of the divine Bridegroom then does not dictate that priests in the Christian dispensation who represent Jesus must be clearly and apparently of the male sex. The image is far too involved for such a single-line application. In fact, a priesthood of men and women, celibate and married, would much more adequately represent the rich biblical nuances of virginity and marital union, simultaneously overlapping in the symbol of God and Jesus as spouse.

Bibliography

H.W. Wolff, *Hosea.* Hermeneia series (Philadelphia: Fortress Press, 1974) pp. xxvi-xxviii, 13-16, 30-64; J.L. Mays, *Hosea.* Old Testament Library (Philadelphia: Westminster Press, 1969) 7-15, 34-60; P.G. Rinaldi, *I Profeti Minori,* II. La Sacra Bibbia (Roma: Marietti, 1960) 7, 22-23, 27-46; J. Bright, *Jeremiah.* Anchor Bible (Garden City, N.J.: Doubleday, 1965); R. de Vaux, "Jerusalem and the Prophets," *Interpreting the Prophetic Tradition* (New York: Ktav, 1969) 275-300, augmented in *Revue Biblique* 73 (1966) 481-509; R.A.F. MacKenzie, "The City and Israelite Religion," *Catholic Biblical Quarterly* 25 (1963) 60-70; Richard J. Sklba, *The Faithful City.* Herald Biblical Booklets (Chicago: Franciscan Herald Press, 1976); C. Stuhlmueller, *Creative Redemption in Deutero-Isaiah.* Analecta Biblica, 43 (Rome: Biblical Institute Press, 1970) 60-66, 115-122; in the *Jerome Biblical Commentary* (Englewood Cliffs, N.J.: Prentice-Hall, 1968), ch. 15 on Hosea by Dennis J. McCarthy; ch 19 on Jeremiah by G.P. Couturier; ch 22 on Deutero-Isaiah by C. Stuhlmueller; and ch 30 on Canticle of Canticles by R.E. Murphy; Leonard Swidler, "Jesus had Feminine Qualities, too," *National Catholic Reporter* 13 (no. 23; April 1, 1977) 15-16.

41
Reflections on Discipleship
Denise C. Hogan

Concluding an essay on women in the fourth Gospel, Raymond Brown takes a second look at the pericope of Jesus with the Samaritan woman. He reflects that had the disciples, who were amazed to find Jesus conversing with such a one, had the courage to ask, "What do you want of a woman?" (John 4:27), we might not be so straitened to define woman's role in the Church today.[1] This essay is a reflection upon Brown's exegesis, with special reference to his assertion that Jesus included women as "first-class" disciples.[2] It is based upon the conviction that the implications of discipleship include two possibilities of vital importance for Christian women today: the possibility of sacramental ordination and the prospect of a fuller understanding of the meaning of partnership in the Christian community.

Discipleship, as Brown points out, is the primary Christian category for the author of the fourth Gospel.[3] Quite apart from "apostleship," which in its technical sense connotes a specific office in the Christian community, the notion of discipleship is glorified by John, indicating as it does, not a special ecclesiastical charism from God, but a simple, wholehearted and humble following of Jesus in obedience to his word and fidelity to his example.[4] John's Gospel seems to remind us, Brown says, that neither Church office nor Church structure is as important as the radical adherence to Christ which constitutes the sole criterion for participation in the reign of God.

With this in mind, we turn to a brief consideration of two instances of the discipleship of women cited by Brown as clearly evident in the fourth Gospel. This is followed in each case by an analysis of the implications of discipleship for Christian women today.

The first example of female discipleship concerns Mary Magdalene and has its basis in the allegorical parable of the Good Shepherd. John compares the disciples of Jesus to sheep who are able to recognize their shepherd's voice when called by name (John 10:3-5). In the same passage, we are told, Jesus twice refers to the sheep as "his own," the same phrase he uses to refer to his disciples at the start of the Last Supper (John 13:1).

It is of no small significance that John takes care to describe Mary Magdalene responding in the same manner. That is, she recognizes the risen Jesus when he appears to her (before all others)[5] and calls her by name. The Gospel tells us that it was then that Mary knew Jesus, and it was then that Jesus gave her a quasi-apostolic role: to go and tell the others—a task she eagerly and joyously fulfilled, using the standard apostolic proclamation: "I have seen the Lord!" In this, Mary Magdalene is but a hairsbreadth away from satisfying the Pauline conditions for apostleship: seeing the risen Lord and receiving a commission to preach him to the world.

This episode and its interpretation deserve closer examination. In receiving a direct commission from Jesus, Mary Magdalene, as the long tradition of the Western Church holds, was granted the honor of the apostolate. She proceeded to evangelize her "coapostles" with the Good News of the Resurrection.[6] Further, she received her apostolic commission expressly on the basis of her faithful discipleship, and in exercising her apostolic office she fulfilled a genuine missionary function. This is of particular importance inasmuch as in the Palestine of that time, the testimony of a woman was not accepted as reliable. And while it may be impossible to conclude from the evidence afforded by this episode that Jesus intended women to be included among the sacramentally ordained, we are certainly warranted in the assumption that Jesus *did* intend that women preach—a function ordinarily reserved to the ordained. In commissioning Mary, Jesus abrogated the law and surpassed another of the "ancient juridical structures"[7] which served to hamper the realization of feminine dignity and forbade full female participation in public and religious activities.

Pondering this incident from the point of view of the Christian feminist, one takes heart at the fact that at least some glimmer of hope exists for those women who are convinced of their call to the sacramental priesthood. Mindful of the significance of Jesus' command to Mary, they can recognize in her the triumph of woman over her habitual consignment to a particular social category and particular functions in society and its institutions. The immanentist view of woman which confines and regulates her to a narrow sphere of existence is most clearly illustrated by the old aphorism that there is a "woman's place." That "place" is a field of operations presumably reserved for her in the divine scheme of things and corresponding to the fulfillment of a particular set of functions in the world of men. This kind of mythic thinking reflects the age-old tendency of societies and institutions to maintain certain traditional patterns of thought and behavior. This is done in the fear that challenging or changing such patterns is tantamount to inviting chaos and disaster by undermining the order which the traditions both establish and prolong.[8]

In studying the scriptural passage cited above, and with particular reference to the question of female ordination, we would do well to recall the report of the Pontifical Biblical Commission to the Vatican's Doctrinal Congregation. This report stresses that Jesus' activities and his attitude toward women should be examined in light of his intention to bring about an unmistakable "departure point" from the previous state of affairs; "the reign of God, inaugurated by his preaching and his presence, brings with it a new order and a full restoration of feminine dignity."[9] Granting, as the Commission's report also states, that the biblical texts are not principally concerned to define the role of women, we must still ask ourselves what they do reveal to us about Jesus' attitude and intentions. Christians believe that Scripture constitutes the written record of God's revelation to humanity. Dare we say that we have plumbed the depths of its divine message, particularly as it relates to the question of the role of women in the Church? The Church itself teaches that ". . . there is a growth in the understanding of the realities and the words which have been handed down . . ." and that ". . . as the centuries succeed one another, the Church constantly moves forward toward the fullness of divine truth. . . ."[10] Recalling the exegesis of John which we have been considering and its explication of the concept of discipleship, including the full discipleship of women granted to them by Jesus himself, we must also ask whether the Church can afford to overlook such actions of Jesus and still remain faithful to his word. To insist that women cannot receive the call to ordination seems precariously close to an insistence that God cannot issue that call.

Further, since "theology rests on the written word of God, together with tradition,"[11] it is of the utmost importance for the correct interpretation of Scripture that its limitations as well as its enduring truths be fully appreciated. The Biblical Commission expressed just such an appreciation in its recent report, with the reminder that in regard to the role of women, the biblical texts themselves are not particularly helpful. From the feminist point of view, this means that essential to the correct understanding of the texts is the recognition (with all its ramifications) that the revelation of God in Scripture is still expressed in human language. As such it reflects historically and culturally conditioned notions at the same time that it contains within itself the seeds of greater understanding. We have to remember also that Scripture scholars themselves tell us that the connection between theology and revelation is so close as to be at times indistinguishable. As Elisabeth Schüssler Fiorenza observes, "This hermeneutic insight is far-reaching when we consider that Scripture as well as theology is rooted in a patriarchal-sexist culture and shares its biases and prejudices."[12] This does not mean, however, that Scripture is without value to us in coming to some understanding of Jesus' attitude and, by implication, his intentions.

Christian feminists are willing to concede the merit of arguments which claim that the question of female ordination cannot be solved solely by reducing it to a matter of justice, as though ordination were a God-given right.[13] They are also mindful that the Church holds that "problems of sacramental theology, especially when they concern the ministerial priesthood . . . cannot be solved except in the light of Revelation,"[14] and that the human sciences alone cannot suffice in these cases.

Nevertheless, these same feminists also recognize that the Church *does* use the findings of the human sciences in its approach to the solution of certain pastoral problems associated with sacramental theology. They wonder, too, why questions concerning the ministerial priesthood, more than questions concerning baptism, marriage or any other sacrament, are solvable only in the light of Revelation. The question becomes more pressing when we realize that the written record of Revelation is not without its sexual prejudices. The Pontifical Biblical Commission itself has declared: "It does not seem that the New Testament alone will permit us to settle in a clear way and once and for all the problem of the possible accession of women to the presbyterate."[15] If the Mary Magdalene story has any relevance at all, at least a part of its message must be that Christian discipleship carries with it the further possibility of exercising the apostolic vocation in its fullness.

Turning to a second instance of female discipleship in the fourth Gospel, we consider Brown's treatment of the Mother of the Lord. According to the exegete, both John and Luke tell us that discipleship constitutes the true family of Jesus, and that his natural family become his true family through the grace of this calling.[16] The order of relation is reversed and a new order inaugurated, one based not on blood, but on faith and obedience to Jesus. The position of Mary in relation to her Son assumes a new importance and must be seen in a new light.

John speaks of Mary in only two instances: at Cana and on Calvary. In neither instance does he use her personal name. Rather, he refers to her as the mother of Jesus, his way of insisting, we are told, that her primary importance lies not in her maternal relation to Jesus, but in her symbolism for the meaning of true discipleship.[17] At Cana, her request is granted because Jesus is willing to anticipate the "hour" of his glorification dictated by God. He reminds his mother that his primary relation is not to her as mother, but to God whom he calls Father. This is a bond which transcends all human relationships. Additionally, he reminds her of the only title by which she may command his intervention, that is, not as her son, but as her Lord. This, Brown tells us, is the significance of Jesus' use of the term "woman," in addressing Mary on this occasion.[18]

On Calvary, Jesus again addresses his mother as "woman," and grants her the role of mother to the Beloved Disciple. In recognizing the Disciple as the child of his mother, Jesus is claiming him and all disciples to be his true sisters and brothers. Mary's role at this most important juncture, at Jesus' "hour," is not that of mother to Jesus but that of mother to the Beloved Disciple. By explicitly denying Mary involvement in his ministry on the basis of her physical motherhood, Jesus is reinterpreting who his mother and family are, and reinterpreting them precisely in terms of discipleship.[19]

This reinterpretation of Mary the mother of Jesus, like that of Mary Magdalene, is of great importance for understanding the role and "place" of women in the Christian community. Like Mary Magdalene, whose primary claim to fame (though its historicity is open to question) is that she was a reformed prostitute and thus a woman of the flesh *par excellence*, Mary the mother of Jesus has been presented to generations of Christians primarily in her maternal role as biological mother. While the Church has always honored Mary as the symbol of humble faith and obedience (discipleship), she has nevertheless remained in popular devotion as first and foremost the loving, nurturing mother, standing ready to intervene between a sinful people and a just God. By embracing her primary identity in the scheme of salvation as that of disciple rather than that of mother, Mary expands the horizons of possibility for all Christian women and personifies their God-given ability to transcend identification with the merely physical or with any role in which they are defined as purely relational beings. She holds out to them the possibility of embarking upon their Christian ministry, whatever it might be, in full partnership with the other disciples. In Brown's words, "A man and a woman stood at the foot of the Cross as models for Jesus' 'own,' his true family of disciples."[20]

That the Scriptures should contain this pearl of information and that it should be illustrated in the life of the Mother of God offers immeasurable consolation to those women who wish to serve the Lord in capacities other than those defined by sexuality, whether as consecrated virgin or consecrated mother. The notion of Mary as disciple gives a new dimension to the lives of Christian women who have heretofore been expected to fit themselves to one of the traditional feminine roles. Mary herself takes on a new richness when she is seen as disciple, and the age-old patriarchal and Patristic emphasis upon her (and woman's) role as bride is counterbalanced by the recognition of her simultaneous vocation to discipleship. The Declaration of the Vatican congregation with regard to the ordination of women relies heavily upon the nuptial theme of Christ as Bridegroom and the Church as his Bride, with the usual emphasis upon the strong, protective love of the Groom for the Bride. This imagery is used to buttress the argument that the maleness of Christ is essential to the economy of salvation and that the sacramental sign of ordination is attached to human sexuality rather than to human personhood.[21] The concept of discipleship as the primary Christian category allows for an emphasis on personhood and partnership and opens the way for the use of other scriptural language which also "expresses and affects man and woman in their profound identity."[22] Using the insights of the fourth Gospel, we may assert that Christian identity rests on discipleship and is not primarily sexual. The mythic notion of woman as essentially sexual and consequently both inferior and evil provides the basis for Canon 968, which forbids the ordained ministry to women. The law is reflective not only of the age in which it was formulated, but also of the collection of myths surrounding woman which have persisted in the minds of men from earliest times.[23] As an example of positive law it is, as Pierre Grelot says in another context, "not the consequence of an ideal principle derived from revelation; it provides the framework for an actual situation determined by the culture of the times."[24] Similarly, the Declaration, with its mythic view of the "place" and role of women, its static view of tradition and its unwillingness to recognize the value of the human sciences, ignores the facts of history and the new realization of woman's identity and worth.

We are fast approaching the time when, after the example of Jesus, we must formulate new laws which abrogate and transcend the old, and which bring with them "a full restoration of feminine dignity."[25] Both at Cana and on Calvary Jesus responded to the demands of the "hour" dictated by God, in the first instance by the anticipation and in the second by the completion of his redemptive mission. In each case, he reminded a woman, his mother, that her relationship to him was primarily that of discipleship. In each case, also, he involved her as disciple directly in his activity. After his death, the risen Jesus revealed himself first to a woman and commissioned her as his disciple to carry the Good News to others, a distinctly apostolic activity. Recognizing Jesus' intention to depart from the old order and acknowledging his inclusion of women into full discipleship, we may allow ourselves the hope that the full implications of that discipleship—full priesthood and full partnership in the Christian mission—may also be recognized as open to women and as in direct conformity with both Jesus' words and his actions in their regard. The hour has come for the Christ to be fully glorified in his humanity.

Notes

1. Raymond E. Brown, S.S., "Roles of Women in the Fourth Gospel," *Theological Studies*, Vol. 36, No. 4 (Dec., 1975), p. 699.

2. *Ibid.*

3. *Ibid.*, p. 694.

4. Hartman points out that in the New Testament the primary meaning of the term is that of follower or adherent, and that in many cases it is impossible to say whether it refers to the smaller or the larger group of Jesus' followers. See: Louis F. Hartman, C.SS.R., *Encyclopedic Dictionary of the Bible*. A Translation and Adaptation of A. van den Born's *Bijbels Woordenboek*. Second Revised Edition, 1954-1957. (New York: McGraw-Hill Book Company, Inc., 1963), s.v. "Disciple."

5. The tradition that Jesus first appeared to Mary Magdalene has a good chance of being historical. See: Brown, *op. cit.*, p. 692, n. 12.

6. In the liturgy of the Western Church, Mary Magdalene was given th honor of being the only woman besides the Mother of God on whose feast the Creed was recited, specifically because she was revered as an apostle. Brown cites the use of the term "apostle" with reference to Mary Magdalene by Rabanus Maurus, her ninth-century biographer. *Ibid.*, p. 693, n. 14.

7. Biblical Commission Report, Part I, 3.

8. The term "myth" is used in the technical sense as referring to a living social force which is only indirectly related to historical fact. A social myth strengthens certain traditions and endows them with greater value and prestige by tracing them back to an earlier, higher and in some cases divinely ordained order of events. See: Bronislaw Malinowski, *Myth in Primitive Psychology* (New York: W.W. Norton and Company, Inc., 1926), p. 13.

9. Biblical Commission Report, Part I, 3.

10. "Dogmatic Constitution on Divine Revelation," par. 8, in *The Documents of Vatican II*, ed. Walter M. Abbott, S.J. (New York: Guild Press, 1966), p. 116.

11. *Ibid.*, par. 24, p. 127.

12. Elisabeth Schüssler Fiorenza, "Feminist Theology as a Critical Theology of Liberation," *Theological Studies*, Vol. 36, No. 4 (Dec., 1975), p. 611.

13. Declaration, par. 38.

14. *Ibid.*, par. 34.

15. Biblical Commission Report, Part IV, sec. 2.

16. Brown, *op. cit.*, p. 698.

17. It is important to note that Brown makes clear that discipleship is not the only symbolism in which Mary can be seen, and that in becoming a disciple, Mary did not become simply one among many. Rather, she has "an eminence as the mother of the ideal Disciple," Brown, *op. cit.*, p. 698, n. 28.

18. This view is corroborated by Bruce Vawter in his commentary on the Gospel of John. See: Bruce Vawter, S.M., "The Gospel According to John," in *The Jerome Biblical Commentary*, Vol. II, ed. Joseph A. Fitzmyer, S.J. and Raymond E. Brown, S.S. (Englewood Cliffs, N.J.: Prentice-Hall, 1968), p. 427.

19. This is a close paraphrase of Brown, *op. cit.*, p. 698.

20. *Ibid.*, p. 699.

21. Declaration, pars. 29, 30. Krister Stendahl speaks to his assertion in a pithy manner when he says: The masculinity of God and of God-language is a cultural and linguistic accident, and I think one should also agree that the masculinity of Christ is of the same order. To be sure, Jesus Christ was a male, but that may be no more significant to his being than the fact that presumably his eyes were brown. Incarnation is a great thing. But it strikes me as odd to argue that when the Word became flesh, it was to re-enforce male superiority. Quoted in: Casey Miller and Kate Swift, "Women and the Language of Religion," *Christian Century*, Vol. 93 (April, 1976), p. 355.

22. Declaration, par. 29.

23. For a treatment of the origin of certain of these myths, see: H.R. Hays, *The Dangerous Sex. The Myth of Feminine Evil* (New York: Pocket Books, 1964).

24. Grelot is speaking of the Old Testament tradition of two moralities, one for men and the other for women, which reflected the social point of view rather than any considerations of sexual morality, and which contained no recognition of marriage, for example, as an agreement between two equal partners. However, the application of his words to the Canon Law of the Church is a logical one. See: Pierre Grelot, "The Institution of Marriage: Its Evolution in the Old Testament," *Concilium*, 1970 (Vol. 55, American Edition), p. 43.

25. Biblical Commission Report, Part I, sec. 3.

42
Misunderstanding of Sexuality and Resistance to Women Priests

Sidney Callahan

Within the Church we have a disagreement over whether women should be ordained to the priesthood. Both sides are accused of unworthy motives, but it seems clear that both groups are trying to be faithful to the will of Jesus Christ for the Church. We are all straining to hear God's message, much as scientists attempt to understand and make sense of natural events as signals of reality. As a Christian and a psychologist I believe that God is the ultimate reality and aim of both the theological and scientific quest. The way things are in a natural world which God has created can be of use in discerning what God wants us to do and be. This is especially true when we are arguing about "natural resemblances," "perceptible signs," and "symbols imprinted upon the human psychology."

My case for the ordination of women is simply that I think God wills it as a fitting and appropriate action, faithful to the Lord. Those who would exclude women seem to be unfortunately caught up in a basic misunderstanding of sexuality. Sexual identity and sexual social roles and sexual function have not been kept distinct in their analysis, but more damaging by far has been the elevation and exaggeration of the sexual symbolism of the gospel message. A selective reading of Scripture has been made so that the mystery of salvation has been sexualized, all the while recognizing that God is beyond sexuality and that Jesus is "the firstborn of all humanity." Indeed Jesus' example of treating women with a revolutionary equality is given as the basis for encouraging women's equality in all of society and human culture with the exception of the priesthood. The contradiction and exceptions in the argument are curious. Why is there such a clinging to male gender as so central symbolically that only a male can have a "natural resemblance" to Christ as priest?

The motivation in my opinion is not due to any hardness of hearts but rather to a soft romanticism seeking to protect the importance of mystery, transcendence and symbols with inadequate but very old tactics.[1] In many other religions the arbitrary refusal or irrational demand has often been identified with the holy, when and if Divinity has been apprehended as irrational. In the same way the perception of a principle of dichotomy or absolutely opposite categories is, according to Levi-Strauss and Piaget,[2] a feature of the primitive mind. Day-night, good-evil, earth-sky and, in some cultures, male-female are seen as polar opposites. The need for categorization, clarity and order is so great that many persons and cultures resist the ambiguity of any in-between states.[3] But the evolution of mind and knowledge progresses beyond the surface categorizations of dichotomy, polarity and juxtaposition to deeper structures of unity and complexity.[4] The mystery of life and reality is indeed more awesome and subtle, requiring a more complex scheme than any dichotomy.

Sexuality is an example of a simple polar categorization which is now beside the point. Not only is there obviously a wide diversity of social sex roles possible in varying cultures,[5] but even the psychobiological development of sexual identity is far more complicated than appears on the surface. There exists a relay stage system of sexual development in which first genetic factors, then hormonal influences, then morphological and socio-cognitive factors alternate and mutually influence each other.[6] If one or another influence is delayed, misfires or is affected by an environmental agent a human person is still produced.[7] Sexual differentiation and sexual identity is analogous to an information-processing system in which different signals are given to activate and suppress latent potentials. It seems to be the case that we are all programmed more to a basic species model, and that sexual differentiation can be seen as a fairly minor part of the incredibly complicated growth process, unless a culture chooses to exaggerate differences. Generally the lack of sexual differentiation in the early embryo, infants and small children is again manifest in old age. We begin and end androgynously. The brief period of mating and sexual reproduction is usually the most sexually differentiated period of the life cycle. Even at this period males, as seen in the example of many animal species, are fully capable of nurturance, and always individual within-sex differences are more pronounced than between-sex differences.[8]

Sexual identity is submerged in personal, species and population identity and is ill-suited for bearing the weight of much symbolism in the Church's life. If nature is being scientifically misunderstood and distorted by specific culture-bound perceptions, then a "natural resemblance" will be seen which is as "perceptible" as the Emperor's new clothes. In fact the gospel message seems to be giving a very different view, always and everywhere downplaying the importance of gender identity and reproduction in favor of personal affirmations and personal conduct. Jesus is constantly shown requiring personal adherence and disregarding ascribed conditions such as sexual identity, blood relationship, status and class. Jesus is also shown as conceived outside natural sexual conception, transcending sexual mating and reproductive behavior, and finally possessing a mysterious transfigured risen body in a state in which there is no marrying. If male gender was so essential to the economy of salvation, then the savior's birth, sexual behavior and promised heaven should have been quite different, as it was among the pagan religions. Instead of Divine couples and sexual intercourse we have creation by fiat and the word made flesh. If God is beyond sexuality, and Jesus transcends sexuality and the risen life transcends sexuality as we know it, how can male sexuality in the priesthood be a sacramental sign of the firstborn of the new humanity? It is as symbolically counterproductive and constraining as would be the requirement for animal sacrifices in and only in the temple in Jerusalem.

The question of change and the time sense of the Church is also an issue here. Catholicism has ever tried to conserve the best of the historical past and to be responsive to the Holy Spirit's promptings and instruction. But in this matter of ordaining women, and in this document in particular, the focus is all on a questionable past model discussed within a static sense of time. There is too little emphasis upon being faithful to Jesus as the risen Christ who makes all things new and awaits us in the future. Since no one knows the day or the hour or the time scheme of salvation, the Church may be in existence for 700 more centuries; should a mere nineteen hundred years' practice determine the future? In that future it might better be remembered that in the Church's infancy for thirty seconds it imposed Mosaic practices, for forty minutes it condoned slavery and for its first few hours it excluded women from the priesthood. Women, like the Gentiles and slaves before them, seemed different and unsuitable while they were being excluded and barred from full participation.

In actual fact, an all-male priesthood and hierarchy is handicapped by exaggerating the importance of sexual difference and symbolism. Without intimacy with women and fully equal personal working cooperation, sex is seen as a more intimate decisive aspect of personality than it is. Distance creates an overblown romanticism and regression to a primitive dichotomous sexual categorization. In this situation nuptial imagery becomes strangely salient when it is really only one strand in a rich symbolic tapestry including among others word, light, water, rock, vine, way, joy, friend, servant, shepherd. A distorted romantic symbolism might be acceptable by some, but in this case it is actively obscuring the fullness of God's message. The mystery of life and personal identity does not need the nostalgic remnants of a pagan sexual mystique to sustain wonder. The word become flesh transcends all dichotomies. The infinite graciousness, greatness and variety of God will be perceived more fully and clearly when the priesthood is personal and open to all those whom God saves and chooses for sacramental service.

Notes

1. David Burrell, "The Vatican Declaration: Another View," *America*, Vol. 136, No. 13 (April 2, 1977), p. 289.

2. Claude Levi-Strauss, *The Savage Mind*, tr. by George Weidenfeld (Chicago: The University of Chicago Press, 1966); Jean Piaget, *The Language and Thought of the Child*, tr. by Marjorie Gabain (New York: The World Publishing Company, 1966).

3. Mary Douglas, *Purity and Danger: an analysis of concepts of pollution and taboo* (London: Routledge & Kegan Paul, 1966; Mary Douglas, *Natural Symbols: Explorations in Cosmology* (New York: Pantheon Books, 1970).

4. Howard Gardner, *The Quest for Mind* (New York: Alfred A. Knopf, 1973).

5. Ann Oakley, *Sex, Gender & Society* (New York: Harper & Row, 1972).

6. R.C. Friedman, R. M. Richart and R. L. Vande-Wiele, *Sex Differences in Behavior* (New York: Wiley, 1974); B.C. Rosenberg and Brian Sutton-Smith, *Sex and Identity* (New York: Holt, Rinehart and Winston, Inc., 1972).

7. John Money and Anke A. Ehrhardt, *Man & Woman: Boy & Girl* (Baltimore: The Johns Hopkins University Press, 1972).

8. Eleanor Emmons Maccoby and Carol Nagy Jacklin, *The Psychology of Sex Differences* (Stanford, California: Stanford University Press, 1974).

43
Bishop and Presbyter
as Representatives
of the Church and Christ

Edward J. Kilmartin

The Declaration affirms this principle: "In actions which demand the character of ordination and in which Christ himself . . . is represented, exercising his ministry of salvation . . . his role must be taken by a male."[1] Why? Because sacramental signs "must be perceptible" to the senses. They must "represent what they signify by natural resemblance." Hence if the minister is not male the natural resemblance is lacking. The minister would not be "image of Christ."[2]

What are the ministerial functions which have these characteristics? The text refers to actions which the priest performs as "image and symbol of Christ himself who calls, forgives and accomplishes the sacrifice of the Covenant."[3] Nevertheless only the role of the priest in the Eucharist is developed: The priest "alone has the power to perform" the sacrifice of Christ. In this activity the celebrant is said to act "not only through the effective power conferred on him by Christ, but *in persona Christi*, taking the role of Christ to the point of being his very image, when he pronounces the words of consecration."[4]

How is the function of the priest as representing the Church related to the role of representing Christ? It is stated that the priest, in his official acts, represents the Church: he "acts *in persona Ecclesiae*, that is to say, in the name of the whole Church and in order to represent her."[5] Furthermore this role is situated in a relationship of dependence on the priest's ability to represent Christ: "It is true that the priest represents the Church . . . But . . . because he first represents Christ himself who is the Head . . . of the Church."[6] The Commentary on the Declaration explains this ordering by reasoning that otherwise the priest would be a delegate of the community; the Church would be source of official authority: "When the priest presides over the assembly, it is not the assembly that has chosen or delegated him for his role . . . It is Christ who calls it together . . . and the priest presides 'in the power of Christ the Head.' "[7]

The Declaration thus explicitly names one ritual act in which the priest directly represents Christ: the proclamation of the account of institution during the eucharistic prayer. It states that in other rites which call for the character of ordination the priest is "image and symbol of Christ." These are described from the viewpoint of Christ's activity in calling, forgiving and offering sacrifice. Moreover the Declaration assumes that if the priest first represents the Church in the sphere of sacramental activity for which ordination qualifies, it must be concluded that the Church, not Christ, is the source of this ministry.

Elsewhere in this volume the question of the signification of the account of institution in the eucharistic prayer is discussed. However some observations on the position taken by the Declaration will be made since they are integral to the argument of this essay. This will be done within the scope of a more general consideration of the role of the priest as representing the Church and Christ in the sacramental activity for which ordination qualifies a baptized member of the Church.

The Declaration's assertion that the priest first represents Christ and then the Church in activity for which the character of ordination qualifies is based on a consideration of the ultimate source of the priest's activity: Christ the Head of the Church. On the other hand the affirmation that the priest directly represents Christ when he pronounces the "words of consecration" is founded on an interpretation of the signification of the account of institution in the sacramental rite itself. Still the text does not treat the implications of these two points of view. In fact by insisting on the priest's being "image and symbol" in other sacramental activities, it gives the impression that in all sacramental rites the celebrant directly represents Christ the Head in the symbolic action itself. The seeming lack of awareness of two different processes which are involved in the analysis of sacramental rites is surprising. It is not our purpose to speculate on why the two processes are confused. However, as a result an important consideration is passed over which, to say the least, renders the reasoning of the Declaration neutral on the question of ordination of women.

The two different processes involved in the analysis of sacramental rites, alluded to in the text, are traditionally used in scholastic theology. The first begins with what is more accessible and progresses toward what is ultimately signified; the second analyzes the actual process in which what is ultimately signified directs the whole process of symbolization.

Since sacramental rites have various levels of signification a simple affirmation that a sacrament signifies something, or "first signifies" something, is not sufficient. One must pay attention to the level of significance at which the statement may be true.[8] Thus beginning with what is most accessible in the case of Baptism it will be seen that the profession of faith, water bath and unction of Confirmation symbolize, respectively, an engagement, purification and consecration. Taken together they constitute the rite of initiation. This rite signifies, first of all, something social and interpersonal, perceptible at the level of human experience: incorporation into the community of believers in Christ. That which is thus symbolized, in its turn, functions to symbolize a spiritual reality: integration into the Body of Christ by the gift of the Spirit. Thus what is *denoted* by the sensible rite also *connotes* a spiritual reality.

The foregoing analysis proceeds from what is immediately accessible and moves to what is ultimately signified within the sacramental rite. But, of course, the actual process of symbolization is reversed: What is ultimately signified directs the whole process. So from the latter point of view one might say that Baptism primarily signifies the gift of the Spirit of regeneration. But from the former point of view it would be correct to say that Baptism first signifies incorporation into the community of believers.

It is also possible to refer to levels of signification which lie above and below the internal structure of a sacramental rite. St. Thomas says that sacraments signify the cause (passion of Christ), the form (grace) and the goal (eternal life) of our sanctification.[9] But both the cause and goal lie above sacramental symbolism. On the other hand the ancient symbolism attached to the many grains of wheat forming one loaf and so signifying the unity of the Church falls below the sacramental level. For if the element of bread directly signified the unity of the Church in the sacramental rite it would have to be considered the cause of this effect—at least from the viewpoint of scholastic theology which understands that sacraments cause by signifying.

These general considerations bring us to the question: On what level of signification which is sacramental can the priest be said to signify Christ "in the exercise of his ministry" and to signify the Church in its activity?

Beginning with what is most accessible it must be said that priests in their liturgical activity directly represent the faith of the Church of which they are leaders. Moreover, participating in the collegial office of the whole Church, priests directly represent the unity of concrete liturgical communities through their communion with one another, and so the common faith of the Church. Thus in their persons and activities they serve in a special way to connote the source of the unity of the whole Church: Christ and the Holy Spirit.

From this standpoint it is necessary to say that the priest first represents (denotes) the Church in its sacramental activity and secondly represents (connotes) Christ the Head of the Church. But this analysis also affirms that from the perspective of what is ultimately signified the priest first represents (connotes) Christ the Head of the Church and secondly represents (denotes) the Church united in faith and love.

The leadership function of the priest in the Church is carried out in various ways to which correspond various modes of the presence of Christ: governing, teaching and liturgical leadership. All these activities are carried out by priests expressing the faith of the Church as members of the collegial body of the pastoral office. As ministers and representatives of the whole Church their activity connotes the pneumatic grounds of the unity of the Church. Hence they act in a special way *in persona Christi*. But they do this since they represent the one Church united in faith and love. So functioning they act in the name of but not merely on the basis of the commission of the local Church. Consequently their commission and authority, as the Commentary states, are not derived merely from the local Church.

This structure holds also for the Eucharist. Presiding over the community priests represent the whole Church and so connote Christ's activity. They act in the name of the whole Church and so serve as transparency for the grounds of unity and activity of the whole Church: Christ and the Holy Spirit.

Since priests, in their official activity, connote the Headship of Christ it is not immediately clear why maleness is required in this ministry in order to preserve the proper symbolic correspondence. Could not a female equally fulfill the symbolic function of connoting the Headship of Christ over the Church in those activities for which the character of ordination is required? An affirmative answer to this question may seem inevitable because women do connote the Headship of Christ in administering Baptism, and they do this by first representing (denoting) the faith of the Church. However according to traditional Catholic theology an exception to the general structure of levels of signification of sacramental rites is claimed for the Eucharist: The priest denotes Christ when pronouncing the account of institution.

A priori such an exception cannot be ruled out because sacramental rites relate to one another analogously, not univocally. Thus, for example, in the unique case of the sacrament of Matrimony the couple are the ministers. What, then, is the theological value of this theology of the "moment of consecration"? Does the priest's activity in this case bypass the first level of signification and so immediately denote Christ's activity?

Since the thirteenth century the account of institution is said to be spoken *in persona Christi* in the Latin Church. The usage is influenced by the Latin patristic writers who employ this phrase in order to attribute words of Scripture to another than the one concretely speaking. They also use it to ground ecclesiastical pardon on Christ. In continuity with this patristic usage theologians of the thirteenth century qualify the account of institution by this phrase to stress its consecratory function in the Eucharist.[10] St. Thomas brings out the implications of this theology of consecration by stressing that the celebrant thus fulfills a ministerial function as instrument of the act of Christ himself.[11]

For St. Thomas *in persona Christi* gives stature to the account of institution and indicates that the priest has a ministerial role in the act of Christ. Moreover St. Thomas understands that in the act of pronouncing the words of institution the priest denotes the action of Christ. He distinguishes this act from other ministerial sacerdotal activity which he understands as action of Christ and so also labels as activity *in persona Christi.*[12] For, speaking of the difference between the form of the sacrament of the Eucharist and those of other sacraments, he states that the other forms are spoken *ex persona ministri*, while the form of the Eucharist is spoken *ex persona Christi ipsius loquentis.*[13] This activity of the priest is distinguished from his activity in reciting the rest of the canon of the Mass which he sees as a rite of the Church and so not necessary for the realization of the sacrament.[14] In reciting the rest of the canon the priest acts *in persona Ecclesiae*. This term is used by St. Thomas to describe the role of the priest presiding over the liturgical prayer of the Church and so acting as organ of the profession of faith of the whole Church.[15]

The teaching that the priest denotes Christ's activity in the Mass at the "moment of consecration" is common in scholastic theology. In its methodological approach to reflection on the Lord's Supper it emphasizes the activity of Christ through the ordained minister. At the same time it totally neglects the structure of the eucharistic prayers of the East and West as well as the epicletic character of these prayers. The defects of this method have been pointed out frequently by modern Catholic scholars.[16]

In the structure of the eucharistic prayer itself the account of institution functions to relate the sacred meal to the event "Jesus Christ" as part of the prayer which includes thanksgiving, liturgical prayer of offering of bread and wine and the epiclesis. The whole prayer is a sacramental word: a word of faith of the Church and form of the ritual action. As a whole, therefore, it denotes the action of the Church which, in turn, connotes the activity of Christ. This is stressed in the epiclesis: the invocation of the Spirit (explicit or implicit) made by the community through the priest with a view to the accomplishment of the mystery signified in the eucharistic celebration.

Another important influence on the development of the concept of the priest denoting Christ in the eucharistic celebration can be traced to the conceptual separation and isolation of the power of orders from the power of jurisdiction. Scholastic theology conceived the power of orders as existing and operating without immediate relation to its ecclesiological grounding. Within this mindset the priest is understood to exercise a power of consecration which is independent of the ecclesiastical context even to the extent of being actualizable outside the liturgy. Only recently in the twentieth century has the possibility of a priest consecrating bread and wine outside the context of the liturgy been generally rejected.

The development of this theology coincides with the concept of the priest functioning as index[17] of Christ in the Eucharist in complete isolation from his index function as confessing believer and representative of pastoral office of the apostolic Church.[18]

Within the eucharistic rite there are certain indexes which connote a real relation to the event "Jesus Christ." Through the account of institution and the sharing of bread and wine the sacred meal of the history of religions assumes a real relation to the Last Supper and the redemptive work of Christ. Furthermore the community of believers itself is the indispensable index: united in the name of Christ with the priest in apostolic succession and so constituting the Church which celebrates the Eucharist.

Within this context the priest is an index: This ministry is linked through the bishop to that of the apostles so that the Eucharist appears as apostolic. Priests provide a historical referent for the celebration as members of the apostolic college of liturgical leaders. Ordination to the pastoral office directly signifies the designation of a person to serve the community in apostolic ministry: Something which can be lived is denoted. It does not directly represent but connotes a relationship to Christ the Head of the Church. The latter relationship could be dramatized independently of the first level of signification, but it would not be a sacramental rite whch belongs to the order of praxis. Consequently priests function on the level of denotation as representatives of the faith of the Church and on the level of connotation as representatives of Christ the Head of the Church.

Liturgical actions do not belong to the order of pure praxis, i.e., they are not destined simply to produce something. Nor do they simply depict a spiritual reality. Rather the praxis connotes a spiritual reality. In our case incorporation into the college of liturgical leaders connotes a sharing in the ministry of Christ the Head of the Church. Corresponding to this the priest in his activity does not dramatize Christ's activity in the Church. Rather through his ecclesial activity, representing the faith of the Church, he connotes Christ's activity.

If one does not pay attention to the various levels of signification of sacramental rites when interpreting the dynamics of liturgical actions, there is a danger that the Christian liturgy will be presented as a sacred drama. This danger is apparent in theological explanations of the Eucharist which describe the priest as directly representing Christ in an activity to which the community *then* relates itself. A curious statement of the Commentary on the Declaration could be interpreted to favor this view of the Mass as a sacred drama. Alluding to the classical usage of *persona*, which means an actor's mask and so by way of metonymy stands for a role, it states that this original meaning describes the activity of the priest in the Mass: "The priest takes the part of Christ, lending him his voice and gestures."[19]

In this presentation it is difficult to avoid the impression that liturgical actions are really sacred dramas with the goal of merely communicating something to the audience. The conceptual separation of the central action of the Mass from the participation of the faithful leads logically to the conclusion that the laity are an audience invited to identify with the drama vicariously in a way analogous to "live theatre."

This presentation might possibly find a home in a typically Reformation theology which sees the Eucharist merely from the viewpoint of Christ's gift of himself to the believer, but it is not consistent with a Catholic theology which teaches that the Eucharist is a sacramental coaccomplishment of the sacrifice of the cross in and by the Church. Christian liturgy differs from sacred drama not merely because of the mystery content but also because the presence of Christ and his saving work take place through the rites which are a form of expression of the faith of the Church. The dynamics of liturgical actions must be presented in such a way that they are clearly seen as social actions in which there is no complete disjunction between the representation of the mystery of salvation and the lives of those involved in the action as "actors," both minister and faithful. This can only be done, from the perspective of the role of apostolic office in the liturgy, by affirming that this office represents Christ by representing the faith of the Church of which Christ is the sharing source along with the Spirit.[20]

Summary and Conclusion

1. The Declaration's explanation of the role of the priest with respect to the Church and Christ is based on Thomistic theology. Logically it leads to the exclusion of women from the priesthood.

2. In this essay an attempt has been made to show that, beginning with the theology of sacramental signification and taking into account the christological and pneumatological-ecclesiological dimensions of pastoral office, the representative functions of the priest are consistent with the ordination of women.

3. The eucharistic theology used by the Declaration to support its position represents a partial tradition which is recognized by most Catholic liturgical scholars as at variance with the authentic whole liturgical tradition of the East and West of the first millenium.

4. The Declaration shows why it is premature, at the level of the official theology of the Roman Catholic Church, to make a decision regarding the ordination of women.

Before any decision based on theological grounds can be taken on the question of ordination of women, a new evaluation by the magisterium of the Roman Catholic Church of the christological and pneumatological-ecclesiological dimensions of the pastoral office is required. It is also imperative that a serious investigation be undertaken in the area of the theology of sacramental signification and the dynamics of the eucharistic celebration.

Notes

1. Declaration, par. 30.
2. *Ibid.*, par. 27.
3. *Ibid.*, par. 33.
4. *Ibid.*, pars. 26-27.
5. *Ibid.*, par. 32.
6. *Ibid.*
7. Commentary, par. 44.
8. M. Amaladoss, "Sémiologie et sacrement," *La Maison Dieu*, Vol. 97, No. 114 (1973), p. 31.
9. *Summa Theologiae*, III, q. 60, a. 3, c.
10. B.-D. Marliangeas, " 'In Persona Christi,' 'In Persona Ecclesiae': Note sur les origines et le developpement de l'usage de ces expressions dans la théologie latine," *La Liturgie après Vatican II*, Y. Congar et al. (Paris: Les Editions du Cerf, 1967), pp. 283-286.
11. *Summa*, III, q. 83, a.1, ad 3.
12. *Ibid.*, q. 22, a.4, c.
13. *Ibid.*, q. 78, a.1, c.
14. *Ibid.*, q. 78, a.1, ad 4.
15. *Ibid.*, q. 64, a.8, ad 2.
16. For example: H.-J. Schulz, "Die Grundstruktur des kirchlichen Amtes im Spiegel der Eucharistiefeier und der Ordinationsliturgie des rö-

mischen und des byzantinischen Ritus," *Catholica*, Vol. 29, No. 4 (October, 1975), pp. 325-340 (especially, pp. 331-334).

17. An *index* indicates something not present but with which it is linked causally or by association. Christian rites must have indexes which relate them to the historical event "Jesus Christ." Because of their connotative structure indexes are sometimes confused with symbols. But symbols as such do not signify a historical referent: The relation between the thing signified and the signifying is one of reason. The relation between the index and the thing indicated is real.

18. This view results in an overdrawn identification between Christ and the priest in which basic sacramental categories such as icon (image), anti-type and type are misunderstood.

Traditional scholastic theology shows an inclination either to completely divorce or completely confuse symbol or image with the reality signified. This is reflected in its explanation of the attitude Christians should adopt toward images of Christ. The VII Ecumenical Council, II Nicaea, explained that icons should not be adored but venerated since they elevate the faithful to the one represented and lead to imitation (H. Denzinger & A. Schönmetzer, *Enchiridion Symbolorum*: Definitionum et Declarationum de rebus fidei et morum, 32 ed., Barcelona: Herder, 1963, p. 201, no. 601). St. Thomas, however, approves the adoration of images of Christ not 'insofar as a thing" but "insofar as image" (*Summa*, III, q. 25, a.3, c.).

19. Commentary, par. 41.

20. E. J. Kilmartin, "Apostolic Office: Sacrament of Christ," *Theological Studies*, Vol. 36, No. 2 (June, 1975), pp. 257ff.

44

The "Ordination" of Queens

J. Massyngberde Ford

Towards the end of the Declaration the writers refer to "ruling power" within the Church. Yet jurisdiction is different from the ability to perform the sacramental and sacrificial duties of the priesthood. Church history can produce examples of lay (male and female) jurisdiction over ecclesial matters not only in the Roman Catholic Church but in other denominations; for example, in the parish of Lynby-cum-Papplewick in Nottinghamshire, England, the lay squire is rector of the tenth century church and the clergyman is subordinate to him, while the incumbent is rector of the eleventh century church in the same Anglican parish.

However, as well as jurisdiction held by Abbesses[1] even over double monasteries, perhaps the outstanding example of female ecclesial jurisdiction is that of Queens. In the ordination, coronation, or consecration of Queens and Empresses, the Church has a very ancient and unbroken tradition of liturgical consecration of a woman to govern men and women, clergy and lay; she is the image of kingship which we predicate of Jesus. The ceremony shows great affinity to that of the consecration of a bishop both in the ceremonies and prayers and in the investiture. Yet very few people, saving the famous John Knox,[2] objected to this ecclesiastical subordination of men to women. The Pauline texts were regarded as no hindrance to this ordination. Queen Elizabeth II of England, I of Scotland, is head of the Anglican church. Thus it is very peculiar that women are not ordained to the priesthood or the bishopric in England. Naturally, the Queen has powers of jurisdiction, not of administering the sacraments, but a bishop also has similar faculties of administration. In the ordination of kings and queens there is no discrimination; only one ceremony is omitted, that of the giving of the spurs, because the queen did not ride out to battle. The queen was a sharer in the regal power *(regalis imperii . . . esse participem)* even if she were the wife of a king.[3] The queen has her officials, her property, her revenue. She could issue charters and take over the regency as need be.

The anointing of monarchs was very important. By it she was inwardly and outwardly changed and became God's office-bearer in the world, a ruler over his people in the divine plan of the cosmos. Any anointing set a person apart.[4] Today and at other stages of history the queen is (was) anointed on the hands (like a priest) on the chest and on the head (like a bishop). At certain points in history, before the sacraments were reduced to seven, the ordination of a monarch was regarded as a sacrament. For example, Robert Grosseteste in 1245 wrote:

The royal anointing was, indeed, a sacrament, and it bestowed upon the King (Queen) insight into the ordering of things temporal and spiritual, and, moreover, made him (her) capable of conducting state affairs *ordinabiliter*. For this reason an anointed King (Queen), unlike an unanointed one, was fortified in all his (her) dealing by Divine and moral power.

Nevertheless, to these glowing words he added:

This privilege of anointing in no way places the Royal dignity above or even on an equality with the priestly, nor does it confer power to perform any sacerdotal office.[5]

On the other hand the Anonymous of York argued that the King had a right to intervene in ecclesial areas and that he could save souls and even absolve from sin.[6] The monarch was the *mediator cleri et plebis* just as a priest was mediator between God and people on the spiritual side.[7] However, the monarch was seen to be anointed like a priest, a *Christus Domini* who was entrusted with the protection of the Church and thus *defensor* or *advocatus ecclesiae*; seen in this light s/he could not be regarded as an ordinary lay person. This position was supported from the Bible by reference to Melchizedek who was both *rex et sacerdos*. The Anonymous of York "analyzed with great acumen, sentence by sentence, the English coronation ordo and compared it with the consecration of bishops."[8] Indeed, to this day the form of the service bears much resemblance to the consecration of a bishop: it is performed on a Sunday or feast day, only bishops take leading parts, the oath is sworn; there is the tradition of the insignia, e.g., the crown (=mitre), the ring, the sword and orb (cf. the crozier), the anointing, the handing over of the Bible, and the recitation of the *laudes regiae*. The monarch wears a kind of stole which originally probably came from the lorum of the Byzantine emperor.[9] Froisart states that Henry IV was vested as a deacon and had buskins of red samite "like those of a prelate." As Schramm observes, "the result of all this was that an unbiased spectator of a fourteenth century coronation could no more regard the King (Queen) of England as a mere layman than could the people who had long believed in miracles."

The oath which the monarchs promise is to govern the People; to cause Law and Justice in Mercy to be executed; to maintain the Laws of God, the true profession of the Gospel, and the Protestant Reformed Religion; and to preserve the rights of the Bishops and the clergy.[10] They swear on the Great Bible.

At the anointing the prayer is as follows:

Be thy head anointed with Holy oil, as Kings, *Priests* and Prophets were anointed.

The Monarch receives the sword "for the terror and Punishment of evil doers, and for the protection, and Encouragement of all, that do well. . . ."[11]

When receiving the ring the Archbishop says:

Receive the Ring of Kingly Dignity, and the Seal of . . . the Catholic Faith: that as You are this day consecrated Head of his Kingdom and People; so being rich in Faith and abounding in good Works, You may reign with Him who is King of Kings. . . .

The ceremony ends with the homage of the clergy and the laity beginning with the Archbishop.

The preface for the Communion contains the exquisite words:

. . . God . . . who makest Kings to be the Nursing Fathers of thy Church, and Queens, her nursing Mothers, and both Defenders of thy Faith, and Protectors of thy Church. . . .

Ratcliff observes that about the eleventh or twelfth century,

by concurrent processes of elaboration, the two Services of the Kings's (Queen's) coronation and the bishop's consecration had acquired a distinct resemblance to each other, it is no matter for surprise that the ceremonies of coronation should be supposed to have been modelled upon those of the bishop's consecration, and that a congruous theory of the King's (Queen's) quasi-ecclesiastical status should be formulated by those who had a political interest in doing so.[13]

The royal vestments still correspond to a bishop's. After the anointing, the Queen dons the *colobium sindonis* (a muslin undergarment like an alb), the *supertunica* or *dalmatica* made of cloth of gold (like a dalmatic worn by a deacon), a rich girdle (cf. the cincture), the *armills* (a piece of silk worn stolewise round the neck and tied to the arms), the royal stole, and the royal robe (which is the imperial mantle corresponding to the bishop's ecclesiastical cope).

Thus ritual and ecclesiastical subordination of man to woman has been known and practiced continually down the age. There was a Jewish Queen, Salome Alexandra. It seems but a little step nowadays to ordain a woman to the priesthood or perhaps even more logically to the bishopric. At least it cannot be denied that in the historic churches a woman may have consecrated supreme headship over men and women. Thus to-day it might be possible to appoint female lay bishops or cardinals whose duties would be that of administration, not of serving through the sacraments. At least this would bring women into the decision-making policies of the Church.

Notes

1. See Joan Morris, *The Lady Was A Bishop* (New York: MacMillan, 1973).

2. John Knox, *The First Blast of the Trumpet against the Monstrous Regiment of Women* in *The English Scholar's Library of Old and Modern Works*, ed. Edward Arber (London, 1878), pp. i-xviii and 1-62.

3. Percy E. Schramm, *A History of the English Coronation* (Oxford: Clarendon Press, 1937), p. 29.

4. *Ibid.*, pp. 8-9.

5. *Ibid.*, pp. 125-26.

6. *Ibid.*, p. 121.

7. *Ibid.*, p. 25.

8. *Ibid.*, pp. 34-5.

9. *Ibid.*, p. 135.

10. *Ibid.*, pp. 34-5.

11. J. Wickham Legg, *Three Coronation Orders*, Henry Bradshaw Society, Vol. 19 (London, 1900), p. 23.

12. *Ibid.*, p. 25.

13. Edward C. Ratcliff, *The Coronation Service of Her Majesty Queen Elizabeth II* (London, 1953), p. 8.

45
Leadership: Secular Gift
Transformed by Revelation

Carroll Stuhlmueller

In Chapter Six the Declaration states: "Thus one must note *the extent* to which the Church is a society different from other societies, *original* in her nature and in her structure" (italics added). The crucial italicized words are difficult to exegete. Does the document mean to say that there are degrees or limitations to "the extent" of originality in Church structure? Or does it emphasize the farthest extent, beyond all other human institutions, reached by the Church in the originality of her nature and structure? The latter explanation is favored by the larger context of the Declaration and so our difficulties are magnified.

In the Bible the structures of religious leadership did not originate through direct revelation from God. They were not newly created *ex nihilo*. All major styles of governing Israel in the Old Testament or of ruling the Church in the New Testament preexisted Israel or the Church. Here we concentrate upon the Old Testament.

Biblical religion did not originate from scratch with an absolutely new creation of Abraham or Moses in a garden of paradise and with a charter of life entirely distinct in language and culture. Rather, in calling Abraham or Moses, David or Ezra, God found these religious leaders within their moment of history and therefore within their culture and total environment. Revelation did not so much consist in new external ways of forming marriage, neighborhood, employment, political order, liturgical style and relaxation, as it centered in a strong, continuing awareness of God as personal Savior (Ex 3). Through this perception of God, embodied in the divine name Yahweh ("He who is always there" as "merciful Savior"), Moses founded a new synthesis or Torah of laws, customs, traditions and folklore from the repertoire of the ancient Near East. In this covenant between Yahweh and his chosen people, institutional forms were purified and strengthened, yet they remained basically the same as with Israel's neighbors.

In fact, the *general* culture or structural life-style of the chosen people was identical with their Gentile neighbors. All spoke the same language, sang the same songs, dressed, worked and recreated in the same way, shared the same basic institutional or tribal values. There was the same emphasis upon community over individual, upon the present moment over the past or future, upon the intuitive element over the rational or speculative, upon family or tribal traditions over doctrinal or philosophical synthesis. Note that we are dealing here with emphases, not with contradictory opposites in describing the culture of Israel and the ancient Near East. Among the most important elements of culture are the system of government and the styles of leadership.

As to leadership in the Old Testament, Moses achieved a blend of such preexisting forms as: a) "heads of families," evident in the patriarchal sagas of Genesis and brought by Abraham from his Mesopotamian origins; b) "elders," received from the Midianite background of his wife and father-in-law (Ex 18:13), and cultic priesthood, shared with all peoples. The offices of judge and king which became prominent in the post-Mosaic period after the conquest can be documented outside of Israel long before their appearance in biblical tradition (Am 2:3; 1 Sam 8:5). Prophecy according to the "charismatic" model of Samuel, Elijah and Elisha, or according to the "classical" model of Amos, Hosea, Isaiah and the others with books to their name, parallels extra-biblical prophecy in Canaan and Mari. We note that the prophet Balaam from Pethor in Aram prominently appears in the Bible long before any biblical prophets.

The origin and evolution of priesthood is closer to our purpose. The secular tribe of Levi, once discredited because of violent injustice (Gen 34:25; 49:5-7), was granted religious privileges because of their loyalty to Moses—again in a form of violence—and because of their blood relationship with him (Ex 2:1; 32:25-29; Deut 33:8-11). The total reversal of Levi's fate from a curse in Gen 49:5-7 to a blessing in Deut 33:8-11 is not due to a special revelation but to an historical act of political importance. Members of tribes other than Levi, especially the royalty, could also function as priests (Judg 17:5; 2 Sam 8:18; Ps 110:4). According to Israel's tribal system non-Levites like Samuel of the tribe of Ephraim (1 Sam 1:1) were granted a place in the genealogy of Levi (1 Chron 6:18), and even Canaanites could be absorbed within Levi and act as priests (1 Sam 7:1; 2 Sam 6:11). These decisions resulted basically from political and religious needs and were not immediately dictated by God.

The history of Levi took a new turn when David conquered Jerusalem and established a double high priesthood, the levite *Abiathar* with ancestry back to Eli at Shiloh and eventually to the age of Moses (1 Sam 22:9-10; 23:6; 2 Sam 8:17), and *Zadok*, very probably a pagan Jebusite priest at Jerusalem who converted to Yahweh after David's capture of the city. The rise to exclusive power by the family of Zadok is due to such influential political figures as David, Solomon and Ezekiel (2 Sam 8:17; 1 Kgs 2:26-27, 35; Ez 44:10-31). The controversy between the *original levites*, who dated back to Abiathar, Eli and eventually to Moses, and the *new Levites* (now spelled with a capital "L") who began with Zadok, even divides the inspired Scriptures between two traditions, Deut 18:6-8 in favor of the former, Ez 40:46; 43:19; 44:10-31 in favor of the latter.

In origin and development, then, the Old Testament priesthood had its history not only within the politics of Israel but also within the political repercussions of the international scene. Its forms were not directly revealed by God to Moses or David but were derived from the culture of the time and were influenced continually by the secular history of Israel. Moses naturally chose as priests those tribesmen who rallied around him. As a master stroke of political compromise David names two high priests and also two general-in-chiefs. During the Babylonian exile representatives of the northern traditions of the former kingdom of Israel united around Second Isaiah and the law code of Deuteronomy, while representatives of the southern tradition of Jerusalem locked arms with Ezekiel who re-codified the Zadokite or Priestly Document. In origin and history the forms of Old Testament priesthood were not immediately due to divine revelation.

Israel, on the other hand, did not slavishly copy her forms of religious leadership from the Gentiles, nor did she allow her traditions to drift according to political currents and economic needs. She may have accepted from others the major lines of her political and religious institutions, but she began at once to purify them and so to elevate the liturgy and piety of the people and the life-style of the priests. This purifying force came immediately from God, especially in the sense of a personal, merciful and providential deity to whom Israel gave the sacred name of Yahweh. This intuition of God was furthered particularly by the classical prophets. In this faith-appreciation of God Israel was "original" and unique; here was the source of the transforming power within all of her civil and religious institutions.

In the Old Testament then the community of Israel was not "original in her nature and in her structure," but her institutions, taken over from non-Israelite neighbors, became uniquely different in their ability to reflect and sustain God's personal redemptive presence among his people.

46
Discrimination or Equality?
The Old Order or the New?
Margaret A. Farley

The Declaration returns in its closing section to the principle of equality which it affirmed in its opening paragraphs. Its concern here, however, is to make clear how it is that the principle of equality among persons is not violated in the Church by the continued exclusion of women from ordained ministry. The basic argument put forth in this regard is that the Church is of "another order" than other societies.[1] While role-differentiation on the basis of sex may constitute unjust discrimination in other spheres of human life, it does not do so in the Church precisely because of the nature of the Church as a special kind of society.

The Declaration gives three characteristics of the "order" of the Church which explain why the principle of equality is not violated even though women are excluded on the basis of their sex from certain roles. First, authority in the Church, unlike other societies, is never a matter of human choice, never a human right, never something "due" a person as a person. Even Baptism "does not confer any personal title to public ministry in the Church."[2] Priesthood is always a wholly gratuitous vocation, given by the Holy Spirit, authenticated by the Church. No persons, then, let alone women, have any claim on the roles or offices of ordained ministry.

Secondly, equality itself, according to the Declaration, does not mean identity or similarity when it is used to describe the relation among persons in the Church. While women and men are equal as persons before God, their roles and functions are not identical. "Equality is in no way identity, for the Church is a differentiated body, in which each individual has his or her role. The roles are distinct and must not be confused; they do not favor the superiority of some vis-à-vis the others, nor do they provide an excuse for jealousy. . . ."[3]

The reason why differentiation of roles is compatible with the principle of equality, according to the Declaration, is that women and men are essentially complementary. Given this premise, equality can in fact be realized only through differentiated functions based on sex. Men as men are suited for ordained ministry and women as women for nonordained ministry. Each, then, is equally affirmed by a separation of roles. The Declaration thus opts implicitly for "similar treatment for similar cases" as its formulation of the principle of equality, justifying the Church's differentiation in treatment of women and men on what it concludes are the differences between them by reason of their sex.

The third characteristic of Church "order" which the Declaration asserts as important for understanding the application of the principle of equality is the recognition of merit based only on love. "The only better gift, which can and must be desired, is love. The greatest in the Kingdom of Heaven are not the ministers but the saints."[4] Any seeming hierarchy among roles, it suggests, is irrelevant because love alone constitutes grounds for superiority, and no one is excluded from such a gift on the basis of sex.

In the Declaration's own terms, then, it is an interpretation of the "new order" of the Christian community which must be assessed if we are to determine the justice or injustice entailed by nonordination of women. Each of the characteristics of Church "order" described by the Declaration must be examined to see if any of them do indeed provide grounds for gender role-differentiation in the ministries of the Church.

1. There can be no argument with the Declaration's description of ordained ministry as a wholly gratuitous vocation, of which authentication by the Church is a constitutive part. No one disputes the fact that a specific call to the office of priesthood is given by the Holy Spirit and mediated through the Church, nor that the Church has the responsibility to discern the legitimacy of any individual's vocation to ministry according to norms which it must formulate and apply. In arguing only this, however, the Declaration misses the point of those who invoke the "right" of persons in relation to ministry. Those who assert such a right in relation to ordination do not argue simply that any person has a right to be ordained. Rather, they maintain that all persons by reason of being persons and being baptized have a right to have their experience of vocation to pastoral office *tested*. Women and men have a right to be judged for acceptance or nonacceptance by the same norms.

The Declaration's exclusion of women from the possibility of an authenticated vocation to ordained ministry must rest on the presupposition that since the law of the Church (based presumably on sound reasons) excludes women as a class from ordination, it is not necessary to test individual cases of women's possible vocation. This is to say that since a call to pastoral office is mediated through the Church in a way that gives no one an *a priori* claim to be admitted to pastoral office, the existence of overriding reasons and Church law excluding women renders it impossible *a priori* that any woman receive an authentic call from the Holy Spirit to such ministry. But to say this is to beg the question of the validity of the reasons and the justice of the laws which exclude women as women from ordination. Only if the reasons can be validated and the laws justified can it be maintained that women as a class have no right to have their experience of a call to ordained ministry tested by the Church community.

2. Other articles in this volume consider various reasons offered by the Declaration as justification of the continued exclusion of women from ordination. The argument which must be addressed in particular here, however,

is the argument by which the Declaration tries explicitly to maintain the principle of equality in the face of the unequal opportunity of women to have their vocations tested. As we have seen, the Declaration attempts to do this by introducing the principle of "complementarity." What we must determine, then, is whether or not complementarity can qualify the meaning of equality in such a way that equality is nonetheless preserved.

First it must be said that the mere assertion of "difference" between women and men cannot justify differential treatment—certainly not in a way that guarantees equality in any ordinary sense of the term. The Declaration itself, for all of its insistence that priesthood does not imply "any personal superiority . . . in the order of values, but only . . . a difference of fact on the level of functions and service,"[5] nonetheless goes on to talk about the "real and pre-eminent place of the priest in the community of the baptized."[6] Even if there are good reasons for opening the office of priesthood to one class of persons and not another on the basis of sex, it is difficult to see how this fulfills the principle of equality in any way beyond a Platonic and Aristotelian notion of "equitable inequalities,"—equal opportunity for equals (men), and proportionately unequal opportunities for unequals (women in relation to men).[7] The Declaration's "similar treatment for similar cases" yields the very weakest form of a principle of equality.

It cannot be assumed, moreover, that there are in fact good reasons for restricting roles in the Church to persons of one sex. If there are not good reasons, then such a restriction constitutes discrimination—an unjust violation of the principle of equality. But how can it be determined whether sexual differentiation of roles does indeed constitute discrimination? As in any issue like this one, we must ask whether the facts of sexual identity are morally relevant when they are brought to bear against claims to equality of treatment. One way to evaluate the moral relevance of sexual differences in relation to equality of opportunity vis-à-vis ordination in the Church is to examine those characteristics which are said to be sex-related and then to determine whether they do indeed justify significant role distinctions.

Though the Declaration affirms that "in human beings the difference of sex exercises an important influence, much deeper than, for example, ethnic differences,"[8] it does not delineate the sex-related characteristics which are relevant to ministry. It builds implicitly, however, on the detailed descriptions provided by other recent Vatican statements such as Paul VI's "Women/Disciples and Co-workers" and the Pastoral Commission of the Sacred Congregation for the Evangelization of Peoples' "The Role of Women in Evangelization."[9] Characteristics such as hopefulness, sensitivity, intuition, fidelity, patience, sympathy, contemplativeness are said to make women suitable for all ministries which are not properly sacerdotal.[10] At first glance, it is difficult to see how this assertion is not discriminatory. The roles open to women on the basis of their "feminine qualities" are limited to the private sphere, and are clearly subordinate to those open to men. Claims to the contrary (that, for example, the roles are not inferior, are of equal importance though different, etc.), as we have seen, have little credibility in a context where, for example, decision-making at all levels is reserved to those in pastoral office.

It must, nevertheless, still be asked whether the characteristics identified as distinctive to women are in fact morally relevant to the circumscription of roles. One way to probe this question is to ask whether a man who has a hopeful, sensitive, contemplative, sympathetic, patient nature should be excluded from ordination. The almost obvious answer to this question points to the conclusion that these characteristics are unsuitable for the ordained ministry only when they appear in women.

In addition, the fundamental question of whether or not distinctive characteristics can in fact be delineated at all for men and women must be raised. Evidence from the behavioral and social sciences, as well as from persons' experience, points overwhelmingly in the direction of our inability to characterize masculine and feminine traits with any accuracy or adequacy.[11] Traditional efforts to do so have proved distortive to our understanding of persons and injurious to human relations. They inevitably end in lists of traits such as those given in the document on Evangelization.[12] Their deficiencies become apparent as soon as they are made exclusively applicable to one sex. Even as general sketches of dominant sex-related features they prove vague, subject to exceptions sufficient to disprove the rule, and importantly culture-conditioned. Short of such listings, there can only be an appeal to biological differences between men and women. The irrelevance of such differences to role-differentiation leads to the sure conclusion that there are no morally significant reasons for excluding persons from major roles in Church ministry on the basis of sex.

3. Finally, we must assess the significance of the Declaration's proposal that it is only the gift of love which determines the superiority or inferiority of persons in relation to one another (and equality in every other respect either is unimportant or can be maintained despite apparent differences in roles). Once again, few would dispute the argument that love, as gift and response, is what ultimately gives meaning and worth to human persons and their lives. To say this, however, neither resolves nor neutralizes the problems raised by the violation of the principle of equality regarding access to ordained ministry. There are, in fact, at least two ways in which the primacy of love gives urgency to the need for structures in the Church which reflect and realize the principle of equality among human persons.

First, the Declaration uses the concept of the gift of love to suggest that anyone seeking access to pastoral office on the grounds of equality of persons can only be motivated by a desire for "social advancement." It admits that "women who express a desire for the ministerial priesthood are doubtless motivated by the desire to serve Christ and the Church," but reminds them that such a desire has no connection with principles of equality.[13]

What the Declaration misses, however, is the relevance of an ethical principle which might be formulated thus: whenever a person has a fundamental duty, he or she has a right to whatever is necessary in order to fulfill that duty. The point is not, of course, that a fundamental duty can never be qualified by lack of capability, etc. It is, rather, that precisely because of a call to service and love, women may argue that they must not be barred from what would allow them to respond faithfully. What demands the elimination of sexual discrimination is not women's own desire or even claim to honor or authority or participation in decision-making, but the claim of those who have a right to be served in and by the Church, those whose needs constitute for women as well as men an urgent call to the duty of ordained ministry, to a love which pours itself out in the "service of God and the Church."[14]

More than this, the Declaration fails to take seriously the relation between justice and love which is deeply embedded in the tradition of the Church. What is required of all Christian persons and of the Church is a just love, a love which corresponds to the reality of those loved and which affirms for individuals and for the community what is needed in order to grow into the fullness of the life of faith. Now it is here that the Declaration's overall interpretation of the "new order" in the Church must be examined. If the Declaration is mistaken in its understanding of this "order," then any affirmation in love of the individuals within that order and of the order as a whole will entail distortions or at least inadequacies in the lives of persons and the community.

On the one hand, the Declaration perpetuates false notions regarding the reality of women. It accepts uncritically a description of the nature of woman which relegates her on the basis of "feminine qualities" to the private sphere (at least in the life of the Church) and to subordinate roles. On this understanding of woman, patterns for relations between persons continue to mirror what must be called not the "new order" of grace but the "old order" of sin.

On the other hand, then, the order in the Church that is presented by the Declaration is an order in which, despite disclaimers, essential human equality remains hidden and distorted by sin. The Declaration argues that New Testament announcements of the equality of all persons in Jesus Christ refer only to the universal call of persons to "divine filiation, which is the same for all,"[15] and not to "specific and totally gratuitous" calls to ministry in the Church. Yet the call to a shared life in Jesus Christ is surely also wholly gratuitous, and it is by God's choice that it is offered to all, without discrimination on the basis even of sex. The reversion, then, within the community of believers to an "old order" marked by domination and exclusion, by male headship and female subordination, can only be just in a sense that takes no account of the new order of grace. Men and women are still given their "due" by affirming them in hierarchically ordered relations based on sexual identity. Here there is no recognition of what is due the children of God, chosen and graced, restored to equality in Christ Jesus. The Declaration builds on an inadequate doctrine of creation an inadequate doctrine of redemption, and it can point, thereby, only to an inadequate doctrine of love.

The Declaration's efforts to hold together the principle of equality and sexual role-differentiation in Church ministries finally fails. We are left with clear inequality of opportunity, an inequality that is not justified by morally relevant factors. This is to say that we are left with sexual discrimination, the violation of rights, and an overall unjust order in the Church (with the further consequence that the prophetic voice of the Church is silenced in relation to society). New perceptions of the nature of women, of the needs of human persons, and of the reciprocal character of interpersonal and social relations are missing. We have here no recognition of the growing moral imperative regarding fundamental values of equality and mutuality. We have here so very little understanding of the "new order" which the Declaration wants to embrace. The Declaration, then, must be critiqued and corrected, in the name of justice and love.

Notes

1. Declaration, pars. 35 and 38.
2. Declaration, par. 36.
3. Declaration, par. 39.
4. *Ibid.*
5. Declaration, par. 30.
6. Declaration, par. 33.
7. See, for example, Plato, *Gorgias* 508a; *Republic* 558c; *Laws* 744 and 757a; Aristotle, *Nichomachean Ethics* 1131a. For a general discussion of various formulations of the principle of equality, see Gregory Vlastos, "Justice and Equality," in Richard B. Brandt, ed., *Social Justice* (Englewood Cliffs, N.J.: Prentice-Hall, Inc., 1962), pp. 31-72.
8. Declaration, par. 31.
9. Paul VI, "Women/Disciples and Co-workers," *Origins*, Vol. IV (May 1, 1975), pp. 718-719; Pastoral Commission of the Sacred Congregation for the Evangelization of Peoples, "The Role of Women in Evangelization," *Origins*, Vol. V (April 22, 1976), pp. 702-707.
10. "The Role of Women in Evangelization," p. 703.
11. See, for example, Margaret Mead, *Male and Female* (New York: William Morrow, 1949), pp. 345-360.
12. See above, note 10.
13. Declaration, par. 38.
14. Declaration, par. 36.
15. *Ibid.*

Appendices

APPENDIX I

Commentary on the Declaration of the Sacred Congregation for the Doctrine of the Faith on the Question of Admission of Women to the Ministerial Priesthood

(This commentary appeared simultaneously with the Vatican Declaration from the office of the Congregation for the Doctrine of the Faith. It was mimeographed and unsigned.)

Circumstances and Origin of the Declaration

1. The question of the admission of women to the ministerial priesthood seems to have arisen in a general way about 1958, after the decision by the Swedish Lutheran Church in September of that year to admit women to the pastoral office. This caused a sensation and occasioned numerous commentaries [1]. Even for the communities stemming from the sixteenth-century Reformation it was an innovation: one may recall, for example, how strongly the *Confessio Fidei Scotiae* of 1560 accused the Roman Church of making improper concessions to women in the field of ministry [2]. But the Swedish initiative gradually gained ground among the Reformed Churches, particularly in France, where various National Synods adopted similar decisions.

2. In reality, the admission of women to the pastoral office seemed to raise no strictly theological problem, in that these communities had rejected the sacrament of Order at the time of their separation from the Roman Church. But a new and much more serious situation was created when ordinations of women were carried out within communities that considered that they preserved the apostolic succession of Order [3]: in 1971 and 1973 the Anglican Bishop of Hong Kong ordained three women with the agreement of his Synod [4]; in July 1974 at Philadelphia there was the ordination in the Episcopal Church of eleven women—an ordination afterwards declared invalid by the House of Bishops. Later on, in June 1975, the General Synod of the Anglican Church in Canada, meeting in Quebec, approved the principle of the accession of women to the priesthood; and this was followed in July by the General Synod of the Church of England: Dr Coggan, Archbishop of Canterbury, frankly informed Pope Paul VI "of the slow but steady growth of a consensus of opinion within the Anglican Communion that there are no fundamental objections in principle to the ordination of women to the priest-

hood"[5]. These are only general principles, but they might quickly be followed by practice, and this would bring a new and serious element into the dialogue with the Roman Catholic Church on the nature of the ministry[6]. It has provoked a warning, first by the Archbishop for the Orthodox in Great Britain, Athenagoras of Thyateira.[7], and then, more recently, by Pope Paul VI himself in two letters to the Archbishop of Canterbury[8]. Furthermore, the ecumenical sectors brought the question to the notice of all the Christian denominations, forcing them to examine their positions of principle, especially on the occasion of the Assembly of the World Council of Churches at Nairobi in December 1975[9].

3. A completely different event has made the question even more topical; this was the organization under United Nations' auspices of International Women's Year in 1975. The Holy See took part in it with a Committee for International Women's Year, which included some members of the Commission for the Study of the Role of Women in Society and the Church, which had already been set up in 1973. Ensuring respect for and fostering the respective rights and duties of men and women leads to reflection on participation by women in the life of society on the one hand, and in the life and mission of the Church on the other. Now, the Second Vatican Council had already set forth the task: "Since in our times women have an ever more active share in the whole life of society, it is very important that they participate more widely also in the various fields of the Church's apostolate"[10]. How far can this participation go?

4. It is understandable that these questions have aroused even in Catholic quarters intense studies, indeed passionate ones: doctoral theses, articles in reviews, even pamphlets, propounding or refuting in turn the biblical, historical and canonical data and appealing to the human sciences of sociology[11], psychology and the history of institutions and customs. Certain famous people have not hesitated to take sides boldly, judging that there was "no basic theological objection to the possibility of women priests"[12]. A number of groups have been formed with a view to upholding this claim, and they have sometimes done this with insistence, as did the conference held in Detroit (U.S.A.) in November 1975 under the title "Women in Future: Priesthood Now, a Call for Action".

5. The Magisterium has thus been obliged to intervene in a question being posed in so lively a fashion within the Catholic Church and having important implications from the ecumenical point of view. Archbishop Bernardin of Cincinnati, President of the United States National Conference of Catholic Bishops, declared on 7 October 1975 that he found himself "obliged to restate the Church's teaching that women are not to be ordained to the priesthood"; Church leaders, he said, should "not seem to encourage unreasonable hopes and expectations, even by their silence"[13]. Pope Paul VI himself had already recalled the same teaching. He did so at first in parenthetical fashion, especially in his address on 18 April 1975 to the members of the Study Commission on the Role of Women in Society and in the Church and the Committee for the Celebration of International Women's Year: "Al-

though women do not receive the call to the apostolate of the Twelve and therefore to the ordained ministries, they are nonetheless invited to follow Christ as disciples and co-workers . . . We cannot change what our Lord did, nor his call to women"[14]. Later he had to make an express pronouncement in his exchange of letters with Dr Coggan, Archbishop of Canterbury: "Your Grace is of course well aware of the Catholic Church's position on this question. She holds that it is not admissible to ordain women to the priesthood, for very fundamental reasons"[15]. It is at his order that the Sacred Congregation for the Doctrine of the Faith has examined the question in its entirety. The question has been complicated by the fact that on the one hand arguments adduced in the past in favour of the traditional teaching are scarcely defensible today, and on the other hand the reasons given by those who demand the ordination of women must be evaluated.

6. To avoid the rather negative character that must mark the conclusions of such a study, one could have thought of inserting it into a more general presentation of the question of the advancement of women. But the time is not ripe for such a comprehensive exposition, because of the research and work in progress on all sides. It was difficult to leave unanswered any longer a precise question that is being posed nearly everywhere and which is polarizing attention to the detriment of more urgent endeavours that should be fostered. In fact, apart from its non-acceptance of the ordination of women, the document points to positive matters: a deeper understanding of the Church's teaching and of the ministerial priesthood, a call to spiritual progress, an invitation to take on the urgent apostolic tasks of today. The bishops, to whom the document is primarily addressed, have the mission of explaining it to their people with the pastoral feeling that is theirs and with the knowledge they have of the milieu in which they exercise their ministry.

7. The Declaration begins by presenting the Church's teaching on the question. This in fact has to be the point of departure. We shall see later how necessary it is to follow faithfully the method of using *loci theologici*.

Tradition

8. It is an undeniable fact, as the Declaration notes, that the constant tradition of the Catholic Church has excluded women from the episcopate and the priesthood. So constant has it been that there has been no need for an intervention by a solemn decision of the Magisterium.

9. "The same tradition", the document stresses, "has been faithfully safeguarded by the Churches of the East. Their unanimity on this point is all the more remarkable since in many other questions their discipline admits of a great diversity. At the present time these same Churches refuse to associate themselves with requests directed towards securing the accession of women to priestly ordination"[16].

10. Only within some heretical sects of the early centuries, principally Gnostic ones, do we find attempts to have the priestly ministry exercised by women. It must be further noted that these are very sporadic occurrences and are moreover associated with rather questionable practices. We know of

them only through the severe disapproval with which they are noted by Saint Irenaeus in his *Adversus Haereses*[17], Tertullian in *De Praescriptione Haereticorum*[18], Firmilian of Caesarea in a letter to Saint Cyprian[19], Origen in a commentary on the First Letter to the Corinthians[20], and especially by Saint Ephiphanius in his *Panarion*[21].

11. How are we to interpret the constant and universal practice of the Church? A theologian is certain that what the Church does she can in fact do, since she has the assistance of the Holy Spirit. This is a classical argument found again and again in Saint Thomas with regard to the sacraments[22]. But what the Church has never done—is this any proof that she cannot do it in the future? Does the negative fact thus noted indicate a norm, or is it to be explained by historical and by social and cultural circumstances? In the present case, is an explanation to be found in the position of women in ancient and mediaeval society and in a certain idea of male superiority stemming from that society's culture?

12. It is because of this transitory cultural element that some arguments adduced on this subject in the past are scarcely defensible today. The most famous is the one summarized by Saint Thomas Aquinas: *quia mulier est in statu subiectionis*[23]. In Saint Thomas's thought, however, this assertion is not merely the expression of a philosophical concept, since he interprets it in the light of the accounts in the first chapters of Genesis and the teaching of the First Letter to Timothy (2:12-14). A similar formula is found earlier in the *Decretum* of Gratian[24], but Gratian, who was quoting the Carolingian Capitularies and the false Decretals, was trying rather to justify with Old Testament prescriptions the prohibition—already formulated by the ancient Church[25]—of women from entering the sanctuary and serving at the altar.

13. The polemical arguments of recent years have often recalled and commented on the texts that develop these arguments. They have also used them to accuse the Fathers of the Church of misogyny. It is true that we find in the Fathers' writings the undeniable influence of prejudices against women. But it must be carefully noted that these passages had very little influence on their pastoral activity, still less on their spiritual direction, as we can see by glancing through their correspondence that has come down to us. Above all it would be a serious mistake to think that such considerations provide the only or the most decisive reasons against the ordination of women in the thought of the Fathers, of the medieval writers and of the theologians of the classical period. In the midst of and going beyond speculation, more and more clear expression was being given to the Church's awareness that in reserving priestly ordination and ministry to men she was obeying a tradition received from Christ and the Apostles and by which she felt herself bound.

14. This is what had been expressed in the form of an apocryphal literature by the ancient documents of Church discipline from Syria, such as the *Didascalia Apostolorum* (middle of the third century)[26] and the Apostolic Constitutions (end of the fourth or beginning of the fifth century)[27], and by the Egyptian collection of twenty pseudo-apostolic canons that was included in the compilation of the Alexandrian *Synodos* and translated into many lan-

guages[28]. Saint John Chrysostom, for his part, when commenting on chapter twenty-one of John, understood well that women's exclusion from the pastoral office entrusted to Peter was not based on any natural incapacity, since, as he remarks, "even the majority of men have been excluded by Jesus from this immense task"[29].

15. From the moment that the teaching on the sacraments is systematically presented in the schools of theology and canon law, writers begin to deal *ex professo* with the nature and value of the tradition that reserved ordination to men. The canonists base their case on the principle formulated by Pope Innocent III in a letter of 11 December 1210 to the Bishops of Palencia and Burgos, a letter that was included in the collection of Decretals: "Although the Blessed Virgin Mary was of higher dignity and excellence than all the Apostles, it was to them, not her, that the Lord entrusted the keys of the Kingdom of Heaven"[30]. This text became a *locus communis* for the *glóssatores*[31].

16. As for the theologians, the following are some significant texts: Saint Bonaventure: "Our position is this: it is due not so much to a decision by the Church as to the fact that the sacrament of Order is not for them. In this sacrament the person ordained is a sign of Christ the mediator"[32]. Richard of Middleton, a Franciscan of the second half of the thirteenth century: "The reason is that the power of the sacraments comes from their institution. But Christ instituted this sacrament for conferral on men only, not women"[33]. John Duns Scotus: "It must not be considered to have been determined by the Church. It comes from Christ. The Church would not have presumed to deprive the female sex, for no fault of its own, of an act that might licitly have pertained to it"[34]. Durandus of Saint-Pourcain: ". . . the male sex is of necessity for the sacrament. The principal cause of this is Christ's institution . . . Christ ordained only men . . . not even his Mother . . . It must therefore be held that women cannot be ordained, because of Christ's institution"[35].

17. So it is no surprise that until the modern period the theologians and canonists who dealt with the question have been almost unanimous in considering this exclusion as absolute and having a divine origin. The theological notes they apply to the affirmation vary from "theologically certain" (*theologice certa*) to, at times, "proximate to faith" (*fidei proxima*) or even "doctrine of the faith" (*doctrina fidei*)[36]. Apparently, then, until recent decades no theologian or canonist considered that it was a matter of a simple law of the Church.

18. In some writers of the Middle Ages however there was a certain hesitancy, reported by Saint Bonaventure without adopting it himself[37] and noted also by Johannes Teutonicus in his gloss on *Caus.* 27, q. 1, c.23[38]. This hesitancy stemmed from the knowledge that in the past there had been deaconesses: had they received true sacramental ordination? This problem has been brought up again very recently. It was by no means unknown to the seventeenth- and eighteenth-century theologians, who had an excellent knowledge of the history of literature. In any case, it is a question that must be

taken up fully by direct study of the texts, without preconceived ideas; hence the Sacred Congregation for the Doctrine of the Faith has judged that it should be kept for the future and not touched upon in the present document.

The Attitude of Christ

19. In the light of tradition, then, it seems that the essential reason moving the Church to call only men to the sacrament of order and to the strictly priestly ministry is her intention to remain faithful to the type of ordained ministry willed by the Lord Jesus Christ and carefully maintained by the Apostles. It is therefore no surprise that in the controversy there has been a careful examination of the facts and texts of the New Testament, in which tradition has seen an example establishing a norm. This brings us to a fundamental observation: we must not expect the New Testament *on its own* to resolve in a clear fashion the question of the possibility of women acceding to the priesthood, in the same way that it does not on its own enable us to give an account of certain sacraments, and especially of the structure of the sacrament of Order. Keeping to the sacred text alone and to the points of the history of Christian origins that can be obtained by analyzing that text by itself would be to go back four centuries and find oneself once more amid the controversies of the Reformation. We cannot omit the study of tradition: it is the Church that scrutinizes the Lord's thought by reading Scripture, and it is the Church that gives witness to the correctness of its interpretation.

20. It is tradition that has unceasingly set forth as an expression of Christ's will the fact that he chose only men to form the group of the Twelve. There is no disputing this fact, but can it be proved with absolute certainty that it was a question of a deliberate decision by Christ? It is understandable that partisans of a change in discipline bring all their efforts to bear against the significance of this fact. In particular, they object that, if Christ did not bring women into the group of the Twelve, it was because the prejudices of his time did not allow him to: it would have been an imprudence that would have compromised his work irreparably. However, it has to be recognized that Jesus did not shrink from other "imprudences", which did in fact stir up the hostility of his fellow citizens against him, especially his freedom with regard to the rabbinical interpretations of the Sabbath. With regard to women his attitude was a complete innovation: all the commentators recognize that he went against many prejudices, and the facts that are noted add up to an impressive total.

21. For this reason greater stress is laid today on another objection: if Jesus chose only men to form the group of the Twelve, it was because he intended them to be a symbol representing the ancestors of the twelve tribes of Israel ("You who have followed me will also sit on twelve thrones and judge the twelve tribes of Israel": Mt 19:28; cf. Lk 22:30); and this special motive, it is added, obviously referred only to the Twelve and would be no proof that the apostolic ministry should thereafter always be reserved to men. It is not a convincing argument. We may note in the first place how little importance was given to this symbolism: Mark and John do not mention it. And in Mat-

thew and Luke this phrase of Jesus about the twelve tribes of Israel is not put in the context of the call of the Twelve (Mt 10:1-4) but at a relatively late stage of Jesus' public life, when the Apostles have long since been given their "constitution": they have been called by Jesus, have worked with him and been sent on missions. Furthermore, the symbolism of Mt 19:28 and Lk 22:30 is not as certain as is claimed: the number twelve could designate simply the whole of Israel. Finally, these two texts deal only with a particular aspect of the mission of the Twelve: Jesus is promising them that they will take part in the eschatological judgment[39]. Therefore the essential meaning of their being chosen is not to be sought in this symbolism but in the totality of the mission given them by Jesus: "he appointed twelve; they were to be his companions and to be sent out to preach" (Mk 3:14). As Jesus before them, the Twelve were above all to preach the Good News (Mk 3:14; 6:12). Their mission in Galilee (Mk 6:7-13) was to become the model of the universal mission (Mk 12:10; cf. Mt 28:16-20). Within the messianic people the Twelve represent Jesus. That is the real reason why it is fitting that the Apostles should be men: they act in the name of Christ and must continue his work.

22. It has been described above how Pope Innocent III saw a witness to Christ's intentions in the fact that Christ did not communicate to his Mother, in spite of her eminent dignity, the powers which he gave to the Apostles. This is one of the arguments most frequently repeated by tradition: from as early as the third century the Fathers present Mary as the example of the will of Jesus in this matter[40]. It is an argument still particularly dear to Eastern Christians today. Nevertheless it is vigorously rejected by all those who plead in favour of the ordination of women. Mary's divine motherhood, the manner in which she was associated with the redeeming work of her Son, they say, put her in an altogether exceptional and unique position; and it would not even be fair to her to compare her with the Apostles and to argue from the fact that she was not ranked among them. In point of fact these assertions do have the advantage of making us understand that there are different functions within the Church: the equality of Christians is in harmony with the complementary nature of their tasks, and the sacramental ministry is not the only rank of greatness, nor is it necessarily the highest: it is a form of service of the Kingdom. The Virgin Mary does not need the increase in "dignity" that was once attributed to her by the authors of those speculations on the priesthood of Mary that formed a deviant tendency which was soon discredited.

The Practice of the Apostles

23. The text of the Declaration stresses the fact that, in spite of the privileged place Mary had in the Upper Room after the Ascension, she was not designated for entry into the College of the Twelve at the time of the election of Matthias. The same holds for Mary Magdalen and the other women who nevertheless had been the first to bring news of the Resurrection. It is true that the Jewish mentality did not accord great value to the witness of women, as is shown by Jewish law. But one must also note that the acts of the Apostles and the Letters of Saint Paul stress the role of women in evan-

gelization and in instructing individual converts. The Apostles were led to take a revolutionary decision when they had to go beyond the circle of a Jewish community and undertake the evangelization of the Gentiles. The break with Mosaic observances was not made without discord. Paul had no scruples about choosing one of his collaborators, Titus, from among the Gentile converts (Gal 2:3). The most spectacular expression of the change which the Good News made on the mentality of the first Christians is to be found precisely in the Letter of the Galatians: "For as many of you as were baptized into Christ have put on Christ. There is neither Jew nor Greek, there is neither slave nor free, there is neither male nor female; for you are all one in Christ Jesus" (Gal 3:27-28). In spite of this, the Apostles did not entrust to women the strictly apostolic ministry, although Hellenistic civilization did not have the same prejudices against them as did Judaism. It is rather a ministry which is of another order, as may perhaps also be gathered from Paul's vocabulary, in which a difference seems to be implied between "my fellow workers" (*synergoi mou*) and "God's fellow workers" (*Theou synergoi*)[41].

24. It must be repeated that the texts of the New Testament, even on such important points as the sacraments, do not always give all the light that one would wish to find in them. Unless the value of unwritten traditions is admitted, it is sometimes difficult to discover in Scripture entirely explicit indications of Christ's will. But in view of the attitude of Jesus and the practice of the Apostles as seen in the Gospels, the Acts and the Letters, the Church has not held that she is authorized to admit women to priestly ordination.

Permanent Value of This Practice

25. It is the permanency of this negative decision that is objected to by those who would have the legitimacy of ordaining women admitted. These objections employ arguments of great variety.

26. The most classic ones seek a basis in historical circumstances. We have already seen what is to be thought of the view that Jesus's attitude was inspired solely by prudence, because he did not want to risk compromising his work by going against social prejudices. It is claimed that the same prudence was forced upon the Apostles. On this point too it is clear from the history of the apostolic period that there is no foundation for this explanation. However, in the case of the Apostles, should one not take into account the way in which they themselves shared these prejudices? Thus Saint Paul has been accused of misogyny and in his Letters are found texts on the inferiority of women that are the subject of controversy among exegetes and theologians today.

27. It can be questioned whether two of Paul's most famous texts on women are authentic or should rather be seen as interpolations, perhaps even relatively late ones. The first is 1 Cor 14:34-35: "The women should keep silence in the churches. For they are not permitted to speak, but should be subordinate as even the Law says". These two verses, apart from being missing in some important manuscripts and not being found quoted before the

end of the second century, present stylistic peculiarities foreign to Paul. The other text is 1 Tim 2:11-14: "I do not allow a women to teach or to exercise authority over men". The Pauline authenticity of this text is often questioned, although the arguments are weaker.

28. However, it is of little importance whether these texts are authentic or not: theologians have made abundant use of them to explain that women cannot receive either the power of magisterium or that of jurisdiction. It was especially the text of 1 Timothy that provided Saint Thomas with the proof that woman is in a state of submission or service, since (as the text explains) woman was created after man and was the person first responsible for original sin. But there are other Pauline texts of unquestioned authenticity that affirm that "the head of the woman is the man" (1 Cor 11:3; cf. 8-12; Eph 5:22, 24). It may be asked whether this view of man, which is in line with that of the books of the Old Testament, is not at the basis of Paul's conviction and the Church's tradition that women cannot receive the ministry. Now this is a view that modern society rejects absolutely, and many present-day theologians would shrink from adopting it without qualifying it. We may note however that Paul does not take his stand on a philosophical level but on that of biblical history: when he describes, in relation to marriage, the symbolism of love, he does not see man's superiority as domination but as a gift demanding sacrifice, in the image of Christ.

29. On the other hand there are prescriptions in Paul's writings which are unanimously admitted to have been transitory, such as the obligation he imposed on women to wear a veil (1 Cor 11:2-16). It is true that these are obviously disciplinary practices of minor importance, perhaps inspired by the customs of the time. But then there arises the more basic question: since the Church has later been able to abandon prescriptions contained in the New Testament, why should it not be the same with the exclusion of women from ordination? Here we meet once again the essential principle that it is the Church herself that, in the different sectors of her life, ensures discernment between what can change and what must remain immutable. As the Declaration specifies, "When she judges that she cannot accept certain changes, it is because she knows that she is bound by Christ's manner of acting. Her attitude, despite appearances, is therefore not one of archaism but of fidelity: it can be truly understood only in this light. The Church makes pronouncements in virtue of the Lord's promise and the presence of the Holy Spirit, in order to proclaim better the mystery of Christ and to safeguard and manifest the whole of its rich content."

30. Many of the questions confronting the Church as a result of the numerous arguments put forward in favour of the ordination of women must be considered in the light of this principle. An example is the following question dealt with by the Declaration: why will the Church not change her discipline, since she is aware of having a certain power over the sacraments, even though they were instituted by Christ, in order to determine the sign or to fix the conditions for their administration? This faculty remains limited, as was recalled by Pius XII, echoing the Council of Trent: the Church has no

power over the substance of the sacraments[42]. It is the Church herself that must distinguish what forms part of the "substance of the sacraments" and what she can determine or modify if circumstances should so suggest.

31. On this point, furthermore, we must remember, as the Declaration reminds us, that the sacraments and the Church herself are closely tied to history, since Christianity is the result of an event: the coming of the Son of God into time and to a country, and his death on the Cross under Pontius Pilate outside the walls of Jerusalem. The sacraments are a memorial of saving events. For this reason their signs are linked to those very events. They are relative to one civilization, one culture, although destined to be reproduced everywhere until the end of time. Hence historical choices have taken place by which the Church is bound, even if speaking absolutely and on a speculative level other choices could be imagined. This, for instance, is the case with bread and wine as matter for the Eucharist, for the Mass is not just a fraternal meal but the renewal of the Lord's Supper and the memorial of his Passion and thus linked with something done in history[43].

32. It has likewise been remarked that in the course of time the Church has agreed to confer on women certain truly ministerial functions that antiquity refused to give them in the very name of the example and will of Christ. The functions spoken of are above all the administration of baptism, teaching and certain forms of ecclesiastical jurisdiction.

33. As regards baptism, however, not even deaconesses in the Syriac-speaking East were permitted to administer it, and its solemn administration is still a hierarchical act reserved to bishop, priest and, in accessory fashion, deacon. When urgently required, baptism can be conferred not only by Christians but even by unbaptized people whether men or women. Its validity therefore does not require the baptismal character, still less that of ordination. This point is affirmed by practice and by theologians. It is an example of this necessary discernment in the Church's teaching and practice, a discernment whose only guarantee is the Church herself.

34. As regards teaching, a classical distinction has to be made, from Paul's Letters onwards. There are forms of teaching or edification that lay people can carry out and in this case Saint Paul expressly mentions women. These forms include the charisms of "prophecy" (1 Cor 11:15). In this sense there was no obstacle to giving the title of Doctor to Teresa of Avila and Catherine of Siena, as it was given to illustrious teachers such as Albert the Great or Saint Laurence of Brindisi. Quite a different matter is the official and hierarchical function of teaching the revealed message, a function that presupposes the mission received from Christ by the Apostles and transmitted by them to their successors.

35. Examples of participation by women in ecclesiastical jurisdiction are found in the Middle Ages: some abbesses (not abbesses in general, as is sometimes said in popularizing articles) performed acts normally reserved to bishops, such as the nomination of parish priests or confessors. These customs have been more or less reproved by the Holy See at different periods: the letter of Pope Innocent III quoted earlier was intended as a reprimand to the

Abbess of Las Helgas. But we must not forget that feudal lords arrogated to themselves similar rights. Canonists also admitted the possibility of separating jurisdiction from Order. The Second Vatican Council has tried to determine better the relationship between the two; the Council's doctrinal vision will doubtless have effects on discipline.

36. In a more general way, attempts are being made, especially in Anglican circles, to broaden the debate in the following way: is the Church perhaps bound to Scripture and tradition as an absolute, when the Church is a people making its pilgrim way and should listen to what the Spirit is saying? Or else a distinction is made between essential points on which unanimity is needed and questions of discipline admitting of diversity: and if the conclusion reached is that the ordination of women belongs to these secondary matters, it would not harm progress towards the union of the Churches. Here again it is the Church that decides by her practice and Magisterium what requires unanimity, and distinguishes it from acceptable or desirable pluralism. The question of the ordination of women impinges too directly on the nature of the ministerial priesthood for one to agree that it should be resolved within the framework of legitimate pluralism between Churches. That is the whole meaning of the letter of Pope Paul VI to the Archbishop of Canterbury.

The Ministerial Priesthood in the Light of the Mystery of Christ

37. In the Declaration a very clear distinction will be seen between the document's affirmation of the datum (the teaching it proposes with authority in the preceding paragraphs) and the theological reflection that then follows. By this reflection the Sacred Congregation for the Doctrine of the Faith endeavours "to illustrate this norm by showing the profound fittingness" to be found "between the proper nature of the sacrament of Order, with its specific reference to the mystery of Christ, and the fact that only men have been called to receive priestly ordination". In itself such a quest is not without risk. However, it does not involve the Magisterium. It is well known that in solemn teaching infallibility affects the doctrinal affirmation, not the arguments intended to explain it. Thus the doctrinal chapters of the Council of Trent contain certain processes of reasoning that today no longer seem to hold. But this risk has never stopped the Magisterium from endeavouring at all times to clarify doctrine by analogies of faith. Today especially, and more than ever, it is impossible to be content with making statements, with appealing to the intellectual docility of Christians: faith seeks understanding, and tries to distinguish the grounds for and the coherence of what is taught.

38. We have already discarded a fair number of explanations given by mediaeval theologians. The defect common to these explanations is that they claimed to find their basis in an inferiority of women vis-à-vis men; they deduced from the teaching of Scripture that woman was "in a state of submission", of subjection, and was incapable of exercising functions of government.

39. It is very enlightening to note that the communities springing from the Reformation which have had no difficulty in giving women access to the pastoral office are first and foremost those that have rejected the Catholic doctrine on the sacrament of Order and profess that the pastor is only one baptized person among others, even if the charge given has been the object of a consecration. The Declaration therefore suggests that it is by analyzing the nature of Order and its character that we will find the explanation of the exclusive call of men to the priesthood and episcopate. This analysis can be outlined in three propositions: 1) in administering the sacraments that demand the character of ordination the priest does not act in his own name (*in persona propria*), but in the person of Christ (*in persona Christi*): 2) this formula, as understood by tradition, implies that the priest is a sign in the sense in which this term is understood in sacramental theology; 3) it is precisely because the priest is a sign of Christ the Saviour that he must be a man and not a woman.

40. That the priest performs the Eucharist and reconciles sinners in the name and place of Christ is affirmed repeatedly by the Magisterium and constantly taught by Fathers and theologians. It would not appear to serve any useful purpose to give a multitude of quotations to show this. It is the totality of the priestly ministry that Saint Paul says is exercised in the place of Christ: "We are acting as ambassadors on behalf of Christ, God, as it were, appealing through us"—in fact this text from 2 Corinthians has in mind the ministry of reconciliation (5:18-20)—"you have received me as an angel of God, even as Christ Jesus" (Gal 4:14). Similarly Saint Cyprian echoes Saint Paul: "The priest truly acts in the place of Christ"[44]. But theological reflection and the Church's life have been led to distinguish the more or less close links between the various acts in the exercise of the ministry and the character of ordination and to specify which require this character for validity.

41. Saying "in the name and place of Christ" is not however enough to express completely the nature of the bond between the minister and Christ as understood by tradition. The formula *in persona Christi* in fact suggests a meaning that brings it close to the Greek expression *mimema Christou*[45]. The word *persona* means a part played in the ancient theatre, a part identified by a particular mask. The priest takes the part of Christ, lending him his voice and gestures. Saint Thomas expresses this concept exactly: "The priest enacts the image of Christ, in whose person and by whose power he pronounces the words of consecration"[46]. The priest is thus truly a *sign* in the sacramental sense of the word. It would be a very elementary view of the sacraments if the notion of sign were kept only for material elements. Each sacrament fulfils the notion in a different way. The text of Saint Bonaventure already mentioned affirms this very clearly: "the person ordained is a sign of Christ the mediator"[47]. Although Saint Thomas gave as the reason for excluding women the much discussed one of the state of subjection (*status subiectionis*), he nevertheless took as his starting point the principle that "sacramental signs represent what they signify by a natural resemblance"[48], in other words the need for that "natural resemblance" between Christ and the person who

is his sign. And, still on the same point, Saint Thomas recalls: "Since a sacrament is a sign, what is done in the sacrament requires not only the reality but also a sign of the reality"[49].

42. It would not accord with "natural resemblance", with that obvious "meaningfulness", if the memorial of the Supper were to be carried out by a woman; for it is not just the recitation involving the gestures and words of Christ, but an action, and the sign is efficacious because Christ is present in the minister who consecrates the Eucharist, as is taught by the Second Vatican Council, following the Encyclical *Mediator Dei*[50].

43. It is understandable that those favouring the ordination of women have made various attempts to deny the value of this reasoning. It has obviously been impossible and even unnecessary for the Declaration to consider in detail all the difficulties that could be raised in this regard. Some of them however are of interest in that they occasion a deeper theological understanding of traditional principles. Let us look at the objection sometimes raised that it is ordination—the character—not maleness, that makes the priest Christ's representative. Obviously it is the character, received by ordination, that enables the priest to consecrate the Eucharist and reconcile penitents. But the character is spiritual and invisible (*res et sacramentum*). On the level of the sign (*sacramentum tantum*) the priest must both have received the laying on of hands and take the part of Christ. It is here that Saint Thomas and Saint Bonaventure require that the sign should have natural meaningfulness.

44. In various fairly recent publications attempts have been made to reduce the importance of the formula *in persona Christi* by insisting rather on the formula *in persona Ecclesiae*. For it is another great principle of the theology of the sacraments and liturgy that the priest presides over the liturgy in the name of the Church, and must have the intention of "doing what the Church does". Could one say that the priest does not represent Christ, because he first represents the Church by the fact of his ordination? The Declaration's reply to this objection is that, quite on the contrary, the priest represents the Church precisely because he first represents Christ himself, who is the Head and Shepherd of the Church. It indicates several texts of the Second Vatican Council that clearly express this teaching. Here there may well be in fact one of the crucial points of the question, one of the important aspects of the theology of the Church and the priesthood underlying the debate on the ordination of women. When the priest presides over the assembly, it is not the assembly that has chosen or designated him for this role. The Church is not a spontaneous gathering. As its name of *ecclesia* indicates, it is an assembly that is convoked. It is Christ who calls it together. He is the head of the Church, and the priest presides "in the person of Christ the Head" (*in persona Christi capitis*). That is why the Declaration rightly concludes "that the controversies raised in our days over the ordination of women are for all Christians a pressing invitation to meditate on the mystery of the Church, to study in greater detail the meaning of the episcopate and the priesthood, and to rediscover the real and pre-eminent place of the priest

in the community of the baptized, of which he indeed forms part but from which he is distinguished because, in the actions that call for the character of ordination, for the community he is—with all the effectiveness proper to the sacraments—the image and symbol of Christ himself who calls, forgives, and accomplishes the sacrifice of the Convenant."

45. However, the objectors continue: it would indeed be important that Christ should be represented by a man if the maleness of Christ played an essential part in the economy of salvation. But, they say, one cannot accord gender a special place in the hypostatic union; what is essential is the human nature—no more—assumed by the Word, not the incidental characteristics such as the sex or even the race which he assumed. If the Church admits that men of all races can validly represent Christ, why should she deny women this ability to represent him? We must first of all reply, in the words of the Declaration, that ethnic differences "do not affect the human person as intimately as the difference of sex". On this point biblical teaching agrees with modern psychology. The difference between the sexes however is something willed by God from the beginning, according to the account in Genesis (which is also quoted in the Gospel), and is directed both to communion between persons and to the begetting of human beings. And it must be affirmed first and foremost that the fact that Christ is a man and not a woman is neither incidental nor unimportant in relation to the economy of salvation. In what sense? Not of course in the material sense, as has sometimes been suggested in polemics in order to discredit it, but because the whole economy of salvatio has been revealed to us through essential symbols from which it cannot be separated, and without which we would be unable to understand God's design. Christ is the new Adam. God's covenant with men is presented in the Old Testament as a nuptial mystery, the definitive reality of which is Christ's sacrifice on the Cross. The Declaration briefly presents the stages marking the progressive development of this biblical theme, the subject of many exegetical and theological studies. Christ is the Bridegroom of the Church, whom he won for himself with his blood, and the salvation brought by him is the New Covenant: by using this language, Revelation shows why the Incarnation took place according to the male gender, and makes it impossible to ignore this historical reality. For this reason, only a man can take the part of Christ, be a sign of his presence, in a word "represent" him (that is, be an effective sign of his presence) in the essential acts of the Covenant.

46. Could one do without this biblical symbolism when transmitting the message, in contemplating the mystery and in liturgical life? To ask this, as has been done in certain recent studies, is to call into question the whole structure of Revelation and to reject the value of Scripture. It will be said, for example, that "in every period the ecclesial community appeals to the authority it has received from its founder in order to choose the images enabling it to receive God's revelation." This is perhaps to fail even more profoundly to appreciate the human value of the nuptial theme in the revelation of God's love.

The Ministerial Priesthood in the Mystery of the Church

47. It is also striking to note the extent to which the questions raised in the controversy over the ordination of women are bound up with a certain theology of the Church. We do not of course mean to dwell on the excessive formulas which nonetheless sometimes find a place in theological reviews. An example is the supposition that the primitive Church was based on the charisms possessed by both women and men[51]. Another is the claim that "the Gospels also present women as ministers of unction"[52]. On the other hand, we have already come across the question of the pluralism that can be admitted in unity and seen what its limits are.

48. The proposal that women should be admitted to the priesthood because they have gained leadership in many fields of modern life today seems to ignore the fact that the Church is not a society like the rest. In the Church, authority or power is of a very different nature, linked as it normally is with the sacrament, as is underlined in the Declaration. Disregard of this fact is indeed a temptation that has threatened ecclesiological research at all periods: every time that an attempt is made to solve the Church's problems by comparison with those of States, or to define the Church's structure by political categories, the inevitable result is an impasse.

49. The Declaration also points out the defect in the argument that seeks to base the demand that the priesthood be conferred on women on the text Galatians 3:28, which states that in Christ there is no longer any distinction between man and woman. For Saint Paul this is the effect of baptism. The baptismal catechesis of the Fathers often stressed it. But absolute equality in baptismal life is quite a different thing from the structure of the ordained ministry. This latter is the object of a vocation within the Church, not a right inherent in the person.

50. A vocation within the Church does not consist solely or primarily in the fact that one manifests the desire for a mission or feels attracted by an inner compulsion. Even if this spontaneous step is made and even if one believes one has heard as it were a call in the depths of one's soul, the vocation is authentic only from the moment that it is authenticated by the external call of the Church. The Holy Office recalled this truth in its 1912 letter to the Bishop of Aire to put an end to the Lahitton controversy[53]. Christ chose "those he wanted" (Mk 3:13).

51. Since the ministerial priesthood is something to which the Lord calls expressly and gratuitously, it cannot be claimed as a right, any more by men than by women. Archbishop Bernardin's declaration of October 1975 contained the sound judgment: "It would be a mistake . . . to reduce the question of the ordination of women to one of injustice, as is done at times. It would be correct do to this only if ordination were a God-given right of every individual; only if somehow one's human potential could not be fulfilled without it. In fact, however, no one, male or female, can claim a 'right' to ordination. And, since the episcopal and priestly office is basically a ministry of service, ordination in no way 'completes' one's humanity"[54].

52. The Declaration of the Sacred Congregation for the Doctrine of the Faith ends by suggesting that efforts in two directions should be fostered, efforts from which the pastors and faithful of the Church would perhaps be distracted if this controversy over women's ordination were prolonged. One direction is in the doctrinal and spiritual order: awareness of the diversity of roles in the Church, in which equality is not identity, should lead us—as Saint Paul exhorts us—to strive after the one gift that can and should be striven after, namely love (1 Cor 12-13). "The greatest in the Kingdom of Heaven are not the ministers but the saints", says the Declaration. This expression deserves to be taken as a motto.

53. The other direction for our efforts is in the apostolic and social order. We have a long way to go before people become fully aware of the greatness of women's mission in the Church and society, "both for the renewal and humanization of society and for the rediscovery by believers of the true countenance of the Church". Unfortunately we also still have a long way to go before all the inequalities of which women are still the victims are eliminated, not only in the field of public, professional and intellectual life, but even within the family.

Notes

1. Note especially: J.E. HAVEL, *La question du pastorat féminin en Suède*, in *Archives de sociologie des religions*, 4, 1959, pp. 207-249; F.R. REFOULÉ, *Le problème des femmes-pretres en Suède*, in *Lumière et Vie*, 43, 1959, pp. 65-99.

2. No. 22 (W. NISEL, *Bekenntnisschriften und Kirchenordnungen* . . . , München, 1939, p. 111): "quod . . . foeminis, quae Spiritus sanctus ne docere quidem in Ecclesia patitur, illi [papistae] permittunt ut etiam Baptismum administrarent".

3. The position of the Catholic Church on this point was made clear by Leo XIII in the Letter *Apostolicae Curae* of 13 September 1896 (Leonis XIII Acta, 16. 1897, pp. 258-275).

4. Earlier, in 1944, his predecessor Bishop Hall called a woman to the priesthood, but she had to refrain from exercising the ministry because of the energetic intervention of the Archbishops of York and Canterbury, who for ecumenical motives repudiated the action of the Bishop of Hong Kong.

5. Letter of 9 July 1975 to the Pope, in *L'Osservatore Romano* (English edition), 2 September 1976.

6. Cardinal Willebrands stated this to some United States Episcopal Bishop in September 1974, according to the account published in *Origins—NC Documentary Service*, 9 October 1975.

7. Italian translation published in *L'Osservatore Romano*, 16-17 June 1975.

8. Letters of Paul VI to Dr Coggan, 30 November 1975 and 10 February 1976: cf. *AAS* 68(1976), pp. 599-601.

9. At the WCC's Assembly in New Delhi in 1961, the Department of

Faith and Order was asked to prepare, in collaboration with the Department on Cooperation of Men and Women in Church, Family and Society, a study on the theological questions raised by the problem of women's ordination (cf. *Nouvelle-Delhi 1961*, Neuchâtel, 1962, pp. 166, 169). On the discussion of the problem at the Nairobi Assembly, see E. LANNE, *Points chauds de la Ve Assemblée mondial du Conseil oecuménique des Eglises a Nairobi . . . ,* in *Revue théologique de Louvain*, 7, 1976, pp. 197-199: *Les femmes dans l'Eglise*.

10. Second Vatican Council, Decree *Apostolicam Actuositatem*, 9.

11. This intrusion of sociology into hermeneutics and theology is perhaps one of the most important elements in the controversy. This has been rightly stressed by B. LAMBERT, *L'Eglise catholique peut-elle admettre des femmes à l'ordination sacerdotale*, in *Documentation Catholique* 73, 1976, p. 774: "en corrigeant dans l'interprétation de la Tradition et de l'Ecriture ce qui était lié à des formes socio-culturelles, historiquement nécessaires et conditionnées, mais aujord'hui dépassées, à la lumière de l'évolution de la société et de l'Eglise".

12. The very phrase (reported in *Le Monde* of 19-20 September 1965) used by J. DANIELOU during the Council at a meeting of the Alliance Internationale Jeanne d'Arc. He returned to the subject, introducing perhaps more shades of meaning, in the interview he gave at the time of his promotion to Cardinal, *L'Express*, 936, 16-22 June 1969, pp. 122, 124: "Il faudrait examiner où sont les vraies raisons qui font que l'Eglise n'a jamais envisagé le sacerdoce des femmes."

13. *Origins—NC Documentary Service*, 16 October 1975: "Honesty and concern for the Catholic community .˙. . require that Church leaders not seem to encourage unreasonable hopes and expectations, even by their silence. Therefore I am obliged to restate the Church's teaching that women are not to be ordained to the priesthood."

14. *AAS* 67 (1975), p. 265.

15. Letter of 30 November 1975: *AAS* 63 (1976), p. 599.

16. Cf., for example, the theological conversations between Catholics and Russian Orthodox at Trent, 23-28 June 1975: *L'Osservatore Romano*, 7-8 July 1975; *Documentation Catholique*, 71, 1975, p. 707.

17. 1, 13, 2: *PG* 7, col. 580-581; Harvey edition 1, 114-122.

18. 41, 5: CCL 1, p. 221.

19. In the Letters of Saint Cyprian, 75: CSEL 3, pp. 817-818.

20. Fragments published in *Journal of Theological Studies*, 10 (1909), pp. 41-42 (No. 74).

21. *Panarion*, 49, 2-3: GCS 31, pp. 243-244;—78, 23 and 79, 2-4; GCS 37, pp. 473, 477-479.

22. St. Thomas, *Summa Theol.*, 2[a], 2[ae], q. 10, a. 12; 3[a] pars, q. 66, a. 10; q. 72, a. 4 and a. 12; q. 73, a. 4; q. 78, a. 3 and a. 6; q. 80, a. 12; q. 82, a. 2; q. 83, a. 3 and a. 5; —cf. *In IV Sent. Dist.* 20, q. 1, a. 4, q.[a] 1 ff; *Dist.* 23, q. 1, a. 4, q.[a] 1, etc.

23. St. Thomas, *In IV Sent. Dist.* 19, q. 1, a. 1,q[a] 3 ad 4[um]; *Dist.* 25, q. 2, a. 1, q[a] 1; cf. q. 2, a. 2, q[a] 1, ad 4; *Summa Theol.*, 2[a], 2[ae], q. 177. a. 2.

24. *Dictum Gratiani in Caus.* 34, q. 5, c. 11, ed. FRIEDBERG, t. 1, col. 1254; cf. R. METZ, *La femme en droit canonique médiéval*, in *Recueil de la société Jean Bodin*, 12, 1962, pp. 59-113.

25. Canon 44 of the collection called after the Council of Laodicea: H.T. BRUNS, *Canones Apostolorum et Conciliorum* . . . t. 1, Bertolini, 1839, p. 78; St. Gelasius, *Epist. 14, ad universos episcopos per Lucaniam, Brutios et Siciliam constitutos*, 11 March 494, no. 26: A. THIEL, *Epistolae Romanorum pontificum* . . . , t. 1, Brunsbergae, 1868, p. 376.

26. Chap. 15: ed. R.H. Connolly, pp. 133 and 142.

27. Lib. 3, c. 6, nn. 1-2; c. 9, 3-4; ed. F.X. Funk, pp. 191, 201.

28. Can. 24-28; —Greek text in F.X. FUNK, *Doctrina Duodecim Apostolorum*, Tübingen, 1887, p. 71; T. SCHERMANN, *Die allgemeine Kirchenordnung* . . . , t. 1, Paderborn, 1914, pp. 31-33; —Syriac text in *Octateuque de Clément*, Lib. 3, c. 19-20; Latin text in the Verona ms., Bibl. capit. LV, ed. E. TIDNER, *Didascaliae Apostolorum, Canonum Ecclesiasticorum, Traditionis Apostolicae Versiones Latinae*, Berlin, 1965 (TU 75), pp. 111-113. The Coptic, Ethiopian and Arabic versions of the *Synodos* have been translated and published chiefly by G. HORNER, *The Statutes of the Apostles or Canones Ecclesiastici*, Oxford University Press, 1915 (=1904).

29. *De Sacerdotio* 2, 2: *PG* 48, 633.

30. *Decretal. Lib. V*, tit. 38, *De paenit.*, can. 10 Nova A. FRIEDBERG, t. 2, col. 886-887: *Quia licet beatissima Virgo Maria dignior et excellentior fuerit Apostolis universis, non tamen illi, sed istis Dominus claves regni caelorum commisit.*

31. e.g., *Glossa in Decretal. Lib. 1*, tit. 33, c. 12 *Dilecta*, V° *Iurisdictioni.*

32. *In IV Sent., Dist. 25*, art. 2, q. 1: ed. Quaracchi, t. 4, p. 649: *Dicendum est quod hoc non venit tam ex institutione Ecclesiae, quam ex hoc quod eis non competit Ordinis sacramentum. In hoc sacramento persona quae ordinatur significat Christum mediatorem.*

33. *In IV Sent. Dist. 25*, a. 4, n°1; ed. Bocatelli, Venice, 1499 (PELLECHET—POLAIN, 10132/9920), f° 177ᴿ: *Ratio est quod sacramenta vim habent ex sua institutione: Christus autem hoc sacramentum instituit conferri masculis tantum, non mulieribus.*

34. *In IV Sent., Dist. 25, Opus Oxoniense*, ed. Vivès, t. 19, p. 140; cf. *Reportata Parisiensia*, ed. Vives, t. 24, pp. 369-371. *Quod non est tenendum tamquam praecise per Ecclesiam determinatum, sed habetur a Christo: non enim Ecclesia praesumpsisset sexum muliebrem privasse sine culpa sua actu qui posset sibi licite competere.*

35. *In IV Sent., Dist. 25*, p. 2; ed. Venice, 1571, f°364ⱽ: . . . *sexus virilis est de necessitate sacramenti, cuius causa principalis est institutio Christi . . . Christus non ordinavit nisi viros . . . nec matrem suam . . . Tenendum est igitur quod mulieres non possunt ordinari ex institutione Christi.*

36. Details of these theological notes can be found in E. DORONZO, *Tractatus Dogmaticus de Ordine*, t. 3, Milwaukee, Bruce, 1962, pp. 395-396; Cf. also F. HALLER, *De Sacris Electionibus*, 1636, quoted in J.P. MIGNE, *Theologiae Cursus Completus*, t. 24, col. 821-854; many present-day objections are surprisingly anticipated in this work, which goes so far as to qualify as *periculosa in fide* the opinion that would admit women's ordination in general, and as *haeretica* that which would admit them to the priesthood, col. 824; cf. also H. TOURNELY, *Praelectiones Theologicae de Sacramento Ordinis*, Parisii, 1729, p. 185, notes as an error *contra fidem* this assertion with regard to episcopate, priesthood and diaconate. Among canonists: X. WERNZ, *Ius Decret.*, t. 2, Romae, 1906, p. 124 *iure divino* (he quotes sever-

al writers); P. GASPARRI, *Tractatus Canonicus de Sacra Ordinatione*, t. 1, Parisiis, 1893, p. 75; *Et quidem prohibentur sub poena nullitatis: ita enim traditio et communis doctorum catholicorum doctrina interpretata est legem Apostoli: ed ideo Patres inter haereses recensent doctrinam qua sacerdotalis dignitas et officium mulieribus tribuitur.*

37. St. BONAVENTURE, *In IV Sent., Dist. 25*, art. 2, q. 1, ed. Quaracchi, t. 4, p. 650: *Omnes consentiunt quod promoveri non debent, sed utrum possint, dubium est* (the doubt arises from the case of the deaconesses); he concludes: *secundum saniorem opinionem et prudentiorum doctorum non solum non debent vel non possunt de iure, verum etiam non possunt de facto.*

38. This canon deals with deaconesses. At the word *ordinari*, Johannes Teutonicus states: *Respondeo quod mulieres non recipiunt characterem, impediente sexu et constitutione Ecclesiae: unde nec officium ordinum exercere possunt . . . nec ordinatur haec: sed fundebatur super eam forte aliqua benedictio, ex qua consequebatur aliquod officium speciale, forte legendi homilias vel evangelium ad matutinas quod non licebat alii. Alii dicunt quod si monialis ordinetur, bene recipit characterem, quia ordinari facti est et post baptismum quilibet potest ordinare.*

39. Cf. J. DUPONT, *Le Logion des douze trônes*, in *Biblica*, 45, 1964, pp. 355-92.

40. The documents cited in notes 26-28 above. Note also the curious *Mariale*, falsely attributed to Albert the Great, quaest. 42; ed. Borgnet, t. 37, pp. 80-81.

41. I. DE LA POTTERIE, *Titres missionnaires du chrétien dans le Nouveau Testament* (Rapports de la XXXIème semaine de Missiologie, Louvain, 1966), Paris, Desclée de Brouwer, 1966, p. 29-46 cf. pp. 44-45.

42. Council of Trent, sess. 21, c. 2 and Pius XII, Constitution *Sacramentum Ordinis*, 30 November 1947, quoted in the Declaration.

43. Cf. Ph. DELHAYE, *Rétrospective et prospective des ministères féminins dans l'Eglise*, in *Revue théologique de Louvain* 3, 1972, pp. 74-75.

44. *Epist.* 63, 14: ed. Hartel, CSEL t. 3, p. 713: *sacerdos vice Christi vere fungitur.*

45. St. Theodore the Studite, *Adversus Iconomachos* cap. 4; *PG* 99, 593; *Epist. lib. 1*, 11: *PG* 99, 945.

46. *Summa Theol.*, III, q. 83, a. 1, ad 3um.

47. Above, note 32: *persona quae ordinatur significat Christum mediatorem.*

48. *In IV SENT., Dist. 25*, q. 2, a. 2, q^a 1, ad 4um: *signa sacramentalia ex naturali similitudine repraesentent.*

49. *Ibid. in corp. quaestiunculae: Quia cum sacramentum sit signum, in eis quae in sacramento aguntur requiritur non solum res, sed significatio rei.*

50. II Vatican Council, Constitution *Sacrosanctum* on the Liturgy, no. 7; Pius XII, Encyclical *Mediator Dei*, 20 November 1947, *AAS* 39 (1947), p. 528.

51. Cf. *Concilium* 111, 1976, *La femme dans l'Eglise*, French edition, pp. 19, 20, especially 23: "Au temps de Paul, les fonctions de direction étaient réparties et reposaient sur l'autorité charismatique".

52. *Theological Studies* 36, 1975, p. 667.

53. *AAS* 4, 1912, p. 485.

54. In *Origins—NC Documentary Service*, 16 October 1975.

APPENDIX II
Biblical Commission Report
Can Women Be Priests?

The Pontifical Biblical Commission was asked to study the role of women in the Bible in the course of research being carried out to determine the place that can be given to women today in the church.

The question for which an answer is especially sought is whether or not women can be ordained to the priestly ministry (especially as ministers of the eucharist and as leaders of the Christian community). In making this biblical inquiry, one must keep in mind the limits of such a study.

1. In general the role of women does not constitute the principal subject of biblical texts. One has to rely often on information given here and there. The situation of women in the biblical era was probably more or less favorable judging from the limited data that we have at our disposal.

2. The question asked touches on the priesthood, the celebrant of the eucharist and the leader of the local community. This is a way of looking at things which is somewhat foreign to the Bible.

A) Surely the New Testament speaks of the Christian people as a priestly people (I Peter 2, 5.9; Apoc. 1, 6; 5, 10). It describes that certain members of this people accomplish a priestly and sacrificial ministry (I Peter 2, 5.12; Rom 12, 1; 15, 16; Phil 2, 17). However it never uses the technical terms *hiereus* for the Christian ministry. *A fortiori* it never places *hiereus* in relationship with the eucharist.

B) The New Testament says very little on the subject of the ministry of the eucharist. Luke 22, 19 orders the apostles to celebrate the eucharist in memory of Jesus (cf. I Cor 11, 24). Acts 20, 11 shows also that Paul broke the bread (see also Acts 27, 35).

C) The pastoral epistles which give us the most detailed picture of the leaders of the local community (episkopos and prebyteroi), never attribute to them a eucharistic function.

3. Beyond these difficulties resulting from a study of the biblical data from the perspective of a later conception of the eucharistic priesthood, it is necessary to keep in mind that this conception itself is now placed in question as one can see in the more recent declarations of the magisterium which broaden the concept of priesthood beyond that of eucharistic ministry.

PART I

WOMAN'S PLACE IN THE FAMILY

(1) "In the Beginning."

In Genesis, the "beginning" serves less to present the beginning of history than the fundamental plan of God for mankind. In Genesis 1, man and woman are called together to be the image of God (Gen. 1, 26f) on equal terms and in a community of life. It is in common that they receive rule over the world. Their vocation gives a new meaning to the sexuality that man possesses as the animals do.

In Gen. 2, man and woman are placed on equal terms: woman is for man a "helper who is his partner" (2, 18), and by community in love they become "the two of them one body" (2, 24). This union includes the vocation of the couple to fruitfulness but it is not reduced to that.

Between this ideal and the historical reality of the human race, sin has introduced a considerable gap. The couple's existence is wounded in its very foundations: love is degraded by covetousness and domination (3, 16). The woman endures pains in her condition as mother which nevertheless put her closely in contact with the mystery of life. The social degradation of her condition is also related to this wound, manifested by polygamy (cf. Gen. 4), divorce, slavery, etc. She is nevertheless the depository of a promise of salvation made to her descendants.

It is noteworthy that the ideal of Gen. 1 and 2 remained present in the thought of Israel like a horizon of hope: it is found again explicitly in the book of Tobias.

(2) The Symbolism of the Sexes in the Old Testament

The Old Testament excluded the sexual symbolism used in Eastern mythologies, in relation to the fertility cults: there is no sexuality in the God of Israel. But very early, the biblical tradition borrowed traits from the family structure to trace pictures of God the Father. Then also it had recourse to the image of the spouse to work out a very lofty concept of the God of the covenant.

In correlation with these two fundamental images, the prophets gave value to the dignity of women by representing the people of God with the help of feminine symbols of the wife (in relation to God) and of the mother (in relation to the human partners of the covenant, men and women). These symbols were used particularly to evoke in advance the eschatological covenant in which God is to realize his plan in its fullness.

(3) The Teachings of Jesus

Considering the social and cultural milieu in which Jesus lived, his teaching and behavior with regard to women are striking in their newness. We leave aside here his behavior (cf. the following reports). Questioned about divorce by the Pharisees (Mk. 10, 1-12), Jesus moves away from the rabbinic casuistry that, on the basis of Deut. 24, 1, discriminated between the respective rights of men and women.

Reminding the Pharisees of the original plan of God (Gen. 1, 27 and 2, 24), he shows his intention of establishing here below a state of things that realizes the plan fully: the reign of God, inaugurated by his preaching and his presence, brings with it a full restoration of feminine dignity. But it brings also a surpassing of the ancient juridical structures in which repudiation showed the failure of marriage "by reason of the hardness of hearts." It is in this perspective that the practice of celibacy "for the sake of the kingdom of God" (Matt. 19, 12), for himself and for those "to whom it is given" (19, 11) is understood. His attitude toward women should be examined from that point of departure.

Thus Jesus inaugurates in the framework of the present world the order of things that constitutes the final horizon of the kingdom of God: that order will result, in "a new heaven and a new earth," in a state in which the risen will no longer need to exercise their sexuality (Matt. 21, 31). Consequently, to represent the joy of the kingdom of heaven, Jesus can properly use the image of the virgins called to the wedding feast of the bridegroom (Matt. 25, 1-10).

(4) From the Mother of Jesus to the Church

Considering the historical existence of Jesus, son of God sent into the world (Gal. 4, 4 etc.), one might take a look at his beginnings.

The evangelists, Matthew and especially Luke, have made clear the irreplaceable role of his mother Mary. The value proper to femininity that the Old Testament presented are recapitulated in her, so that she accomplishes her unique role in the plan of God. But in the very accomplishment of this maternal role, she anticipates the reality of the new covenant of which her son will be the mediator. In fact she is the first one called to a faith that concerns her son (Luke 1, 42) and to an obedience in which she "listens to the word of God and puts it into practice" (Luke 11, 28, cf. 1, 38).

Moreover, the Spirit who brings about in her the conception of Jesus (Luke 1, 35, Matt. 1, 18) will make a new people spring up in history on the day of Pentecost (Acts 2). Her historic role is therefore linked to a resumption of the feminine symbolism used to evoke the new people: from then on, the church is "our mother" (Gal. 4, 20). At the end of time, it will be the "spouse of the Lamb" (Apoc. 21). It is by reason of this relationship between Mary, concrete woman, and the church, symbolic woman, that in Apoc. 12 the new humanity rescued from the power of sin and death can be presented as giving birth to Christ, her first born (Apoc. 12, 4-15), expecting to have as posterity "those who keep the word of God and have the testimony of Jesus."

(5) Woman in the Church

Nuptial symbolism is specifically taken up again by St. Paul to evoke the mystery of Christ and his church (Eph. 5, 22-33). But it is first of all the relationship between Christ and the church, his body, which casts light on the reality forming the basis for Paul's approach.

Despite an institutional framework which implies the submission of women to their husbands (cf. Eph. 5, 22; Col. 3, 18; I Pt. 3, 1), Paul reverses the perspective to emphasize their mutual submission (Eph. 5, 21) and love (5, 25.33) for which Christ's love is the source and model: charity (cf. I Cor. 13) becomes the measure of conjugal love. It is through it that the "original perfection" (that is to say the fullness of the plan of God for the human couple) can be attained (cf. Eph. 5, 31 citing Gen. 2, 24). That supposes between man and woman not only an equality of rights and duties explicitly affirmed (I Cor. 7, 3-4), but also an equality in adoptive sonship (Gal. 3, 28, II Cor. 6, 18) and in the reception of the Spirit who brings about participation in the life of the church (cf. Acts 2, 17-18).

Marriage, having thus received its full meaning, thanks to its symbolic relationship with the mystery of Christ and the church (Eph. 5, 32), can regain also its indissoluble solidity (I Cor. 7, 10-12; cf. Luke 16, 18).

At the heart of a sinful world, maternity has a saving value (I Tim. 2, 15). Outside conjugal life, the church grants a place of honor to consecrated widowhood (I Tim. 5, 3) and it recognizes in virginity the possible meaning of eschatological witness (I Cor 7, 25-26) and of a more complete freedom to consecrate oneself to "the business of the Lord" (I Cor. 7, 32ff.). Such is the background against which theological reflection on the place and function of women in society and in the church takes place.

PART II

THE SOCIAL CONDITION OF WOMAN ACCORDING TO BIBLICAL REVELATION

I. The Bible, especially the New Testament, teaches very clearly the equality of man and woman in the spiritual domain (relationships with God) and in the moral area (relationships with other human beings). But the problem of the social condition of woman is a sociological problem that must be treated as such:

1. In terms of the laws of sociology: physical and psychosomatic data of feminine behavior in an earthly society;

2. In terms of the history of the societies in which the people of God lived during and after the composition of the Bible;

3. In terms of the laws of the church of Christ, his body, whose members live an ecclesial life under the direction of a magisterium instituted by Christ, while belonging to other societies and states.

II. The biblical experience shows that the social condition of woman has varied, but not in a linear manner as if there were continual progress. Ancient Egypt experienced a real flourishing of woman before the existence of Israel. The Israelite woman experienced a certain flourishing under the monarchy, then her condition became subordinate once more. In the time of Christ the status of woman appears, in Jewish society, inferior to what it is in Greco-Roman society where their lack of legal status is in the process of disappearing and in which "women handle their business themselves" (Gaius).

In relation to his contemporaries, Christ has a very original attitude with regard to woman which gives renewed value to her situation.

III. Christian society is established on a basis other than that of Jewish society. It is founded on the cornerstone of the risen Christ and is built upon

Peter in collegiality with the twelve. According to the witness of the New Testament, especially the Pauline epistles, women are associated with the different charismatic ministries (*diaconies*) of the church (I Cor. 12, 4; I Tim. 3, 11, cf. 8): prophecy, service, probably even apostolate . . . without, nevertheless, being of the twelve. They have a place in the liturgy at least as prophetesses (I Cor. 11, 4). But according to the Pauline corpus (I Cor. 14, 33-35; cf. I Tim. 2, 6-15) an apostle such as Paul can withdraw the word from them.

This Christian society lives not only on the government of the twelve who are called apostles in Luke and elsewhere in the New Testament, but also on the liturgical sacramental life in which Christ communicates his spirit as high priest no longer according to Aaron but according to Melchisedech, king and priest (Heb. 8; cf. Ps. 110).

Sociologically speaking, in Jewish society, therefore for Christians until the break, the consecrated priesthood of Aaron (Lev. 9) assured an authentic liturgical and sacrificial life in the temple of stone. But Christ is the true high priest and the true temple (John 2, 21). He was consecrated and sent (*hagiazein, apostellein*) by the Father (Jn. 10, 26), and he consecrates himself in order to consecrate the apostles in the truth that he himself is (Jn. 17, 17.19). It is a fundamental characteristic of the society that is the church in the midst of other societies, that it dispenses eternal life through its own liturgy.

IV. The problem is to know whether in Christian society ruled by the apostles—the twelve, Paul, Titus, Timothy—and by their successors (bishops, presbyters, *higoumenes*) women can be called to participate in this liturgical ministry and in the direction of local communities, as the queens of the Old Testament, especially widows, were called to participate in the royal functions of anointed kings. In fact in the New Testament no text formally supports this hypothesis, even though one may note the role of widows in the pastoral epistles (I Tim. 5) and what Luke says of Anna in the Temple (*latreuein*). This study is no longer a matter of sociology, but of the labors of our third section (condition of woman in cult).

PART III

ECCLESIAL CONDITION OF WOMAN

Old Testament

In the Old Testament, the Yahwist religion was not reserved to men alone, as is said elsewhere. Women as well as men could have sacrifices offered, participate in worship. Nevertheless, contrary to the customs of the contemporary pagan peoples, the worship of the second temple was exclusively reserved to men of the tribe of Levi (not only the function of priests, but also that of cantor, porter, etc.).

Moreover, there are women who bore the name of prophetess (Maria, Deborah, Huldam, Noiada), while not playing the role of the great prophets. Other women exercised an important function for the salvation of the people of God at critical moments of this people's history (for example, Judith, Esther) (cf. section 2).

(Amendment of Father Wambacq:) "In the Old Testament, the Yahwist religion was not a religion in which women were excluded, as is sometimes held. Women as well as men could participate in worship. Contrary to the usages of the contemporary pagan peoples, the official exercise of the temple worship was reserved to men, in the second temple to those of the tribe of Levi."

THE GOSPELS

In striking contast to the contemporary usages of the Jewish world, we see Jesus surrounding himself with women who follow him and serve him (Luke 8, 2-3). Mary of Bethany is even described as the examplary disciple "listening to the word" (Luke 10, 38-42). It is the women who are charged with announcing the resurrection "to the apostles and to Peter." (Mark 16, 7).

The fourth gospel stresses this role of witness attributed to women: the Samaritan woman, whose mere conversation with Jesus had astonished the apostles, goes carrying her witness to Jesus to her fellow citizens. After the resurrection, the evangelist emphasizes the role of Mary Magdalene whom tradition will call "the apostle of the apostles."

ACTS AND PAUL

As Christianity spread, women took a notable part. That again distinguished the new religion sharply from contemporary Judaism.

Some women collaborated in the properly apostolic work. This is shown at numerous points in the Acts and the epistles. We shall limit ourselves to a few of them.

In the establishment of local communities, they are not content with offering their houses for meetings, as Lydia (Acts 16, 14-15), the mother of Mark (Acts 12, 12), Prisca (Rom. 16, 5), but, according to Phil. 4, 2, for example, Evodia and Syntyche are explicitly associated with "Clement and the other collaborators of Paul" in the community. Of the 27 persons thanked or greeted by Paul in the last chapter of the Epistle to the Romans, nine or perhaps 10 are women. In the case of several of them, Paul insists on specifying that they have tired themselves for the community, using a Greek verb (kopian) most often used for the work of evangelization properly so called.

The case of Prisca and her husband Aquila whom Paul calls "his collaborators in Christ" and of whom he says that "to them are indebted not only himself but all the churches of the Gentiles" (Rom. 16, 3-4), shows us concretely an example of this "collaboration": their role in the story of Appollo is well known (Acts 18, 24-28).

Paul mentions explicitly a woman as "deacon" (*diaconos*) of the churcn of Cenchrees, who "was also," he says, "for many Christians and for himself a protectress" (Rom. 16, 1-2). In the pastoral epistles, the women indicated after the bishops and the deacons probably had a status of *diaconos* (1 Tim. 3, 11). Also notable is the case of Junias or Junio, placed in the rank of the apostles (Rom. 16, 7), with regard to whom one or another raises the question of whether it is a man.

PART IV

REPLY TO THE QUESTION ABOUT THE EVENTUAL ORDINATION
OF WOMEN TO THE PRIESTHOOD

(1) The Ministry of Leadership According to Jesus
and the Apostolic Church

In establishing the kingdom of God, Jesus, during his ministry, chose a group of 12 men who, after the fashion of the 12 patriarchs of the Old Testament, would be the leaders of the renewed people of God (Mk. 3:14-19); these men whom he destined to "sit upon twelve thrones judging the twelve tribes of Israel" (Mt. 19:28) were first sent to "proclaim that the kingdom of heaven is at hand" (Mt. 10:7).

After his death and resurrection, Christ confided to his apostles the mission of evangelizing all nations (Mt. 28:19, Mk 16:5). These men would become his witnesses, beginning at Jerusalem and reaching to the ends of the earth (Acts 1:8, Lk. 24:47). "As my Father sent me," he told them, "I also send you" (Jn. 20:21).

Upon leaving the earth to return to his Father, he also delegated to a group of men whom he had chosen the responsibility to develop the kingdom of God and the authority to govern the church. The apostolic group thus established by the Lord appeared thus, by the testimony of the New Testament, as the basis of a community which has continued the work of Christ, charged to communicate to humanity the fruits of his salvation.

As a matter of fact, we see in the Acts of the Apostles and the epistles that the first communities were always directed by men exercising the apostolic power.

The Acts of the Apostles show that the first Christian community of Jerusalem knew only one ministry of leadership, which was that of the apostles: this was the *urministerioum* from which all the others derived. It seems that, very early, the Greek community received its own structure, presided over by the college of seven (Acts 6:5). A little later there was a question for the Jewish group about a college of presbyters (ibid. 11:30). The church at Antioch was presided over by a group of "five prophets and teachers" (ibid. 13:1). At the end of their first missionary journey, Paul and Barnabas installed presbyters in the newly founded churches (ibid. 14:23).

There were also presbyters at Ephesus (ibid., 20:17), to whom were given the name of bishop (ibid. 20:28).

The epistles confirm the same picture: There are *proistamenoi* in I Thess. 5:12 (cf. I Tim. 5:17 *"hoi kalos proetotes presbyteroi"*), of Christian *presbyteroi* (I Tim. 5:1, 2, 17, 19; Titus 1, 5; James 5, 4; I Pet. 5:1, 5), of *episkopoi*, of *hegoumenoi* (Heb. 13:7, 13, 24. cf. Lk. 22:26).

I Cor. 16:16 recommends "submission" to Christians regarding those of the "house of Stephanas" who were sent for the service of the saints.

Whatever this last designation may be, (verse 17 speaks of Stephanas, Fortunatus and Achaikos), all that we can know of those who held a role of leadership in the communities leads to the conclusion that this role was always held by men (in conformity with the Jewish custom). (N.B. The *"presbytides"* mentioned in Titus 2:3 were elderly women, and not priestesses.)

The masculine character of the hierarchical order which has structured the church since its beginning thus seems attested to by scripture in an undeniable way. Must we conclude that this rule must be valid forever in the church?

We must however recall that according to the gospels, the Acts and St. Paul, certain women made a positive collaboration in service to the Christian communities.

Yet one question still always be asked: What is the normative value which should be accorded to the practice of the Christian communities of the first centuries?

(2) The Ministry of Leadership and the Sacramental Economy

One of the essential elements of the church's life is the sacramental economy which gives the life of Christ to the faithful. The administration of this economy has been entrusted to the church for which the hierarchy is responsible.

Thus the question is raised about the relationship between the sacramental economy and the hierarchy.

In the New Testament the primordial role of the leaders of the communities seems always to lie in the field of preaching and teaching. These are the people who have the responsibility of keeping the communities in line with the faith of the apostles.

No text defines their charge in terms of a special power permitting them to carry out the eucharistic rite or to reconcile sinners.

But given the relationship between the sacramental economy and the hierarchy, the administration of the sacraments should not be exercised independently of this hierarchy. It is therefore within the duties of the leadership of the community that we must consider the issue of eucharistic and penitential ministry.

In fact there is no proof that these ministries were entrusted to women at the time of the New Testament. Two texts (I Cor. 14:33-35 and I Tim. 2:11-15) forbid women to speak and to teach in assemblies. However, without mentioning doubts raised by some about their Pauline authenticity, it is possible that they refer only to certain concrete situations and abuses. It is possible that certain other situations call on the church to assign to women the role of teaching which these two passages deny them and which constitute a function belonging to the leadership.

Is it possible that certain circumstances can come about which call on the church to entrust in the same way to certain women some sacramental ministries?

This has been the case with baptism which, though entrusted to the apostles (Mt. 28:19 and Mk. 16:15f.) can be administered by others as well. We know that at least later, it will be entrusted also to women.

Is it possible that we will come to this even with the ministry of eucharist and reconciliation which manifest eminently the service of the priesthood of

Christ carried out by the leaders of the community?

It does not seem that the New Testament by itself alone will permit us to settle in a clear way and once and for all the problem of the possible accession of women to the presbyterate.

However, some think that in the scriptures there are sufficient indications to exclude this possibility, considering that the sacraments of eucharist and reconciliation have a special link with the person of Christ and therefore with the male hierarchy, as borne out by the New Testament.

Others, on the contrary, wonder if the church hierarchy, entrusted with the sacramental economy, would be able to entrust the ministries of eucharist and reconciliation to women in light of circumstances, without going against Christ's original intentions.

For the votes of the Commission, see above, p. 25.

PONTIFICAL BIBLICAL COMMISSION[1]

President: Franjo Cardinal Šeper, Prefect of the
             Sacred Congregation For the Doctrine
             of the Faith

Secretary: Msgr. Albert Deschamps, Titular Bishop of Tunis

Members: Rev. Jose Alonso-Diaz, SJ
             Rev. Jean-Dominique Barthelemy, OP
             Rev. Pierre Benoit, OP
             Rev. Raymond Brown, PSS
             Rev. Henri Cazelles, PSS
             Msgr. Alfons Deissler
             Rev. Ignace de la Pitterie, SJ
             Rev. Jacques Dupont, OSB
             Msgr. Savatore Garofalo
             Rev. Joachim Gnilka
             Rev. Pierre Grelot
             Rev. Alexander Kerrigan, OFM
             Rev. Lucien Legrand, MEP
             Rev. Stanislas Lyonnet, SJ
             Rev. Carlo Martini, SJ
             Rev. Antonio Moreno Casamitjana
             Rev. Ceslas Spicq, OP
             Rev. David Stanley, SJ
             Rev. Benjamin Wambacq, OPraem

Technical
Secretary: Rev. Marino Maccarelli, OSM

[1]*Annuario Pontificio*, 1977, p. 1073.

AUTHORS

Madeleine I. Boucher received the M.A. in English Literature from the Catholic University of America and the Ph. D. in Biblical Studies from Brown University. She is Assistant Professor of New Testament in the Department of Theology at Fordham University, and a member of the Executive Board of the Catholic Biblical Association of America. She is the author of *The Mysterious Parable: A Literary Study*.

Bernadette Brooten is a Ph. D. candidate at Harvard University in the field of New Testament and is writing a dissertation on "Women in Early Church Office and Within the Organizational Structures of the Synagogue." Ms. Brooten also studied theology for three years at the University of Tuebingen in West Germany.

Sidney deS. Callahan holds degrees from Bryn Mawr College and Sarah Lawrence College and is currently a doctoral candidate in psychology at C.U.N.Y. She is the author of many essays and four books, including *The Illusion of Eve: Modern Women's Search for Identity* and *Parenting: Principles and Politics of Parenthood*.

Francine Cardman is Associate Professor of Church History at Wesley Theological Seminary in Washington, D.C. She holds a Ph. D. in Historical Theology (Patristics) from Yale University. Publications include *The Preaching of Augustine* (translation of "The Lord's Sermon on the Mount"), ed. by Jaroslav Pelikan, and "Tradition, Hermeneutics and Ordination," in *Sexism and Church Law*, ed. by James Coriden. She is a member of the Executive Board of the North American Academy of Ecumenists.

Anne Carr, BVM, is Assistant Dean and Assistant Professor at the Divinity School of the University of Chicago, where she received the Ph. D. Author of *The Theological Method of Karl Rahner*, she presented a paper at the Ordination Conference in 1975 ("The Church in Process," published in *Women and Catholic Priesthood*, ed. by A.M. Gardiner) and is a member of the Task Force on the Status of Women of the Catholic Theological Society of America.

Elizabeth Carroll, RSM, is Staff Associate at the Center of Concern, Washington, D.C. With degrees from Pittsburgh and Toronto, and a Ph. D. from Catholic University of America, she has served as professor, dean and president of Carlow College, Pittsburgh; as president of the Pittsburgh Sisters of Mercy and of the Leadership Conference of Women Religious.

Juliana Casey, IHM, obtained the S.T.D. from the Universiteit Katholieke te Leuven, Louvain, Belgium. She is currently Assistant Professor of New Testament at St. Meinrad School of Theology in Indiana. She served as a member of the Theological Commission of the Archdiocese of Detroit from 1963-1966.

Adela Yarbro Collins received the A.B. degree in Religion from Pomona College. A member of Phi Beta Kappa, she has received the Fulbright, Woodrow Wilson and Danforth Fellowships. She received the Ph. D. with distinction in New Testament from Harvard University in 1975 and is currently Assistant Professor of New Testament at McCormick Theological Seminary in Chicago.

Bernard Cooke's educational career included St. Louis University (A.B. and M.A.), St. Mary's College in Kansas (S.T. Lic.), and the Institut Catholique de Paris (S.T.D.). For more than a decade he was chairman of the theology department at Marquette University; currently he teaches at the University of Calgary. His most recent publication is *Ministry to Word and Sacraments*. He is married to Pauline Turner.

Mary Rose D'Angelo has a B.A. from Fordham University and the M. Phil and Ph. D. degrees from Yale University. She has taught Scripture at Hartwick College and Liturgy at The School of Theology, The University of the South. During Spring of 1977 she was a Research Fellow at the Yale Divinity School.

John R. Donahue, SJ, Associate Professor of New Testament at Vanderbilt Divinity School, received his Ph. D. from the University of Chicago and has taught at Woodstock College. He is the author of *Are You the Christ? The Trial of Jesus in the Gospel of Mark*. He has been a member of the Executive Board of the Catholic Biblical Association and is currently a member of the Editorial Board of the Journal of Biblical Literature.

Michael A. Fahey, SJ, is associate professor of theology and director of graduate studies in the department of theological studies at Concordia University, Montreal. He studied at the University of Louvain and received his doctorate from the University of Tuebingen. The author of a book on Cyprian of Carthage as well as numerous articles, he is consultant theologian from the Orthodox and Roman Catholic Bilateral Conversations in North America.

Margaret A. Farley, RSM, is currently Associate Professor of Ethics at Yale Divinity School. She received her Ph. D. in Religious Ethics from Yale University. She is the co-author of *A Metaphysics of Being and God* and has published articles in such periodicals as *Journal of Religion* and *Theological Studies*.

M. Nadine Foley, OP, is currently a member of the General Council of the Adrian Dominican Congregation. She holds a Ph.D. in philosophy from the Catholic University of America and an S.T.M. from Union Theological Seminary. She was the co-ordinator of the task force which organized the conference Women in Future Priesthood Now—A Call to Action in 1975.

Elisabeth Schuessler Fiorenza studied at the Universities of Wuerzburg and Muenster, earning a Licentiate in Pastoral Theology and a Doctorate in Theology. Her books include *Die Getrennte Schwestern*. An Associate Professor at the University of Notre Dame, she has been associate editor of the *Catholic Biblical Quarterly, Journal of Biblical Literature*, and *Horizons*.

J. Massyngberde Ford received her B.A. from the University of Nottingham, a B.D. from King's College, London, and her Ph.D. from Nottingham. She has taught at Makerere University College in East Africa and is currently on leave from the University of Notre Dame, teaching at the University of Santa Clara. She writes on Neo-Pentecostalism in the Catholic Church and on Death and Sickness as well as in her special field of Scripture.

Mary Ann Getty, RSM, teaches at Carlow College, Pittsburgh, Pa., where she is the chairperson of the Theology Department. She received her S.T.L. and S.T.D., with a specialization in New Testament, from the University of Louvain, has taught in women's studies programs and lectured throughout the U.S. on the ordination of women and women in ministry.

Jean M. Higgins received her B.A. at Capetown University, South Africa, and her Ph. D. from Marquette University. She is an Assistant Professor of Religion, teaching historical theology, at Smith College and has chaired the Women's Caucus—Religious Studies of the American Academy of Religion for the past two years.

Denise C. Hogan received her Ph. D. in theology from Boston University; her dissertation was entitled: "Woman and the Christian Experience: Feminist Ideology, Christian Theology and Spirituality." She is currently teaching at Southern Vermont College in Bennington.

Robert W. Hovda is a priest of the diocese of Fargo, North Dakota, and has worked since 1965 on the staff of The Liturgical Conference, Washington, D.C. Presently its editorial director, he is the author of *Strong, Loving and Wise—Presiding in Liturgy, Dry Bones*, and other works.

Dorothy Irvin received her M.A. from Duquesne University and her Dr. Theol. in Old Testament studies at the University of Tuebingen in West Germany. She was taught at such institutions as the University of Detroit, the University of Dayton, and Tuebingen. Book review editor of the *Journal of Ecumenical Studies*, she is the author of the forthcoming *Mytharion*.

Robert J. Karris, OFM, received his Th. D. from Harvard Divinity School in New Testament Studies. He is now Associate Professor of New Testament Studies at Catholic Theological Union in Chicago, as well as editor of four biblical series and the New Testament book review editor for *Catholic Biblical Quarterly.*

Christopher Kiesling, OP, resides at Aquinas Institute of Theology in Dubuque, where he was professor of sacramental theology from 1956-76. He is editor of *Cross and Crown* and Formation Director of Scholastics in the Dominican Central Province. His writings include *Confirmation and Full Life in the Spirit.*

Edward J. Kilmartin, SJ, is Professor of Liturgical Theology at the University of Notre Dame. He is Executive Secretary of the National Conference of Catholic Bishops' Committee for Dialogue with Orthodox and Other Eastern Churches. He contributes regularly to such journals as *Theological Studies* and is the author of *The Eucharist in the Primitive Church.*

Paul J. LeBlanc holds the M.A. and the M. Div. degrees. He is an associate pastor at the Church of St. Pius V in the Bronx and a member of the New York Liturgical Commission and editor of its newsletter. He also edits *Liturgical Prayer* and is a member of the adjunct faculty of Maryknoll Seminary, where he teaches sacramental theology.

E. Ann Matter received her Ph. D. from Yale University. She is Historian of Christian Doctrine and Spirituality in the Department of Religious Thought at the University of Pennsylvania. She has presented papers at the 1976 Berkshire Conference and the 1977 SEMA Conference.

John L. McKenzie received his S.T.D. from Weston College in Massachusetts. He is currently Professor of Old Testament Studies at De Paul University. A former president of both the Catholic Biblical Association and the Society for Biblical Literature, he is the author of such books as *The Two-Edged Sword* and *The Power and the Wisdom.*

Francis G. Morrisey, OMI, holds licentiates in both philosophy and theology as well as a doctorate in canon law and an M.A. in religion. He is currently the Dean of the Faculty of Canon Law at St. Paul University in Ottawa. He has been the editor of "Studia Canonica" since 1967 and has served as president of the Canadian Canon Law Society.

Carolyn Osiek, RSCJ, has been Research/Resource Associate in Women's Studies at Harvard Divinity School, where she is also a doctoral candidate in the field of New Testament and Christian Origins. She has recently been appointed Assistant Professor of New Testament at the Catholic Theological Union in Chicago.

Anne E. Patrick, SNJM, doctoral student in religion and literature at the University of Chicago Divinity School, has written and lectured widely on religious dimensions of the women's movement. From 1973 to 1975 she chaired the Committee on Women in Church and Society of the National Assembly of Women Religious.

Pheme Perkins received her B.A. from St. John's College in Annapolis and her M.A. and Ph. D. from Harvard University. She is currently Associate Professor of Theology at Boston College and serves as Associate Editor of the *Catholic Biblical Quarterly* and a member of the Editorial Board of the *Journal of Biblical Literature.* Her publications include articles on Gnosticism.

Bernard P. Prusak received a B.A. in Classical Languages from Seton Hall University, an S.T.L. from the Gregorian University and a J.C.D. from the Lateran University in Rome. He is currently an associate professor in the Religious Studies Department of Villanova University and Co-Editor of *Horizons*, the journal of the College Theology Society.

Sonya A. Quitslund received her M.A. and Ph. D. from the Catholic University of America. She is now assistant professor of religion at George Washington University. The founder of the Christian Feminists, she is a core commissioner of Women's Ordination Conference. Her publications include *Beauduin A Prophet Vindicated.*

Thomas P. Rausch, SJ, completed the S.T.M. at the Jesuit School of Theology at Berkeley and his Ph. D. at Duke University. His dissertation focused on the questions of priesthood and ministry. Currently he teaches in the Department of Religious Studies at Loyola Marymount University.

Rosemary Radford Ruether holds a B.A. from Scripps College and an M.A. and Ph. D. from Claremont Graduate School. Currently she teaches at Garrett-Evangelical Theological Seminary. Her many publications include *The Church Against Itself, The Radical Kingdom, Liberation Theology,* and with Eugene C. Bianchi, *From Machismo to Mutuality.*

Sandra M. Schneiders, IHM, received an S.T.L. from Institut Catholique in Paris and an S.T.D. from Gregorian University in Rome. She is currently assistant professor of New Testament and Spirituality at the Jesuit School of Theology at Berkeley and Executive Co-ordinator of the Institute for Spirituality and Worship.

Mary Ellen Sheehan, IHM, received her B.A. from Marygrove College, her M.A. from St. Louis University and an S.T.D. from the Catholic University of Louvain, Belgium. She is currently Associate Professor of Systematic Theology at St. John's Provincial Seminary in Michigan as well as a member of the Archdiocese of Detroit Theological Commission.

Carroll Stuhlmueller, CP, received his doctorate in Sacred Scripture from the Pontifical Biblical Institute in Rome. He has been a Visiting Professor at L'Ecole Biblique in Jerusalem and is now professor of Old Testament at the Catholic Theological Union in Chicago. He has published extensively and is on the editorial board of *The Catholic Biblical Quarterly* and *The Bible Today*.

Arlene Anderson Swidler took a B.A. at Marquette University and M.A.'s in English from the University of Wisconsin and Theology from Villanova University. Co-founder of the *Journal of Ecumenical Studies*, she is the author of *Woman in a Man's Church* and editor of *Sistercelebrations*.

Leonard Swidler received a Ph.D. in history from the University of Wisconsin and an S.T.L. from the Catholic Theological Faculty of the University of Tübingen. He is co-founder and editor of the *Journal of Ecumenical Studies*, Professor of Religion at Temple University, and author of *Freedom In the Church* and *Women In Judaism*.

George H. Tavard, AA, professor of theology at the Methodist Theological School in Ohio, is the author of *Woman in Christian Tradition* as well as of several essays on related topics especially "Sexist Language in Theology?" in *Woman. New Dimensions*, ed. by W. Burghardt.

Thomas L. Thompson did graduate study in theology, Bible and religion at Oxford and Tuebingen Universities and received his Ph. D. from Temple University. The author of several books and articles on the Old Testament and related topics, including *The Historicity of the Patriarchal Narratives*, he is currently writing a book on the literary structures of Genesis.

Pauline Turner received her undergraduate education at Mercyhurst College in Pennsylvania and received M.A.'s in English and Theology at Marquette University. She has taught at Marquette and the University of Windsor, and is now teaching part-time at the University of Calgary.

Helen M. Wright, SND, received her Ph. D. from St. Michael's College at the University of Toronto. She is currently Assistant Professor in the Department of Ecclesiology at the Washington Theological Coalition; formerly she was Director of the Training Center for Educational and Pastoral Ministry at Emmanuel College in Boston.